MONOGRAPHS ON BRITISH ECONOMIC INSTITUTIONS

General Editor: Professor E. Victor Morgan

THE LONDON CLEARING BANKS

Already published in this series:

THE STOCK EXCHANGE
Its History and Functions

Professor E. V. Morgan and *W. A. Thomas*

THE BUILDING SOCIETY MOVEMENT

E. J. Cleary

INVESTMENT AND UNIT TRUSTS IN BRITAIN AND AMERICA

H. Burton and *D. C. Corner*

THE LONDON DISCOUNT MARKET

W. M. Scammell

THE LONDON CLEARING BANKS

Edward Nevin

Professor of Economics,
University College of Swansea

and

E. W. Davis

Research Associate
University College of Wales, Aberystwyth

ELEK BOOKS · London

Published by

ELEK BOOKS LIMITED
2 All Saints Street, London N.1.

ISBN 0 236 17611 0

PRINTED BY Unwin Brothers Limited
THE GRESHAM PRESS OLD WOKING SURREY ENGLAND

Produced by 'Uneoprint'

A member of the Staples Printing Group (UO7252)

Contents

Foreword

Because of a series of misfortunes and interruptions, the writing of this book has been spread over a period of more than six years, and it is indicative of the pronounced state of flux in which the British clearing banks find themselves that the form of the final section of the book is now significantly different from that which it would probably have taken had it been completed five or six years ago. The British banking system, in other words, is currently in a Forth Bridge situation: any portrayal of it is likely to be rendered obsolete before its completion, so rapid and confused are the changes being wrought in it in response to its evolving environment.

We have divided the story of the clearing banks into three broad sections. The first section, from roughly the mid-seventeenth century to the first World War, we have called the formative era when goldsmith-bankers emerged, gave way to country banks and finally crystallised into the structure we now call the London Clearing Bank system. The second section takes the story from the first World War to the early 1950s; this we have called (for lack of a better title) the Macmillan era. It is tempting to see this period now as the middle-age of the system, the era in which it became Establishment and when some of its arteries hardened. Following the analogy, some might be tempted to treat our third section, from the late 1950s on—which we name the Radcliffe era—as the old age of the London clearing banks. Certainly its previous dominance in the British credit system has been dramatically challenged—we believe permanently. Certainly critics (such as the National Board for Prices and Incomes) have implied that in its long era of pre-eminence fatal attitudes of over-confident complacency and introspective cartel-mindedness have enabled newer, more dynamic institutions to seize opportunities and develop business which should have been theirs and which will now never be regained.

The business of writing this book (and, we hope, of reading it) will instil, if nothing else, a healthy caution towards the writing of over-hasty epitaphs for the London clearing banks. In this context, at least, it is not true that we learn nothing from history except that we learn nothing from history; one unmistakable feature of these institutions over the whole stretch of time between the goldsmiths and the enormous, merged monsters of today is their capacity to adapt and change as official rules and regulations come forth and multiply and as the world in which they operate moves on in form and fashion. *Natura non facit saltum,* Marshall tells us, but the closing chapters of this book display (not always, perhaps, intentionally) a process of flux and doubt and uncertainty which suggests that the 1970s are likely to be an unusually long step, if not a sudden leap, in the progress of the clearing banks. This is a story, in other words, with no clear ending—happy or otherwise.

We have referred to the lengthy gestation from which this book has emerged. We must therefore express our deep gratitude to the authorities of the University College of Wales, Aberystwyth, where most of it was experienced, for the resources put at our disposal in order that the gestation should be made possible and the product here emerge. (For one of the authors, at least, this is an expression of gratitude which repeats others made more than once in the past.) We should also record our thanks to the editor of this series and its publishers for having endured this over-long period of waiting with patience and understanding. We are grateful, too, to officials of the Midland Bank and of Messrs Glyn Mills & Co. for much assistance and advice, the latter especially on the historical side, and most especially to Mr D. E. Fair, of the National Commercial Banking Group, who gave most generously of time, effort and advice. A number of others have given help which has been greatly appreciated; we should in particular mention Mr Cyril Pohl who worked as a research assistant on the project for a time during its initial stages and to whom some valuable material on the earlier history of the banks is due. Finally, perhaps we may record our thanks to Mrs Sheila Jacobs for having battled with the typing of a succession of drafts, the meaning of whose contents was seldom illuminated by the legibility of the hand in which they were written.

April 1970

E. T. N.

E. W. D.

PART I

THE FORMATIVE ERA (–1918)

CHAPTER ONE

The Precursors of British Banking

1. The earliest beginnings

The description of an activity as the oldest profession in the world is not perhaps one which involves the happiest associations. Whatever human occupation may be held to possess the strongest claim to this title, however, it is certain that many of the activities nowadays associated with the somewhat nebulous word 'banking' are in fact of great antiquity. The use of money itself, of course, can be discovered in the very earliest records of human existence(1) but there are many instances of transactions involving the use of credit in primitive communities even before the introduction of a monetary system. Loans in kind were effected through, for example, borrowing seed which was repaid (with, in effect, interest) from the resultant crop; similarly, they could be effected by means of a deferment of payment in kind to artisans for the production of implements until their application in harvesting or hunting had brought in the produce with which the debt could be extinguished. In the Banks Islands in the Pacific strings of shells were employed much more extensively as a means of recording debts than as a medium of exchange and their use as a money of account probably preceded their use as a means of exchange.(2)

The use of negotiable paper instruments also has a long history. During the reign of the Emperor Wu-Ti, around 140 BC, a form of 'paper money'—made in fact of white stage skin or pasteboard—was in use and the record of subsequent Chinese dynasties is full of instances of note issues.(3)

Almost all these early experiments involved private bilateral credit arrangements or, alternatively, the issue of various types of notes by the legal money-issuing authority. If 'banking' is understood to mean the organised and systematic dealing in debts by private (i.e. non-sovereign) agencies on a multilateral basis, the record, so far as Western Europe is concerned, must be said to begin at a much more recent point of history. In the earliest stages, the role of the king, or equivalent, was certainly crucial; given the political and civil uncertainties of the times, no private credit was likely to possess the backing—which a sovereign's power to exact ultimate sanctions could provide—necessary to support the growth of continuous and multilateral credit dealing. Or, for that matter, the persuasive power necessary to induce its emergence.

In fact, until the beginning of the thirteenth century royal borrowing was largely confined to the particular and restricted channels of the more affluent ecclesiastical dignitaries and institutions, usually on the security of land. Until the development of trade with the gradual evolution of economies away from the traditional subsistence or barter basis, the Church could be the only major source to which the sovereign could turn with much prospect of success for liquid resources on any adequate scale. As the revenue of European sovereigns increased, the securing of their 'overdrafts' in this way became less necessary, and perhaps less easy of negotiation. Certain classes of laymen, particularly merchants, were becoming owners of significant quantities of working capital and consequently acquiring an ability to furnish credit; royal dependence on ecclesiastical sources of credit therefore diminished. At first, laymen were no more than supplementary sources of credit, but by the early thirteenth century they were supplanting the Church in this sphere. Another factor tending to promote this development was the doctrine embodied in a group of papal decrees promulgated by Alexander III in 1163; these declared that loans on mortgage were a form of usury, a view which assisted in gradually redirecting the financial activities of monasteries towards such devices as the purchase of perpetual rent-charges from borrowers, a form of mortgage lending more suited to the requirements of small landowners than of those of kings.

The Church at this time was not infrequently a financial intermediary rather than an ultimate source of credit; ecclesiastical lenders were in fact often obliged to borrow elsewhere in order to meet the sovereign's requirements for loans. Lay lenders preferred to obtain security through the acquisition of control over taxes, tolls and tariffs but would also lend willingly on the security of valuables such as jewellery or plate. Unlike land, such valuables could be swiftly and easily foreclosed; on the other hand, the income from land pledged as security did not go to amortise the debt and generally constituted a pure gain to the lender.

Certain mints in Europe were kept in operation at this time by bullion supplied on credit by merchants and money-changers but the charging of substantial seigniorage on the coins in which such debts were ultimately repaid probably served to render the debt burden less onerous. By 1200, many rulers in Europe were also resorting to 'tax farmers' as their revenues expanded. This device, used by ecclesiastical landlords as well as governments, was a means of obtaining a guaranteed sum in place of the fluctuating proceeds of taxes thus 'farmed out'; in effect it was a means by which credit was extended to the state by privileged private entrepreneurs. Credit was obtained from tax-farmers in a second sense when a king borrowed upon the *anticipated* revenues of future years.

In this early period the English Crown's borrowing was fairly sporadic, apart from Henry II's credits from William Cade of St Omer, a Flemish merchant and usurer who lent to merchants in England and overseas and on occasions financed the transportation of Flemish soldiers and other royal employees.(4) Later, Henry borrowed from the Jewish community, which was to be taxed and fined out of existence as a source of credit by Richard I and King John. A great variety of lenders was beginning to make its appearance.

Henry III's biggest creditor was his brother Richard, Earl of Cornwall, who lent interest-free but obtained various concessions in return for his financial co-operation, a notable example being his undertaking the recoinage of the entire English currency in 1247 in return for the 'farm' of the Royal Mint, lending some £6,666 to provide the initial silver bullion.(5)

2. The medieval kings as debtors

From the reign of Edward I onwards official borrowing became more regular and systematic, its purpose becoming the regular easement of temporary cash deficiencies. Until the mid-fourteenth century, the Crown's credit with successive lenders was good, the more intensive borrowing being roughly coincidental with the advent of medieval Europe's greatest period of prosperity. Along with an enrichment of the sources of available credit, in other words, went an increased demand by government for funds. The latter arose from the gradual replacement of feudal vassals by paid armies and officials as sources of political support and military service. Other forces impelling official borrowing were the static or only slowly expanding nature of traditional revenues, the fact that to be taxed was out of the ordinary and—a source of political weakness—the need to obtain the consent of the sovereign's more powerful subjects to taxation.

During the reign of Edward I, loans frequently came to be contracted on the security of future revenues. Initially monasteries and military orders (e.g. the Templars and Hospitallers) were the important lenders, but in the course of the thirteenth century merchants (and magnates to a lesser extent) were becoming the main lenders. Large-scale commercial enterprises entailed the accumulation of fixed assets both at home and on the continent; the latter were liable to seizure by the rulers in whose domains they were situated if the goodwill of the princes concerned, or their protection from the ill-will of native competitors, was forfeited.[(6)] There were, however, more positive incentives to exhibit willingness to lend to a ruler: the banker to a prince might anticipate not only interest but privileges also—exemptions from certain taxes or levies, protection from extortion or diplomatic support for his operations elsewhere. Princes additionally had the power to confer titles of nobility and to exercise their influence in matters relating to wardships or marriage.

Withdrawal from government lending, however, was correspondingly difficult; it might well jeopardise any chances of repayment of advances outstanding. Lending at long-term was relatively uncommon: a succession of short term loans would more usually perform the functions achieved by what would nowadays be referred to as funded debt. Rulers were unwilling to mortgage their revenues too far into the future; merchants, on the other hand, were not anxious to lock up their resources in an illiquid form. Among the psychological reasons for maintaining what was by modern standards a wastefully high degree of liquidity were the implications of the slowness and difficulty of transport.

Specific taxes, tolls and duties were frequently earmarked for debt-servicing but this did not necessarily mean that the debts concerned were, as it were, overdrafts secured by the abrogation of state control over revenue sources. An export duty imposed on wool in 1275 was assigned to the exclusive disposal of the Riccardi for nineteen years, in return for which they undertook to make advances to the government as and whenever required; the assignees in this and similar cases, however, had to account to the king for all receipts under that heading. The tax farmer, by contrast, was under no such obligation and merely paid a fixed rent; on occasion he anticipated revenue by extending loans to the sovereign—often interest-free—in return for favours. Their existence is in large measure attributable to an absence of a potential supply of qualified and honest tax collectors which the government could employ.

The inauguration of permanent indirect taxes in the later Middle Ages added to the amount of revenue which could be assigned or farmed and therefore borrowed in advance of receipt. Tax farming, in practice, was a means of securing credits rather than of ensuring the regular collection of revenues. It was a symptom of mismanagement; sources of revenue earmarked for the 'amortisation' of tax-farmers' advances passed out of the hands of the state on progressively unsatisfactory terms.

3. The continental bankers

Italian competition in lending to the states of North-West Europe was negligible until about 1275 but the monarchs engaged in the Third and, more particularly, the Fourth Crusades came into contact with the advanced credit facilities offered by the Genoese and Venetians. Merchants from Italian cities were coming to frequent the fairs of Champagne in France by the 1190s, and by 1270 the more important among them had permanent representatives at the fairs which, although initially overwhelmingly concerned with commodity sales, were becoming mainly financial in character. Even in the context of commodity exchanges, however, they displayed some considerable sophistication. The exchanging of merchandise without the use of money, which was developed in them, was not barter but a system of clearings. Goods were bought and sold on credit entered in a banker's books which lasted the period of the fair; when it closed the clearing was made, thus obviating the use of money except for the final sums needed to effect a balance.(7) At this general settlement, merchants received payments owing to them and discharged their debts, while the bankers were able to offset debits and credits against one another so that only net balances needed to be settled by coin or bills payable at a later fair.(8)

There is some ground for supposing, indeed, that in 959 Baldwin III, Earl of Flanders, noticing that a scarcity of money obstructed trade with France, abolished export and import duties and established markets and fairs precisely in order that goods could be exchanged without money.(9) Rulers, bishops and municipalities of Northern France and the Low Countries borrowed at these fairs, while financial settlements—the offsetting of mercantile debts—between houses were also negotiated. The Papacy itself stimulated financial contacts by Italians north of the Alps by encouraging prelates to borrow from Roman financiers in order to make various non-routine payments to the Holy See. It would subsequently extend its spiritual and diplomatic support to merchants when they travelled north to collect money from defaulting ecclesiastical debtors. Italian firms also collected papal taxes on behalf of the Curia and rendered other financial services. The money lenders of Venice had in fact became deposit-keepers as an adjunct to the money-changing business.(10) Money-changers were in effect the financial intermediaries of medieval Europe.(11)

From around 1267 Italian firms from Siena, Lucca, Florence, Piacenza and Pistoia began to open branches or to settle in England. They divided between themselves the profits from collecting papal levies which they subsequently repatriated.(12) This activity, together with the growing importance of commerce arising from the English wool trade, was the main incentive for their settlement in England. Their superior efficiency arose out of better techniques, more capital—originally arising both from deposit-keeping and the savings of Italian entrepreneurs—and greater mutual cohesion, and they were also successful in securing deposits from non-business investors. Their English depositors consisted of the more substantial merchants and both lay and ecclesiastical magnates; probably only a minority of them were in fact deposit-keepers, however, in contrast to the situation in Italy. Most landowners employed the merchants simply for making payments overseas.(13)

The Italian merchants also adopted procedures whereby debtors made their settlements into a creditor's account rather than to him personally. Transfers between depositors were effected by the adjustment of accounts which merchants held with each other or by ledger transfers of credit. Although involved primarily in general mercantile business, they might perform other services on behalf of their customers—such as the purchase of military equipment abroad. The advantages to a depositor of dealing with the Italian houses were numerous—the avoidance of the need to store coin personally, the convenience of a London account, the ability to direct debtors to pay into a place of safe-keeping, and the ability to effect transfers of claims quickly and with minimal risk of loss. The payment of interest on deposits was by no means general; almost the only advantage to the merchant of accepting deposits was that wool transactions might be financed with them. For similar reasons they competed for the privilege of transferring papal revenues to Avignon.

In the early fourteenth century, a number of bankruptcies occurred among these Italian houses; thirty to forty years later, the Crown began to encounter difficulties in finding willing financiers, the supply of funds falling below governmental requirements. By the mid-fifteenth century, royal finances were experiencing acute and increasing difficulty. Only through the exploitation of royal lands and of the Crown's prerogative rights—and only to a negligible extent through borrowing—was an improvement effected under Edward IV and Henry VII.

4. The role of bullion

From the mid-fourteenth century onwards, technological difficulties conspired to cause a failure in the output of European gold and silver mines, with the result that bullion supplies became inadequate; with a falling price level, trade depression set in.(14) Other factors associated with this economic contraction included an apparently declining agricultural productivity in the fourteenth century; this set a limit on population expansion, which slowed down in the early 1300s and spectacularly collapsed in 1348-9 under the impact of the Black Death. Another element in the situation was probably a tendency for agricultural prices to fall more rapidly than those of the handicraft industry because of the lower elasticity of supply in the agricultural sector.(15) Mining output, also, is known to have fallen appreciably.(16)

From 1326 onwards, an adequacy of coin—even amounting, possibly, to a slight over-sufficiency—turned to shortage, a development which was reflected in repeated ordinances, proclamations and parliamentary petitions against the export of gold or silver bullion, money or plate, the last being in 1449.(17) While population may have declined by 30-40 per cent over this period, it seems possible that the volume of coin in circulation may have contracted by as much as 80 per cent. Hence there developed a real shortage of money, unrelieved by either population contraction or a more economical use of credit sources.

From around 1380-1420 (at least) bullion—particularly gold—was undervalued at the Mint relative to its free market price; widespread clipping and exporting followed as a consequence, suggesting that the Mint ratio was out of line with that of competing continental mints, although the payment of papal levies was cited at the time as a source of bullion loss. In 1378-9, Parliament demanded import controls on luxuries and in an attempt to lessen the use made of trade credit also demanded export prohibitions on wool unless 10 per cent of its value in bullion were immediately imported by the merchant.(18)

The deterioration of English public credit at this time is well illustrated by the experiences of Edward III while on campaign in the Netherlands in 1340-41. At Malines and Louvain he was reduced to pledging the persons of the Earls of Derby and Northampton as hostages for his debts, and various crowns of both the King and his wife were pledged to various towns in return for loans. These were dealings of a very unusual type except in Germany or in much earlier times, however; normally such security would not have been sought by professional lenders.

Borrowing by the Tudor governments in Antwerp was a fairly recurrent feature of their finances from the reign of Henry VIII, among whose unsuccessful expedients was the attempted raising of a loan on the security of lead stripped from the roofs of ecclesiastical buildings.(19) Accepted securities of a more orthodox character for borrowing in Antwerp were usually those of Italian mercantile firms established in London, particularly the house of Vivalde and Bonvyce.(20)

Until around 1550 there was in fact a foreign predominance in the emerging London money market which was thereafter diluted by increasing native participation.(21) Nevertheless, Gresham had raised state loans in London as well as Antwerp: in 1561, a loan of £30, 000 at 10 per cent was raised for Queen Elizabeth from twelve Englishmen, while in 1560 Gresham in a letter to Cecil expressed confidence that large loans to the Government could be raised in England at an interest rate of 5 per cent at the outside.(22) Further evidence of the growing importance of London as a capital market was the royal loan of £15, 000 at 10 per cent raised in 1589 from over a hundred subscribers, nearly all English.(23)

In the 1590s, large sums were raised by means of Privy Seal demand notes. These were printed and issued to collectors who entered on the note the name of the lender and the sum advanced and provided a receipt; they were payable on demand at the Exchequer on or after the date of redemption. In effect they constituted an order to the 'Exchequer of Account' or audit department to pay the lender or whatever person to whom the bill had been assigned. 'Assignment' was thus practised in Elizabethan times, the assignee endorsing the demand note and the 'collector' receipting it, although the Bill of Exchange payable to order was not legally recognised as assignable until post-Restoration times.(24) Nevertheless, the assignment of a bill of exchange by means of a written endorsement was known much earlier than this. Thomas Madox gives an example of such a transaction between two Jews during the reign of Edward I in 1289.(25) At that time the device was apparently fairly well known; as the assignment was written on the back or 'dorsal' portion of the parchment, the process later became known as 'endorsement'.(26)

Certainly mercantile debts had become assignable by means of a Bill of Exchange by the fourteenth century through the practice of Italian merchants, many of whom lent to the Crown.(27) The English were using the Bill of Exchange before the end of the fifteenth century, but it was economically unimportant until Tudor times; it grew in significance, however, in the late Tudor period.(28) Those Elizabethan goldsmiths who specialised as bullion merchants and money lenders were fairly frequent subscribers to Privy Seals, although they dealt mostly in plate and jewellery.

After the time of the Black Death (1348-9) and the later pestilences of 1361, 1368, 1381 and 1396, the consequent rise in the rate of commutation of feudal services for money had helped to create an independent class of small landowners and a fairly free market in land as an outlet for investment. The new landowners, and the traders in the towns with whom they dealt, usually converted a proportion of their annual income—now received in the form of money—into the only fairly accessible asset which was generally more easily marketable than land: jewellery and gold and silver plate. This new type of demand called into existence a class of specialised dealers in precious articles—the goldsmiths.[29] Financially they were overshadowed by merchants, brokers and scriveners but were, institutionally, the forerunners of the goldsmith banking house of Stuart London.

Of the great advancers to the State at this time, however, the 'exchanging merchants' were the most significant: they transported coin and bullion between England and Western Europe and delivered money internationally by bills of exchange. They would lend money on a Privy Seal payment order: this, signed by the Lord Treasurer, could be issued by the Exchequer of Receipt to an Army paymaster serving abroad. The latter would give or send it to the merchant who gave money for it in exchange and later presented the order for redemption at the Exchequer of Receipt. English merchants would 'make the money over' by the transfer of coin to the Army paymaster, selling English goods, particularly wool, locally for cash or by bills of exchange drawn on Flemish merchants. They would levy a charge called 'collibos' for this service and/or as recompense for damage and loss sustained by them while delivering the money.[30]

Besides Privy Seal demand notes there also existed 'bills obligatory'; these were promissory notes given by a Royal intermediary as sealed acknowledgement of a loan. They were often called 'Sealed Bills' in consequence and were first issued around 1575. They were repayable to the lender, his heirs, executors or 'assigns' and generally had a life of three months or more.

5. The emergence of trade credit

From the time of Elizabeth I onward, Englishmen were tending to be classified, according to their financial activities, into money-lenders, money-changers, bullion merchants and financial middlemen. Among the last could be distinguished four professions: goldsmith, broker, scrivener and merchant. These latter groups are important types: the origins of the activities nowadays collectively labelled 'banking' are to be found in their transactions. In the early part of the reign of Elizabeth I 'banker' meant 'exchange specialist'; during the reign of her successor, brokers and scriveners had become important financial intermediaries and they later evolved into actual money-lenders.

'Retailing brokers' or 'pawnbrokers' were the most extortionate money-lenders; Malynes in *Lex Mercatoria* records that their most favourable rate was 6d on 20s per 28 days ($32\frac{1}{2}$ per cent per annum). He was one among many who advocated the erection of *monts de piété* to undercut them. The pawnbrokers, it was held, borrowed and then relent at extortionate rates to the poor; not infrequently they were also dealers in stolen property.

Other brokers, known as 'sworn broggers', were those authorised by a magistrate to practise their trade of bringing together potential borrowers and lenders. By the 1690s they had evolved into stock jobbers or bullion dealers, the scope for such evolution being facilitated by the formation of the great merchanting companies and by the proliferation of various types of marketable government paper. The economic importance of this market was underlined by an Act of 1711; this forbade brokers to receive above 2s 9d per cent in fees connected with buying or selling 'tallies, orders, Exchequer bills, Exchequer tickets, Bank bills, or any share or interest in any joint stock enterprise.'

A scrivener was originally a clerical intermediary of Tudor and Jacobean times who specialised in drawing up bonds (sealed undertakings to repay), bills obligatory and contracts between merchant and merchant, borrower and lender, or buyer and seller.(31) As early as 1615, however, the Jacobean scrivener had anticipated the goldsmith as a deposit-keeper in accepting sums for the express purpose of relending and he continued so to function even when the goldsmith-bankers were firmly established. As late as 1713, an Act of Parliament cites him first in a list of financial middlemen; a comparable prominence is accorded him in an 'Act for the Restraining of Excessive Usury' in 1660.

Neither goldsmith nor broker solicited deposits in Jacobean times or earlier. Occasionally merchants kept deposits, even as early as the reign of Elizabeth I, but only for personal use in regular mercantile activity. Some examples occurred in the late 1600s of merchants going into partnership so as to receive deposits as a principal activity. These deposits were invested in various commercial enterprises while the depositors received as security 'joint bonds',(32) such partnership in a sense anticipating the modern unit trust.

Credit entered very widely into trade with rural entrepreneurs but in these cases the entrepreneurs themselves, rather than financial specialists, were the immediate source of credit. The wool-brogger of Tudor and early Stuart England was an important provider of trade credit and has been described as the banker of the cottage weaver.(33) In a sense he was functionally a precursor of the country banker; he advanced money on future wool supplies and sold wool on credit to the clothier. Such trade credit was characteristic of pre-Tudor times;(34) certain variants, such as 'dry exchange', formed a means of evading anti-usury legislation.(35)

The business of wool-broggers probably received some impetus from the dissolution of the monasteries and from the subsequent confiscation of guild lands during the reign of Edward VI. Small farmers had obtained seed, cattle and sheep on credit from the guilds and monasteries and are known to have sold long wool futures to the monasteries, thereby easing seasonal deficiencies in purchasing power. The monasteries in turn had obtained credit from Flemish and Italian merchants and had done so since the thirteenth century. This source of credit having disappeared, farmers were obliged to look elsewhere for accommodation.(36) Counterparts of the wool brogger also existed in the tin-mining and distributing industry.(37)

6. The goldsmiths

Besides the expansion of English trade in Tudor times, an important factor in the emergence of banking was the change which took place in public opinion with regard to usury in the later Tudor and early Stuart period.(38) The medieval condemnation of usury had rested in reality on the fact that in a large barter, subsistence-type economy borrowing arose predominantly because of personal emergencies and distress; the lender, who suffered no real hardship as the result of a temporary loss of money—regarded, with some considerable justification in such an environment, as a sterile asset—could not be justified in seeking to profit from the misfortunes of his fellow-men. The changing environment was rendering this doctrine irrelevant rather than invalid. The emergence of a growing, money-using commercial economy transformed the nature of the borrowing transaction on both sides. On the one hand, profitable trade or investment, rather than human distress, was increasingly a motivating-force for borrowing; on the other hand, the existence of investment outlets implied that the loss of control over money could involve a lender in a very real opportunity-cost. As a result, the giving and taking of interest gradually ceased to involve moral turpitude and this greatly helped to facilitate the development of financial intermediaries. An Act of 1545 legalised the taking of interest up to a 10 per cent maximum; this was repealed in 1552, but the 10 per cent upper limit was re-established in 1571. Under an Act of 1673, the upper limit was lowered to 8 per cent.

While the use of bills of exchange was becoming widespread in Elizabethan times, banks or other institutions carrying on a discounting business were non-existent in England prior to the reign of Charles I. Richard Dafforne, in his *The Merchants Mirrour* (1636), regarded such banks of discount as unnecessary in England, even though he conceded that they fulfilled a useful function in Venice and the Low Countries where they had been operating from as early as the Tudor period. In truth, it might be said that possibly the only function which such institutions would have been especially capable of performing would have been the discounting of 'outland' bills—a business already competently carried on in other hands. In respect of inland bills, their evolution and adoption may well have been delayed by the adequacy of such entrepreneurs as 'corn-bodgers' and 'wool-broggers' in the sphere of trade credit. According to John Marius in the second (1655) edition of his *Advice concerning Bills of Exchange*, inland bills had been known for 24 years—i.e. only since about 1630. By 1655, transference by endorsement of order bills of exchange had become common; in Marius's first (1622) edition only bills to '(name) or assigns' and to '(name) or bearer' are mentioned.(39)

The earliest known English goldsmith's receipts for money deposited is that given by Lawrence Hoare in 1633. Some London goldsmiths had accepted money and plate on trust prior to the Civil War but this was by no means a major part of their activity. A state document of 1628, however, refers to (i) 'working goldsmiths' and (ii) those who carried on the newly-established business of money-exchanging, bullion dealing, and dealing in plate and jewels. Originally, goldsmiths kept money deposited with them on trust, with no authority to re-invest. With or without reinvestment, however, these deposits were a source of profit to the goldsmith, provided that (a) the coinage was not appreciably debased and (b) the seigniorage levied on newly minted bullion was insufficient to offset the divergence between home and foreign mint ratios; the latter condition meant that a profit could be made by the illicit melting down of the heaviest coins and the export of the proceeds as bullion. An English agent, writing in 1652 from Amsterdam to Sir Robert Stone of London, describes how he was informed of the manner by which heavy coins were in fact sorted out in London and exported.(40) Goldsmiths also kept stocks of the more important foreign coins to meet their customers' requirements. As will be shown in more detail in the succeeding chapter, these foreign exchange dealings lay at the heart of the evolution of goldsmiths into bankers.

By the first quarter of the seventeenth century, then, many of the essential functions going to make up the business of banking had begun to appear in Britain and had done so in a variety of quarters. As that century progressed occasional and, in a sense, special events were to give this evolutionary process a sharp push forward. An injudicious interference with bullion deposited at the Mint by Charles I in 1640, by shaking confidence in the Mint as the safest of safe deposits for coin and bullion, almost certainly accelerated the movement of the goldsmiths into public favour as custodians of deposited wealth. Similarly, the First Dutch War (1651-4) and the administrative system of Parliamentary Committees greatly increased the scope of certain goldsmiths for profitable activity, the 'sub-treasuries' set up at Goldsmiths' Hall and Haberdashers' Hall effecting payments for the government out of revenues received.(41)

Even without these special events, however, it is clear that men and institutions were developing banking activities in response to the deeper-seated, long-run trends implied by the growth of the British economy. Banking, like all economic activity, emerges from the existence of three essential ingredients: an exchangeable asset which is scarce and sought-after, potential suppliers of that asset and eager demanders of it. The emergence of a predominantly monetary economy supplied the first in the form of coin and bullion. Indeed, the opening of England to the international monetary system of the day brought many varieties of that asset into the market and hence created the possibility of profit-making as a result of discrepancies in their relative values; as has been noted, the exploitation of disparities in the weights and values of the coinage, internally and externally, was a key factor, in the process of which, at this time, the goldsmiths were beginning to leave behind them their original role of keepers of precious metal or workers in it.

The supply side of the mechanism had been established on a substantial basis by the emergence of a monied class whose wealth sprang from real property and the profits of the growing wool trade. The demand side, also, sprang from the financial needs implied by the expansion of England's interest in the international textile trades and of the incipient industries whose acceleration in the following century was to merit the label of a revolution. An asset, a supply, a demand: given these ingredients the economic system will always evolve the institutional arrangements required to organise their inter-relationships and to profit by them. By the middle of the seventeenth century this process had clearly begun to take on a firm and recognisable shape and pattern in English banking.

REFERENCES

1. A. del Mar, *A history of money in ancient countries*, Bell, London 1855, pp. 22-7.

2. P. Einzig, *Primitive money*, Eyre and Spottiswoode, London 1949, pp. 372, 376 and 412-3.

3. See del Mar, *loc. cit.*

4. C. H. Haskins, 'William Cade', *English History Review*, Vol. XXVIII, 1913, pp. 730-1.
5. E. B. and M. M. Fryde, *Cambridge Economic History of Europe*, Vol. III, Chapter 7.
6. R. L. Reynolds, 'Origins of modern business enterprise: medieval Italy', *Journal of Economic History*, Vol. XII, 1952, p. 365.
7. A. del Mar, *History of monetary systems*, Effingham Wilson, London 1895, pp. 228-9.
8. E. Victor Morgan, *A history of money*, Penguin Books, Middlesex 1965, p. 156.
9. James Anderson, *History of Commerce*, Vol. I, London 1787, p. 98, quoted by del Mar, *ibid.*, p. 228.
10. C. F. Dunbar, *Quarterly Journal of Economics*, Vol. VI, 1892, p. 310 and *Economic Essays*, London 1904, p. 145.
11. M. Postan, 'Credit in medieval trade', *Journal of Economic History*, Vol. I. No. 2, 1938.
12. W. E. Lunt, *Financial relations of the Papacy with England to 1327*, Cambridge, Mass., 1939, Appx. VI, pp. 641-650.
13. N. Denholm-Young, *Seignorial administration in England*, Oxford University Press, London 1937.
14. W. C. Robinson, 'Money, population and economic change in late medieval Europe', *Economic History Review*, Series 2, Vol. XII, 1959, pp. 63-76.
15. On this point see H. A. Miskimin, 'Monetary movements and market structure: forces for contraction in 14th and 15th Century England', *Journal of Economic History*, Vol. XXIV, No. 4, December 1964, pp. 471-2.
16. J. E. Nef, 'Mining and metallurgy in medieval civilisation', *Cambridge Economic History of Europe*, Vol. II, 1952, pp. 430-92.
17. See R. Ruding, *Annals of the coinage of Britain and its dependencies*, 2nd edition, London 1819, Part II, p. 136 *et seq.*
18. *Ibid.*, p. 220.
19. R. H. Tawney and E. Power, *Tudor Economic Documents*, Vol. II, 1924, pp. 138-42.
20. R. D. Richards, *The early history of banking in England*, P. S. King & Son, London 1929 (Reprints of Economic Classics, Kelly, New York 1965), p. 3.
21. *Review*, Vol. I, No. 2, January 1928, p. 342.
22. Richards, *loc. cit.*
23. H. Buckley, 'Sir Thomas Gresham and the foreign exchanges', *Economic Journal*, Vol. XXXIV, 1924, pp. 589-601.
24. W. S. Holdsworth, *A history of English Law*, London 1925, Vol. VIII, Ch. 4.

25. *History and antiquities of the Exchequer of the Kings of England,* Vol. I, London 1769.

26. del Mar, *ibid.*, p. 229.

27. Sir Edward Bond, 'Extracts from the Liberate Roll relative to loans supplied by Italian merchants to the Kings of England in the thirteenth and fourteenth centuries', *Archaeologia,* Vol. XXVIII, 1839, pp. 207-326; R. J. Whitwell, 'Italian bankers and the English crown', *Transactions of the Royal Historical Society,* N.S., Vol. XVII, 1903; W. E. Rhodes, 'The Italian bankers in England and their loans to Edward I and Edward II', in T. F. Tout and J. Tait, *Historical Essays,* Longmans Green, London 1907.

28. E. Power, 'The English wool trade in the reign of Edward IV', *Cambridge History Journal,* Vol. II, No. 1, 1926.

29. E. T. Powell, 'The evolution of the money market', *The Financial News,* London 1915, pp. 4 and 9-11.

30. R. H. Tawney, *Wilson's Discourse upon Usury,* pp. 73-4.

31. See H. C. Gutteridge, 'The origin and historical development of the profession of Notaries Public', *Cambridge Legal Essays,* 1926.

32. Richards, *op, cit.,* p. 16, n.1.

33. R. H. Tawney, *ibid.,* p. 49.

34. M. Postan, *op. cit.*

35. W. Forbes, *A methodical treatise concerning bills of exchange,* London 1703.

36. R. H. Tawney, *The agrarian problem in the 16th Century,* London 1912, pp. 109-10.

37. G. R. Lewis, *The Stannaries,* London 1968.

38. On this see R. H. Tawney, 'Religious thought on social and economic questions in the 16th and 17th centuries', *Journal of Political Economy,* Vol. XXI, Nos. 4-6, 1923 and *Religion and the rise of capitalism,* John Murray, London 1926, pp. 36-55; E. Roll, *A history of economic thought,* Faber and Faber, 2nd ed. London 1945, Chap. I, pp. 49-51.

39. See also John Scarlett, *Stile of Exchanges,* London 1682 and A. P. Usher, 'The origin of the bill of exchange', *Journal of Political Economy,* Vol. XXII, 1914, pp. 566-76.

40. R. D. Richards, *op. cit.,* p. 37; see also Sir A. Feaveryear, *The pound sterling,* 2nd ed. London 1962, pp. 76-122.

41. W. O. Scroggs, 'English finances under the Long Parliament', *Quarterly Journal of Economics,* Vol. XXI, 1907, pp. 463-87.

CHAPTER TWO

The Goldsmith Bankers

1. The exchanging goldsmiths

Prior to the Civil War, the business of investment of spare cash balances was almost entirely in the hands of the scriveners.(1) Originally public letter-writers and skilled copyists, they had gradually evolved into a body of legal practitioners specialising in the art of drawing up documents—for example, those relating to conveyancing. This last field of activity they had abandoned by the beginning of the eighteenth century in favour of the receiving of clients' money on deposit and its re-investment at the scrivener's discretion, an activity originally incidental to the drawing up of documents such as mortgage deeds. They were, therefore, of some significance in the early development of banking, anticipating the 'exchanging goldsmiths' as deposit keepers. The nature of their operations, however, led them to develop professions such as stock-jobbing, stock-broking and accounting rather than banking,(2) although there were some cases of provincial scriveners evolving into country bankers in the eighteenth century.

Scriveners also lent money, for periods running into years, upon the security of title deeds to manors and other land for purposes of fixed investment. They were generally men of smaller means than goldsmiths, however, having as a group a reputation for extortionate and unfair business dealings; consequently they commanded less public confidence than the goldsmiths. These factors, and the probability that their main fields of operation—particularly the post-Restoration estate market—were distinctly lucrative, may explain why they tended to abandon the deposit-keeping business to the goldsmiths.(3)

The beginning of the differentiation of the trade of goldsmithery into 'working goldsmiths' and 'exchanging goldsmiths' was probably discernible during the later years of Queen Elizabeth I's reign. The nobility of Elizabethan times had been accustomed to holding a large proportion of their ready money in the form of jewellery and plate. Under these conditions goldsmiths had prospered and attained an increasing importance. Apart from their normal trade as working goldsmiths, their activities appear to have comprised mainly the exchanging and valuing of money and bullion, and the negotiation of bills drawn on places abroad.

A considerable decline in the turnover of the goldsmith trade was apparent in the early 1620s,(4) largely because of the decaying economic power of the noble land-owning class relative to that of the urban middle class; the latter were using their improved economic position to finance commercial enterprises and to initiate money-lending businesses rather than to acquire plate and jewellery. In 1637 an attempt was made by the Crown to nationalise foreign exchange dealings through a revival of the office of Exchanger; the considerable alarm expressed by the goldsmiths suggests that by this time many of them were beginning to reduce their dependence upon plate-dealing and that their operations in bills of exchange and foreign coin were of correspondingly greater importance to them.(5)

In 1628, a state document advocating the retention of the Royal Exchanger distinguishes between those still primarily engaged in goldsmithing proper and those expanding their activities.(6) The former are described as 'working goldsmiths' and the latter as 'goldsmiths about the Cittie Exchanges'; the document adds that the business of exchange was 'a new kind of trade sprung up lately among them'.

This transition in the nature of their business had received impetus from the flow of foreign coins—particularly from Holland, France and Portugal—into Britain and its domestic circulation as a result of the increasing overseas trade of the early Stuart era. As a consequence, large quantities of English and foreign coins were accumulated by the goldsmiths and substantial reserves were kept to satisfy the demands of traders travelling overseas—a service which the goldsmiths found very profitable. Alternatively, the coins were melted into bullion for the manufacture of jewellery or, on the other hand, the bullion (mainly gold in the first half of the seventeenth century) was sold to the Mint for coining. Scope was also found for speculation arising out of the disparities in values observed not only in international currencies but in domestic currency as well. The English merchant could make more money by exporting gold than by exporting any other commodity. Silver, too, was undervalued at the English Mint. Thus a document written in Amsterdam in 1652 stated:

> It is the goldsmiths, especially those in Lombard Street, who are the greatest merchants and London cashiers, and who will receive any man's money for nothing, and pay it for them the same or the next day, and meantime keep people in their upper rooms to cull and weigh all they receive, and melt down the weighty and transport it to foreign parts.(7)

Another document of an earlier date had upbraided

> the money-changers in Lombard Street (who) by culling, buying and selling at a dearer rate (than) the King's Mint have been thereby exceeding great gainers and have sold it again to Dutchmen, by which means they have exhausted many millions of our treasure.(8)

Apart from the interest of these documents as early appreciations of the mischief it was believed Lombard Street could do to the economy, they provide a plausible explanation for the goldsmiths' willingness to accept deposits of cash.

Although the wealthiest goldsmiths of the reigns of Elizabeth I and James I are known to have advanced money both to the Crown and to private customers, at that time such activity was financed not out of deposits but from profits acquired in the course of their normal trade; goldsmiths of this time did not generally accept money on deposit. Such merchants as had large sums of cash tended to deposit them in the Tower of London under the care of the Master of the Mint. As was mentioned in Chapter 1, however, in 1640 Charles I, in need of money as always, requisitioned some £200, 000 deposited in the Tower and popular belief in the security of the Mint was severely shaken. For a time many merchants reverted to the practice of keeping their own cash, but the general insecurity accompanying the Civil War(9) encouraged them to look for some safer depository.

Hence many turned to the goldsmiths who, with the facilities they possessed for the safe storage of their own valuables, were a logical choice. Minor as this development might have appeared at the time, the goldsmith's acceptance of such money deposits in trust, returnable on demand, was the first really significant stage in the evolution from goldsmith to banker.

At first the goldsmith charged a small fee for acting as custodian of deposits which he had no authority to reinvest. The money was sealed in bags or chests and was returnable on demand; a receipt was issued for the sum concerned, which receipt was assignable neither to order nor to bearer, having only the function of a left-luggage ticket. Before a goldsmith accepting coin on deposit could become a banker in the modern sense, the receipts issued by him had to lose their correspondence with particular deposits and become instead generalised claims against a portion of his total assets; when this occurred the legal status of the goldsmith would have changed from that of bailee to that of debtor. When a depositor gave a goldsmith authority to reinvest the sum deposited—usually in the form of loans to customers—at his own discretion and for his own profit, in return for a consideration, the goldsmith was transformed in accordance with existing legal rulings into the depositor's debtor.(10)

2. From goldsmith to banker

Under pressure from changing economic circumstances the goldsmiths had already demonstrated a readiness to offset the decline in their domestic trade of goldsmithing proper by expanding their activities so as to include dealings in foreign coinage and bills of exchange; they thereby met the needs of the developing financial classes and simultaneously promoted their financial expertise. It was not surprising, therefore, that the more ambitious of them should seek to profit by this latest opportunity arising from the political uncertainties of the age.

Recognition of the distinct development from goldsmith to banker is believed to have arisen during the Protectorate. The pamphleteer Sir Ralph Maddison did not mention goldsmith-bankers in *Englands looking in and out* (1640) but he did so in the 1654 edition of his economic tract entitled *Great Britains Remembrancer*, while the anonymous author of *The Mystery of the New-Fashioned Goldsmiths*(11) dated the start of goldsmith banking at about 1646, thirty years prior to his date of publication. The ledgers of Alderman Backwell, particularly the Dunkirk Ledger, show that Backwell conducted a big banking business in Cromwellian times. (12)

By 1660 it appears that the goldsmiths were receiving considerable sums of cash on deposit. A tract published in that year states that

> Some Goldsmiths in Lombard Street keep at this day many great Merchants' of London cashes and some noblemen's cash: by this credit of other men's monies the goldsmiths of Lombard Street are in the nature of Bankers and have a great stock of treasure by them. (13)

The new business continued to increase and it was not long before demand deposits were followed by time deposits; as the ledgers of Backwell show, the latter were a feature of goldsmith banking in the years immediately following the Restoration, and it was probably at about this time that the goldsmiths began to pay interest on sums left in their hands. Pepys records in his Diary for 30th March 1666:

> I out to Lumbarde Street and there received £2, 200 and brought it home; and, contrary to expectation, received £35 for the use of £2, 000 of it for a quarter of a year, where it hath produced me this profit and hath been a convenience to me as to care and security of my house and demandable at 2 days warning, as this has been.

At an early stage in their development as bankers the goldsmiths had discovered the fundamental principle of modern banking—i.e. that it was necessary to regulate till-money so as to keep only a proportion of their assets as a reserve against day-to-day outgoings, and possible to employ the rest at profit. Probably because of a desire to compete more effectively for deposits, therefore, the goldsmiths had begun to pay interest; they also widened the circle of their depositors to include landowners, among others, as well as merchants. As a consequence they developed the additional function of receiving rents on behalf of depositors. The fact that interest was paid on money 'at call', even when deposited for as little as one month at a time, caused money to flow into their deposits on a scale which, by the standards of the time, was a large one. The goldsmiths had in fact created a form of asset, comparatively safe and easily convertible into cash, a combination of safety and liquidity which was in sharp contrast to mortgages arranged through the agency of a scrivener.[14]

Among the earliest of these goldsmith bankers were Richard Blanchard and Sir Francis Child, at the Marygold by Temple Bar, and examination of surviving Child ledgers shows quite clearly the change from goldsmithing to banking.[15] In 1663, 60 new accounts were opened, of which 41 were goldsmith accounts and 9 banking, the other 10 being mixed accounts containing entries of both types of business. The following year the figures were 48, 25 and 16 respectively, indicating that the banking business was expanding. In December 1664 the Great Plague appeared in London and its effect was such that the number of new accounts opened in 1665 dropped to only 9. The numbers grew slowly in succeeding years but it was not until 1679 that the figures rivalled those of the years before the Plague. By that time the purely banking accounts exceeded the purely goldsmith accounts, and in 1681 the figures for new accounts opened were: banking 206, goldsmith 27 and mixed accounts 20. Despite this change of emphasis, however, the older traditional side of the business remained an important factor until the end of the century.

In the initial stages, as has been seen, the goldsmith merely accepted money for safe custody and gave in exchange a receipt which took the form of a promise to repay on demand. The practice soon arose, however, whereby from time to time these receipts were presented for part payment, the face value of the receipts being reduced on each occasion. In this way the goldsmith bankers became known as 'keepers of running cashes' and these running cash accounts (demand deposits) were the precursors of the modern current account. In July 1663 a Mr Martyn deposited £56 with Mr Child. An account was opened in the ledger and credited with this sum as 'Rcd. being left here £56'. The debit side shows that Mr Martyn withdrew £16 on 4th October and two sums of £10 each in the following January, the account being closed in May with the withdrawal of the balance of £20, recorded as 'paid in full'.

By about 1660 the growth of the practice of keeping 'running cashes' had led to the goldsmiths' receipts becoming assignable and passing from one person to another in place of money. Eventually such 'promissory notes' were issued by the goldsmiths in the form of loans and were not necessarily backed by deposits of coin and bullion, and, as one historian observes, 'When this stage was reached the goldsmith had become a duly recognised purveyor of currency.' (16) The earliest of the Backwell ledgers, dated 1663, provides evidence of this and reveals that in the early years of the post-Restoration regime many customers paying in Backwell notes were credited with their face value. (17) Ultimately, of course, the promissory note was to develop into the modern banknote—which in fact still retains some similarity with its forerunners. The earliest promissory notes are made out to X or bearer, as in the earliest surviving example provided by Childs: (18)

November 28: 1684.

I promise to pay unto ye Rig^t Honble ye Ld North &

Grey or bearer ninety pounds at demand for Mr. ffran

Child & myself

£90 Jno Rogers

The development of the goldsmith's promissory note is closely related to the evolution, and eventual legal recognition, of the assignability of the bill of exchange. As a by-product of his business in foreign coins and at least twenty years before he became a recognised deposit keeper, the goldsmith had acquired experience of carrying out big transactions on behalf of both English and foreign merchants involving the remittance of money abroad and also of providing funds for trade by dealing in bills of exchange.

The development of assignability in the bill of exchange and the goldsmiths' familiarity with this developing practice was thus readily adaptable to the promissory note—all the more so because businessmen and, indeed, lawyers of the day did not recognise any distinction between the two under the custom of merchants. The Common Law Courts of Stuart England did not regard outland and inland bills of exchange and promissory notes payable to X or bearer as assignable, although contemporary evidence (19) reveals that between 1622 and 1651 it had become common in England to transfer by endorsement bills of exchange payable to order and that loans could be obtained by assigning bills of exchange to the 'cashkeepers' of goldsmith bankers. (20)

3. The emergence of the cheque

In the latter half of the seventeenth century it appears that not only was the bill of exchange payable to order freely transferred from one person to another by endorsement, and the practice of repeated endorsements customary, but that the quality of complete assignability had emerged—such assignments being recognised as legal by the Common Law Courts before the end of that century. (21) Moreover, since there was originally thought to be no real difference between the promissory note to order and the inland bill to order, the promissory note was in effect accepted as a bill of exchange and was transferable by repeated endorsements; under the custom of merchants, such notes payable to order were also regarded as negotiable instruments.(22) As Richards observes, 'Side by side with, even as it were under cover of, the inland bill of exchange, the promissory note developed into a negotiable instrument',(23) although legal recognition of this status was not finally accorded until the Promissory Notes Act of 1704.(24)

A parallel process governed the development of the early cheques or drawn notes which, also under the custom of merchants, were accepted as bills of exchange. These provided a further method by which a customer could withdraw money which he had deposited. The earliest known 'cheques'(25)—or 'drawn notes', as they were called, to distinguish them from the goldsmiths' receipt notes—are in the custody of the Institute of Bankers and read as follows:

> Mr Morris & Mr Clayton,
>
> Pray pay the bearer hereof Mr Delboe or order ffour
> hundred pounds I say £400:-:- for Yrs: Nic^{o}: Vanacker
> London the 16th of February 1659

> Mr Morris Pray pay unto Mr Oliver Chadwell (a goldsmith in
> Towerstreet) the som of Syxtie pounds the value received
> of Mr Thomas Colebrook & place to the acc^{o}: of
>
> Yrs: Nicholas Vanacker
>
> Amberley December
> the 13th — 1665
> At the fflying horse in Cornehill London

Possibly the most human of these drawn notes was that of a customer of Sir Francis Child—the young son of the first Duke of Beaufort. Addressed to his father's banker and dated 'Chelsey, 23rd September 1686', it reads:

> Pray do mee the favour to pay his bird-man four guineas for a paire of parakeets that I had of him. Pray dont let anybody either my Ld or Lady know that you did it and I will be sure my selfe to pay you honestly againe.
>
> Arthur Somerset.

Some controversy has arisen over the origin of the cheque. It appears most likely that the key to its origin lies in the fact that it was accepted as a bill of exchange.(26) Thus, in the early stages the depositor probably addressed a letter to his goldsmith authorising the payment to the creditor of the sum due. The creditor would then take this 'note' to the goldsmith and there receive the sum in cash. Marius, writing about the middle of the seventeenth century, reveals how this was done.

> When a bill of exchange is due, and the party to whom it is payable, or his servant comes for the money to the party who hath accepted

> the bill, and ought to pay the same, demanding payment thereof, and he writes him a note to go to a goldsmith, or to such a place to such a man, and there orders the money to be paid.[27]

Since bills of exchange to order and to bearer were well known to the business community of the mid-seventeenth century, it was a natural step to the next stage when the debtor drew his 'bill' or 'note' in favour of his creditor 'or order' or in favour of him 'or bearer'.[28]

This appears to be the simplest and most likely explanation of the origin of the cheque, although a resemblance has been noted between the 'drawn note' and the still earlier demand note drawn on the Exchequer as well as the later 'Auditor of the Receipts' note.[29] The demand notes drawn on the Exchequer were made by persons such as government officials or pensioners who had claims on the Exchequer and who were paid by means of debentures; like the earliest cheques, they began with the name of a person—an Exchequer official, usually a teller—followed by the phrase 'Pray pay'. By means of these notes, which were in use some thirty to forty years before the first 'drawn note', servants were able to draw money at the Exchequer on behalf of their masters; sometimes the notes were made out to persons other than servants and occasionally they were assigned by endorsement. The Auditor of the Receipts note, on the other hand, employed from 1660 until 1834, was endorsed on payment orders issued by the Exchequer; it gave a teller at the Exchequer authority to pay part or all of the order together with the interest due upon the sum which the order represented. Both types of notes thus served for the tellers of the Exchequer of Receipt the function which cheques serve for a banker; this fact, together with the probability that these Exchequer devices were well known to the goldsmiths and their customers, has been adduced to suggest that these notes were the precursors of the cheque itself.

The employment of the promissory note and the early 'cheque' was a natural product of, on the one hand, the goldsmiths' concern to attract and accommodate a growing number of customers spread throughout the various parts of the country and society and, on the other, an increasing inclination on the part of the latter to avoid the burdens and risks of the transport of cash.

By the 1670s the majority of Sir Robert Vyner's depositors consisted of a large number of minor London tradesmen—drapers, butchers, saddlers, brewers, watchmakers, cooks, apothecaries and so on. Gilbert Whitehall held the accounts of London mercers, cordwainers and Nottinghamshire and Huntingdonshire gentlemen. Vyner's customers, like Backwell's, included patrician noblemen and ecclesiastics, such as Sir John Wynne of Denbighshire and Dr Samuel Parker, Archdeacon of Canterbury, and were drawn from all over the country. Between 1688 and 1693 Childs were banking for the Dukes of Leeds and Beaufort, Lord Exeter, Lord Chief Justice (Common Pleas) Sir Francis Pemberton, Nell Gwyn and the royal wife of William of Orange. Whatever the profession or occupation, the goldsmith was there to ply his trade and spread his growing business.

4. Bankers and the Crown

London after the Restoration, however, with its markets and exchanges, brokers, broggers, traders and merchants, was still the source of greatest profit and its leading goldsmiths were of active assistance to the traders of the day in the business of exchange. More important than the merchants, however—or even than the needy landowners living in excess of their income who according to Sir Dudley North still remained the chief borrowers of money — [30] were the financial needs of the Crown which provide the decisive factor in the evolution of the British banking system.

The Crown had found in the reigns of James I and Charles I that its credit needs were too large and too long-term in nature to allow of easy accommodation through the services of the scriveners, part-time brokers and merchant-financiers who constituted the main financial intermediaries in early Stuart London; these needs were best met largely by the assignment of royal revenues of current years—and eventually even of future years [31] —to syndicates of financiers (customs farmers) in return for a fixed rent and the right to anticipate it by borrowing on tallies, a receipt in the form of a notched stick issued on specific royal revenues. [32] The timing of the royal income was thus largely the concern of the tax farmer. Until 1671 the customs were farmed; so was the excise until 1683 and from 1667 to 1684 the Hearth Tax. The accession of Charles II did not greatly alter the fiscal problem which had occupied so much of the ingenuity and attention of his predecessors; like them he faced the disadvantage of a growing reliance on taxation as his main source of income. The hereditary revenues—the Customs and the newer Excise and Hearth taxes—yielded less than expected and were slow in coming in. The imbalance between calls upon the resources of the Crown and its revenues arose mainly from the expense of the wars with Holland which also depressed the Customs yield through their effect on shipping and trade. Revenue raised from extraordinary taxation to meet the expenses of war also proved to be inadequate and difficult to collect. With an irregular and deficient income, therefore, Charles was obliged to share the experience of common mortals and turn to the moneyed men to help him meet his deficits. To bolster the offices of the customs farmers and make good the lags and short-falls in the receipt of the royal revenue, the Crown began to rely on funds advanced by the leading goldsmith bankers on the security of these actual revenues.

Under the Protectorate the goldsmiths had developed their banking functions; from the author of *The Mystery of the New-Fashioned Goldsmiths* we learn that 'when Cromwell usurped the Government, the greatest of them began to deal with him to supply his wants of money upon great advantages'. [33] Cromwell was not regarded as a particularly stable outcome of the Civil Wars, however, and his regime had largely forfeited the financial and political support of the City by defaulting upon a substantial proportion of the credits raised there during the course of the Civil War in the 1640s. [34] After the King's return, however, according to the author of the *Mystery*,

> he wanting money, some of these Bankers undertook to lend him not their own but other men's money, taking barefaced of him ten pound for the hundred, and by private contracts many Bills, Orders, Tallies and Debts of the king's, about twenty, and sometimes thirty in the hundred, to the great dishonour of the Government. [35]

The use of goldsmith bankers made by Cromwell and Charles I and the latter's employment of Exchequer payment orders as a form of paper money issued to the goldsmiths in return for loans marked the beginning of a radical change in the relationship of the government to the money-market; this was significant in the history of banking in a way which the financial machinery of the earlier monarchs—for example, the customs farmers, who left no linear descendants—is not.[36]

The goldsmith bankers became of outstanding importance to the government, extending loans amounting to tens and hundreds of thousands of pounds on the security of the hereditary revenues and extra-ordinary taxation voted by Parliament. As will be seen, their security usually took the form of paper credits issued on these revenues. In the years after the Restoration Alderman Edward Backwell, probably the most important of the goldsmith bankers, was engaged on royal financial missions at home and abroad; such was his standing that in 1665 in his absence abroad on such a mission, Pepys wrote that 'the king and kingdom must as good as fall with that man at this time'. It was not altogether surprising that the King 'always treated those men very graciously, as his very good servants, and all his Ministers looked upon them as very honest and very valuable men'.[37] To attract loans and otherwise shore up the failing finances, the executive of Charles II adapted the tally—hitherto a non-interest-bearing receipt for a loan which was registered on a branch of the public revenue—so as to bear interest and to be accompanied by a repayment order or 'order of loan' which, by an Act of Parliament, was itself made assignable by endorsement. Thus the 'repayment orders' or 'orders of loan' became negotiable interest-bearing securities. To the receiver of public revenue, or the Exchequer official who was called upon to cash them at maturity, both orders and tallies served as vouchers. If the lender needed payment before the date of maturity of his loan, however, it was possible for him to have his tally and order discounted by another person, usually a goldsmith banker, who ultimately presented it at the Exchequer for payment.

The 'order of loan', which when issued represented an actual advance to the State, was soon developed by the executive of Charles II into an order of an entirely different nature—the 'order of the Exchequer' for which a precedent had been devised by Sir William Killigrew in 1663.[38] These 'orders of the Exchequer' did not represent advances to the State but, like the 'orders of loan', were assignable interest-bearing instruments registered on the public revenue and were used by Exchequer officials for paying debts or raising money. They have been described as the origin of official paper money in England.[39]

According to the Exchequer Registers of Orders for Repayment[40] large numbers of 'orders of loans' and 'orders of the Exchequer' were originally issued to such powerful goldsmith bankers as Sir Robert Vyner, Alderman Backwell, Meynell, Duncombe, Colville, Snow and Whitehall by the various departmental treasurers such as the Treasurer of the Navy, the Treasurer of Tangiers and so on, who either raised loans on their security, usually from these goldsmiths, or gave them to government creditors who nearly always discounted them with the goldsmith bankers. The goldsmiths in turn duly presented these for payment at the Exchequer of Receipt; it appears that the goldsmiths were in this way to some extent using the Exchequer as a central bank for their own cash.

In January 1672, however, the Exchequer of Receipt suspended repayment of loans largely because the annual sum of £1,200,000 granted by Parliament in 1660 for the King's expenses was not only not forthcoming from the existing sources but was in any case less than the average annual expenditure between 1660 and 1671, which amounted to over £1, 570, 000. It was possible, indeed, that the system would have worked reasonably satisfactorily had not the triple strains of war, plague and the Great Fire so hamstrung the collection of taxes that the principal of the debt grew and interest payments lagged.

When the 'Stop' was declared it was soon discovered that practically all the Orders of the Exchequer in circulation were in the hands of a number of goldsmith bankers who also held large numbers of individual tallies and orders of loan which they had secured either through discounting or as collateral for advances to the Government. Of a total government debt of £ $2\frac{1}{4}$ million, the sum of £ 1, 365, 733 was estimated as being due to the goldsmith bankers, carrying £ 81, 944 in annual interest at 6 per cent. The bulk of this sum was in turn owed by the goldsmiths to their customers out of whose deposits the royal loans had been financed.

The stop was not a repudiation, however: after some delay interest payment was resumed—to form eventually (1705) part of the British Funded Debt—and it was ordered that the interest on the debt was to be divided by the goldsmiths among their respective creditors; detailed records of these payments were kept in the Exchequer Assignment Books. Nevertheless, the credit of the Crown was seriously impaired, and an abrupt end was made of the Orders of the Exchequer whose issue had been overdone. Not unnaturally, the 'stop' generated a loud clamour amongst the creditors of the bankers. Great damage was done to Sir Robert Vyner, Backwell and others, although the majority of the goldsmith bankers, whose business was mainly with the 'private sector', appear to have been relatively unaffected. Vyner, who was hardest hit, carried on somehow for twelve years and Backwell for ten, although neither was very active after 1672. Amongst Backwell's creditors were other goldsmith-bankers such as Sir Thomas Vyner, Alderman Francis Maynell, Snow and Hornby; in this respect Backwell was acting as a reserve banker discharging one of the duties of a central bank.

Examination of two Exchequer books, known as 'The Bankers Book of Interest' and 'A booke of entringe of the accompts of Goldsmiths and others' enabled R. D. Richards (41) to provide illuminating evidence of the nature of the Crown's commitment to individual goldsmith bankers such as Sir Robert Vyner, Alderman Backwell, Isaac Meynell, John Portman, Joseph Hornby, Jeremiah Snow, Bernard Turner, Robert Welstead, Thomas Rowe and Robert Ryves, but not all of these would be included in Clarendon's definition of the leading royal bankers who totalled 'not above the number of five or six men'. (42)

Sir Robert Vyner and Alderman Backwell would certainly have been included in this definition, however; the Exchequer records show that on the security of tallies, 'orders of loan' and 'orders of the Exchequer', the Crown's total debt to Vyner and partners was over £ 400, 000 and to Backwell nearly £ 300, 000. One account of Isaac Meynell and partners shows a total debt of over £ 200, 000 and reveals that large sums had been advanced on the Hearth money, Customs, and Wines and Vinegars. Another, of Portmans, refers to transactions in 'orders of loan' registered on the customs, while between Michaelmas 1669 and Michaelmas 1671 Jeremiah Snow is recorded as having advanced £ 28, 404 10s 11d to the Cofferer of His Majesty's Household upon two £ 10, 000 'orders of the Exchequer' registered upon the Additional Excise and two such orders each of £5,000 upon the Country Excise.

Clarendon reveals something of the actual working of this incipient money market. When an Act of Parliament was passed authorising a tax, the bankers were summoned before the King, and the Lord Treasurer declared the need for cash:

> whereupon one said: 'he would within such a time pay one hundred thousand pounds', another more, and another less. . . . They were desirous to have 8 in the hundred, but would leave the interest to the King's own bounty, declaring 'that they themselves paid 6 in the hundred for all the money with which they were entrusted', which was known to be true.(43)

Virtually indispensable to the Crown, these half-dozen goldsmith-bankers had in the space of thirty years emerged as large-scale financial intermediaries, taking in funds not only from London but from the provinces as well, usually at not more than 6 per cent, and relending to the King at 8 per cent plus. Although the legal maximum rate of interest was 6 per cent, at this time, royal loans frequently commanded rates of up to 10 or 12 per cent. As the Crown's borrowing increased, so credit tightened and rates hardened, even, according to the author of the *Mystery*, to 20 or 30 per cent. 'Such rates,' as one historian observes, 'were not entirely incommensurate with the risks of having Charles II as a client.'(44) This view, however, was not altogether shared by opinion of the day.

In 1665-6 Pepys, in his capacity of Secretary of the Navy, tried desperately to raise money for the navy but 'did despair of compassing it... so long as we and the world must be subjected to these bankers'.(45) Indeed, there were many who felt that the goldsmiths, having stumbled upon a profitable line of business, were exploiting it in their own interest. It was supposed—with perhaps some truth—that, apart from their business with the Crown, in their trade as dealers in coin they not only culled out for export the heavier pieces—lending out and paying their note and deposit liabilities with light pieces exclusively—but even resorted to 'clipping' and 'sweating'. Another grudge against the goldsmiths was their tendency to go bankrupt. According to Dr Nicholas Barbon the amount of money lost through the bankruptcies of goldsmiths and bankers was 'not less than two million within 5 and 20 years'.(46) Apart from the exceptional circumstances of the 'stop', which would account for much of this sum, common causes of failure included borrowing short and lending long, inadequate or illiquid securities and, especially, insufficient cash reserves. In 1691 Sir Dudley North observed that goldsmiths and scriveners,

> instead of having Ten Thousand Pounds in cash by them as their Accounts show they should have of other Mens Money, to be paid at sight, have seldom One Thousand in Specie; but depend upon a course of Trade whereby money comes in as fast as it is taken out.(47)

Horsefield has shown that a 10 per cent cash reserve was a not uncommonly quoted ratio even in the 1690s.(48) Although this would possibly have sufficed under conditions of peacetime prosperity, it was probably quite inadequate in turbulent times and would appear to have been largely responsible for the frequent failures. It is not an unreasonable assumption, too, that the more cautious—and in the long run the more successful—bankers maintained cash reserves of around 30 per cent; the balance sheets of Childs reveal that in fact the ratio of cash to deposits was normally about 35 per cent. It was still exceptional, however, for critics discussing the safety of a bank's assets to concern themselves with the liquidity of those assets—still less with their shiftability. One of the few to do so was Sir S. T. Janssen who urged in 1698 that the Bank of England should concentrate on short-term assets and avoid trading and dealing in exchanges.(49) By this time the necessity for an adequate cash reserve was beginning to be recognised, although an attempt in Parliament in 1698 to make the cash ratio 100 per cent was unsuccessful.

Real animosity was reserved, however, for the often extortionate rate of interest which the goldsmiths managed to exact from the Exchequer. The year before the Stop, George Downing had been instrumental in securing a tax of 15s on every £100 lent by the bankers which carried over 6 per cent interest. In 1665, indeed, Downing had persuaded Parliament, when voting the Additional Aid for the Dutch War, to specify that all money raised by the Bill should be appropriated for a specific purpose—the conduct of the war and, further, that a direct appeal should be made to the country at large to place funds with the Exchequer, thus bypassing the goldsmiths.(50) Downing's ambition appears to have been to establish a much improved Exchequer in the capacity of a National Bank along the lines suggested by the Bank of Amsterdam. His policies met with a considerable degree of approval and he was supported by, among others, Josiah Child who deplored 'the late innovated Trade by the Bankers in London'.(51)

5. The demand for public banks

The obvious shortcomings of the financial machinery of the State were reflected in a variety of controversies and schemes for improvement. From the last years of the reign of Charles I and throughout the rest of the century there appeared a body of writings which revealed that not a few appreciated the need for, and advantages of, a well-organised credit system.

As early as 1641 Robinson had recommended the establishment of a deposit bank where money could be deposited on interest at 5 per cent and loaned out to borrowers.(52) Generally, most of these advocates of public banks had as their object the betterment of mankind by the infusion of additional purchasing power which would offset the scarcity of currency and create an expansion of trade. Many of them were concerned at the state of the coinage and its scarcity in the years around the Great Recoinage(53) although, in fact, the problems of war finance provided the greatest stimulus. Sir William Petty, writing in 1682 when a recoinage was contemplated, had observed:

> Qu. 26. What Remedy is there if we have too little money?
> We must erect a Bank, which well computed, doth almost double the effect of our coined money.(54)

Secondary merits seen in public banks included greater safety for depositors and an opportunity for the hoarder and small man to invest profitably; it was also felt that more money would lower the rate of interest, which would not only benefit the State and merchants, so it was thought, but would also enhance the value of land.

In 1650 Potter had advocated that 'Banks of Money should be established in various towns, issue negotiable bills for deposits and thus quicken the revolution of money and credit'.(55) Three years later Samuel Lamb had vaguely sensed something of the importance of the note issue and argued that a bank should accept deposits and issue 'imaginary money' or 'credit upon ticket' at $2\frac{1}{2}$ to 3 per cent.(56) In the rein of Charles II projects multiplied, especially after the 'Stop' and the economic and political crises of the latter half of the seventeenth century. Cary had joined Potter, Cradocke, Lewis and Murray in suggesting numerous banks scattered throughout the country. Cary's proposal was for the establishment of a bank or 'Grand Chamber' in London and 'lesser Chambers' in other towns. These banks were to issue depositors with assignable interest-bearing notes payable to order and to advance money 'upon reasonable security, either Rent, personal or Goods'; the notes given in any one Chamber of the Bank were to be 'demandable in any other together with the interest due till payment'.(57)

Horsefield(58) had defined four broad categories within which most of these schemes can be placed. First, Lombard banks which sought to base credit on goods, in that goods of all kinds were to be taken in and circulating credit issued on the strength of them. Such was the influence of these schemes that the by-laws of the Bank of England included, both in 1694 and 1698, provisions for sale 'by inch of candle (of) all jewels, plate, bullion, or other goods, chattels or merchandise and whatsoever which shall be pawned into this corporation'. Secondly, there were plans to capitalise government revenue, of which the Bank of England was a result. By contrast, the Bank of Scotland was a product of schemes in a third category, namely those for banks based on commercial obligations, which were in fact the forerunners of later commercial banks.

Finally, there were schemes for banks based on the security of land and whose liabilities would consist of notes which were optimistically expected to pass from hand to hand and maintain their face value because they were backed by land securities. In the first instance no provision was made for encashment. A spate of these schemes occurred in 1695/6 of which that founded by Asgill and Barbon is at least an honest example. Certainly the most notorious was the Office of Land Credit launched by a professional promoter, 'Dr' Hugh Chamberlen, 'physician in Ordinary' to Charles II. His other designations included 'obstetrician and man-mid-wife'; it was, perhaps, in the practice of this last profession that he mysteriously absconded with the proceeds of his scheme. In the same year Parliament attempted to establish a land-bank for raising a loan of £$2\frac{1}{2}$ million, but only a very small amount was subscribed and the project collapsed.

Apart from the complicated nature of many of these schemes and the occasional transparency of the risks involved, public opinion remained basically cautious. The last half of the seventeenth century did not lend itself to the serious study of projects which did not offer a return of a quick profit; this was an era of lotteries and booms in the stocks of the great joint-stock trading companies. Even so, by the end of the century an often bitter experience had demonstrated something of the nature of banking and its problems.

Schemes for Lombard banks and land-banks were a not illogical expression of men's search for visible security and of their concern with the solvency rather than the liquidity of banks. Even so, emphasis was beginning to be laid on convertibility and by 1697 the need to concentrate on self-liquidating assets was specifically stated.(59) Concern over the security of bank assets was reflected in a fairly rapid shift of thought—perhaps encouraged by the decease of the instigator of the Stop—towards believing that a government-backed bank was the safest kind; on the other hand, there was no shortage of capital owing to the repression of the usual outlets by the war with France.

The adoption of William Paterson's third scheme for a Bank of England in 1694 was not so much a recognition by the government of its intrinsic merits but rather an appreciation of the fact that it was the best offer going, bearing in mind the urgent need to finance the war with France. The subscription of £1,200,000 was raised without difficulty and under its charter of incorporation the new bank was empowered to borrow money on the security of revenues authorised by Parliament, to deal in bullion and bills of exchange and to act as pawnbroker. By the end of the year the Bank had advanced the whole of its capital to the State, mostly in the form of bills taken by the Exchequer in return for tallies and used to pay government creditors. The creditors in turn could either cash them at the Bank, leave them on deposit or, most important, accept Bank notes upon whose ready acceptance and circulation the Bank depended, having parted with much of its capital. Thus began the Bank of England which, with the later Bank of Scotland, survived while all other rivals, including the Orphan's Bank and Million Bank, went down in the general deflation and uncertainty surrounding the Great Recoinage.

6. The contribution of the goldsmith bankers

While the discussions about public banks had been proceeding the goldsmith bankers had been developing an efficient system of private banking in London. The extent of the damage done to the goldsmiths by the 'Stop' has been exaggerated: the royal goldsmiths certainly suffered, but nevertheless showed remarkable resilience. Several important bankers, in fact, were not touched; goldsmith bankers such as the Childs, Hoares, Heriots, Johnsons, Mawsons, Sweetaples, Whites, Pinckneys and Goslings do not appear to have been much involved with the various types of Treasury Exchequer payment orders.(60) There were, besides, a number of rich goldsmiths in reserve ready to develop the banking side of their business; indeed, some of the clerks of the failing houses started business on their own account. Of these perhaps the most outstanding was Charles Duncombe, erstwhile apprentice to Alderman Backwell. By the time of the death of Charles II, Duncombe had loans outstanding to the extent of £390,000, had been appointed 'Register and Comptroller' of Excise and, after 1683, Cashier.(61) On January 10th, 1689, nearly five weeks before the Crown was settled on William and Mary, Duncombe advanced a loan to the new regime at 6 per cent and partly as a result of this his loans to the late King were honoured and interest allowed as if nothing had happened. Backwell's servant had learned his lessons well.

Most of the goldsmith bankers, however—and especially the smaller ones—were not involved in dealings with the Crown; instead, they concentrated on the private business which was relatively unaffected by the risks of royal finance. There had been about thirty goldsmiths who 'kept running cashes' in 1670; according to the *Little London Directory* of 1677 there were then more than forty.(62) Somehow they survived the trade depressions, financial crises and political upheavals of the latter half of the century, including the days of the Popish plot when 'almost all the bankers of Lombard Street are gone off like crackers one after another'(63) and—such was the number of bank failures—when the Queen asked each morning, 'Who is broke today?'(64)

It was these goldsmith bankers who were to emerge into the famous banking firms of London, some of which still exist today. The firm of Blanchard and Child of the Marygold at Temple Bar was taken over by Glyn Mills and Company in 1924 and still continues as Childs Branch. Coutts and Company, now affiliated with the National Provincial Bank, dates from 1692. Hoares of the Golden Bottle in Chepe removed to Fleet Street in 1790 where the business continues to be run by the Hoare family. The firm of Duncombe and Kent, at the Grasshopper in Lombard Street, is now part of Martin's Bank Ltd. Barclay's Bank was incorporated in 1896 by the amalgamation of twenty private banks, among which was Goslings and Sharpe, descended from the famous goldsmith's shop of 'Ye Three Squirrels' which flourished under Major Henry Pinckney in Cromwell's time.

It is difficult to assess the goldsmiths' importance as financial intermediaries. Between 1650 and 1672, very large sums were lent to the government from the deposits held by the bankers and during these years equally large sums were paid to the bankers as interest. The private banking of the goldsmith bankers was related to the fiscal needs of the State and the bankers became the financial experts who mobilised capital for both trade and the Exchequer. Their greatest achievement, however, probably lies in the establishment of themselves as a comparatively secure and profitable outlet for funds which would otherwise have lain idle in sterile hoards. The first beginnings of a banking habit were thereby created, paving the way in succeeding centuries for industrial revolution and progress. They acted as a magnet for money; the funds they attracted, albeit irregular and on a minute scale compared with later years, having entered the goldsmiths' rough but ready mechanism, could be channelled from trades in surplus to trades in deficit, relieving seasonal and other fluctuations. Inevitably there were mistakes and disasters, doubtful dealings and extortionate charges, and always an eye for a quick profit; nonetheless their value to business and the economy in general was considerable. Their construction and operation of a credit system not only served the expanding financial needs of a growing nation; in itself it created opportunities for expansion.

In the history of British banking the goldsmiths' development of the promissory note and cheque, demand and time deposits, balance sheets and cash reserves, provided the primitive but nevertheless essential elements of a modern banking structure. In their evolution they had provided precedents which the directors of the Bank of England were to adopt and subsequently embellish—particularly in the case of the note issue—and for which no model had been suggested by the Bank of Amsterdam or any of the other leading continental banks. As one of the founders and first directors of the Bank of England, Sir Theodore Janssen, wrote in his *Discourse concerning Banks* in 1697, 'The Custom of giving notes hath so much prevailed amongst us that the Bank could hardly carry on Business without it.'

REFERENCES

1. E. Lipson, *Economic History of England*, Vol. III, Cambridge University Press, London 1931, p. 235.

2. H. C. Gutteridge, 'The origin and historical development of the profession of Notaries Public in England', *Cambridge Legal Essays* (Ed. P. H. Winfield and A. D. McNair), Heffer, Cambridge 1926, pp. 128-33.

3. D. C. Coleman, 'London scriveners and the estate market in the later seventeenth century', *Economic History Review*, Series 2, Vol. IV, No. 2, 1951, pp. 221-30.

4. J. D. Gould, 'Trade Depression in the early 1620s', *Economic History Review*, Series 2, Vol. III, 1954-5, p. 81.

5. E. T. Powell, 'The Evolution of the Money Market 1385-1915', *The Financial News*, London 1915, pp. 58-9.

6. State Papers Domestic, Charles I, 107, No. 17.

7. State Papers Domestic in the Public Record Office, 1651-2, No. 21.

8. *Ibid.*, Charles I, 65/74, 43/4.

9. E. T. Powell, *op. cit.*, pp. 59-60.

10. E. T. Powell, *op. cit.*, pp. 62-8.

11. *The Mystery of the New-Fashioned Goldsmiths or Bankers* published in 1676 (incorporated in J. B. Martin's *Grasshopper in Lombard Street*, 1892, pp. 285-95).

12. Backwell Ledgers, in Custody of Glyn Mills.

13. Quoted by S. W. Shelton, Archivist & Review Editor, Glyn Mills.

14. E. T. Powell, *op. cit.*, pp. 59-60; see also H. D. Macleod, 'A history of banking in Great Britain', Chap. 1, sec. (i), p. 2 in 'A history of banking of all the leading nations', *Journal of Commerce and Commercial Bulletin*, Vol. 2, New York 1896.

15. Glyn Mills Archives.

16. R. D. Richards, *The Early History of Banking in England*, P. S. King and Son, London 1929, p. 40.

17. Glyn Mills Archives.

18. *Ibid.*

19. Malynes in his *Lex Mercatoria*, first published in 1622, does not mention the assignability of the English bill of Exchange nor the terms 'to order' or 'to bearer'. John Marius in 1651 in the first publication of *Advice concerning Bills of Exchange*, pp. 7-10, describes the custom in detail.

20. P.R.O., Ch. P., before 1714 (Mitford), 64/81.

21. Carter v. Downich (1686), Carth., p. 83; Jordan v. Barloe (1701), 3 Salk., p. 67.

22. Richards, *op. cit.*, pp. 47-8. See also W. Cranch, 'Promissory Notes before and after Lord Holt', *Select Essay A.A.L.H.*, III.

23. *Ibid.*, p. 47.

24. J. Milnes Holden, *The History of Negotiable Instruments in English Law*, The Athlone Press, University of London, 1955, pp. 73-87.

25. Although there is an isolated reference to a 'cheque' in Childs' ledger for 1680, the expression does not appear to have become current usage until very much later. S. W. Shelton, Glyn Mills & Co.

26. Holden, *op. cit.*, pp. 204-10.

27. Marius, *op. cit.*, p. 6.

28. Holden, *op. cit.*, p. 207.

29. Richards, *op. cit.*, pp. 52-55.

30. Sir Dudley North, *Discourses Upon Trade* (1691), pp. 6-7.

31. R. Ashton: *The Crown and the Money Market 1603-40*, Clarendon Press, Oxford 1960, pp. 43-44. In 1628, part of the revenues up to two years ahead had been pledged; by 1630 the figure was seven years; by 1631 eleven and by 1637 fourteen years ahead.

32. Usually a hazel wand which, after the requisite number of notches had been cut, was split, one half being retained by the Exchequer, the other being given as the receipt.

33. Ashton, *op. cit.*

34. M. P. Ashley, *op. cit.*, pp. 98-9.

35. *Ibid.*, from Powell, *op. cit.*, p. 60.

36. R. Ashton, *op. cit.*, pp. 186-7.

37. *The Life of Edward, Earl of Clarendon* (ed. 1827), iii, pp. 8-9.

38. J. K. Horsefield, *British Monetary Experiments, 1650-1710*, London 1960, p. 96.

39. W. A. Shaw, 'The Treasury Order Book', *Economic Journal*, Vol. XVI, 1906.

40. P.R.O., Recs. Ex. R., E. 403/2430-2435.

41. Richards, *op. cit.*

42. *Ibid.*, pp. 8-9.

43. *Ibid.*

44. Powell, *op. cit.*, p. 60.

45. Arthur Bryant, *Pepys*, Vol. I, p. 282.

46. Dr. Nicholas Barbon, *A Discourse of Trade*, 1690, p. 29.

47. North, *op. cit.*, p. 20.

48. Horsefield, *op. cit.*, Appendix 5, p. 263.

49. Sir S. T. Janssen, *A second Part of a Discourse concerning Banks*, 1698.

50. C. Wilson, *England's Apprenticeship 1603-1763*, Longmans, London 1965, pp. 214-5.

51. *Ibid.*, p. 215 (Quoting from H. Roseveare, unpublished thesis *The Advancement of the King's Credit 1660-1672*).

52. H. Robinson, *England's Safety in Trades Increase* (1641), reprinted in W. A. Shaw, *Select Tracts and Documents illustrative of English Monetary History, 1626-1730* (1896).

53. Horsefield, *op. cit.*, p. xvii.

54. Sir William Petty, *Quantulum cumque concerning Money*, 1682.

55. W. Potter, *The key to Wealth*, 1650, pp. 71-72.

56. S. Lambe, *Seasonal Observations*, 1657.

57. J. Cary, *Essay towards the Settlement of a National Credit*, 1696, pp. 3-5.

58. Horsefield, *op. cit.*, pp. xvii-xviii.

59. Sir S. T. Janssen, *A Discourse Concerning Banks*, 1697, p. 8.

60. Richards, *op. cit.*, p. 64.

61. E. Hughes, *Studies in Administration and Finance 1558-1825*, Manchester University Press, 1934, pp. 164-6.

62. F. G. Hilton Price, *A Handbook of London Bankers*, gives list.

63. Letter of Ormonde to Earl of Arran. March 10 (1682) Ormonde MSS. V 430-1, VI 542.

64. Verney Memoirs, IV 27-8.

CHAPTER THREE

Country Banking

1. The origins of country banking

The London goldsmith bankers had made no effort to extend their business into the provinces largely because of difficulties of communication and transport; even had these been absent, however, there still remained a practical deterrent in the limitation on the size of partnerships. Until 1826 the Charter of the Bank of England prevented the establishment of joint-stock banks in England and Wales. Outside London, however, the expansion of trade and business which was the forerunner of the Industrial Revolution was creating a need for monetary services. At first this was perhaps no more than mere money-changing or the provision of small coin as wages, but with the growth of the Industrial Revolution from the mid-eighteenth century the needs became more specialised and urgent. Manufacturers and traders in the North and Midlands in need of capital to develop and operate new enterprises were eager for funds to finance their investments. Money was needed for both fixed capital formation and working capital and in the absence of its supply by the London private bankers or the Bank of England it was left to businessmen themselves to meet their own needs.

Three main types of individual seem to have developed into early country bankers: industrialists, financial intermediaries—i.e. scriveners—and remitters of funds between London and the country, principally traders and local collectors of government revenue. Country banking was thus 'less an innovation than a specialisation in existing financial techniques'.(1) To meet the need for more and better coinage—a need not fulfilled by the Mint and eighteenth century government—traders and industrialists throughout the country issued their own tokens and notes; in the first instance they did so usually in order to pay wages to their employees, but in doing so they thereby served a common apprenticeship to banking. William Blow Collis, for example, a mercer and draper in Worcester around 1762 (when he was described as 'mercer and banker') issued notes between 1760 and 1775 when a severe shortage of small change encouraged issues of this kind.(2) Legislation was introduced in 1775 to prohibit the issue of small notes below £1 and this was extended to notes of less than £5 from 1777. The issue of tokens, however, continued until forbidden by Parliament in 1817.

In general the efforts of entrepreneurs to overcome the shortage of currency arose from a desire to meet the routine needs of their business, but the movement into full banking, and the use of paper money, was given impetus by the suspension of cash payments by the Bank of England in 1797. An unfavourable balance of payments, outflows of Bank of England bullion and the strains of wartime finance had already given cause for public nervousness about the position of the Bank. The landing of a handful of Frenchmen on the Pembroke coast towards the end of February of that year had precipitated a liquidity panic resulting in the suspension of cash (i.e. gold and silver) payments by the Bank; although originally intended to be of short duration, the suspension lasted for over twenty years. Shortly afterwards both the Bank of England and the country bankers were authorised by Parliament to issue notes of low denomination, and this greatly stimulated the private issue and circulation of paper money.(3)

Apart from the shortages of coin and the financial difficulties of the 1780s and 1790s there were other strong incentives for entrepreneurs in expanding industries to undertake banking activities of various degrees. Through the circulation of notes on his own credit, the issue of drafts and the acceptance of deposits from the general public, the industrialist-turned-banker was not only providing a local means of payment but was receiving, on the credit of his own name, a supply of capital to assist his own industrial enterprise. In the iron and steel industry, Messrs Taylors and Lloyds, bankers at Dale End, Birmingham, became full-blown bankers in 1765, paying interest at 2 per cent on deposits within four months of opening their account.(4) In 1804 Samuel Galton, switching from gun-making to banking, established a triple partnership with his son and Joseph Gibbins, and their office in Steel-house Lane became the banking house of the gun trade.(5)

As in Birmingham — the centre of numerous metal trades — so in most of the provincial towns, the private banker emerged during the great expansion of British trade and industry in the second half of the eighteenth century. The Finches of Dudley, long established as nail ironmongers and merchants, had issued tokens as early as 1648 and had entered banking by 1791. The 'Miners' Bank' of Truro was founded by 1759, and Praed's Cornish Bank by 1774, the partners of both being involved in the Cornish copper industry. John Morgan, proprietor of the Carmarthen Furnace Bank, had already issued a number of copper tokens to assist his business in tin when during the 1790s he turned to full banking.(6) The textile industries, too, were productive of bankers since they faced the need to pay a considerable labour force, preferably with small change, and to finance the interval between various stages of production, concern with which led many into banking. In East Anglia Gurney and Co. were established as bankers in 1775, but long before this they had been advancing money to their employees in woollen manufacturing and to entrepreneurs in other trades. In the south-west other clothiers and traders—including the Barings—turned to banking, either to augment their existing business or to seek in banking a more attractive return on their capital.

Money scriveners provided another major source of country bankers. The scrivener was a specialist in land conveyancing and in mortgages but in his capacity as attorney he was accustomed to receiving clients' money on deposit, to be invested at interest with other clients who wished to borrow for the purposes of land investment.(7) By 1750 bankruptcies of scriveners and money scriveners began to increase, an indication of the expansion of their activities. By the early years of the nineteenth century, however, money scriveners as a distinct profession were disappearing, although attorneys continued to act as agents for investment and to be bankrupted as money scriveners.

Of equal importance as an origin of country banking were those activities which involved the remittance of funds, primarily through the discount of bills, usually to London but often abroad. Towards the end of the seventeenth century there had arisen the practice of using bills issued against the assets of London bankers to effect payments between London and the country in order to avoid the inconvenience and risk of the transport of coin.

The importance of the bill in the development of country banking must not be overlooked. Indeed, it has been suggested that the country banks of the eighteenth century were primarily organisations for dealing with bills — not only for discounting them, but for presenting them for acceptance, holding them in safe keeping, and collecting payment on maturity. According to Hawtrey:

> Their note issues and deposits were originally incidental to these functions; traders made their bills payable to the banks, and were willing to leave the proceeds of discount or collection on deposit, or to draw them out in the convenient form of bank notes.(8)

It is more probable, however, that these functions were carried out by merchants and traders themselves, some of whom later extended their activities to include note-issue and the acceptance of deposits. General merchants and overseas traders were in fact a fruitful source of merchant banking activity. The really important trader-bankers were those whose business involved them in considerable trading beyond the merely retail sphere—that is, commodity dealers in cloth and iron, or importers of tea and wine.(9)

In 1774, for example, John Shore, the son of a Sheffield factor, established the bank of Parker, Shore and Co. Again, Clarke, Richardson and Hodgson (later known as Richardson, Holt and Co.) were drapers, wine merchants and mercers at Whitby who in 1786 added banking to their other interests. Even earlier, in 1778, Thomas Peirson, a draper of the same town, founded a banking firm later known as Frankland and Wilkinson. Yorkshire's marked diversity of development also provided a fruitful ground for a full extension of banking.(10) To the basic occupation of agriculture had been added a great textile industry and an important iron and steel trade. Initially, in this county, as in other parts of the realm, banking was for many years a mere adjunct to some other principal trade and many of the early banks arose directly out of a trading partnership. In Liverpool, of fourteen banks of any importance, ten came from merchant houses. Heywood's Bank developed in this way out of the sugar trade and other trading activities—including the slave trade. By 1773 Arthur Heywood's banking activities had developed into a specialist bank known as Arthur Heywood, Sons and Co., but he continued to trade under his own name as a merchant.(11) In Lancashire the ubiquity of the bill of exchange in everyday payments provided a practical banking apprenticeship for most businessmen; for those who embarked on full banking a ready-made network of credit existed.

In addition to these commercial remittance activities there were the collection and remittance of Crown revenues by local receivers. Officials of canal companies and receivers of land and assessed taxes extended credit on money passing through their hands. At least six of a list of country bankers in 1784 were tax-receivers; these usually remitted to London by buying bills from local merchants drawn on London, the bills being sent to a London agent who paid them over to the government departments. Owing to the delay in making over cash they were effectively borrowing money on discount at the public expense, thereby expanding their local cash reserves with which they were able to make loans or buy Exchequer Bills.

After 1750, as regular banking emerged, ample evidence was provided of close connections between country banks and public finance.[12] Joseph Berwick, a Worcester draper, for example, was receiver-general of the land-tax for the county for several years before he began banking proper in 1781. Undoubtedly, in the lags between receipt and delivery of these funds, the country banker found a regular and profitable source of income which added both deposits and prestige to his business. In fact, the banker did not need to be directly responsible for the collection of taxes in order to benefit from public money so long as the revenue officials accepted his notes or kept their accounts with him.[13]

Industrialists and traders, scriveners and tax-collectors—these were the people involved with large transactions in credit and coin, bills and notes, deposits and advances which readily led to the evolution of country banking. Some bankers, indeed, could attribute their ancestry to a combination of more than one of these occupations. One such—a late example—was Thomas Rushton, who became a partner in the banking partnership of Hardcastle Cross & Co., of which his father, a solicitor, was also a partner. Thomas himself was admitted as a solicitor in 1831 and remained in that practice until 1879. He was also for many years a partner in an iron foundry but retired from that shortly after he became the managing partner in the bank in 1858.[14]

With the first great advance of the industrial revolution the needs of industry and trade had led to the evolution of the country banker as primarily a specialist in local trades and industry, to bolster which, or as a side-line to which, was grafted the occupation of amateur banker. According to Edmund Burke not more than a dozen banks existed outside London in 1750, and only Smith's of Nottingham can be shown to have provided banking services before this date.[15] In 1784, the earliest list available—Baileys' British Directory for 1784—reveals 119 banks outside London in England alone,[16] while the secretary of the Association of English Country Bankers reckoned in 1797 that there were about 230. Allowance had to be made, however, for the fact that many of these banks were very small, new or short-lived. By 1804 there were reckoned to be between 470 and 480 and many towns with modest populations ran to three, six or seven separate banks;[17] in 1808-9 it was usual to speak of about 800 banks. In 1808 official statistics became available when all note-issuing banks were required to take out licences; from these it is known that by the end of the Napoleonic wars only three counties—all Welsh—had no licensed banks, while 26 had three or more. Yorkshire had 64, Devon 49 and Somerset 42; in 1821 Thomas Richardson remarked that 'I should conceive there are bankers or bankers' agents within 10 miles of every place, almost.'[18]

There were dangers in such expansion, as the figures for bankruptcies show. Between 1750 and 1830 at least 343 firms whose proprietors styled themselves 'bankers' failed in the country; 334 of them failed between 1790 and 1826, and of these 67 failed in the three years 1814-16 and 60 between July 1825 and June 1826.[19] Many could trace their ruin to the uncertain circumstances of a wartime era and especially to the aftermath of the Napoleonic wars. One underlying cause of all such failures, however, lay in the over-expansion of banking services, particularly in the late eighteenth and early nineteenth centuries—the period of the suspension of cash payments. In the early 1800s Abingdon, with about 4, 500 people, had three banks; Boston, with perhaps 7, 000, had six; Exeter had seven, although it had a population of only about 18, 000.[20] In 1836 John Harding (of Harding and Co.) had stated before the Select Committee on Joint Stock Banks that Driffield, a village of 2, 500 inhabitants, possessed four banks and that there was no possibility of success for all of them—a condition of affairs which, he alleged, was true of all the towns and many villages of the East Riding.[21] Business optimism had ridden high—often too high—on the first wave of the industrial revolution and when the tide receded whole industries and regions, as well as individuals, were left stranded. A major weakness of country banking lay in its evolution from, and subsequent reliance upon, particular trades and industries which were often vulnerable to trade cycles and long-term decline created by technological development and changing patterns of consumption. Just as local trades and industries frequently provided the cradle of country banking, so in many cases they were to provide its coffin. The joint-stock banks, eventually based on a more diverse clientele, were to prove more successful.

2. Links with London—the correspondent system

The country banks were linked indirectly with each other and with the London money market in a system of unit banking by the common economic and business influences to which the provinces and capital alike were subject. Direct links with the London money market were forged by the country banker's need to provide for his customers some of the essential financial services whose operation was dependent on London bankers and the lack of which would have lost him many of his clientele. Of these services, the most relevant to the growth of country banking was the increasing use of the bill of exchange drawn on London, as well as other forms of paper credit based directly upon the capital. By the early eighteenth century the London bill was becoming an accepted method of payment between country towns and London. By the end of the century it was appearing at every stage in the growing cotton industry of Lancashire and was no less evident in expanding industries elsewhere. The various aspects and methods of the remittance of funds were a prime concern to the country banker and, as has already been seen, remittance activities often led to banking. When local banks appeared in the second half of the eighteenth century, their principal function was the remittance of funds and their most vital feature was a regular link with the London money market. At this point the bulk of a country banker's business was usually handled by a single agent, a London banker.

A natural product of this connection was the exercise of increasing influence over the country banker by his London agent, since country banks accumulating resources in excess of what could be invested profitably in their districts employed these surplus resources with their London bankers. On the other hand, when local resources were inadequate to meet local demands for funds, the country banker looked to London for short-term credit for the discounting of bills and for the grant of bank drafts. When money was scarce or advice needed, the country banker tended to turn to London, much as the London banks tended to turn to the Bank of England.

The choice of a London banker as agent was usually settled by the personal or business connections of the country bankers; in some cases the bond was even sealed by an interlocking partnership.[22] In a few instances the country bank set up its own London office, as did Smith and Payne of

Nottingham and Taylors and Lloyds of Birmingham (a type of foundation known as a 'pig-on-pork' bank from the fact that its acceptances were in the name of the original parent bank), the main function of some of these offices being not to replace but to supplement the ordinary London banker-agent. The majority of country bankers, however, relied on agency agreements with London bankers.

With few exceptions the London banks established before 1750—the goldsmith bankers and their descendants—did not participate very fully in country correspondence. The outstanding London agents were the firms founded in the second half of the eighteenth century which tapped the country business from the beginning of its rapid expansion in the 1780s; the older firms, being perhaps more conservative and cautious, preferred the known business profits, and risks, of the capital.(23)

The country banker was able to ensure that debts between different parts of the country were to a large extent settled through the London account, simply by ordering debits to the account with the agent. He was able to issue his own notes payable at the London agents and also drew upon them bills of exchange which they collected for his credit. In 1798, for example, Oakes of Bury St Edmunds instructed Ayton & Co. to pay to the Exchequer two amounts of £10,000 and £12,000 in respect of taxes collected by Orbell Oakes in his capacity as Receiver-General for West Suffolk.(24) A thrifty banker, however, would keep an eye on payments from his London funds, since such payments incurred commissions, reduced profits and weakened reserves; as J. W. Gilbart observed in 1827, 'It is the object of the country bank to receive as much and to pay as little as possible in London'(25) Such payments could be reduced by inter-bank settlements but it was left to the joint-stock banks to develop this technique.

There were more interesting aspects of the London agent's routine business of handling his correspondents' cheques and bills of exchange. In 1855, for example, Lacons Youells (Norwich and Yarmouth) instructed Glyns not to pay drafts without specific advice, as a clerk had absconded with two blank signed drafts. Glyns were asked to detail anyone applying for money on these drafts and were informed that the absconding clerk 'may be immediately identified by his eyebrows which meet on his nose'.(26)

A not unnatural development of the employment of a London account, through which a considerable and regular volume of business was carried out, was that the country banker came to regard his London balance as part—and the most important part—of his cash reserve.(27) Stephens Harris and Stephens at Reading banked with Willis Percival & Co. in Lombard Street, and in their 1815 'General Statement', in which assets totalled some £173,000, cash stood at £8,327 while 'Balance in Hands of Willis Percival and Co.' stood at £13,334. Five years later, cash stood at £10,561 with £23,739 in Lombard Street, and in 1840 they were still keeping the bulk of their cash in hand with their London agent.(28)

The ability to overdraw an account was one of the perquisites of the agency system and in general there seems to have been no difficulty about occasional overdrafts up to £10,000 or even £20,000 for banks whose total assets were generally less than £200,000. Persistent overdrafts were disliked by the bank in London. Lending long was not the bankers' business; furthermore, suspicions could justly be entertained as to the regularity of the affairs of the customer concerned. Thus in 1831 H. S. Thornton, a partner in Williams Deacon & Co., addressed a banker in Frome, for whom his bank was the London agent:-

> January 21st, 1831.
>
> If you wish to prevent us from refusing your notes for the future, it will be necessary that you should yourself take immediate steps for reducing the (overdrawn) account. We consider it extremely improper that you should have taken a considerable sum from the bank in which you are a partner, thereby compelling us to come under advances in the manner we have, and at the same time exposing your partners to the greatest risk of bankruptcy... We expect you will lose no time in converting sufficient property.[29]

The threat of refusal of payment of the country bankers' notes, and the allusion to the disastrous consequences of this action, depending on the customer's willingness to reform, revealed something of the influence exercised by the London agent. The extent of this influence was often considerable, particularly when the country banker was dependent on his agent for overdraft facilities, and it extended from simple advice to strict instruction as to the conduct of local business. It is possible to exaggerate the influence of the London banker, however, since in many cases his advice was too late to be of any real use. It was all too frequently in the capacity of undertaker rather than doctor that the agent was obliged to act for his country client.

3. The means of payment

The principal function of the country banker was to supply means of payment, transfer and remittance, thereby endeavouring to fill the gap left by the failure of the Mint and the Bank of England to supply money for everyday needs. The main way in which this was done was the issue of printed notes, except in Lancashire where they were comparatively insignificant. Some banks economised on the use of gold in the years before the suspension of cash payments by lending their own notes, particularly those in rural areas and those established in Newcastle, Bristol, Birmingham and Sheffield; other lent only in drafts, bills of exchange, coin or Bank of England notes.

The banks operating in Lancashire and the West Riding—the two fastest-growing areas of Britain—concentrated on supplying and discounting bills which formed the medium through which industrial development was financed. Largely because of the acute shortage of silver and base coin in Lancashire, they circulated as money while bills of denominations as low as 6d or 1s were used to pay wages; retailers who received these exchanged them with the manufacturers for larger bills drawn on London.[30]

The use of the bill of exchange in the settlement of industrial or trading debts was not confined to these regions. A Midland or North Country manufacturer who had a payment to make to London or elsewhere often did so by means of a draft or bill of exchange. His banker drew a bill with a life of approximately two months on the banker's London correspondent, knowing that he would be put in funds at the appropriate time so that either he could meet the bill, if presented to him, or his account with his London correspondent could be debited by the latter if it were presented there for redemption. The drawer of the bill endorsed it in making payment and it could pass from hand to hand (with successive endorsements making the bill a sounder security the nearer it reached redemption) as a form of credit currency. The manufacturer paid interest to his banker for the privilege of using this device to delay payment in coin. A country bank could discount bills for its customers but the extent of its lending was limited by the amount of its note issue and deposits and the need to maintain a cash reserve.(31)

In the West Riding and Lancashire of the eighteenth century these bills were the sole paper currency, performing the function not only of banknotes but also—particularly the smaller denominations—to a great extent that of coin, for which they could be readily discounted. They were at least comparable to a banknote in both soundness and liquidity and their predominance in the north-west perhaps explains the late development of banking there; hence the reference by one historian to

> the relative immunity of Lancashire and the West Riding from the panics of those parts of England in which the paper currency rested on the reputation not of the traders, but of a number of small, and not always well-managed, banks of issue.(32)

A second means of payment at this stage was of course the bank cheque, but in fact this remained insignificant in country banking until the second quarter of the nineteenth century. The stamp duties payable on drafts and cheques drawn on a locality more than ten miles (after 1828, fifteen miles) from the bank concerned discouraged a full development of payment by cheque, although this was partially offset by the establishment of bank agencies.(33) A complete realisation of the benefits of this particular instrument was enjoyed by the joint-stock banks, particularly after the Bank Charter Act of 1844 restricted private note issues.

In the more sophisticated financial and commercial world of London the cheque was better known and had been since the seventeenth century; nevertheless, although increasing, its use was still not common in comparison with banknotes and bills of exchange. Early in the eighteenth century the Bank of England had begun to encourage its customers to write their 'drawn notes' on 'check' (chequered) paper.(34) London private bankers in the 1770s mostly ceased to issue notes, using instead Bank of England notes and cheques. The use of the cheque in eighteenth- and early nineteenth-century London, however, resembled less the modern method of paying debts by transfer of a claim upon a bank than an order to the banker—in the manner illustrated in Chapter 2—to pay out money, coin, notes, bills of exchange to the holder of an account or to some person named by him.(35)

As the eighteenth century progressed the increasing use of paper media in London—notes, drafts and bills, and also, but to a lesser extent, cheques —created a need for a regular system of clearing. Hitherto it had been the practice of a London private banker receiving a cheque to send it to the paying bank, together with private bank notes, drafts and bills, by a clerk on foot and to secure Bank of England notes in exchange. Undeniably a laborious and slow procedure, it involved the handling of unnecessarily large sums of cash to settle outstanding balances and a considerable risk of robbery. The first step towards establishing a regular system of clearance was taken by the 'walks' clerks themselves; some time around the mid-eighteenth century, they began to appreciate the advantages to themselves of meeting at a convenient place—usually a coffee house—and exchanging their drafts on each other, settling only the balance in cash. This informal and unauthorised exchange continued for some years until about 1770, when the practice of clearing was accorded official recognition by the private bankers of the City; in 1773 a room was hired for the purpose in the 'Five Bells', Dove Court, off Lombard Street. It was to be the best part of a century before cheque clearings became the main feature of the Clearing House, but the institution of the clearing, by economising on the volume of cash needed in settlement of a given turnover, had already permitted a considerable saving in the quantity of money which the banks were obliged to leave lying idle in their tills. This was of particular importance to bankers in the City; because of their extensive bill dealings and mercantile custom, they were more subject to wide variations from day to day in the value of claims presented against them than their counterparts in the West End.

Cheques, therefore, were of no great concern to the private country banker, although to the mid-nineteenth century banker in the provinces they were to assume considerable importance. Bankers' drafts—transfers through the London agents—together with bills of exchange and banknotes were however used for many routine payments in business. For small payments the third major means of payment—private note issues—was largely used in most areas outside London, especially between 1797 and 1825, and the issues 'provided the most direct contact between the banks and that overwhelming majority of the community which did not keep banking accounts'.[(36)] Country banknotes were issued to customers in return for cash deposits; until the 1790s, they were often interest-bearing up to a maximum rate of around 3 per cent. They were negotiable, made out to order or bearer, and might be payable on demand or on up to 20 days' notice. The suspension of cash payments by the Bank of England in 1797 greatly increased the importance of country banknotes, partly because of the consequent Parliamentary permission for the provision of currency of small denominations and also because of the practical, if not legal, encouragement of the ready substitution of notes for gold.[(37)]

In England and Wales the Act of 1777 had prevented the issue of anything less than a five pound note by any bank; until 1793 the Bank of England had not issued in smaller units than £10. Anticipating a vacuum in the currency after suspension, Parliament had authorised first the Bank of England and then the private banks to issue notes for less than £5. As gold became scarcer, Bank of England £1 and £2 notes were used more for paying wages and in retail trade, especially in the London area and in South Lancashire where they had no local competitors. Their circulation rose gradually to between £4 million and £5 million by 1800.[(38)]

Country banknotes, too, were issued for denominations as low as 10s, 5s and even 2s 6d; in 1808, when denominations of less than £1 were prohibited by Act of Parliament, they were common throughout much of the country and were widely used in the payment of wages. One of the Birmingham Lloyds recalled in 1858 that when £1 notes were permitted, bank notes were very frequently taken by labourers. In 1832 Beckett, the Leeds banker, said that wages were paid to the extent of two-thirds or three-quarters in gold and silver and the remainder in country notes. The prohibition in 1826 of notes of less than £5 undoubtedly reduced the scope for private issues, but notes continued to be used for wages.[39] Not least of the drawbacks attached to notes was the ease of forgery. In the period 1812-21 there had been 201,206 forgeries of Bank of England notes (£1 and £2) alone. In the early years of the suspension, however, ordinary wage-earners and small traders knew little of paper money and learned its use only slowly. Nevertheless the age gradually became 'one of bank-notes and tradesmen's tokens and Spanish dollars stamped with the head of King George III and put into circulation by the Bank of England'.[40]

A variety of causes induced bankers to issue their own notes and to continue to circulate them until the last private issuing bank, Fox Fowler & Co., was absorbed in 1921. Sometimes they issued notes because Bank of England notes were regarded locally as inferior or because they were more expensive to supply. Most bankers, however, accepted Gilbart's description (1827) of notes as 'the grand source of profit' and declared that their replacement by Bank of England paper and gold would damage them seriously.[41] Vincent Stuckey, perhaps with an excess of zeal, told the 1841 Committee that the loss of his note issue would reduce his profits by 'at least one half'.[42] Unlike the later joint-stock banks, country banking generally was based upon the issue of notes, the attraction of deposits being only a secondary aim. Moreover, in 1832 Forster, a Walsall banker, had drawn attention to the free publicity provided by private note issues. 'It gives a sort of éclat to the establishment; it answers the purpose of the address card of a Tradesman; it makes the bank notorious and makes it a subject of conversation, and brings deposits and customers.'[43] Walter Bagehot in his *Lombard Street* also confirmed that the operation of a successful note issue advertised the credit of a banker and set in motion a flow of deposits towards him.[44] Sentiments such as these are no doubt appreciated today by the Scottish banker. His eighteenth-century ancestor, at any rate, considered a note issue to be the chief function of a bank, essential to provide it with the necessary funds additional to the proprietor's subscribed capital; it was not until the end of that century that deposit banking was actively encouraged.[45]

Reliable statistics of the volume of private note issues are not available, although there is no lack of information on the Bank of England circulation. In 1790 its average of notes outstanding for the four quarters had been £11 million and it was slightly more in 1795. During the last half of 1796 and the first quarter of 1797, when the directors were deliberately restricting the issue, it was down to £9.7 million. After that it grew slowly but steadily, reaching £15 million in the first quarter of 1800, £16 million in the first quarter of 1801 and £17 million in the third quarter of 1802; in the first and second quarters of 1804 it reached a peak of £17.6 million which it did not exceed until 1809.[46]

No figure for the country-bank note-issue can be more than an informed guess. One such was that offered to the Bullion Committee in 1810 by J. H. Tritton, a London banker and agent for many country banks. He gave £30,000 as an average circulation, multiplied this by 721 (the number of issuing banks) and arrived at a figure of around £20 million as the total circulation of private banks, including those in Scotland which were reckoned to have out some £2 million in notes.[47] By 1808, when licences to issue were first required, licences were held in every county of England and Wales with the exception of Radnorshire. After 1825, Bank of England issues greatly exceeded private issues; in 1833, when returns of the private circulation including joint-stock banks were first made, the former were nearly double the latter. But in their hey-day—the period of the suspension of cash payments—country bankers appear to have supplied about as much of the ordinary currency of the country as did the Bank of England and the Mint.(48)

There were temptations and pitfalls, however, in the opportunities provided for private note issues. Issuing banks generally were none too secure. Between 1816 and 1824, a period of comparative calm, less than 2 per cent of them failed yearly but in the troubles of 1816 some 6 per cent had gone and in 1825 and 1826 the percentage rose to over 10.(49)

From 1819 the prospect of the resumption of cash payments exerted a deflationary influence upon the supply of credit. Country note issues appear to have contracted as local bankers took precautions, acquiring stocks of gold and keeping greater reserves locally and in London. Following three years of agricultural depression, however, the government embarked on a policy of reinflation including, in 1822, a decision to extend the power of private bankers to issue small notes (£1 and £2 notes) until 1833, the date of the renewal of the Bank of England Charter. This step was an open invitation to over-issue, especially as the Bank of England—in an imprudent effort to employ the very large reserves it had accumulated against the expected reduction of the country circulation—promptly reduced its rate of 4 per cent and extended the currency of eligible bills from 65 to 95 days.(50) The country bankers could hardly do other than follow these changes in the credit situation; a fall in the rate of interest, by reducing the profitability of London balances and investments in bills and bonds, obliged them to employ their resources more extensively and often, of course, at greater risk. Falling rates of interest and increasing public confidence, however, led to an increase in the demand for money; since, in anticipation of the Resumption in 1821, the Bank of England had been contracting its circulation of small (under £5) notes, due to come to an end in 1823, this demand could readily be met by the country banker through the issue of his own notes.

By 1808 the Government had required country bankers to license their note issues and to pay stamp duty on their notes. Even allowing for the fact that stamped notes were not necessarily issued, the statistics of these licences are still a worthwhile indicator of the expected demand for them. In 1824 the country bankers stamped twice as many notes as in 1820, while the 1825 stampings were 30 per cent above those of 1824 and more than 100 per cent above those of 1822. According to Clapham, between 1822 and 1825 there was a minimum extra issue of 20 to 25 per cent, not including bills of exchange.(51) Over-issue was undoubtedly a major danger in country banking; together with other factors it played a significant part in the crisis of 1825 which brought the ruin of many, and the eventual replacement of all, private country banks.

Banking activity generally, however, had tended to over-expand in the years of the suspension period. Note issue was the most conspicuous feature of the extension of the country bankers' credit and over-issue was the manifestation of over-extension. Nevertheless it is unwise to exaggerate this as an isolated factor: several other factors were involved. The Bank of England itself had discounted heavily before the crisis. Country bank advances were often made for doubtful ventures and much business was done on dubious security. There was a spate of speculation in foreign loans. No limit was set by Parliament to the quantity of notes which might be circulated nor, indeed, was there any central control over the exercise of issue powers, other than the formal requirement to take out a licence and to stamp notes. The Industrial Revolution, the French Wars, the suspension of cash payment—all had created needs for finance which the country bankers had helped to meet at the cost of an over-expansion which was to cull out many of the weaker and less stable firms. The crisis of 1825 and the collapse of credit in much of the country's banking system highlighted the dangers of unrestricted note-issues; in fact, however, there were other faults—not only in country banking but in the entire financial and business structure.

4. The employment of funds

The regulation of the means of payment—especially the note issue—and the extension of bank credit were both likely to depend on the bankers' estimate of what constituted an adequate reserve. By lending, the bank created deposits which its customers could draw upon; if it lent too much, their payments to customers of other banks would exhaust its cash reserves. No hard rule seems to have been adopted; it would seem, as Cantillon observed in 1755, that the appropriate ratio depended on the nature of the liabilities and on their stability or lack of it.(52) To a considerable extent it would also depend on the nature of the country bankers' assets—that is, on their liquidity. In general, bankers in industrial areas would tend to keep greater reserves than those in agricultural areas, while London bankers on the whole tended to keep a higher reserve than their country counterparts. In times of alarm—and there were many such throughout the eighteenth and early nineteenth centuries—high reserves might be maintained. If the unsettling effects of competition, with the advent of the joint-stock banks, led to any tendency to move to higher reserves, this was probably offset by improved communications with London following the introduction of the railways and also by the establishment of Bank of England branches from whom, in emergency, coin and Bank of England notes could often be obtained more speedily than from London.

Country banks had to provide for payment of their notes both at their country office and at their London office or agent; without this latter facility they would have lost much business. Thus the reserve of a country banker was really in two parts.(53) Till money—strictly Bank of England notes and coin—was needed in the country to pay notes presented there, to repay deposits, and perhaps to settle balances in local clearings. In London, a balance with a banker would provide against notes presented for payment there, bills and drafts issued to customers and the balance of London clearings. In addition, the banker usually kept London assets which were readily saleable in the London market—bills, government and other securities—to replenish either local reserves or the balance with the London agent. To a modern banker these would be 'shiftable' assets, forming in part a secondary ratio and in part a holding of 'investments'.

It was common practice for country bankers to count as cash not only local till money of coin and Bank of England notes but also credit balances with London agents, consisting of country banknotes, bills and drafts, coin and Bank of England notes; local holdings of country banknotes, bills of exchange and drafts would also be counted as cash. The sum of all these assets might approximate one third of the total and would be broadly comparable with the Bank of England cash ratio, although the ratio of local holdings of 'hard' cash—i.e. coin and Bank of England notes—might be as low as one tenth or even one twentieth. In an age of war-time crises, uncertainty and sudden rumours, such local reserves were frequently inadequate; this was especially so when, to counter the speed of wagging tongues in a distant country town, a bank depended on a coach and pair with coin and Bank of England notes from London. With the odds all too often against the timely arrival of the horse-drawn carriage, resort could only be had to the mercy of local competitors or proclamations of confidence by local dignitaries and tradesmen. Thus in Cheltenham in early 1826 a local hatter declared:

> John Church's will, as others do,
> Take Hartlands' notes and Turners' too.(54)

No consistency was apparent in the keeping of reserves; there is no evidence of any precise ratio, whether to deposits or note-liabilities or both. The fairly rigid ratios observed by modern banks are a comparatively recent innovation; in any event, for many eighteenth- and nineteenth-century bankers, only very high ratios would have withstood all the crises of those early years and ratios of such a level would have crippled the bankers' ability to earn profits.

Apart from the cash reserve there were two main outlets for the resources of the country banker. Advances to the public, including the partners themselves, were the most important; supplementary to this came investments in London assets, including short and long-term government securities, bills of exchange and bank drafts drawn on London and balances with London bankers and bill brokers. The art of successful banking may be defined as an appropriate combination of the competing claims of profit and liquidity. 'In ascending order of liquidity and descending order of earning-power come advances to the public, investments (predominantly in government securities), bills and money at call, and, finally, cash and money at the Bank of England'.(55)

The motive behind the establishment of many country banks was often the mobilisation of capital from the public in order to finance the business of the partners. Many reliable industrial and trader bankers borrowed, often heavily, from their own banks; this was undoubtedly one of the flaws of country banking, an inherent weakness which was often highly prejudicial to sound banking, particularly since accounts had to be neither audited nor published. Many such bankers were prudent men, but against them were others who most certainly were not. Allen of Manchester owed about £40,000 to his firm at its failure in 1788; in Plymouth, in 1823, one of the partners of Elford's bank was overdrawn by £29,517, another by £11,667, and by the time of bankruptcy, in 1825, the clerks, too, had overdrawn by more than £4,700.(56)

Industrial banks for the most part held the bulk of their assets locally, quite often in firms or industries which had given birth to the bank itself, and had relatively small holdings of government stock. Money market assets were held primarily for immediate purposes—for drafts and discounts, and to procure means of payment for local use. The rural bankers, not being specifically based on any one industry, employed a smaller proportion of their resources in local advances and a larger proportion in

London assets than was commonly the case with their brethren in industrial areas. 'Between these two extremes, sometimes inclining one way, sometimes the other were the trading bankers; they employed considerable resources locally, but also kept substantial reserves.'(57)

Instructions as to the regulation of advances might often be specified in the original deed of partnership, in an accompanying agreement, or occasionally in the course of business. Any individual partner's ability to advance to any one customer would be subject to agreed limits beyond which the approval of other or all partners was necessary, just as today branch managers of the joint-stock banks may advance up to certain limits without reference to head office. The banker, too, was happier when the money was 'turned over' frequently, preferring an active debit account to a dormant loan on however good a security. An attempt to open an account with an overdraft often met with a refusal; as early as 1782 Stevenson Salts had laid it down that money should be lent 'to none but those who occasionally lodge cash with you'.(58)

The advance most favoured by country bankers in lending to the public was that made by way of discount or purchase of bills of exchange. The bills drawn on local traders which a country bank received in the course of its business would not be readily marketable outside the district and so would often be held till maturity. Bills on London, however, were a suitable asset for any bank, whether in London or in the country. Any bank with a surplus of bills on its hands became a seller of bills on London and it was for the supply of facilities for the market in such bills that the London discount market evolved.(59)

Country banking from its beginning was bound up with the great development of trade in inland bills of exchange in the eighteenth century. In the early stages of their development, many country bankers were localised in districts which, from the nature of their economic life, commonly provided the banker with an excess of deposits for which no local use could be found. As a result, an employment of surplus funds could be found only in the purchase of bills through London agents or through the services of a London bill broker. With the beginnings of industrialisation and the growth of trade, banks grew up in manufacturing districts where borrowers predominated; this demand was met by the country banker largely through the discount of his customers' bills in return for bank-notes. The country (industrial) banker in turn despatched these bills to his London agent (or bill broker) who generally resold them to the London agent of a rural bank, the latter discounting them on behalf of his banker-customers in agricultural areas on a commission basis since, except at harvest time and certain other seasons, the agricultural bank invariably had a substantial surplus to employ.(60)

London, indeed, provided a ready market for bills of exchange; until 1810, however, it was a market in which dealers acted as 'brokers', buying and selling on behalf of others rather than operating on their own account. At this stage, preceding the further specialisation which led to the London bill market of the nineteenth century, both London and country bankers found markets for funds only by the outright purchase and scale of bills in which the bill broker was increasingly appearing as intermediary. The purchase of bills amounted to a quite substantial part of the business of the city of London; in the last twenty or thirty years of the eighteenth century, about a quarter of Taylors and Lloyds of Birmingham's total resources appear to have been used in this way. If other Birmingham banks were working in the same way, the amount of Birmingham money so placed in London may well have been over £100,000.(61)

The period after 1810, as Richardson, Overend and Co.'s 1814 accounts show, saw a marked expansion of bill market business, both with country bankers and with merchants. An increase in business with the country banks arose partly from the continued growth in their number—which by 1814 amounted to well over 900; the main influence, however, was undoubtedly the great expansion of their note issues. It appears, too, that many banks were beginning to substitute bills for Government securities, and other more dubious securities, in their investment portfolios.(62)

With the transformation of the bill-brokers into bill-dealers holding bills on their own account with the help of borrowed money, the short-term loan to the bill market largely replaced the purchase of bills. The straight loan to a bill-broker is shown first in the Taylor and Lloyd accounts in 1812, when £12,000 was placed with Sanderson and Co. In 1818 the business began to increase and Richardson, Overend and Co. appear as borrowers of £7,000.(63) It was not until about 1827, however, that the practice of lending money at call or short notice to bill brokers on the security of bills really took root.(64) The country bankers were in fact beginning to use the discount houses—which many bill-brokers had by then become—much in the same way as the banks use them today: that is, in a broking capacity as suppliers of bills for the bank's portfolios and as an outlet for call money. The bill broker was expected to guarantee a bill which he sold to a bank and when taking a straight loan he would usually deposit sufficient bills as cover for the call money with the country bank's London agent.

One of the advantages of bills, and a probable cause of their popularity, was that the banker obtained a negotiable asset, the liquidity of which made it practically identical with hard cash and which would in any case automatically reimburse the holder on maturity. Occasionally the banker would take additional security, although the range of securities available and their liquidity was very small until well on into the nineteenth century.

A flexibility in taking securities which would be comparatively commendable today was then often practised with disastrous results. The 1836 Committee on the Joint-Stock Banks was astonished to find that in the deeds of settlement of existing banks advances on real property were in no instance forbidden.(65) In that same year G.C. Glyn, reporting to the Governor of the Bank of England on the accounts of the London firm of Esdaile and Co., agent to many country banks and then in a perilous state, wrote, 'The house labours under the great disadvantage of having a large amount of Assets so locked up as they cannot be realised or rendered available for the purpose of the house within any reasonable period.'(66) The London private bankers—particularly those of the West End, with their high proportion of landed gentry as customers—may have paved the way for this practice. In 1847, as crisis reared up before the city, Lord George Bentinck remarked that 'Messrs Drummond are calling in their mortgages'.(67) The crisis of 1825 was partly precipitated by the dangerous facility with which the country bankers, competing for business, advanced money on anything and everything.

These banks might fill their portfolios with paper quite incapable of negotiation outside their respective localities. The Northumberland and

Durham Bank, for example, as late as 1857 held about £250,000 of small bills on Newcastle shopkeepers, 'bills which were probably good in themselves, but which were not available out of Newcastle'. E. T. Powell records the remark of a relative of Thomson Hankey's that 'Nothing is easier to conduct than the business of a banker, if he will only learn the difference between a mortgage and a bill of exchange.'(68) It was a lesson which the Bank of England itself was hardly fit to teach, with £300,000 out to the Duke of Rutland, £200,000 to the Marquis of Bath and £130,000 to the Duke of Devonshire, to mention but a few.(69)

Generally bankers disliked lending substantial sums on long-term, as on mortgage, although they might repeatedly renew short-term advances on bills, promissory notes, bonds etc. Railway stock was usually accepted as really good security, while a popular means of securing an account was the personal bond of the borrower, backed in all probability by a guarantor acceptable to the bank. Promissory notes, too, with or without a guarantor were also readily acceptable to bankers during the Napoleonic wars, particularly for advances to customers.

Apart from advances and (investment in) bills of exchange which provided the major outlet for funds, the country banker with ample resources in London was rarely content to leave them wholly, or almost wholly, as a balance with his agent there, especially when, after the 1825 crisis, London agents began to abandon the practice of paying interest on deposits.(70) Partly as a result of this latter tendency, the country banks began to turn to the bill-brokers, but throughout the latter part of the eighteenth century and during the early part of the nineteenth, investment in the Funds provided a valuable outlet for surplus cash. At the sacrifice of some liquidity, this provided the banker with profitable assets which could also be regarded as a second-line reserve supplementing balances with his London agent. Long-term securities—government and Bank of England stocks—were the most popular, but use was also made of short-dated securities such as East India Bonds and Exchequer Bills. The wars with France, and the need to finance the armed forces, led to the introduction of other short-term paper—Navy, Victualling and Transport Bills, and Ordnance debentures—which by the early nineteenth century were added to Exchequer Bills to form part of the floating debt. To supplement these, considerable trading was also done in Stock Exchange securities, which until about the 1830s were regarded as a normal part of bank reserves.

By the end of the eighteenth century, for example, Berwick and Co. of Worcester had rather more than 12 per cent of their resources in 'Investments' of which just under half comprised a recent purchase of Consols. James Oakes and Co., at Bury St Edmunds, were also in the market for Consols at about this time, but they seem to have been investing, as other private banks did then and later, in life assurance policies as well. In Birmingham, Taylor and Lloyds in their earliest days were holding South Sea Annuities and East India Bonds. In 1781, when the War of American Independence had occasioned some years of government deficit, Lloyds were holding Navy Victualling Bills, Long Annuities and Exchequer Bills. In 1774 they were still holding their East India Bonds while at the same time dabbling in Navigation Shares, probably those of the Birmingham Canal. By 1800 their total investment in canal shares had risen to £8,000.(71)

Speculation in foreign bonds was no less popular among country bankers, although many of these securities were of distinctly doubtful value.

According to E. T. Powell, in the period 1818-1832 about £40 million in foreign loans were issued on the London market, but of 126 foreign government loans issued between 1823 and 1826, no fewer than sixteen were in default within a few years.(72) Between 1827 and 1833, Hentys of Worthing were holding Bank of England stock, Consols, Exchequer Bills, annuities and local government bonds, but fully one-third of their total investments consisted of foreign bonds—Brazilian, Danish and Russian. Taylors and Lloyds had gone into American bonds as early as 1817; by 1821 loans to foreign countries were mainly to the solid and creditworthy European states—Russia, Prussia and Denmark. Rothschilds, Barings and Goldsmids were especially prominent in such lending.(73)

The South American rush of 1824-5, however, resulted in loans of upwards of £18 million on most of which dividends ceased to be paid in 1826 or 1827.(74) The Republic of Poyais, in Honduras, floated a loan of £200,000 while a Peruvian 6 per cent loan was so attractive that the bonds were sold by auction, at as high as 90, from the benches of the Royal Exchange. Heavy speculation in such bonds was a contributory factor to the boom and crash of 1825, but part of their attraction to the country banker (compared with the distinct suspicion with which the modern banker would treat them) can be attributed to the absence of UK government stocks of convenient maturities. 'There were not available successive maturities at reasonably near dates, such as would have allowed a banker to hold maturities for almost every year through the following 10 or 15 years'.(75) A portfolio confined to British stocks would have placed its holder at a considerable disadvantage, especially since such investments necessarily went into the undated Consols.

5. The sources of funds

The ability of any bank to employ money depended on its own ability to attract capital. Its partners supplied the initial capital, their share of any undistributed profits and their general creditworthiness in the community; the general public, on the other hand, brought their deposits and accepted and circulated banknotes, bills and drafts. Other country banks might provide funds by rediscount, while the London agent frequently provided overdraft facilities and, in difficult times, loans and security. Bill brokers, too, were appearing as suppliers of funds.

As befitted unit banks, the deposits of the country banks were drawn from a broad cross-section of local life. Customers were drawn from all sections of the community but predominantly from the lower middle-classes and upwards. The mainstays of country banking business tended to be businessmen needing regular and increasing supplies of cash, manufacturers with workmen to pay, traders with bills to discount, and a middle-class group of clergy, widows, country gentlemen, farmers, spinsters, traders and so on with regular incomes and savings to invest. Lloyds of Birmingham was typical of a provincial town bank with a background of manufacturing and trading.(76) In 1775 the first twenty customers, in alphabetical order out of a total of 277, were described as follows.

Publican	Plater
Barber	Victualler
Watch-chain-maker	Factor and Chapman
Hinge-maker	Thimble-maker

Malt-Mill-maker	Thimble-maker
Curry-comb-maker	Whip-maker
Baker	Joiner and carpenter
Butcher	Toy-maker
Victualler	Split-ring-maker
Victualler	File-cutter

Statistics on total country bank deposits are subject to the validity of individual guesses. G. W. Norman, in evidence before the 1840 Select Committee on Banks of Issue, had suggested £40 million as an average for the preceding years, while the following year Stuckey had reckoned that it might be around £25 to £30 million. Both are uncertain estimates; in any event 'deposits' to the country banker meant sums left on deposit at interest (time deposits); the expression did not include current accounts, which were described as 'credit balances'. Deposits, in both senses of the word, were of course vital to any bank; the country bankers, like the London goldsmiths before them, relied upon the payment of interest as the normal incentive to attract customers, although interest was in fact only allowed on deposit accounts (time deposits); interest was not paid on current accounts (other than bill accounts) until about the 1830s, when increasing competition from the joint-stock banks led to a revision of established practice in the matter. No single rate was quoted throughout the country; it varied with the amount deposited, the time for which funds were left on deposit and with the custom of individual regions and local banks. In 1786 Fletcher, Parsons & Co. of Oxford allowed 3 per cent on money left for twelve months and 2½ per cent on deposits for shorter periods. In 1779 the Exchange Bank of Bristol held money for which it had given interest notes of 2, 3, 4 and 5 per cent, while in 1793 rates of 3 to 3½ per cent were widely quoted. But country people, according to George Rae, preferred a steady average rate.(77) They disliked, and probably would not tolerate, variations of rates reflecting movements of London rates and in the foreign exchanges, although with the progress of the nineteenth century the influence of London money rates increasingly penetrated to the country. Until then, however, local custom and the tradition of the bank concerned would have as much influence as the other main determinants—that is, the time left on deposit and, of course, the restrictions imposed by the Usury Laws until their removal in 1833.

By 1825, investment outlets were enlarged by the first, albeit comparatively minor, boom in railways, when money-rates became flexible in the middle decades of the nineteenth century; the lender-borrower relationship between London agent and country banker also provided a ready network by which London rates on capital could extend to the country. By 1849 it was apparently thought natural in making a new agency agreement for any advance to be 'at the then Bank or market rate of interest'.(78) Acceptance of London rates still continued to be patchy in many parts of the country but there was increasingly a general acceptance of some link with Bank Rate.

While deposits provided the ordinary working funds of the country banker, the bank's initial capital, provided by the partners themselves, was required primarily to put money into the till, to cover outlays on offices and so on, to open an account with a London agent and to act as a reserve. Except in extraordinary circumstances—such as a long-term loan—this capital was not employed in advances. 'Banks' which did in fact so use their capital were little more than money-lenders—bankers only in their aspirations—since the function of a banker is not to lend his own capital but to employ claims upon himself in the settlement of debts.

The basic distinction between the private country banker and his nineteenth century joint-stock successor was the fact that up until 1826 the Bank of England's charter provided that capital for the establishment of a bank of issue could not be drawn from more than six partners. This did not prevent public banks for the deposit of capital from being established, but by virtue of the fact that the right of note issue was usually regarded as indispensable, it remained an effective deterrent until the 1820s. This not only restricted the scale of its activities but led to a lack of specialised services which the joint-stock banks were later to exploit. Considerable difficulty was also experienced in separating the banking business from the other private partnerships of any kind; a private banker's personal wealth and the assets of his non-banking concerns were liable to be called upon to settle his banking debts, a disadvantage which deterred many of the more prosperous aspirants.(79)

A primary purpose of the capital of a bank was to act as a reserve against loss to noteholders and so on, although in many cases the amount of the reserve was quite inadequate. Apart from reserves of cash or liquid assets required for normal day-to-day management, the maintenance of a definite reserve fund as a cover against bad debts does not seem to have been normal practice amongst country bankers until a comparatively late date. Nor does the increase of capital beyond its initial level—through the accession of new partners, ploughing back profits or calls on existing partners—seem to have been common until the 1840s or later. Around that time, for example, the partners of Hardcastle Cross and Co. in Bolton only drew interest on their capital at 4 per cent and left the rest of the profit in the business, with the result that the capital grew steadily. In 1859 it was £100,000; by 1869 it was £261,000 (despite the death of a partner which took out £33,000) and by 1875 the books showed a capital of £360,000, although this latter figure was subject to deduction owing to earlier debts. In 1872 the profit for the year was put to Special Guarantee account to meet a possible loss, while the books from 1874 also show signs of pre-occupation with reserves for bad debts.(80)

Bearing in mind the rough and ready nature of the country banking of the time and the existence of unlimited liability, the stress often placed upon capital and reserves was not without relevance. Even so, Vincent Stuckey in his evidence to the Bank Charter Committee of 1832 remarked: 'I scarcely know any security but in the general feeling of its good management and the property of its partner'. Even personal riches were of little use if the firm was blatantly mismanaged and extended its lending to long-term advances and/or on illiquid securities. Attwoods, Spooner and Co., for example, collapsed through financing its partners by huge overdrafts, while Sir C.R. Price of Marryat & Co. took over certain ironworks for a debt and worked them at a continuous loss, paying the penalty in the shape of suspension.(81) The capital of Greenway, Smith and Greenways stood at £35,000 in 1875, although this took no account of the fact that by that time the Greenways had begun the systematic overdrawing of their accounts. The following year they withdrew the whole of their capital. Their financial system was peculiarly their own. When a partner drew money out of the bank for private purposes, the amount was treated as an advance to a customer and the firm credited with interest on it at 5 per cent, which in turn was divided among the partners as bank profit—although in fact it was never received from anyone and never earned. It was admitted by one of the partners during the bankruptcy proceedings that the larger the overdrafts of the partners, the larger was the division of profits between them. In addition to their own overdrafts of well over £100,000, they had made various advances and overdrafts to a total of over £100,000 in a tannery, disastrously mismanaged by a cousin, which had succeeded in making a loss in every year of business.(82) Malpractice and mismanagement on such a scale were by no means universal, of course, but nonetheless chaotic book-keeping and unrealisable assets were the ruin of a great many country bankers. The failings and virtues of country banking, therefore, extended to fields other than the management of the note issue.

6. Conclusion

Banking generally had tended to over-expand in response to the demands created by the Industrial Revolution and the period of the suspension of cash payments, the expansion often being achieved on an insecure and ill-managed basis. With the post-war slump after the false security permitted in previous years, many firms found that they would have to pay the price of reckless—or, on the other hand, too cautious—management or simply the changing needs of the economic environment. To illustrate the weaknesses of country bankers, however, is not to deny their undoubted merits. Walter Bagehot could imagine 'nothing better in theory, or more successful in practice, than private banks as they were in the beginning. A man of known wealth, known integrity and known ability, is largely entrusted with the money of his neighbours. The confidence is strictly personal. His neighbours know him, and trust him because they know him.'(83)

Personal attributes and qualifications of this kind were well suited to the needs and nature of eighteenth-century country banking and, with the eventual growth of confidence in the new joint-stock banks, they were largely inherited by branch managers. Isolated in regions at best poorly served by communications, the enterprise of individual country bankers helped to meet the demand of local trades and industries; in their relations with their London agents, they established channels by which finance could be extended from one region to another. Amateur banking it often was, but given the legal restrictions of the age, the paucity of reliable communications and the rudimentary development of bankers' skills, their achievement was not inconsiderable. Country banking partnerships were to continue for a good many years yet but, forced to compete with the much greater resources of the joint-stock banks, their decline was inevitable. The disasters of the suspension period and immediately afterwards—particularly the 1825 crisis—had left in men's minds a certain suspicion against a paper circulation and country banking generally. As a popular lyric put it,

> A guinea it will sink and a note it will float
> But I'd rather have a guinea than a one pound note.

Parliamentary opinion overwhelmingly inclined to the view that the over-issue of small denomination notes by the country bankers was the root of the financial troubles of the period and that no institution could be expected to administer its own issue competently.[84] Accordingly, in 1826 notes of denominations under £5 were prohibited. This was expected to ensure a substantial gold circulation as a basis to the credit system, while at the same time the restriction was accompanied by the threat not only of the new joint-stock banks but also of the Bank of England's determination to dominate the currency circulation through the extension of its own note issue.

The disasters of English banking between 1790 and 1826 had been very slightly reflected in Scotland; it was only natural, therefore, that opinion favourable to the Scottish system of joint-stock banks and branches should gain ground. J. W. Gilbart, first manager of the London and Westminster Bank, obviously did not share Bagehot's sentiments when he declared somewhat bitterly that 'the apostles of the principles of joint-stock banking found the mass of the population bowed down in superstitious homage to those idols of gold, of silver, of wood, and of brass, which were railed before their eyes in the persons of the country bankers'.[85] But public disillusion was growing—very much so after the events of 1825-6, when the failure of nearly a hundred banks hurt many pockets. Lord Liverpool's specific for the illnesses of English banking was to pillory the note-issues of the country banker and legislate for a system which, it was hoped, would catch something of the Scottish success. William Paterson would no doubt have approved. So, christened by law and blessed by the progress of Dr Watt's invention, the joint-stock bankers prospered.

REFERENCES

1. L. S. Pressnell, *Country Banking in the Industrial Revolution,* Clarendon Press, Oxford 1956, p. 12.
2. W. F. Crick and J. E. Wadsworth, *A Hundred Years of Joint Stock Banking,* Hodder and Stoughton, London 1936, p. 46. Legislation was introduced in 1775 to prohibit the issue of small notes below £1—and extended to notes of less than £5 from 1777-97. The issue of tokens continued until forbidden by Parliament in 1817.
3. Pressnell, *op. cit.,* p. 16.
4. R. S. Sayers, *Lloyds Bank in the History of English Banking,* Clarendon Press, Oxford 1957, p. 89.
5. *Ibid.,* pp. 51-2.
6. Pressnell, *op. cit.,* p. 28.
7. *Ibid.,* p. 37.
8. R. G. Hawtrey, *A century of Bank Rate,* Longmans Green, London 1938, p. 5.
9. Pressnell, *op. cit.,* p. 47.
10. Crick and Wadsworth, *op. cit.,* p. 200.
11. G. Chandler, *Four centuries of Banking,* Batsford, London 1964, pp. 171-185.
12. Pressnell, *op. cit.,* p. 60.

13. *Ibid.*, p. 61.
14. *The Three Banks Review*, No. 56, December 1962, p. 41.
15. Pressnell, *op. cit.*, p. 4.
16. *Ibid.*, p. 6.
17. J. Clapham, *The Bank of England*, University Press, Cambridge 1944, Vol. II, p. 1.
18. Evidence to the Select Committee on the Duties of the Receivers-General of the Land and Assessed Taxes, BPP, 1821 (630 and 667), viii, p. 103. Quoted by Pressnell, *op. cit.*, p. 11.
19. Pressnell, *op. cit.*, p. 443.
20. Clapham, *op. cit.*, vol. II, p. 1.
21. Crick and Wadsworth, *op. cit.*, p. 201.
22. Pressnell, *op. cit.*, pp. 105-116.
23. Clapham, *op. cit.*, Vol. I, p. 165 and Pressnell, *op. cit.*, p. 105.
24. Sayers, *op. cit.*, p. 117.
25. J. W. Gilbart, *Practical Treatise on Banking*, London 1827, p. 31.
26. Sayers, *op. cit.*, p. 118.
27. *Ibid.*, p. 121.
28. *Ibid.*, p. 121.
29. *The Three Banks Review*, No. 69, March 1966, pp. 33-5.
30. T. S. Ashton, 'The Bill of Exchange and Private Banks in Lancashire, 1790-1830', *Economic History Review*, Vol. XV, Nos. 1 & 2, 1945, pp. 25-35.
31. Hawtrey, *op. cit.*, p. 9.
32. T. S. Ashton, *An Economic History of England: the 18th Century*, Methuen, London 1964, pp. 185-6.
33. Pressnell, *op. cit.*, p. 168.
34. Clapham, *op. cit.*, Vol. I, pp. 142-3.
35. *Ibid.*, pp. 221-3.
36. Pressnell, *op. cit.*, p. 136.
37. *Ibid.*, p. 142.
38. Clapham, *op. cit.*, Vol II, p. 3.
39. Pressnell, *op. cit.*, pp. 153-4.
40. Clapham, *op. cit.*, Vol. II, p. 4.
41. Gilbart, *op. cit.*, p. 26.
42. Stuckey to Commission, 1841, QQ 554-8 and 571-4, quoted by Pressnell, *op. cit.*, p. 157.
43. Forster to Commission 1831-2, Q. 60, quoted by Pressnell, *op. cit.*, p. 157.

44. Walter Bagehot, *Lombard Street*, Smith, Elder and Co., London 1910, p. 881.

45. *The Three Banks Review*, No. 67, September 1965, p. 35.

46. Clapham, *op. cit.*, Vol. II, p. 5.

47. Pressnell, *op. cit.*, p. 146.

48. *Ibid.*, p. 160.

49. Clapham, *op. cit.*, vol. II, p. 90.

50. W. T. C. King, *History of the London Discount Market*, Routledge, London 1936, p. 35.

51. *Ibid.*, p. 97.

52. R. Cantillon, *Essai sur la nature du commerce*, 1755, English ed., Higgs H., London 1892, pp. 229-303, cit. by Horsefield, *op. cit.*, p. 72.

53. Pressnell, *op. cit.*, p. 197.

54. Sayers, *op. cit.*, p. 208.

55. Pressnell, *op. cit.*, p. 287.

56. *Ibid.*, p. 292.

57. *Ibid.*, p. 288.

58. Quoted by Sayers, *op. cit.*, p. 96.

59. Hawtrey, *op. cit.*, p. 10.

60. King, *op. cit.*, p. 6.

61. Sayers, *op. cit.*, pp. 180-1.

62. King, *op. cit.*, pp. 26-7.

63. Sayers, *op. cit.*, p. 181.

64. King, *op. cit.*, pp. 67-70.

65. E. T. Powell, *The Evolution of the London Money Market 1385-1915*, Cass, London 1966, p. 284.

66. *The Three Banks Review*, No. 70, June 1966, p. 42.

67. Disraeli, *Life*, p. 451.

68. Powell, *op. cit.*, p. 286.

69. *Ibid.*, p. 292.

70. Pressnell, *op. cit.*, p. 411.

71. Sayers, *op. cit.*, pp. 185-6.

72. Powell, *op. cit.*, p. 326.

73. Sayers, *op. cit.*, pp. 186-7.

74. Clapham, *op. cit.*, Vol. II, p. 93.

75. Sayers, *op. cit.*, p. 188.

76. *Ibid.*, p. 89.

77. Quoted by Pressnell, *op. cit.*, p. 162.

78. Pressnell, *op. cit.*, pp. 252-3.

79. Sayers, *op. cit.*, p. 126.

80. Stuckey, *Evidence to Secret Committee on Joint-Stock Banks*, 1836, Q. 1447.

81. *The Three Banks Review*, No. 56, December 1962, p. 42.

82. Powell, *op. cit.*, p. 288.

83. Bagehot, *op. cit.*, 9th ed., p. 267.

84. Feaveryear, *op. cit.*

85. J. W. Gilbart, *Logic of Banking*, p. 170.

CHAPTER FOUR

Joint-Stock Banking

1. Emergence and evolution

In 1589 Drake had set out to sea, a departure which was part and parcel of what has been described as 'a mere joint-stock speculation'. In Elizabeth's reign, and even before, the advantages of joint-stock enterprises in raising capital for risky trading ventures were widely appreciated. After the collapse of the South Sea Co. and the passing of the 'Bubble' Act of 1719, however, the only way in which a joint-stock company could legitimately be formed (until the Act's repeal in 1825) was through a special charter from the Crown. An expensive undertaking at best, it was all the more difficult because Parliament resented anything which smacked of the exclusive privileges sold by the Stuarts. The idea that a company was synonymous, or at least coextensive, with monopoly persisted well into the nineteenth century and Parliament was thus antagonistic towards any proposal or petition for a joint-stock company—with the notable exception of canal companies, for which over a hundred Acts were passed before 1800. The fields of enterprise in which a joint-stock company could legitimately and economically embark continued to be, long after Adam Smith, 'a matter of much doubt and debate, and by many thought to be narrowly circumscribed'.(1)

The usual commercial unit in industry and trade was therefore an individual or a small partnership, often a family business, and this was the basis of English country banking. A second stage gradually arrived as enterprises grew larger and required more extensive capital funds. For activities other than banking (except in Scotland), partnerships tended to increase the number of members, embodying the terms of their association in a deed of co-partnership issuing share capital (not transferable) and becoming 'common law' companies, although they were still no more than partnerships writ large. They possessed no corporate entity and the members were individually liable for all debts of the firm; joint-stock companies formed by charter, on the other hand, comprised a legal entity responsible for its debts in its corporate capacity only and possessing the ability to transfer its shares. Despite the 'Bubble' Act, 'common law' companies continued to increase in strength and numbers, especially in insurance but occasionally in manufacturing, forming the direct predecessors of the modern trading company. The boom years after 1800 provoked vigorous efforts to widen the sphere of joint-stock organisation, inspiring the opinion that 'companies might be extended to every branch of trade and manufacture' although, as yet, to do so without benefit of Parliament was to court action by the Attorney-General.

Prominent amongst the examples of successful (and legal) joint-stock enterprise was that provided by the Bank of England and the banks of Scotland. By the early nineteenth century their success was apparent, although in Scotland the legal basis was very different from that prevailing in England. The Bank of Scotland, the first joint-stock bank in Scotland, was established one year after the foundation of the Bank of England; by Act of Parliament it had been given a monopoly of joint-stock banking for 21 years. With the expiry of this term the monopoly was not renewed; the result was that in Scotland there was henceforth no legal barrier to the setting up of other joint-stock banking companies. Under Scots law there was in any case a generally available form of legal incorporation in the 'contract of co-partnery'. In 1727 the Royal Bank of Scotland was established by royal charter and it was followed in 1746 by the British Linen Bank.

Similar progress, even if on a 'common law' basis, would have been open to the private bankers of England had it not been for the fact that, in relation to English banking, the law was much more restrictive. From 1708 to 1825 the Bank of England's charter established that it would not be lawful:

> for any body politic or corporation whatsoever erected or to be erected other than the said Governor and Company of the Bank of England, or for other persons whatsoever united or to be united in covenant or partnerships, exceeding the number of six persons, in that part of Great Britain called England, to borrow, owe, or take up any sum or sums of money on their bills or notes, payable at demand, or at any less time than six months from the borrowing thereof.

Hence English law fulfilled the intention—emphasised again in the Bank Act of 1742 by the phrase 'the privilege of exclusive banking'—of preventing the foundation of joint-stock banks or the extension of banking partnerships into 'common law' companies. The eighteenth-century legislators and bankers held the right of note-issue to be the definitive function of a bank, of course, ignoring the significance of deposit banking without note-issue. This latter function was not specified in the monopoly clause of the Bank's charter and was later to prove a loophole of particular importance for London banking; by the end of the eighteenth century the private bankers of the capital had ceased to issue their own notes and were concentrating on deposit banking instead. Even so, the spirit of the law, if not its exact letter, was sufficient to discourage joint-stock deposit banking in the capital and the provinces, where country bankers (except in Lancashire) would not have dreamed of banking without note-issue.

Banking apart, by 1825 many company promotions were being floated 'in shoals like herring from the Polar Seas' with or without Parliamentary approval, including one to drain the Red Sea for the treasure abandoned after the crossing of the Israelites. The pressure of petitions upon Parliament was such that in that year the 'Bubble' Act was repealed, a development which gave added encouragement to the proponents of English joint-stock banks of issue.

A leading spokesman for the campaign in favour of joint-stock banking had been Thomas Joplin, a Newcastle timber merchant with local experience of banking disasters who had made a study of currency problems. It was not unnatural for him and others to take note of the more favourable progress of the Scottish banking system. The joint-stock banks of Scotland did not fail; they were better agents for the mobility of capital and they served the small man better. Joplin's pamphlets of 1822 and subsequent agitation pressed for a relaxation of the monopoly of the Bank of England and exposed the fallacy of the view that the clause of the 1742 Act (embodying the Charter of the Bank of England) which forbade joint-stock issues thereby prohibited joint-stock deposit banking.

Ricardo, too, was active in support of reform and his speeches in Parliament had some influence on Lord Liverpool's administration. The legal position, however, remained disputed and nobody dared to oppose the Bank of England as long as the interpretation of the law remained doubtful.(2) Private bankers, metropolitan and provincial, were well represented in the House and had fiercely opposed any inauguration of joint-stock banking, but the crisis of 1825-6 ensured a sympathetic hearing for the arguments put forward by Joplin. The events of that year set in hand schemes which the government had already considered and matured. Lord Liverpool had his own views on currency and banking: 'The £1 note, especially when issued from the factory of a country banker, he had always disliked: it had only been kept alive since the resumption of cash payments as a concession to parliamentary opinion.'(3) Branch banks of England were an old hobby of his; he knew all about Scotland, where there had been two or three bank failures but none among the older or the fully-developed joint-stock banks and not one in Edinburgh or Glasgow. Nothing could be done, however, without the assent of the Bank of England in view of the fact that the privileges contained within its Charter did not expire until 1833. Public opinion was against such privileges—as the East India and Hudson Bay Companies had already discovered—and the Directors of the Bank were therefore persuaded, with difficulty, to agree to the establishment of joint-stock banks of issue. The Bank, however, whilst apparently making considerable concessions, in fact retained the kernel of its monopoly; the London area—the focus of the country's financial business—was exempt from the provisions of the new Act.

The Act of May 1826 'For the better regulation of co-partnerships of certain Bankers in England' (7 Geo. IV. c. 46) permitted the establishment of banking co-partnerships with any number of shareholders and a right of note issue outside a radius of 65 miles of London within which the new banks were not to open offices. The shareholders remained liable jointly and severally for debts of the co-partnership; any legal action had to be taken by, or made against, two or more members appointed as 'public officers' and judgements against such officers were to operate against all the partners.(4) It is important to remember that as yet the new joint-stock banks were legally only extended partnerships with unlimited liability. Another irksome restriction was that the new banks were not allowed to draw bills on their London agents payable on demand or for less than £50 in amount. To the Governor of the Bank of England at that time 'it was a Feather they had, and that they chose to keep it'.(5) And so they did, at any rate until 1833, when the new banks were allowed to draw bills on London on demand and for less than £50.

On the other hand, no restriction was placed upon the volume of note issues; this would appear surprising in view of the supposed causes of the 1825 crisis, but the prohibition of notes of under £5 denomination was thought to guard against excesses. Furthermore, no provision was made as to share denominations or the amounts to be paid up on shares, nor was any attempt made to lay down directions regarding the deeds under which the co-partnerships were to operate.(6)

The first true joint-stock bank in the provinces opened at Lancaster in 1826, to be followed shortly by others at Norwich, Huddersfield, Bradford, Workington and Manchester. Stuckey's Bank in Somerset was the first existing private bank to adopt the new system and was among the earliest banks to take advantage of the Act, although in form and practice it comprised an amalgamation of four or five private banks in which Stuckey was a partner.

Considerable opposition was expected at first, not only from the country bankers but from the Bank of England as well. A clause in the 1826 Act specifically allowed the Bank to open branches anywhere in England and this, together with competition expected from the established country bankers, had at first a deterrent effect on new joint-stock banks. The success of the first joint-stock banks in standing up to competition from well-entrenched rivals, however, soon attracted others. By the end of 1833 there were nearly fifty joint-stock banks in England, with proprietors numbering about 10,000; by 1836-7 a hundred had been established, most of them issuing their own notes and conducting business in much the same way as private bankers.

Other country bankers who might have followed Stuckey's example were in fact more concerned with criticising the undoubted weakness of some of the new joint-stock banks or with lobbying against the Bank of England's new branches, but with the passing of time some of these fears were allayed. Thomas Attwood of Birmingham had no complaints and Forster of Walsall was even appreciative. Vincent Stuckey objected to 'poaching' by the branches, but felt that they lacked the local knowledge of effective competition in country districts, while in the mid-1830s bankers generally were beginning to appreciate William Beckett's sentiments that the Bank's branches had 'added to the safety of banking'. (7)

Such resentment would have been nothing in comparison with the clamour which would surely have arisen had the country bankers known that Bank of England branches were to be used as a stalking-horse for a Bank take-over of the nation's note issue. Such an idea was already being discussed at the beginning of 1826, when bank failures and commercial bankruptcies were still continuing. The Court of the Bank of England had received a report from a special committee appointed to report on branch policy which advised that it was highly expedient: it would greatly increase the Bank's own note circulation, give it 'a much more complete control than it now possesses over the whole paper circulation and enable it to prevent a recurrence of such a convulsion as we have lately seen', would probably lead to a 'very large' increase of deposits and would protect the Bank against the competition of 'large banking companies' should the government encourage their formation. (8) Such ambitions were confirmed by Horsley Palmer in his correspondence with the Governor of the Bank of Ireland in 1831 and the Royal Bank of Scotland in 1833 when sounding out support for 'one issue instead of many'—'the principle you know to be a favourite theory of mine'. (9)

Until 1826 the Bank's business had been directly confined to the London area but within the 65-mile radius the Bank's notes were widely circulated, while within the metropolitan area a complete monopoly of joint-stock banking was considered to be held. The Act of 1826, although permitting joint-stock banks in the provinces, was thought to pose no real threat to the Bank of England; the bulk of its business was in the exempt London radius, while the Bank itself had received the additional and quite handsome 'sop' of branches.

It was thus common opinion that the terms of the Bank of England's charter prohibited the establishment of joint-stock banks in London. It was the opinion of Thomas Joplin, however—and he had made a careful study of the Bank's charter—that such was not the case.[10] In 1832, the year before the renewal of the charter, a petition was presented to Parliament by various interested parties requesting that all doubts surrounding the legality of opening joint-stock banks in London as banks of deposit be removed by explicitly granting that right. Accordingly, when the Bank's charter came up for renewal in 1833 a special declaratory clause was inserted in the Act—to the great disgust of the Bank of England—to establish Joplin's contention that banking co-partnerships might be set up even in London as long as they did not issue notes. 'Whereas doubts had arisen' on a certain matter of importance—in short, since the Bank's monopoly of joint-stock banking within the radius might mean only a monopoly of note-issue there—it 'declared and enacted' that companies might carry on 'the trade of business of Banking in London' provided they circulated no notes.[11] This was, perhaps, the really substantive change in the legal basis of joint-stock banking.

One of the parties largely responsible for the insertion of this clause comprised a group of 'Noblemen and Gentlemen' with a strong proportion of Scots—notably Bute and Lord Stuart de Rothesay, as well as a Stewart, an Arbuthnot and a Douglas who were eager to see a joint-stock bank started in London. Their successful intercession was the signal for a radical change in the capital's banking pattern; ten days before the Act received royal assent on 29th August, the group of noblemen and gentlemen had completed a final draft of their prospectus for a non-issuing London joint-stock bank entitled 'The London and Westminster Bank'.[12]

The rivalry and open opposition expressed in relation to joint-stock banks was even more evident in the case of the London joint-stock banks, for in the capital the private bankers and the Bank of England were very well entrenched. In March 1834 the London and Westminster opened in Throgmorton Street with a paid-up capital of £50, 000 and J. W. Gilbart as manager. By 1840 the London Joint Stock Bank, the Union Bank, the London and County and the Commercial Bank had set up business in London. Access to the Clearing House was denied by the London clearing bankers, however, while the Bank of England also refused to open a drawing account; for a brief period in the 1830s, it even refused to discount bills payable at the new banks.

Unlike their country counterparts, the London joint-stock banks were not allowed the right to act through public officers; in any legal action—say for the recovery of some small debt—they were obliged to quote the name of each and every 'shareholder' and a mistake in so doing would render the claim void.[13] Since the number of shareholders could run into hundreds, the difficulties may be imagined. This handicap was not removed until 1844 and the new banks were at first obliged to make all contracts in the name of trustees.[14]

Apart from this, under common law a man could not sue himself; thus, if two banking co-partnerships, whether in London or the provinces, possessed one or more members in common (a not unlikely occurrence, especially in London), they could not go to law against each other.[15] Furthermore, a co-partnership could not sue one of its members, nor could a member take legal action against the bank—a hopeless position when one remembers that the bulk of shareholders were usually customers of the bank so that the need for either action might easily arise. The collapse of the Northern and Central Bank in 1837 left the liquidators with an almost impossible task arising from these anomalies which were not remedied until the amending legislation of 1838. (1 & 2 Vict. c.96, and 2 & 4 Vict. c. 111.) To cap it all was the discovery that all joint-stock organisations which contained members of the clergy as partners were illegal, on the ground that spiritual persons could not take part in any trading concern, a defect which was not removed until 1841.(16)

The success of the joint-stock banks, particularly in London, was therefore remarkable in the light not only of legal difficulties but also the stern opposition of the City private bankers—who were more powerful than country private bankers—together with the Bank of England and the discrimination of the latter in favour of the private bankers. To a London private banker dishonouring a cheque which overdrew the balance of a small client the 'only receptacle for such accounts' was the London and Westminster.(17)

Public opinion, however, was on the side of the joint-stock banks; the series of bank failures, especially during the 1825 crisis, had undermined public confidence in private bankers, particularly the country bankers. The new joint-stock banks with prominent directors and a large body of shareholder proprietors, all fully liable for the debts of their banks, were more attractive to the public than the obscure and smaller private banks. Favourable opinion was also enhanced by the innovation and circulation of annual statements. Furthermore, the joint-stock banks, in their struggle with the private banks and the Bank of England, had met their competition by offering customers better terms than their established rivals, notably in the payment of interest on deposits and even on current accounts. In the 1830s and 1840s, when the new joint-stock banks in the country and in London were seeking business, competition in rates on deposits was intense.(18) Such practices undoubtedly attracted business away from the private bankers and added fuel to the fire of opposition, although it is probable that the greater part of this business was drawn from new sources hitherto untapped by the private banks and the Bank of England.(19)

The competition which the early joint-stock banks faced from the entrenched private banks encouraged them to seek ways of providing better and quicker services for their customers and as a result agency arrangements were made by some of the joint-stock banks with similar banks in other districts. Favourable discount rates would also be accorded to banks with whom such friendly understanding was reached. Despite their persisting legal and practical handicaps, the early joint-stock banks nonetheless managed to establish a strong basis for a growing popularity with the public.

The most significant successes were achieved in the provinces where conditions were more conducive to the growth of joint-stock banking. The opportunities provided by the development of industry and trade were increased by the weakness and failures of the old country bankers, many of whom had been outgrown by the firms or industries to which they owed their origins. The provincial private banks themselves were lacking both in quality of personnel and adequacy of resources; an inadequate local monopoly in the provision of credit was particularly vulnerable to competition from branch banking facilitated by improved transport. In the industrial towns in particular, the facilities offered to both depositors and borrowers by the private banks were poor.[20] There was a need for more broadly-based enterprises to match the demands of such areas—enterprises which could take in deposits from the agricultural hinterland and channel loanable funds into the industrial growth areas. Many of the country bankers sold out to their new rivals; some, like Stuckey, adopted the joint-stock pattern; many others failed or retired. Long before Bagehot was to prophesy the doom of private banking in *Lombard Street,* the 1836 Secret Committee on joint-stock banks had observed in its first report that 'a principle of competition exists which leads to the extinction of all Private Banks, and to their conversion into Banking Companies'.[21] Between 1826-7 and 1836-7 the number of country joint-stock banks had risen to 100; by 1841-2, 118 were in operation. At the centre of the banking world stood the Bank of England and ranged close about it was a group of about sixty London private firms. Provincial joint-stock banks still followed the country bankers in maintaining London correspondents and issuing their own notes (except a few in South Lancashire) while London joint-stock banks were beginning to compete for this business at the expense of their private rivals. To some extent, however, the private bankers of the capital were reluctant to enter into any agreement with a provincial joint-stock bank for fear of offending any private country bankers who were among their customers.

2. The beginnings of branch banking

In the light of the Scottish example, some of the joint-stock banks began to open branches, a development which had been impracticable for private country bankers—except for one or two such as Furney and Stuckey—largely because of restrictions on the number of partners and their consequent lack of resources. Such a system seemed likely to provide a more stable structure than the unit banking of the eighteenth to early nineteenth centuries, and one more suited to the needs of a now advanced industrial revolution. Branch banking depended for its success on ready access to Head Office, however, if it were not to degenerate into no more than a modified version of unit banking. In the early stages communications were inadequate and nearly always too slow to meet possible needs; it was not until the development of the railways that branch systems were to approach anything like the cohesion associated with them today.

Apart from the danger of runs on sometimes isolated branches, book-keeping and accounting were still rudimentary; even more serious, there was a real shortage of trained men to act as managers and there were hardly any to spare for tours on branch inspection. Examples of fraud and bad business were not at all unusual. The respected manager of the Rotherham branch of the Sheffield and Rotherham Joint Stock Banking Company from 1836 until 1853, for example, was allowed to run his branch very much as he chose and with scant supervision; as a result, on his retirement the books were found to be quite out of balance, the figures falsified and substantial deficits involved.[22] Private bankers were quite as prone to such failings but the larger joint-stock organisations were eventually able to establish systems of training and inspection which, together with obligatory audits and the publication of accounts, tended to eradicate many of the old vices. Even as late as 1883, however, the Union Bank of Birmingham Ltd was discovered to have been defrauded of large sums of money, the culprit (the manager) having escaped to America.[23] Ten years later the Metropolitan Bank, seeking to consolidate its Welsh business by amalgamating with the National Bank of Wales, unearthed a pretty state of affairs. Not least was the discovery that the general manager and two directors of the National Bank of Wales had feloniously diverted £30, 000 of bank money into their own pockets; it was estimated that this bank had altogether lost approximately £500, 000, a sum which was covered in part by calls on shareholders. For at least six years dividends had been paid out of capital; unsecured loans for large sums had been made to the directors and the general manager, while the balance sheets were shown to be false.[24]

It was no wonder that leading bankers often expressed considerable misgivings about branch systems. Indeed, as early as 1826 Mr. Robert Paul had informed the Parliamentary Committee on the Small Note Currency that bank branches 'were accompanied with so much hazard, require such constant watching and inspection, and involve us altogether in such a degree of superintendence, that, upon the whole, my general impression is that the branches are not the most advantageous part of our business'.[25] Some of the most serious failures among early joint-stock banks were in fact the result of hasty attempts to found a branch system; it was not until later in the nineteenth century, with improved communications and banking techniques, that conditions favourable to large-scale branch expansions were established.

3. Notes and cheques

Legal restrictions and the difficulty of communication prevented a real fusion of London and country joint-stock banking. Joplin had shown the way, but such was the importance attached to the right of note-issue that many banks were deterred from establishing themselves in the capital, where they had in any case to contend with more substantial opposition. The success of the first London joint-stock banks, however, taught a useful lesson on banking without note-issue, hitherto thought to be the life-blood of any bank. From the higher echelons of the financial world downwards there had long been a tendency to overestimate the economic importance of note issue. 'The earliest way to develop credit is to issue notes, ' argued Walter Bagehot.[26] He was undoubtedly right, but banking sentiment for long inclined to the more extreme view that it was the *sine qua non* of the business, ignoring the fact that there were other ways of extending credit. 'From the discussion,' Smart observed, 'one would think that the business of the country was still conducted by bank-notes'—[27] so slight was the attention given to bills, drafts, cheques and other instruments of credit.

The 1833 Act not only gave a great impetus to joint-stock banking by permitting its foundation in London but also confirmed the legality of cheques drawn on them. Cheques had by this time become an important component of the money supply circulating in London and their use by joint-stock companies permitted the speeding-up of commercial transactions. Where cheques were drawn and paid in at different branches of the same bank, they could be sent through the head office for debiting against the customer's account, instead of through the clearing banks—a process which normally took several days. Access to the London Bankers' Clearing House was still denied to the joint-stock banks, however; until 1854 the latter were obliged to present cheques for collection over the counters of the banks on which they had been drawn, receiving coin and Bank of England notes at the time of presentation. Outside London the cheque was still of minor importance, although its use was increasing; it was nominally subject to heavy stamp duties if drawn at a place more than fifteen miles from the bank at which it was payable.

After the minimum legal denomination of bank notes in England had been raised to £5 in 1826, small currency needs were met by gold and subsidiary coins. For larger payments, other than those effected through bills of exchange, Bank of England notes were becoming firmly established in the provinces at the expense of local issues as local bankers abandoned their own note issues, receiving in return a commission payment or a discount account at especially favourable rates with a local branch of the Bank of England. Except under these special arrangements, country joint-stock banks did not usually open an account with the Bank of England nor with its branches. By means of such inducements, however, the Bank through its branches promoted its circulation in the provinces. In January 1830, for example, the new Birmingham Banking Company had been given a discount account on condition that it circulated only coin and Bank notes. In attracting discount business, and especially that of provincial banks, the branches were extremely successful and they were able to use this facility as a lever for promoting the circulation of Bank notes. As early as 1830 in the Bank's eleven branches 'nearly £5½ million of discounting was done for nearly 1,000 clients, more than was done that year in Threadneedle Street'.(28)

Indeed, throughout the country there was a number of large banks—some private, some joint-stock—which had regular agreements with the Bank of England to use its notes exclusively. At Liverpool in 1841 there were seven of these; in Manchester there were three, in Birmingham six, in Newcastle four and in Hull two as well as others at Portsmouth, Swansea and Gloucester. By the end of 1844 there were 43 in all, including some at Plymouth, Bristol, Leeds and Leicester.(29) The experience of these banks and the success of the non-issuing London joint-stock banks were beginning to create in the minds of many an appreciation of the fact that the surrender of a note-issue did not entail the automatic emasculation of banking business. This awareness was to provide a real spur towards both participation in London banking and the promotion of the cheque as a substitute for a note-issue; nevertheless it is probably true to say that the decline of private note-issues would have been more prolonged had it not been for the statutory changes which occurred in 1844.

4. The legislation of 1844

The discussions and controversies surrounding note issues, particularly that of the Bank of England, found their culmination in the Bank Charter Act introduced by Sir Robert Peel in 1844 (7 and 8 Vict. C. 32).(30) The primary intent of the Act was to secure the eventual concentration of the nation's note-issue in the Bank of England, the success of which depended upon the amalgamation movement then in its early stages. The Act laid down that no other bank in England, whether joint-stock or private, which was not at that time issuing notes should be permitted to do so in the future; furthermore, all issuing banks were prohibited from circulating more notes than were outstanding before the Act. It was possible for two private banks of issue to amalgamate and to retain the aggregate of their issues, provided that the membership of the new partnership did not exceed six in number; if an issuing joint-stock bank absorbed a private bank of issue, however, or if two joint-stock banks of issue amalgamated, then the new note-issue was not to be the total of the existing notes in circulation but only the amount permitted to the absorbing bank. Further, if any joint-stock bank of issue amalgamated with a bank, whether joint-stock or private, having an office within the 65-mile radius, or itself opened an office there, the right of issue was forfeited. Finally, if any issuing bank closed its doors, its right of issue lapsed. The Bank of England was entitled to apply for an increase in its own note circulation of up to two-thirds of any issues relinquished under these provisions.

Although the Act as designed by Peel and his supporters was primarily intended to establish the legal tender note circulation of the Bank of England in an unassailable position, no special allowance was made for the growing demand for money; the Act depended upon an increase in the stock of gold to meet such needs, and it was a fortunate accident of history that new gold-mines were discovered in 1851. The chief significance of the Act in the history of joint-stock banking thus lies in the enforced acceleration, albeit unintentional, which it gave to the development of deposits and cheques as a substitute for currency. Now that further expansion of private note-issues was prohibited, expanding commerce and industry had to choose between using an all-metal currency or the development of another form of credit instrument. As a result the use of the cheque, already popular in London, was much extended.

The provisions of the Bank Charter Act also discriminated against mergers involving joint-stock banks, according more favourable treatment to private bank amalgamations. Further restrictions upon the development of new joint-stock banks were imposed in September of 1844 by an Act 'to regulate the Joint Stock Banks in England' (7 and 8.c. 113).[31] This embodied a code which applied to the establishment and conduct of all new joint-stock banks, although those already in existence were not affected by it. In future no bank could be formed without a charter under Letters Patent with a maximum term of twenty years and which could be obtained only by means of a petition to the Crown through the Committee of the Privy Council for Trade and Plantations. The minimum nominal capital was to be £100,000 and a £100 minimum denomination to each share was stipulated; further, all shares had to be subscribed and at least a half of their nominal amount had to be paid up before the company could open its doors. As a result, smaller investors were largely excluded from contributing to bank development and the number of possible shareholders was reduced. Additional requirements were that the deed of partnership should be in a form approved by the Privy Council and that it should contain clauses which, amongst other things, forbade the company to purchase or lend upon the security of its own shares, required that a statement of assets and liabilities should be published once a month and stipulated that annual accounts were to be examined by auditors elected by the shareholders.

Some of these provisions undoubtedly had real merit. The 1836 Committee appointed to enquire into the operation of the Act of 1826 had observed that deeds of settlement were often loosely drawn up, giving excessive powers to directors and management; there was often a wide and misleading disparity between the nominal amount of shares and the actual amount subscribed; the paid-up capital was sometimes inadequate; there was no legal obligation to ensure that dividends were paid only out of the banking profits and only after bad or doubtful debts had first been written off.[32]

There were a number of failures of joint-stock banks around 1836. Contributory causes, apart from those already mentioned, included an abuse of the rediscounting facilities which, as has been seen, had undergone a substantial growth with the emergence of the London bill market. By the 1830s the business was flourishing, encouraged by the increasing recourse to the market by the joint-stock banks; by the latter, re-discounting had come to be regarded largely as a means of enabling them to accept new business beyond the limits set by their direct obligations (i.e. deposits and notes issued). A bank could raise money by re-selling bills of exchange discounted for its customers, but in endorsing the bill in order to do so it rendered itself liable to pay out the face value of the bill in the event of its being dishonoured by the drawee. The real weakness was not the practice itself, some merits of which have already been discussed, but the frequent lack of discrimination in the quality and quantity of the bills 're-discounted after endorsement'.(33) (Injudicious discounting was a vice to which early private bankers had not been much prone, partly because of the smaller scale of the practice and also, perhaps, because of an innate prudence in their make-up.) A further evil associated with the practice was that the ease with which money could be raised by (often doubtful) re-discounts in itself created a tendency to work on inadequate cash reserves, the bank in an emergency relying on further re-discounts to raise funds.(34) Losses arising from this source—including fraud on the part of borrowers—were frequently concealed from the scrutiny of shareholders by maintaining dividends through paying them partly or wholly out of capital.(35)

Nonetheless, some of the provisions of the Joint-stock Banks Act of 1844 were unnecessarily irksome. The new procedures for the formation of companies and the regulation of deeds of settlement imposed severe constraint on the establishment of any new bank; furthermore, the fact that existing banks were exempt from restrictions—good as well as bad—considerably strengthened the competitive position against which any new establishment would have to battle.

5. Consolidation and limited liability

Largely as a result of the 1844 code and the provisions of the Bank Charter Act, only three joint-stock banks were founded in the decade after 1844; even until 1857—when the code was repealed—very few new joint-stock banks were attempted. The directors of the Stourbridge and Kidderminster Bank displayed uncommon perception when they remarked during their Annual General Meeting of 1844 that 'For ten years at least the advantages of our circulation are secured without danger of opposition from new and competing banks of issue.'(36) The position of the established joint-stock banks had in fact been strengthened, albeit unwittingly, by the legislation of 1844, since an incidental but nonetheless important effect of the legislation had been to provide virtual security from new joint-stock competitors. In addition, economic conditions proved hardly conducive to the formation of new banking enterprises. Bad harvests in England and Ireland had necessitated large imports of wheat with a consequent adverse effect on the balance of payments; this was reflected in outflows of gold from the Bank of England, limitations of its note-issue and a deflationary effect on prices. Heavy demands for capital to finance the railway boom also severely strained the financial system of the country, culminating in heavy speculation in railway companies which broke in 1847.

In January of that year railway calls for funds amounted to £4½ million for home use and £1.65 million for foreign use, so that a great deal of capital was locked up in a temporarily unproductive use; combined with the abnormal grain imports, an adverse balance of international payments—temporary but nonetheless serious—was created. In the final quarter of 1847 more bankruptcies occurred than in any quarter since 1826. Failures of first-rate commercial firms during September alone were reckoned as producing liabilities of from £10 million. By October the banking system, joint-stock and private, was beginning to feel the effects of the crisis. The Royal Bank of Liverpool was lent £300,000 in Consols by the Bank of England, but this was not enough to avert disaster. The city of Liverpool, indeed, after London, was the hardest hit and merchants there, as elsewhere, bore the brunt of the crisis.

Joint-stock banks generally withstood the panic without too much damage and, indeed, emerged with greatly enhanced prestige. The joint-stock banks in London and the provinces consolidated their position, partly by tapping new resources and partly at the expense of the private banks; the numbers of the latter fell from 208 banks of issue at the time of the Bank Charter Act of 1844 to 157 in 1857.[(37)] Of those that disappeared, roughly a half failed and the remainder lost their identity in mergers. Of the 72 joint-stock banks of issue in 1844, 63 remained in 1857, six had failed, and three had merged.

The 1850s, the decade of gold, witnessed the attainment of British industrial and commercial supremacy and a corresponding expansion in the services provided by the established joint-stock banks. The London joint-stock banks, whose deposits increased five-fold between 1844 and 1857, were spreading their branches. The London and Westminster, for example, had four branches in 1850 and seven in 1865; by 1851 the London and County had twenty London branches as well as a hundred in the Home Counties. Even so, only a few of the joint-stock banks had opened branches on a large scale. By 1864, the National Provincial of Birmingham had 119 branches, the London and County 127 while the Manchester and Liverpool District had 34. All the rest, some 114, had an average of only about four each. Many private banks had one or two sub-offices, although only three of them had as many as ten.[(38)]

In the years after 1844, opposition was increasingly expressed to the legislation of that year and particularly to the Joint-stock Bank Act which had virtually put an end to the creation of new joint-stock banks and greatly increased the tangle of banking laws. Banking companies could now be incorporated under four different legal classifications: first, those under the Act of 1826; secondly, those newly formed under the Joint-stock Bank Act of 1844; thirdly, those under neither of the Acts—for example, the London joint-stock and other non-issuing joint-stock banks established before 1844; finally, those previously existing banks which had taken advantage of Section XLV of the 1844 Act to become incorporated under the Act. A leading article in *The Economist* observed:

> The ingenuity of the law officers of the Crown; experience as elicited by the Banking Committees of both Houses of Parliament; the admini-

> strative and constructive ability of Sir Robert Peel—seem all to have been exhausted in the framing of this Act. Yet, alas for legislative contrivance in matters of trade, its chief, almost its only fruit (except the crop of banks established during the last two years), was the Royal British Bank.[39]

A series of business failures (including that of the Royal British Bank, one of the very few new joint-stock banks to be registered under the 1844 Joint-stock Bank Act) brought matters to a head early in 1857. In August of that year, therefore, an Act (20 & 21 Vict. c. 49) was passed repealing the whole of the code of 1844 and enacting in its place a much simpler and more permissive set of provisions. In essence, these provided for a return to the situation before 1844 except that the important modifications resulting from the Bank Charter Act were not affected—and, in particular, there was to be no resumption of former rights of note-issue. The £100 minimum denomination for shares in banking companies was the only clause of the 1844 Code which was retained, while all new banks, together with the few established since 1844, were required to register under the provision of the new Act which also incorporated the provisions of the Companies Acts of 1856 and 1857. There was one significant exception to this latter feature, however; banking companies were still denied the privilege of limited liability. Many, indeed, did not want it.

With the repeal of the code of 1844, the period of comparative freedom from new competitors enjoyed by the joint-stock banks came to an end. It had been long enough, however, for many of them to become firmly established. The London joint-stock banks, indeed, had increased their deposits from just under £9 million in 1847 to over £43 million in 1857. Even in London the opposition of the private bankers was beginning to fade. Something of the old suspicion with which the private banker viewed his joint-stock rival had been allayed by the steadiness of the latter in withstanding the panic of 1847; by the time of the 1857 crisis, in fact, the joint-stock system was as reliable as any in the banking world.

In 1854, six London joint-stock banks, headed by the London and Westminster, were at last admitted to the London Bankers' Clearing House, and by the outbreak of the first World War eleven more had been admitted at varying intervals.[40] A country cheque clearing was begun in 1858 on the basis of plans elaborated by Lord Avebury (then Mr J. Lubbock) in order to satisfy the country bankers; these had resorted to the same method of pressure as had the London joint-stock bankers—that is, they had threatened the establishment of their own clearing house. In accordance with the 1854 agreement between the private clearing bankers and the London joint-stock banks, clearing by transference of Bank of England notes was replaced by settlement in the form of cheques drawn on the banks' accounts at the Bank of England. As a consequence, the importance of banknotes as a means of settlement was much reduced and this also tended to moderate public demand for notes. The introduction of the country clearing reduced the use of notes still further. Cheques from the country banks (not drawn on themselves) were cleared by their London correspondents and this practice encouraged a large-scale and more widespread use of cheques.[41] By 1867, the membership of the clearing house was 13 private and 111 joint-stock banks while the Bank of England itself had become a member three years before.

6. Limited liability

In the struggle for full legal franchise one privilege, limited liability, now enjoyed by other business companies had not yet become a recognised attribute of banking companies. In theory, most co-partnerships could limit risk by a clause in their deeds which required that the company should be wound up if more than a quarter of the capital were lost. In practice, however, the provision was almost entirely ignored, with the result that the failure of a company usually meant not only the loss of the shareholders' capital but risk to their private property as well. The hardships which often resulted provoked support for the notion of limited liability in banking. Vincent Stuckey had expressed support for the idea before the 1836 Committee; in the same year William Clay had advocated in Parliament the granting of limited liability to bank shareholders. In 1849 leave was sought by a private member to bring in a bill to achieve this, but the motion was withdrawn in the face of government opposition. Althorp, apparently, had meant to offer limited liability to non-issuing banks in the legislation of 1833 but, as he wrote to the Governor of the Bank of England, finding 'the opposition of the Country Bankers too strong for me on the question of Limited Liability, my colleagues have decided that I must not persevere in this question'.(42) Banking opinion generally was none too enthusiastic about such proposals but tended instead to endorse the view that 'the law may safely be left as it is'.(43)

This lack of enthusiasm on the part of the banking fraternity may at first sight appear surprising but behind it lay a profound distrust of the effects which the transition from full to limited liability might have on their customers and hence their deposits. Offsetting, and indeed over-riding, the need to bolster the confidence of shareholders in the banks—which in any case could be met by attractive dividends and bonus issues—was the fear of undermining the equally important confidence of customers. The private banking tradition, which perforce was the inheritance of the joint-stock banks, had largely depended for its goodwill—or so it was thought—upon the unlimited liability of the partners whose personal fortunes were thereby staked on the success of the enterprise. It was felt that any lessening of the proprietors' liability would arouse the suspicion of depositors as to the bank's solvency—especially if other banks did not follow suit. Apart from this difficulty, it was apparent that the adoption of limited liability would require the publication of balance sheets—a step which most of the old joint-stock banks were reluctant to contemplate.

Nevertheless, the protagonists of limited liability remained staunch to their cause. One Governor of the Bank of England had echoed Gilbart in criticising unlimited liability; he had pointed out that in the event of mismanagement, any shareholders who became aware of it would not expose it for fear of precipitating unlimited liability on themselves, whereas if liability was limited they would act.(44) *The Economist*, too—perhaps with undue optimism—held that:

> the principle of limited liability would ensure a better class of shareholders and a better class of directors—that it would necessarily tend to greater caution on the part of the public in dealing with banks, and thus enforce a more circumspect management.(45)

In 1858 a short bill (21 & 22 Vic. c. 91) was passed; this was in the nature of an addition to the Act of 1857, enabling new banks to be formed with limited liability except as regards note-issues. Existing banks were allowed the same right but like the new limited liability banks they were required to publish a statement of assets and liabilities twice a year and to display it in every branch of the bank. Thus it was possible for banking co-partnerships to incorporate themselves as either limited or unlimited companies; for the reasons already given, however, most of the old-established joint-stock bankers were still reluctant to commit themselves to limited liability. As the *Bankers' Magazine* remarked,

> But that any joint stock bank which, under the existing law, is enjoying a safe and profitable business, will desire to exchange their unlimited for limited liability, looking at the price they may have to pay for a doubtful advantage, is more than improbable.(46)

For another twenty years this opinion was to prove well-founded.

New banks, with much less at risk, were less affected by such doubts but under the 1857 Act they were still subject to the difficulty of complying with the minimum share denomination of £100. This restriction was removed in 1862 by the Companies Act, a consolidating measure which greatly simplified the existing laws affecting companies generally, including banks. As a result there was a pronounced increase in limited liability banking both in London and in the provinces. Twenty-four new banks were established in the fifteen years to 1875, a trend which was augmented by conversions of existing banks—particularly private banks—into limited joint-stock enterprises. Many amalgamations and re-arrangements took place, reducing further the area of private banking facilities; in the process famous old private banks such as Jones, Lloyd and Co. and Heywood, Kennard and Co. were absorbed by joint-stock banks. Some of the leading provincial bankers, such as Lloyd's of Birmingham and J. M. Head and Co. of Carlisle, also converted into limited liability companies. Lloyd's prospectus of 29th March 1865 stated that

> The recent alterations in the law affecting Banking Partnerships, and the growing requirements of the Trade in this District, have determined Messrs. Lloyds and Company and Messrs. Moilliet and Sons to extend the basis of their present Partnerships by Converting them into a Joint-Stock Company with limited liability.

Banking opinion nevertheless remained divided, despite the permissive powers made available to the banks by the Acts of 1858 and 1862. Many of the larger, established joint-stock banks were still reluctant to risk the change in form to limited liability; in the 1870s the majority of them were still unlimited liability companies. Their reluctance had been stiffened by the collapse in 1866 of Overend-Gurney, for long a private firm and the most famous of the London discount houses, which had adopted limited liability only a few months before it failed with liabilities of over £10 million. Those joint-stock banks not of limited liability form were thus faced with an acute dilemma. On the one hand, public confidence in private firms was declining and the publication of accounts by limited liability companies was in increasing favour; on the other hand, the adoption of limited liability might arouse the gravest suspicions as to the bank's solvency, particularly after the Overend-Gurney affair. Since the new legislation there had been a spate of company formation, often excessive and top-heavy, which culminated in many business failures. One cause of the trouble—and an old one at that—was the incompatibility of fat profits and sound securities. This had been illustrated very well by a leading article of *The Times* on the very day of the Overend crash:

> The Finance Companies raised their capital, or, in other words, obtained subscriptions from the public, on the Faith of the profits which they promised.... They were bound to make profits enough to provide handsome dividends and maintain the value of their shares, and they can only get those profits out of ventures proportionately exceptional.... In other words, they took up the whole of some great speculation—say, a railway or other such work—and found the money for it on condition of getting a lion's share of the ultimate profits.... Good negotiable securities on which money could at any moment be raised, would not have brought all this interest with them.... A finance company, with its assets represented by an unfinished railway, is naturally in difficulties. It may possess property to the extent, perhaps, of its paid-up capital, but it is not property on which money can be raised. Its only remaining resource is a 'call', and the prospect of a call puts its shareholders in such a fright that they are ready not only to give their shares away, but to pay anybody for taking them.(47)

'Black Friday' had burnt itself deep in the memory of the City—and in that of quite a few other places too—and there was much nervousness over dabbling in new company structures. Many of the new limited companies had been hard hit by speculation in their shares; a bear operation leading to a fall in a Stock Exchange quotation could lead in a matter of hours to a substantial withdrawal of deposits, often with embarrassing consequences. This state of affairs was only eased in 1867 with 'Leeman's Act' of that year designed to put an end to purely speculative dealings in bank shares.

It was another disaster—that involving the City and Glasgow Bank, with large liabilities and wholly inadequate assets—which finally broke down old antipathies to limited liability formation. In the case of the City and Glasgow, an unlimited liability bank, the shareholders were obliged to meet heavy losses out of their own pockets. Not altogether unexpectedly, there was a collapse of public confidence in bank shares and a consequent decline in their market values. Clearly public opinion was now decidedly in favour of the limited liability principle and the final solution was found in the Act of 1879 (42 & 43 Vict. c. 76) which provided a new legislative principle of 'reserved liability'. 'Reserved liability' represented the difference between the nominal and the paid-up value of shares, the difference being callable only in the event of the company being wound up. In order to make the Act available to unlimited companies whose shares were fully paid up and who yet desired to have some reserve liability available in case of winding up, such companies were to be permitted to increase the nominal amount of their capital, the increase not being capable of being called except in the case of winding up.(48)

During the next five years the principle was widely adopted as the old joint-stock banks took advantage of the Act, all the London joint-stock banks, for example, registering under reserved liability by 1882. An apparent consequence of the greater security in banking was the impetus given to really large-scale enterprises: the number of branch banks which had risen by about 35 per cent to 2,413 in the nine years to 1881, increased by a further 40 per cent, to 3,383, in the ensuing decade.(49) One result of the change was to make the annual (or more frequent) publication of bank balance sheets a general practice and this furthered the amalgamation process by revealing the financial position of provincial banks. Some of the provincial banks were unwilling to register under the Act but their hesitation placed them at a disadvantage in comparison with more progressive rivals, a fact which was reflected particularly in a decline in market quotations of the shares of banks still operating under unlimited liability.(50) In these ways the adoption of limited liability strengthened the position of the larger joint-stock banks who were prospective purchasers and thus gave added impetus to the amalgamation movement which marked the closing years of the century.

7. Branch expansion and the amalgamation movement

In 1826 Lord Liverpool had declared that 'the solid and more extensive banks would not fail, in time, to expel the smaller and weaker'.(51) At this time, extension of branches was being sought by early banks as a method of obtaining a widespread note-issue. In addition, of course, it was a means of snapping up the business of a failed or struggling bank, of getting a foot into a town before a competitor who was rumoured to be coming, of responding to a call from influential residents, or—with the more venturesome joint-stock banks—of breaking into quite a new district, perhaps a town for which access and new business had been provided by the opening of the railways.

A typical example of early branch expansion is provided by the Gloucestershire Banking Co. which acquired three branches in 1831 by absorbing Hartlands of Cheltenham, Tewkesbury and Evesham and two more in 1842 by the absorption of Cripps and Co. at Cirencester and Stow. There was a further period of 'digestion' and consolidation before a branch was opened in 1853 at Moreton-in-Marsh, where the opening of the railway was thought to promise more business. In ensuing years the company spread westwards into Ross and Hereford, thereby maintaining and extending the agricultural connections of the bank.(52) Again, the West of England and South Wales District Bank, founded at Bristol in 1834, believed in branch expansion from its foundation; in its first twenty years it proceeded to open branches wherever it could, although not in places where one or other of the joint-stock banks was already established. More usually, vigorous branch expansion led to quite severe competition; in the 1830s and 1860s especially, banks were racing each other to establish branches in chosen areas. In 1833, one year after the establishment of the Bank of Birmingham, for example, the Commercial Bank of England, the Northern and Central Bank of England and the National Provincial Bank of England all established offices in Birmingham, which was already the home of Lloyds as well as the Birmingham Banking Co. It might have been thought that this proliferation would have amply served the needs of Birmingham but such was thought to be the demand for banking services that two more joint-stock banks were started: the Birmingham Town and District Bank and, shortly afterwards, the Birmingham and Midland Bank, forerunner of the present Midland Bank.

The typical early joint-stock bank resembled the large private bank in its prime, with perhaps half-a-dozen branches within 20 or 30 miles of the Head Office, although there were, of course, many exceptions—in 1836, for example, the Halifax Joint-Stock Banking Co. had no branches at all while, at the other extreme, the Wilts and Dorset already had 24. Once a joint-stock bank was founded, several years could elapse before it ventured into further expansion. At the same time there existed the advocates of rapid expansion, particularly the joint-stock banks founded in the 1830s, who regularly swallowed old private firms and small joint-stock banks. There were dangers in too rapid a 'digestion', of course, for a new acquisition might be in a more shaky state than was initially realised and could (and often did) have hidden liabilities which could seriously damage the purchasing bank. Prior knowledge of such a state of affairs would often mean that the buyer was in a position to force down the price (usually reckoned on a basis of so many years' profits). Alternatively, the prospective purchaser could stand aside and let the firm fail, thereby probably picking up something of its custom for not much more than the cost of its premises.

In their initial stages joint-stock banks could establish themselves and provide for further expansion not only by buying up private banks but by opening branches in districts poorly served by banking. By the end of the nineteenth century there were few such virgin territories left; from this time on, a bank intent on further expansion was obliged to enter another bank's area, ideally by taking over that bank itself, securing thereby not only its custom, goodwill and premises, but its staff as well. In the later stage of the amalgamation movement, many of the remaining small banks found themselves in a seller's market, such was the keenness to establish branches.

There was a variety of reasons tempting both the old private banker and the small joint-stock bank to sell out. In many instances the old private customer of the private banker had outgrown the bank and had been transformed into a joint-stock company with a large issue of debentures. Small banks with no large branch systems to bring in deposits were vulnerable to the inroads made by a few big customers. Given the trend towards larger industrial and business units, a small bank—even with a few branches—confined to one region or area was liable to find itself called upon to meet quite heavy seasonal demands for finance, whether from cotton importers or loom manufacturers, and the accommodation required in any one district might vary considerably from one season of the year to another. A bank with large resources, and particularly the larger joint-stock banks, could maintain branches in both districts to take advantage of these seasonal variations, thus keeping its money fully employed all year. A further advantage of a network of branches—and one which tended to be abused—was the opportunity provided of working to a minimum of till-money, since gold and Bank of England notes could be obtained at a few hours' notice; the isolated small bank, on the other hand, had either to keep cash lying idle in the safe or run the risk of delay in meeting a sudden demand. Such were the influences which persuaded small firms like the Shropshire Banking Co., to name but one of hundreds, to sell out to a more powerful concern.

Although the displacement of private banks by joint-stock banks made continual progress, branch systems were largely local until the 1870s. By about 1880, however, the nineteenth-century system of communications had been practically completed and the way was established for inter-regional expansion and amalgamation. By 1886 the London and County had 165 branches, the National Provincial 158 and the Capital and Counties 99. Apart from these three, the leaders in branch expansion, the remaining 112 joint-stocks had an average of ten branches each, although six of them now had more than 50. Even as late as 1890, however, there were still nearly 80 private country banks of issue, with average issues ranging from £376 to £67,881.[53] There was a growing awareness that the future lay with the larger banks. The increased scope of banking facilities and the keenness of competition among bankers had undoubtedly tended to reduce the rate of profit on a given capital; hence, apart from the actual direct effects of competition, there was less and less incentive for the private or small joint-stock banker to stay in the banking business; by investing his money elsewhere he could obtain at least an equivalent return with probably a great deal less trouble and—especially before the introduction of limited liability in banking—with much less risk.

In the cheap money era of 1892-7, the amalgamation movement among the smaller banks was accentuated by the need to obtain an outlet for money which was unlendable in London at 2 per cent.[54] Today most branch systems are divided into 'borrowing' and 'lending' branches, the head office acting as agent for the diversion of funds, but in the nineteenth century—or indeed in the late eighteenth century—many banks found themselves in one or other category but not in both; accordingly they were forced to depend on their London correspondents to find or place funds for them at a commission. This was hardly the most economical or profitable means of handling money, especially as banking systems grew larger and the use of cheques increased. Before its amalgamation with the London and Westminster, for example, the London and County Bank was hindered because its branches were largely in agricultural districts (i.e. 'lending' branches) and the Chairman had to express regret that 'we have no large manufacturing towns like Manchester, Bradford, or Newcastle, which absorb enormous sums of money'.[55] Parr's Bank, on the other hand, according to its chairman 'had channels in our northern banking system for the lucrative employment of money which London bankers have not'.[56] This was in 1877. Eventually—although in this instance not until the twentieth century—the situation was rationalised, as were others, by a merger of giants. The London and County amalgamated with the London and Westminster in 1909 and the combined bank merged with Parr's about ten years later.

Branch expansion had originally been sought as a means of circulating a widespread note-issue. It was Bagehot's contention that note issues created the English money market; they made it worthwhile to set up small banks out of which the deposit business grew:

> The system of deposits gradually grows out of a note issue, because there is no increase in confidence required. It is that way that at first the note issuers created the system of deposit banking, and that the system of deposit banking created that wonderful superfluity of money which we have in London.

The private bankers of the capital, with the near monopoly of the Bank of England's note issue in the London area, had tended in the eighteenth and nineteenth centuries to concentrate on deposit banking and were developing the cheque in association with it.

Deposit banking, of course, came in with the goldsmiths; deposits were, and are, vital to any bank, but a note issue had usually been ranked in prior place as an element of profitable banking. The primary aim of private country banks, as has been seen, was the issue of notes, the attraction of deposits being only a secondary aim. Most of the new provincial joint-stock banks had also begun with similar intentions, but it was not long before the value of branch systems was appreciated as a means in itself of gathering deposits. This shift of emphasis had been evident even before 1844 in the discounting agreements made by provincial banks with the branches of the Bank of England and also in the successful example of the note-issuing banks of London and Lancashire. The trend was undoubtedly accelerated by the restrictions imposed on private note issues by the Bank Charter Act of 1844 and the consequent promotion of cheques.

Joint-stock banking thus became primarily deposit banking and the acquisition of deposits, and of outlets for deposits, became the motives for expansion. In the 1840s and 1850s this was the cornerstone of branch expansion as joint-stock bankers went out to attract deposits from small traders, shopkeepers and manufacturers. There was a steady improvement in banking science; the old practice of reliance upon a small number of large customers was suspect and bankers were beginning to appreciate that a great number of small accounts was a much safer foundation. Steadily the principle was evolving that a small capital and large deposits formed the elements of successful and profitable banking.

The acquisition of deposits necessarily meant the attraction of depositors and the most obvious means of achieving this was to offer substantial rates of interest on all credit balances. There were other supplementary incentives, however, whose importance to the public could not be safely underestimated. These included a readiness to accept small accounts, more convenient opening hours, the transfer of money free of charge (by arrangements with joint-stock banks in other districts) and the exchange of local notes, also free of charge. Such service was not a policy of private bankers as a whole.

In most country districts it was the practice to pay interest on credit balances, but the allowance made by the private country banker was often minimal. It was not difficult for the new joint-stock banks to pay interest from the beginning on all credit balances and to push the rates up, thereby luring away custom from rivals and at the same time attracting new business from as yet untapped sources. The Leicestershire Banking Company opening for business in 1829, for example, began a vigorous search for business, after the manner of many of the new banks, by offering attractive rates of interest. Bills were to be discounted at 4 per cent, current accounts were to be allowed 3 per cent when in credit and charged 5 per cent when overdrawn, while deposit receipts of two months and upwards were granted 3 per cent. Within six months it was discovered that these rates were unprofitable and the allowance on credit balances was reduced to $2\frac{1}{2}$ per cent.[(57)] Allowances of between 2 and 3 per cent upon credit balances and charges of from 4 to 5 on overdrafts and discounts seem to have been common.[(58)]

In London, however, a different practice prevailed from that in the country. The distinction between deposit and current accounts, of course, had long been known to London bankers, but the private bankers of the capital had made no allowance of regular interest, even on deposit accounts, since the beginning of the nineteenth century. The safe-keeping of the customer's money was regarded as adequate recompense, while an additional argument related to the danger of requiring the private banker to pay rates which would oblige him to bank up to the hilt—that is, forcing him to lend at higher rates and, therefore, greater risk simply in order to meet the burden of interest payments on deposits. This was a danger, however, which the joint-stock banks were prepared to face. In 1834, to the annoyance of the London private bankers, the London and Westminster had re-introduced interest on deposit accounts, and two years later the London Joint Stock Bank announced in its prospectus of December 1836 that interest would be paid on current accounts as well as on deposit accounts. This was altogether a novelty—a monstrous one to the private banker—and was an obvious device to attract deposits; its success is difficult to assess, however, since deposits do not appear to have been affected when this particular practice was abandoned as being too expensive in the early 1850s. The payment of interest on deposit accounts, of course, remained part of joint stock practice, as it is today.

Price competition in rates on deposits thus became a feature of the joint-stock banks' struggle to acquire larger deposits and it inevitably sharpened the competition which the private bankers were having to meet from the expanding branch systems of the joint-stocks. In 1839 the County of Gloucester Banking Co. was giving its managers discretion to bid 3 per cent in the face of competition, although it was not long before they, as well as many others, reached agreements with local rivals on rates for new deposits. Such agreements became common as banks began to realise the dangers of too zealous a degree of competition; the head offices of branch systems would in fact often allow local managers to enter into agreements with rivals on local rates even though these might be out of line with rates quoted by other branches of the same bank. Branch expansion, too, fell within the scope of local agreements. In 1836, for example, both the Wilts and Dorset Bank and the North Wilts Bank were organisations struggling for a footing in new neighbourhoods; appreciating the disadvantages of overlapping branches, however, they agreed to keep out of certain towns which fell within each other's territory. As late as 1913-14 Lloyd's kept a list of towns in which, should it desire to open a branch, it had agreed to warn other banks.[59] Needless to say such agreements were not regarded as binding if one or other bank felt strong enough to break them.

By the middle of the nineteenth century, the force of competition had brought a fair degree of both uniformity and flexibility into the rates allowed on deposit accounts by the various joint-stock banks, the usual payment being one per cent below the Bank of England's discount rate. This was, as yet, however, only a rough and ready guide, subject in practice to numerous qualifications and shades of interpretation according to size of balance, the required period of notice of withdrawals and also local traditions which—especially in districts approximately self-contained for banking purposes—tended to keep rates fixed for year after year. Towards the end of the century, however, London rates were having much more influence. Local managers were finding that big customers took their deposits to London when rates in the City rose much beyond the more sticky country rate; at the other end of the scale, the lower Bank rate fell, the more uniform were deposit rates in any locality, since local managers found it easier to agree on maximum rates if London rates were low.[60] Rates on loans and overdrafts were also increasingly tied to those obtaining in London; all bankers, however, tended to charge a minimum, usually 5 per cent, below which Bank rate would not be followed.

With the turn of the century it became usual for local banks in any one town to be offering common rates on deposits, although both these and rates on overdrafts and loans would be subject to fine adjustments in special circumstances. The domination of the larger joint-stock banks was in fact creating a situation in which a national uniformity of rates was inevitable. Increasing in size and power, with their head offices now based on London, these banks were becoming less inclined to indulge in price competition, especially since they were now more directly governed by London rates and conditions. In 1898 Sir Thomas Salt had expressed the hope that 'before my banking days are done I may see anything like vulgar competition between large banks given up altogether'.[(61)] Official agreement on rates on deposit accounts came with World War I; after the war, as a general rule, the 'Town Deposit Rate' fluctuated with Bank Rate, while the standard country rate was a steady $2\frac{1}{2}$ per cent.

8. Balance sheets and reserves

One effect of the Act of 1879 and the adoption of reserved liability by the larger joint-stock banks was the publication of bi-annual balance sheets and a general movement towards more publicity. This in itself was a stimulus to amalgamation; many of the old private banks were reluctant to divulge their accounts, especially as their capital and reserve funds would appear puny when set beside the reserved liability of the large joint-stock banks; such, at any rate, were the grievances expressed at a meeting of the Association of English Country Bankers in November 1887. For most of the 1880s, therefore, private bankers were reluctant to follow the example of the joint-stock banks and their secrecy was contrasted unfavourably with the publicity of the latter.

It was the Baring Crisis of November 1890 which provided the sharpest spur to greater publicity. Goschen, then Chancellor of the Exchequer, complained in a series of speeches of the inadequacy of bank reserves—particularly those of private banks—and called for frequent publication of balance sheets as a precaution against undue depletion of cash reserves.

Largely as a result of this criticism, the London joint-stock banks determined to publish monthly statements and the country joint-stock banks quarterly statements, and private bankers reluctantly began to follow their example. Thus, Foster's of Cambridge wrote to Hodgkin Barnetts in Newcastle on the latter's decision to begin publication of their balance sheets in 1891:

> Like yourselves, we feel very forcibly the strong objections to this publicity but fear we must follow the fashion though we cannot approve it.[(62)]

With the expansion of branch banking into really large systems, banks had been able to work to lower cash reserves. The prospect of calls upon individual branches could be more readily assessed and anticipated in the light of not only the funds available from the branch concerned but also those diverted to the head office from surplus branches within the system. Improving communications and ready access to head offices, together with re-discounting facilities in the London bill market and the emergence of the Bank of England as 'lender of last resort', had resulted in a tendency to work to a minimum of till money. The potential harm of this was more apparent in the earlier years and in the smaller branch systems where, if indiscreet management committed itself to doubtful advances on illiquid security, a bank could find itself obliged to suspend payment. The publication of balance sheets, however, necessarily meant the disclosure of the ratio of cash to deposit liabilities. The focus of public attention upon what had always been a sensitive point amongst bankers encouraged the banks to become 'ratio conscious' and the concept of a regular cash ratio as a practical guide in banking operations was steadily evolved. The ratio usually quoted was 10 per cent, although in fact most of the large joint-stock banks could in ordinary circumstances work quite safely to a lower ratio than this. It should be borne in mind, however, that this figure represented a monthly average of the amounts shown in the balance sheets of the various banks on the day of the week selected by each bank for its 'make-up'. All that the managers of the banks had to do was to see that these weekly amounts averaged about the percentage of the current accounts and deposits at which the bank aimed; in their day-to-day lending, they would rarely consider themselves rigidly bound by the ratio. The publication of monthly balance sheets ceased on the outbreak of the first World War but following the recommendations of the Cunliffe Committee of 1918 the monthly returns were resumed in 1921 in a greatly improved and more comprehensive form. Thus the cash ratios of the commercial banks eventually became the principal medium for the operation of Bank of England policy.

9. The overall structure

Although the day of the small country banker, whether joint-stock or private, was clearly nearing its end, until about 1880 the majority of British banks were predominantly local in character. Those which had gone beyond the limits of their own localities, however, were already surpassing all others in size. The freedom from legislative obstacles, the growing dominance of the cheque and the completion of the railways and the development of the telegraph were reflected during the latter years of the nineteenth century in the movement towards ever larger and more widespread banks. As may be seen from Table 1, even by 1884 some 90 provincial joint-stock banks could already claim over a thousand branches.

The further development could not be in doubt. The wider the range of a branch system, the lower the cost of providing banking services and the more certain the outlets at home and abroad for profitable finance. Amongst the foremost advantages was the speedy and cheap clearing of cheques, a process which could be expensive for a local bank which had to maintain agents in the clearing centre. Once a bank could clear quickly and cheaply it could attract deposits by offering the service of administering a drawing account instead of a cash interest payment.

Moreover, the large-scale development of the cheque changed the technique of credit provision; in association with the deposit banking which it made possible, it almost entirely displaced the inland bill of exchange. With the vast increase in their deposits it became a matter of indifference to the joint-stock banks whether they financed their customers by discounting bills or by granting loans or advances; to the customer, on the other hand, the flexibility of the overdraft system, usually in association with the cheque, had definite attractions. The banker could allow his customer a simple loan or overdraft, possibly with collateral security, but without any

TABLE 1

The Banking System of England and Wales, 1884

	Number	Branches	Capital and Reserve £000	Note Circulation £000	Deposits £000
1. Bank of England (September 24)	1	11	18, 295	25, 102	29, 372
2. London Banks:					
a. *Private*	35	10	?	nil	68, 000*
b. *Joint-stock*	21	52	18, 147	nil	76, 654
	56	62	?	nil	144, 654
3. London and Provincial Banks:					
Joint-stock	6	517	9, 000	nil	69, 738
4. Provincial Banks:					
a. *Private*					
(i) Issuing	100	330	?	1, 439	78, 561
(ii) Non-Issuing	72	103	?	nil	
	172	433	?	1, 439	
b. *Joint-stock*					
(i) Issuing	45	523	15, 749	1, 541	54, 456
(ii) Non-Issuing	46	529	18, 728	nil	80, 887
	91	1, 052	34, 477	1, 541	135, 343

* Estimates: the private banks did not publish balance sheets, while 11 provincial joint-stock banks did not give full figures.

Source: W. F. Crick and J. E. Wadsworth, *A hundred years of joint-stock banking*, Hodder and Stoughton, London 1936, p. 34.

possibility of the assignment of the debt to another creditor. The acceptor of a bill, on the other hand, became the debtor of an unknown creditor against whom default was an act of bankruptcy. For a trader who obtained an advance from his banker and paid cash instead of drawing a bill, his financial liability remained a purely private matter between his banker and himself, and traders soon learnt to prefer the ease and privacy of the system. Again, the cheque quickly proved far superior to the inland bill of exchange in favour of the 'open credit' system as the standard method of finance.(63)

The increase in size, with resources diffused throughout the widest possible variety of industrial, professional and personal borrowers, meant that bankers were able to economise on idle reserves and maximise profitable outlets for finance by diverting funds from areas in surplus to those in need. Costs were also brought to a minimum as overheads were reduced and operations standardised; a bonus was provided to the customer in the form of the specialist services derived from the exploitation of the division of labour. By the twentieth century competition in services—foreign exchange, trustee and executor business—was beginning to replace competition in prices and size. At the same time it was possible to minimise risks, not only those pertaining to the credit of individuals but also those created by the instability of economic growth.

To achieve the full advantage of economies of scale, it was obvious that much of the old private banking practices would have to be discarded. Agency agreements were expensive, expecially as banks became larger and much business had to be done through London, while accounts could be lost to London-based firms. Moreover, the old correspondent system of the country banks could not compete with branch structures in safety and profitability. In 1866 the National Provincial Bank (with 120 Midland branches) abandoned its London agency and opened a London office at the sacrifice of its note-issue of nearly £450,000 and the profits arising from it. Scots bankers, arriving in London from the mid-1860s, were soon boasting of their extra profits; as the use of cheques increased, the need for a base in London was appreciated all the more, if only to secure admission to the London Bankers' Clearing House. An additional impetus was the urge of the really large provincial banks to obtain access to the expanding foreign business of London. After 1850, indeed, bank deposits tended to increase at a faster rate than the aggregate domestic demand for credit and supplementary outlets were sought in international finance.(64) By 1870 there were over forty imperial and foreign banking companies in London and by 1890 there were nearly a hundred institutions 'now carrying on business as London bankers'. In this category were now placed most institutions of the Imperial, foreign or Anglo-foreign type—for example, the Yokohama Specie Bank, the Bank of New South Wales, the Hong Kong Shanghai Bank, the Anglo-Egyptian Bank and the Imperial Bank of Persia.(65) Banks with London bases vied with each other to secure agencies for foreign banks not represented in London.

The most coveted prize, however, was almost certainly a seat in the London Bankers' Clearing House. In 1884, Lloyds Bank, hitherto confined to the Midlands, took over two famous London banks, while in 1889 the Birmingham Banking Company entered London by absorbing the Royal Exchange Bank. Two years later, the Birmingham and Midland Bank merged with the Central Bank of London, becoming the London and Midland Bank. Country and London banking was at last being welded into a single structure, although at the risk of domination of the nation's financial interests by a small but very powerful group of joint-stock banks. The resources of these half-dozen banks, operating in London and the provinces, were already equal to the total of those of the purely London joint-stock banks. In 1896, in effect in self-defence, several London and provincial private banking firms amalgamated to form Barclay's Bank, so as to be able to compete with the giant banking organisations.

At the end of 1913 there were in Britain some 43 joint-stock banks (including Baring Bros. and Co., Glyn, Mills and Co. and Coutts and Co.) with altogether 5,797 branches and controlling £809 million deposits, while eight private banks published statements with £27 million deposits. Three of the 43 joint-stock banks had more than 500 branches: the London City and Midland led with 679 branches and over £91 million deposits and Barclays had 570 branches and nearly £61 million deposits. There were fifteen other banks with over 100 branches.(66) In 1914, the amalgamation movement embarked on its final stage. In that year Lloyds absorbed the Wilts and Dorset Banking Co. which had a hundred branches in territory already well represented with Lloyds branches. 1917-18 saw a series of rapid and extensive amalgamations including, in 1917, the affiliation of the Belfast Banking Co. with the London City and Midland Bank and, in 1918, the merger of Lloyds, with its £174 million deposits and 888 offices, with the Capital and Counties with £60 million deposits and 473 offices. By the end of the first World War the process of amalgamation had reduced the number of banks of first importance to five, with resources which were nearly two-thirds of the total for the whole country.

The protagonists of such massive banks stressed the consequent gains in safety, efficiency and economy of operation; they also stressed the need to match the increased size of industrial units if banks were to be able to accommodate them. The size of these later banking amalgamations, however, had occasioned fears of the emergence of a banking monopoly. Anxiety was felt lest banking monopolists should provide a less satisfactory service; already there had been some criticism of the narrowing of bank lending coinciding with the trend to mammoth banks. The resultant feeling of uneasiness, and the occasion of the amalgamation of the London Country and Westminster Bank with Parr's Bank in 1918, led to the establishment of a Treasury Committee on Bank Amalgamations.

The Committee reported that further amalgamation between the big banking institutions would tend to reduce competition to an undesirable extent. It also concluded that a further shrinkage of the ratio of capital to liabilities would be undesirable, pointing out that amalgamations tended to result in a writing-down of the combined capital of the amalgamating institutions.(67) There were some grounds, however, for maintaining that British banks had been over-capitalised in the later years of the nineteenth century and that a tendency to operate from a smaller capital base was not altogether undesirable. Bankers' arguments in support of very large institutions were examined and rejected. There did appear, in these latest mergers at any rate, to be a real danger of surpassing the 'optimum' number of branches, certainly if measured in terms of the needs of the economy as a whole. A Bill was in fact drafted to implement the Committee's recommendations but it was withdrawn when the banks undertook to submit all proposed mergers or arrangements for joint working for the approval of the Treasury and the Board of Trade.

By the end of the first World War, then, the British clearing banks had reached what could be regarded as the high plateau of their history. In the span of not quite a century the joint-stock banks had established a system of branch deposit banking which was to serve as a model for monetary authorities throughout the world, and had formed themselves into a pattern which remained without significant amendment for almost half a century thereafter. The Bank of England apart, the 'clearing banks'—i.e. those forming the Committee of London Clearing Bankers—comprised ten major commercial banks, although a further 15 smaller banks—mainly the old-established private banking firms—used the facilities of the clearing through the agency of one of the clearing banks proper. In the fourteen years which followed one of the latter was to disappear through failure while eight others were absorbed by one or other of the clearing banks; the latter in turn were to alter their names somewhat here and there. The evolution was completed by the admission of the District Bank into the Committee of London Clearing Bankers from the first day of 1936.

The pattern which had emerged, then, in that latter year, is shown in Table 2. The eleven banks between them then held a total of over £2, 000 million, of which the 'Big Five' accounted for about 87 per cent. Between them they were believed to account for around 95 per cent of the banking transactions in Britain. It was a structure which was to remain substantially unchanged until the late 1960s.

TABLE 2

The London Clearing Banks, 1936

		Deposits, £ million
1.	Midland Bank Ltd	487
2.	Barclays Bank Ltd	430
3.	Lloyds Bank Ltd	406
4.	Westminster Bank Ltd	368
5.	National Provincial Bank Ltd	321
	Total, 'Big Five'	2, 012
6.	Martins Bank Ltd	93
7.	District Bank Ltd	78
8.	Glyn Mills & Co.	41
9.	National Bank Ltd	39*
10.	Williams Deacon's Bank Ltd	38
11.	Coutts & Co.	24
	TOTAL	2, 325

* Including deposits at 142 branches in Ireland and notes in circulation.

Source: E.H. Phelps Brown and G.L.S. Shackle, 'Statistics of monetary circulation in England and Wales, 1919-1937', Royal Economic Society, *Memorandum No. 74,* September 1938, p. 6.

REFERENCES

1. T. Joplin, *Essay on Banking,* London 1822, p. 42.
2. A. Andreades, *History of the Bank of England,* P.S. King & Sons Ltd.

3. J. Clapham, *The Bank of England,* Cambridge University Press, London 1944, Vol. II, p. 103.

4. T. E. Gregory, *British Banking Statutes and Reports 1832-1928,* Oxford University Press, London 1929, Vol. I, p. xiii.

5. T. E. Gregory, *The Westminster Bank Through a Century,* Oxford University Press, London 1936, Vol. II, p. 148.

6. W. F. Crick and J. E. Wadsworth, *A Hundred Years of Joint Stock Banking,* Hodder and Stoughton, London 1936, p. 16.

7. Clapham, *op. cit.,* Vol. II, p. 113.

8. *Ibid.,* Vol. II, p. 104.

9. *Ibid.,* Vol. II, p. 114.

10. Joplin, *op. cit.,* p. 42.

11. Clapham, *op. cit.,* Vol. II, p. 128.

12. *Ibid.,* p. 128.

13. Crick and Wadsworth, *op. cit.,* pp. 18-9.

14. *Ibid.,* p. 19.

15. *Macleod on Banking,* Vol. II, p. 331 and H. A. Shannon, 'The coming of General Limited Liability', *Essays in Economic History,* ed. E. M. Carus-Wilson, Edward Arnold, London 1954, pp. 362-4.

16. *Macleod on Banking,* Vol. II, p. 332.

17. Ewings, General Manager London and Westminster; meeting 19th Jan. 1870.

18. R. S. Sayers, *Lloyds Bank in the History of English Banking,* Clarendon Press, Oxford 1957, p. 161.

19. Crick and Wadsworth, *op. cit.,* p. 20.

20. W. H. Court, *A Concise Economic History of Britain from 1750 to Recent Times,* Cambridge University Press, London 1964, p. 185.

21. Gregory, *British Banking Statutes,* Vol. II, p. 222.

22. 'Mr Trollope's father-in-law', *The Three Banks Review,* No. 66, June 1965, pp. 25-38.

23. Crick and Wadsworth, *op. cit.,* p. 79.

24. *Ibid.,* pp. 105-6.

25. Quoted by E. T. Powell, *The Evolution of the London Money Market 1385-1915,* Cass, London 1966, p. 290.

26. Report from the Select Committee on Banks of Issue, 1875, Q. 7999, quoted by Gregory, *The Westminster Bank,* p. 256.

27. Quoted by Clapham, *op. cit.,* p. 106 (Smart, II, 340).

28. Clapham, *op. cit.,* Vol. II, p. 115.

29. *Ibid.,* Vol. II, pp. 133-4.

30. Gregory, *British Banking Statutes,* Vol. I, p. 129.

31. *Ibid.*, Vol. II, pp. 229.

32. *Ibid.*, Vol. II, pp. 219-229.

33. W. T. C. King, *History of the London Discount Market*, Routledge, London 1936, pp. 92-3.

34. *Ibid.*, pp. 39-43.

35. J. Sykes, *The Amalgamation Movement in English Banking 1825-1924*, P. S. King and Son, London 1926, Ch. I.

36. Crick and Wadsworth, *op. cit.*, p. 65.

37. Select Committee on Bank Act, 1857, App. 21.

38. J. H. Clapham, *An Economic History of Modern Britain: Free Trade and Steel*, Cambridge University Press, London 1932, p. 341.

39. *The Economist*, 1857, p. 59.

40. Matthews, *Bankers' Clearing House*, London 1921, p. 26.

41. R. M. Holland, 'The English Banking System', *U.S. Monetary Commission*, 1910, p. 280.

42. Clapham, *The Bank of England*, Vol. II, pp. 127-8.

43. *Bankers' Magazine*, 1849, p. 305.

44. Powell, *op. cit.*, p. 291.

45. *The Economist*, 12th Dec. 1857.

46. *Bankers' Magazine*, 1858, p. 213.

47. *The Times*, 10th May 1966.

48. Gregory, *British Banking Statutes*, Vol. I, p. xlix and Vol. II, p. 301.

49. Sykes, *op. cit.*, p. 113.

50. Crick and Wadsworth, *op. cit.*, p. 310.

51. Quoted by Powell, *op. cit.*, p. 411.

52. Sayers, *op. cit.*, p. 228.

53. Clapham, *An Economic History etc.*, p. 341; Clapham, *Bank of England*, p. 351.

54. Powell, *op. cit.*, p. 443.

55. Chairman at Meeting, 1st February 1877.

56. Chairman at Meeting, 26th January 1877.

57. Crick and Wadsworth, *op. cit.*, p. 250.

58. *Ibid.*, p. 206.

59. Sayers, *op. cit.*, pp. 158-9.

60. *Ibid.*, p. 164.

61. *Ibid.*, p. 166.

62. *Ibid.*, p. 226.

63. R. G. Hawtrey, *A Century of Bank Rate*, Longmans Green, London 1938, Ch. II, pp. 54-56.

64. W. Ashworth, *An Economic History of England 1870-1939,* Methuen, London.

65. F. G. Hilton Price, *A Handbook of London Bankers,* London 1890, pp. 311 and 423.

66. *The Economist Banking Number,* Spring 1914.

67. T. Balogh, *Studies in Financial Organisation,* National Institute of Economic and Social Research, Cambridge University Press, London 1950, pp. 10-11.

CHAPTER FIVE

Monetary Theory and Policy

1. Introduction

Nowadays money, banking and the Central Bank are inseparably and inevitably entwined in men's minds; in the late eighteenth century, however, the British public had looked to the Crown and the Mint to supply their currency needs, while the commercial banks and Bank of England were regarded as simply adjuncts to business and government finance. The period of the suspension of cash payments dispelled much of the mythology which had clouded the subject of money, credit and banking by providing an enforced experience of paper money. The Crown having abdicated its responsibility to pay in gold, a sharper eye was turned upon the substitute—particularly as a result of its depreciation in relation to gold.

The ensuing controversy, discussed in the following section, established the need to control both currency and bank credit and led to a critical examination of the responsibilities of the Bank of England. The theoretical and practical attempts to devise an adequate and automatic mechanism for the control of currency and bank credit which stemmed from this controversy are discussed in a later section; they found legislative resolution in the Bank Charter Act of 1844. Until then, the discussion of central banking theory and practice, and in particular the role of the Bank of England, had not conclusively convinced the Bank of the need to undertake any of the obligations with which a central bank is associated today. There had been useful precedents, even before the Suspension; it was not until well after the Bank Charter Act, however, that the Bank's acceptance of a national responsibility and the development of techniques aimed at more effective control and leadership of the money market were finally established.

2. The Bank of England and the control of currency and credit, 1797-1819

In 1800, with England at war with France and the Bank of England operating an inconvertible currency under the restriction of cash payments, public alarm was aroused by a sudden increase in the price of food. As a result there arose in the first decade of the century a controversy over the control of currency and credit; the theoretical issues of this were to dominate monetary discussion until the middle of the century and, together with its practical implications, were to create an increasing awareness of the responsibilities of a central bank. The early years of the nineteenth century were, on the whole, a period of rising prices and prosperity until the prospects of the resumption of cash payments introduced a deflationary trend. The controversy hinged on a fall in the value of paper money suggested by the indicators of a rise in the market price of gold and a depreciation of sterling on the foreign exchanges. The period has been compared by Harbeler to the German inflation of 1914-20.(1) The depreciation was not particularly serious until 1809—no more than 10 to 12 per cent in the period 1800-10—but it served to remind people of the example of the French Assignats, whose value had fallen to the extent of providing a relatively cheap wallpaper.

The re-emergence of a high premium on gold from 1809 onwards and the substantial fall in the value of the British pound on the Hamburg Exchange provided the sharpest spurs to the controversy. Ricardo, Malthus, Huskisson and others joined the attack begun by Thornton, Boyd, Horner and Lord King before them. Their agitation secured the appointment of a Parliamentary committee of enquiry, of which Horner, Thornton and Huskisson were the most prominent members. The prime cause of contention was the issue of whether the paper pound was or was not depreciated; the 'bullionists' insisted that it was and that Bank of England excess issues were to blame, while most, although not all, of the 'anti-bullionists' denied this. The bullionists held that the paper currency was depreciated if issued to excess and the chief test of this was the existence of a premium on gold bullion (i.e. an increase in the market price of gold above the mint price) and a corresponding fall in the external value of sterling. As Boyd put it, 'The premium on bullion, the low rate of exchange, and the high prices of commodities in general (are)... symptoms and effects of the superabundance of paper.'(2) The link between the quantity of money, prices and the exchanges was vital to any understanding of the dangers of credit creation, as Henry Thornton had shown most effectively in 1802 in *An Enquiry into the Nature and Effects of the Paper Credit of Great Britain.*

A more substantial practical demonstration of the bullionists' contentions than had hitherto been provided in England had occurred in 1804 by a considerable depreciation of the Irish pound in relation to the English currency. Bills of exchange on London were sold in Dublin at a premium amounting usually to some 8 per cent. By 1801 this had risen to about 13 per cent, and by New Year's Day 1804 was running at between 17 and 18 per cent. In March 1804 a Parliamentary Committee was convened, Henry Thornton playing a leading part, to investigate the state of the Irish circulation. According to the evidence, the Bank of Ireland alone had increased its issue more than fourfold in seven years; hence it was not surprising that the Committee in their report attributed responsibility for the depreciation to over-issue by the Irish banks, this in turn being due to the suspension of convertibility.(3) The restriction on gold payments had resulted in an excessive circulation of paper beyond that needed to replace the amount of gold withdrawn from circulation. This was believed to be due to the suspension of the automatic check in the form of a gold backing. Forgeries, especially of small notes, had multiplied; excessive discounts and speculative trade had developed and in turn aggravated the over-issue, no longer restricted as it was by the normal mechanism of gold losses. The Committee concluded that stabilisation of the exchange rate was within the scope of the banking authorities through the use of appropriate credit policy and by a readiness to use its reserves when necessary.

To defend their conduct of monetary affairs, bank representatives—and in particular those of the Bank of England—were obliged to employ the theoretical weapons which they had been bequeathed by Adam Smith. Most of the anti-bullionists would have agreed that there were limits to the safe creation of credit, but they were unable to define these limits except in terms of Smith's doctrine of meeting 'the wants of trade'—in other words, 'the demands of the public' in association with the even older 'real-bills' doctrine. Thus they argued that so long as currency was issued by them only in the discount of genuine and short-term commercial paper it could not be issued in excess of the needs of business; no one, they maintained, would borrow at interest funds which he did not need. The 'real-bills' doctrine took no account of the fact that any one bill could be re-discounted for a number of transactions and, depending on its velocity of circulation, could have a greater or lesser inflationary effect. If currency should by chance be issued to excess, it was argued, it would rapidly return to the banks, either in liquidation of bank loans or, under convertibility, for redemption in specie. The bullionists, of course, explicitly rejected Smith's doctrine, the main theoretical prop of their opponents, as being inapplicable to an inconvertible currency and instead argued that through the resultant change in prices commerce would absorb whatever amount was issued. In evidence before the Bullion Committee, the directors of the Bank appeared as obvious subscribers to the 'wants of trade' and 'real-bills' theories and have been justly censured for so doing—all the more since, in pre-Suspension days, they had shown an enlightened appreciation of credit control.

In 1783 the Bank had temporarily restricted credit in order to check a drain on the foreign exchanges—the first occasion upon which it definitely attempted to exercise some control of the market. Ten years later, apparently detecting the difference between an internal and external drain upon its reserves, the Bank restricted its private discounts at a time of acute business failure, so that recourse had to be had to the issue of Exchequer Bills to provide businessmen with liquid assets.

> It had discovered a principle. . . . namely that when speculation is reaching a dangerous level credit should be progressively contracted until a definite fall of the market sets in, but when this occurs there need be no more fear, and advances may be made freely to soften the fall.(4)

In 1795-6 the Bank again cut down its commercial discounts because of heavy Government borrowing from it, and had been criticised by Boyd and many others, including even Henry Thornton, for so doing.(5)

This caution appears to have been set aside with the suspension of cash payments in 1797 after which the criterion of the exchanges was evidently disregarded. Bank policy now consisted simply of meeting the wants of trade by discounting on the security of real bills, subject only to the state of the cash reserve. As long as this was satisfactory, the Bank seems to have thought that its theory and practice of banking needed no improvement, forgetting that inconvertibility had made the state of the cash reserve inviolable.(6) Adam Smith had implicitly assumed the maintenance of convertibility but Bank of England notes were now, of course, inconvertible; hence there was no way of assessing the probability of over-issue other than by the state of the exchanges or by the premium on gold.

The Bank had thus relaxed its discerning watch, lapsing into a passive role, and its head-in-the-sand attitude is apparent from the evidence given by its representatives to the Bullion Committee. John Pearse, the Deputy Governor, after describing the Bank's policy of only discounting 'bills of real value, representing real transactions' and 'all due within the period of two months', said:

> I cannot see how the amount of Bank notes issued can operate upon the price of Bullion, or the state of the exchanges, and therefore I am individually of the opinion that the price of Bullion, or the state of the exchange, can never be a reason for lessening the amount of Bank notes to be issued, always understanding the control which I have already described.(7)

This opinion was firmly endorsed by the Governor, John Whitmore, and was also shared by a future Governor, Jeremias Harman. It was the opinion of the Bullion Committee, however, that:

> this doctrine (of the Bank) directors is a very fallacious one, your committee cannot entertain a doubt. The fallacy, upon which it is founded, lies in not distinguishing between an advance of capital to Merchants, and an additional supply of currency to the general mass of circulating medium.(8)

The Committee concluded in their report of June 1810 that the cause of the high price of gold bullion was over-issue of Bank notes, and that for this and the adverse exchanges,

> no sufficient remedy for the present, or security for the future, can be pointed out, except the Repeal of the Law which suspends the Cash Payments of the Bank of England,(9)

and that towards this date (in not less than two years' time)—and also towards the resumption of cash payments—the Bank should work by curtailing its advances and thus its issues.

Deficient as the Bank's understanding of monetary principles undoubtedly was, their application depended on practical instruments of which the most obvious was Bank (discount) rate. Its significance to the Bank, however, was very far from what it was to be in Bagehot's day and its use in the market depended primarily upon the commercial motives of the Bank. The possible use of the discount rate as a check upon credit expansion had been demonstrated by Thornton in 1797 and again in 1802, although the Bank was limited by the Usury Laws to a rate at which 'there might be a much greater disposition to borrow off the Bank. . . . than it might become the Bank to comply with'.(10) The effectiveness of Bank rate therefore depended upon whether the prevailing rate of commercial profit was higher than the 5 per cent maximum rate enforced by the Usury Laws.

Since it appears that this was frequently the case, Bank credit control necessarily depended on additional restrictions—i.e. some form of quota. This is evident in the admission by Directors of the Bank that they had a customary maximum of accommodation for each individual customer and occasionally applied other limits to the amount discounted (e.g. restrictions on the term of bills). This they had done in 1795 and, as the joint-stock banks were later to discover, these restrictions could be quite stringent in their effect. It was therefore within the power of the Bank in reality to limit credit expansion, if it wished, even if the commercial rate of profit exceeded the 5 per cent maximum, a rate which was indeed commonly quoted by the Bank throughout the restriction. On the other hand, by lowering its credit standards or by extending credit to a greater variety of applicants for commercial loans, the Bank could promote currency expansion without reducing its interest rate. Its own size and influence in the market were in any event often sufficient to determine market rates and as banker to the government the Bank had additional scope for the expansion of its note issue through advances to government, purchases of Exchequer Bills and public stocks in the open market and through advances for new issues of government stocks.

3. The responsibilities of the Bank of England

In 1797 Sir Francis Baring had referred to the Bank as the 'dernier resort' to which all banks had recourse in an emergency. The role was a very relevant one so far as the government was concerned although, as regards banking and commerce, the doctrine appears to have been accorded only sporadic and *ad hoc* recognition by the Bank until the 1870s. Viner, echoing the sentiments of Boyd, Lord King and Ricardo, has argued that while England had an inconvertible paper currency 'special responsibility attached to some agency, and presumably to the Bank of England as in effect a central bank, to keep the currency in good order',(11) even though this might well entail restricting the activities of the country banks and the London private bankers. Viner continues by applying the standards by which we assess the functions and performance of a central bank today, in that the Bank enjoyed special privileges and also, therefore, special obligations—namely 'that a central bank should contract when the rest of the banking system is dangerously expanding in order to check and to offset that expansion'.(12)

Certainly in the years before the Suspension the Bank had managed its credit in a manner resembling that of a modern central bank. It had been criticised for so doing, however, and it is not altogether surprising that the Bank retreated into its comfortable belief in the 'wants of trade' and 'real bills' doctrines. Moreover, the Bank had no mandate from the government to manage its affairs in any other than its accustomed way. Bank notes were not yet legal tender, even after the suspension; by and large the prerogative of currency control was still thought to rest with the Crown. It may be excused, perhaps, for thinking that its special privileges and responsibilities were amply discharged by meeting the financial demands of the state, fulfilling the duty suggested by Adam Smith and, on occasion, even the expectations of Sir Francis Baring.

It has been suggested, with good reason, that the obligatory demands of government war finance compromised the ability of the Bank to secure a reduction in its volume of credit,(13) the inference being that this was the major cause of the Bank's over-issue and the factor largely responsible for the subsequent currency depreciation. Advances to the government rose from £13 million in 1800 to about £14½ million in 1813 and just over £30 million in 1814. (Government transfer payments abroad, as will be seen later, are also held by many to have had a significant effect on the exchanges.) From 1793 to 1801 and from 1812 to 1814 government financial policy was without doubt inflationary, but in the period 1801 to 1811 there was an excess of taxation over 'active expenditure' which was larger than the normal pre-war excess. Even allowing for heavy interest payments and foreign remittances, the government cannot be accused of inflationary expenditure in this period.(14)

If war expenditure was to be provided out of genuine savings afforded by a diminution of private expenditure and not by inflated bank credit, then it would not be unnatural to expect the Bank to have restricted its advances to the private sector at times of peak government borrowing. It had done so in 1795 in order to meet government demands, but apparently made no attempt to do so from 1808 to 1810. Commercial bills under discount by the Bank of England increased from £6. 3 million in 1800 to £13. 3 million in 1807 and from £12. 9 million in 1808 to £15. 3 million in 1809 and £19. 5 million in 1810. As a proportion of total advances, commercial discounts rose from an average of approximately 25 per cent during the years 1794-6 inclusive to 33 per cent during 1797-1800, 42 per cent from 1801 to 1805 and 50 per cent from 1811 to 1815, falling to 19 per cent in 1820 after Resumption.(15) The greater inflationary potential of the Bank's commercial discounts *vis-à-vis* its advances to the government has been stressed by Viner.(16) It appears that the former had a greater velocity of circulation, business transactions velocity being higher than that of the government.

The bullionists attributed the premium on gold and the depreciated exchange solely to the expanded credit of the Bank. Sir John Clapham has argued in relation to the boom of 1808-10, however, that 'prices were up before the supply of notes was increased—that increase was an effect not a cause'.(17) Moreover, little account was taken by the Bullion Committee of the part played by country bank paper or other forms of credit. Since notes were issued by both the Bank of England and the country banks, responsibility for any excess issue could rest with either or both. The bullionists, however, held that the influence of the Bank was such that 'by the increase or diminution of its paper, the increase or diminution of that of every country bank is infallibly regulated'.(18) Country bank notes were convertible into Bank of England notes; this, the bullionists argued, was as effective a restriction on every country bank note issue as convertibility into gold, assuming the exercise of control by the Bank. With their issues geared to those of the Bank and their dependence on their London agents, the country banks were subject to the predominant influence of the Bank's own credit policy.

There was nothing to prevent the country banks taking the initiative in credit expansion, however, and their issues were probably at least as high as Bank of England paper at this time. The Bullion Report admits that the country banks probably had been able to increase their circulation by holding smaller reserves than before the Restriction. Nevertheless the Report contained no criticism of the role of the country banks, maintaining that they were subject to the control of the Bank. In general the bullionists —and Boyd and Ricardo in particular—assumed that it was necessary for the country banks to maintain constant cash (i.e. Bank of England notes) and reserve ratios, but this was an extremely dubious assumption. It was in fact possible for the country banks to reduce their reserve ratios; as long as their reserves were not completely exhausted, they could force their issues while the Bank of England remained passive. That this was highly probable in the event is suggested by the evidence of considerable fluctuations in country bank cash reserves throughout the period of the Restriction and by the fact that they were generally kept at a lower level than that of the Bank of England.

To a varying extent country bank reserves consisted of balances with London private bankers whose reserves in turn, according to Silberling,

> were wholly uncontrolled by law and had never been more than very moderate sums; and their ability to create credits was now but very little controlled by the Bank of England.(19)

Even so, London bankers were bound to keep some form of cash or 'near cash' reserve. The only cash available at this time was the Bank of England note and its nearest equivalent was a demand deposit with the Bank. London bankers, according to Lowe, had formed the habit of opening accounts at the Bank and of rediscounting bills in their portfolios with the Bank, instead of—as in pre-Suspension days—selling Exchequer Bills or government stock on the open market when they needed to replenish their cash reserve.(20) By lowering their cash reserve ratios the London bankers could to a certain extent expand their credits to the country banks, even if the Bank of England did not allow them increased rediscount facilities. Any such expansion, however, would involve a 'persistent drain of their cash to the Bank of England and to hand-to-hand circulation and could not have been carried far without active Bank of England support'.(21)

In 1803 John Wheatley had drawn attention to the fact that in prosperous times rising public confidence would be reflected in a greater public willingness to hold and circulate country bank notes and that this—and not their convertibility into Bank of England notes—determined the size of the country bank note issue.(22) Nevertheless public confidence in country bank notes still rested largely in their known convertibility into Bank notes, although Wheatley's point is a valid one. It was a failing of the bullionists, and of Ricardo in particular, that they 'underestimated the degree of artificial regulation necessary to ensure convertibility, a lesson which was to be learnt at much cost in the generation after the resumption'.(23) Of particular interest is Wheatley's observation of a change in the relationship between the country and London banks, beginning about 1795, by which the latter obtained rediscount facilities at the Bank of England for their country correspondents.(24) John Pearse, the deputy Governor of the Bank in 1810, admitted to the Bullion Committee that a considerable proportion of the bills discounted at the Bank by the London private banks was country bank paper. As Horsefield observes,

> The result was to increase the dangers of crisis; for the attempts of the London banks to stave off disaster from their country correspondents might well lead to an accumulation of unsound business, which would ultimately sweep away simultaneously large numbers of banks.(25)

Since the Suspension of 1797 there had been a large increase in the number of country banks and there had also been signs of an impairment of the Bank's ability to control the primitive but fast-developing English money markets. It is at least probable that the country banks could initiate—and in periods of high public confidence, prolong—a credit expansion; if Bank control was applied, there were likely to be delays and loopholes in its operation, a state of affairs not unknown in more recent monetary history.

4. Depreciation and speculation

Of considerable relevance to an understanding of sterling depreciation was the fact that, under inconvertibility, speculative anticipations of depreciation or appreciation of the currency would affect the willingness of individuals to hold the currency; they would thus influence its velocity of circulation and its value independently of the effects of variations in its quantity. Thornton had shown a sophisticated grasp of this in 1797, and again in 1802, when he demonstrated that while a paper currency is falling in value foreigners generally would expect

> that the paper, which is falling in value, will, in better times, only cease to fall, or, if it rises, will experience only an immaterial rise, and this expectation serves of course to accelerate its fall.(26)

Thornton, echoed by King, Ricardo and other bullionists, however, denied that there had been any loss of confidence in English currency. This was undoubtedly a mistake; there is every reason to suppose that speculation was in fact a significant factor, whether following the movement of the quantity of money and British price levels and/or in attendance upon the hazards and fortunes of the British campaigns abroad.

The opening of the Peninsular War created a great feeling of enthusiasm and optimism in England. At about the same time, in 1808, Brazil, whose trade had previously been a Portuguese monopoly, was thrown open to English merchants. Beveridge's index of output, based on the construction industries, mining, textiles, etc., shows a curve rising from 1808 to a pronounced peak in 1810. By the second quarter of 1808, however, the general price level was higher than it had been since the famine level of 1800-1, and in the first three months of 1810 the index (1790 = 100) reached an all-time peak of 184, compared with 136 in the year before the Suspension. It is uncertain to what extent this was a measure of credit inflation or of a wartime shortage of goods. Bank note circulation rose from £17.1 million in August 1808 to £19.6 million in 1809 and £24.8 million in August 1810, while the bullion reserve fell from £6 million in August 1808 to £3.6 million in August 1809. The price of standard gold bullion jumped from about £4 in 1804-5 to £4 10s and upwards in 1809, compared with £3 17s 10½d in 1797, a rise in the premium of about 15 per cent. Similarly, the price of silver rose from about 5s 7d an ounce to about six shillings in 1811 and 6s 9d in 1812. A similar measure of depreciation was afforded by the sterling exchanges, which from 1808 were 'running against us with all countries'(27)—adverse not merely by the 3-5 per cent of earlier years but by 15 to 20 per cent. Nevertheless speculation may well have played its part. The war news in 1809 had not been good. Sir John Moore lay in his grave at Corunna; even Wellington, after victory at Talavera, had been forced to retreat and worse news was to come from Holland and Austria. Apart from speculation, there were other influences on the value of sterling which the bullionists either overlooked or chose to ignore. Hawtrey cites especially their failure to understand how rapid and large might be the changes in the value of gold and silver themselves as a result of credit movements in the countries which had adopted metallic currencies.(28)

Government transfer payments abroad could clearly have an effect on the exchange value of sterling, although both Wheatley and Ricardo denied this; Silberling and Angell have shown that a close correlation existed between these remittances and the status of the English currency. Even so, the effect of even large remittances abroad would have been moderate unless they had been accompanied by other influences on the value of sterling.

From the second quarter of 1809 Bank issues had increased sharply. In 1810 they averaged £22.5 million against the £16.8 million of 1806-7 and the £17.1 million of 1808, the notes going out mainly in discounts. In 1810 paper under discount had averaged £19.25 million quarterly, although in the following year it was down to £13 million; the corresponding average of total advances was down by only £1.3 million. According to Clapham, however, 'the Bank cannot fairly be accused of stimulating' the boom of 1809-1810;(29) Bank of England accommodation appears to have lagged behind the increase in prices. Cyclical causes apart, country bank credit may have played a significant role, failing effective control by the Bank. In 1808, their discounts were rather lower than in 1807; they rose appreciably in 1809 and markedly in 1810 'because the Bank was giving help when the crest of the trade wave was toppling over'.(30) Such conduct was reasonably in accord with Sir Francis Baring's suggested duty of lender of last resort and, of course, with meeting 'the wants of trade'. The Brazilian market had not turned out as well as expected; Wellington was idle behind the line of Torres Vedras and Napoleon's embargo was hitting hard at Continental export markets. The financial world was nervous; business confidence—and more—was at stake; it was by no means unreasonable to conclude, as Clapham observes, that 'as commercial bankers, it was their duty not to alarm a shaken City by acquiescing in any policy of sudden and drastic limitation of that assistance which only they could now give'.(31)

Commercial bankers they certainly were and organised from their foundation as a profit-making institution. From that point of view nobody doubted the Bank's success; profits from discounting had indeed been good. This divorce of the functions of the Bank has also been adduced to explain its reluctance to assume responsibility of monetary control.(32) In 1810 the Bullion Committee had agreed that the Bank need not reveal the total of its private discounts. Bank dividends rose from a steady 7 per cent in 1788 to 12 per cent in 1805 and 1806 and were maintained at 10 per cent from 1807 to 1822. 'Public opinion seemed to acquiesce in the view that any increased profits resulting from the Restriction belonged to the stockholders.'(33) There is no lack of evidence from both the Bank and the government to suggest that between 1793 and 1811 the Bank was considered an essentially private business, except for the obligation to make loans to the government.

The commercial awareness of the Bank was evident, although it is uncertain to what extent it may have motivated the Bank's conduct or policy. The Court, city men as they were, with their own firms and close connections throughout the financial world, had much more to dread from a financial crash than from inflation. Vested interest cannot be entirely disregarded, although Castlereagh certainly denied its existence; nor, in fairness, should one forget that Boyd, Lord King and possibly Ricardo, with more to fear from currency depreciation, had particular axes of their own to grind.

By and large the war and the suspension of cash payments were the ultimate cause of sterling's depreciation. Credit inflation was undesirable but it is not proved that the Bank of England was the sole active agent in this—only that it did not control it. The country banks probably played an important—if not, indeed, the most important—part in the expansion of commercial credit. Bank discount policy and, in certain years, inflationary government borrowing, however, assisted other factors in producing depreciation. Among these factors may be listed the effects of bad harvest, speculation, subsidies to allies, military expenditure abroad and restrictions on exports imposed by the Continental blockade and the American policy on non-intercourse. It is possible, however, that the Bank could have offset a number of these factors by restricting its advances to the private sector; this the Bank had done in 1795-6 and before and was obviously not doing now. *Laissez-faire* and the 'wants of trade' had taken root in the minds of the Court. The Bank was following a passive role, letting its credit expand—particularly its commercial discounts—in the face of rising premiums on bullion, falling exchanges and rising prices. In the event this was very much for the best. The adoption and execution of the Bullion Committee's recommendations would have involved a great reduction in domestic prices at the cost of 'disorganisation, unemployment and wastage of national resources, which a nation at war cannot afford'.(34) Bank sentiment in its evidence before the Bullion Committee had been simple enough but was nevertheless right in presuming that restriction would do more harm than good. As Hudson Gurney later observed in the House of Commons, 'The activity of our commerce itself had been bent and directed to the purposes of the war.'(35) The Bullion Committee were defeated in the Commons partly because many people, like Canning, although agreeing with their theories could not support restriction of credit while the war lasted.

In 1812 Wellington took Ciudad Rodrigo, then Badajoz and in July entirely defeated the French at Salamanca. That year sterling began to pick up on the foreign exchanges, although the volume of Bank notes in circulation was almost the same as in 1811 and remained constant throughout 1813, rising thereafter. From 1813-15 total advances rose well above the quarterly average for 1810, when commercial discounts had predominated, as government short-term borrowing began to replace commercial discounts. In July 1813 the bullionists needed no proof of sterling's depreciation with the premium on gold nearly 50 per cent. Lord Liverpool thought differently, however, assuring the Lords that there was 'no proof whatever of a depreciation of our paper currency'.(36) By October 1814, gold was down to £4 5s, rising again to £5 7s in the Hundred Days of Napoleon's return from Elba.

After Waterloo the obvious failings in the Bank's understanding of monetary problems were revealed as it applied the policy of meeting the wants of trade to the needs of a peacetime economy—denying, as late as 1819, the need to watch the exchanges or the price of bullion. An excusable fault in war became an unforgivable folly in peace; the result was the first failure at resumption, which 'demonstrated in fact, as clearly as the Bullion Report had demonstrated in theory, that a central bank paying its notes in cash must have a conscious and active policy for the regulation of credit'.(37)

5. Changing views in the Bank

In the years after the Resumption of Cash Payments in 1821, and especially after 1825, monetary discussion was focused upon improving the effectiveness of the Bank of England; there was also a greater willingness to look on its notes as a national currency, together with an acceptance by the public of the idea that in time of crisis the Bank must act. The Bank, for its own part, at some time between 1810 and 1827 took as its policy the view which it attributed to the Bullion Committee. It now devoted itself to safeguarding the convertibility of its notes, ignoring the problem of the country bank note-issue. It was unfortunate for the Bank that 'its newly-won belief was no sooner shaped than shattered, for the crisis of 1825 demonstrated that a convertible currency was none the less capable of being issued to excess and of feeding a commercial cataclysm'.(38)

In the wake of this crisis the Court of the Bank shifted their view towards the current version of the Bullion Committee's theory, associated with David Ricardo. This early model of what was later to become the Currency Principle replaced the test of convertibility with that of correspondence with an all-metallic currency. Ricardo had maintained that a country which had no paper money could never experience a serious commercial crisis from adverse foreign exchanges because the flow of gold abroad would correct the exchanges. Hence he concluded that a currency which acted in all respects like gold, whether it comprised coins, paper or both, would satisfy the requirements of credit control.(39)

The Bank's understanding of this doctrine was translated by the Directors of the Bank into the practical policy of the Palmer Rule, so called from its original definition by J. H. Palmer, Deputy Governor 1828-30, Governor 1830-3. Bank procedure aimed at making the fluctuations in the currency conform with those which would occur under a purely metallic currency, by keeping its security holdings, including discounts, constant. Thus 'when the exchanges were at par and the currency full' the Bank should try to maintain a bullion reserve of one-third of its combined note and deposit liabilities, so that its current assets should be one-third bullion and two-thirds securities. Thereafter it would only be necessary to keep the securities at a constant amount, allowing the note circulation (and deposits) to fluctuate in accordance with the demand for gold. At about the same time Pennington had recommended what was basically the same rule in a memorandum to Huskisson, then Chancellor of the Exchequer, the ideal being to have the currency operate as would 'a purely metallic currency'.(40)

Palmer in 1832 had envisaged a steady level held against notes and deposits together; the influence of the Ricardian view that deposits might be disregarded, however, led inevitably to the association of the fixed level of securities with the note-issue. If deposits were allowed to fluctuate, then as bullion holdings fluctuated the note circulation might remain constant or might fluctuate in the reverse direction. Unless deposits also were kept constant there was nothing to prevent the withdrawal through deposits of all the specie reserves, without calling for any positive corrective action on the part of the Bank.(41)

Another difficulty at once presented itself. Bank securities consisted of government securities—largely Exchequer Bills—and commercial bills of exchange. The Bank could balance an increased supply of the latter by running down its portfolio of government securities, if necessary, or by selling them on the market. The quantity of commercial bills offered to the Bank for discount depended, however, on the relation between Bank rate and the open market rate. If the supply of discounts to the Bank continued to increase, the total volume of securities it held could rise since under the Usury Laws the Bank could not charge more than 5 per cent.[42] It had to choose between continuing to accept bills brought in for discount or limiting them in other ways. In fact it chose to go on discounting, thus virtually abandoning the Palmer rule; it thereby implicitly confirmed an apparent but unpublished decision that in times of crisis the Bank must be prepared to accommodate the market.

Further evidence of the Bank's awareness of its responsibilities is afforded by the evidence given by the Governor and other members of the Court to the 1832 Committee. From this it appears that the Bank no longer regarded itself as being in the same position as other banks. Competition with other banks for commercial discounts was not thought desirable in normal times, nor was it thought advisable that the rate of interest should be lowered 'by competition, on the part of a body like the Bank' because in periods 'when scarcity of money or credit exists in the London commercial money market the Bank becomes the main support of the commerce of the country'.[43] Particular and successful protest was voiced against the restrictions of the Usury Laws.

6. The currency and banking controversy

Emerging out of the period of the restriction of cash payments was a body of orthodox economic doctrine. By now two basic principles were generally accepted. First, since the resumption the standard of value was, and it was felt should be, gold although proponents of a government inconvertible paper or of a silver standard or bimetallism were not slow to proclaim their particular causes in times of crisis; indeed, they may have suggested a threat to the gold standard which later strengthened Peel's hand.[44] Second, the broad outlines of the Quantity Theory of money were generally accepted.

As a result of the controversy raised in the restriction period, the recurrence of financial crises after the resumption and the latest Bank efforts, as embodied in the Palmer rule, to devise an adequate monetary mechanism, renewed discussions were opened concerning the best way of regulating the credit of the country. This second controversy was conducted by two main schools of thought: the Currency School and the Banking School, from the former of whose arguments and postulates much of the form of the Bank Charter Act was to be derived.[45]

The Currency School of whom Lord Overstone, G. W. Norman, Torrens and Wood were most prominent, were the innovators, while members of the Banking School were the defenders of the *status quo*. The former believed in a single bank of issue and attacked the way the Bank had managed the circulation in the 1830s—and in particular the Palmer Rule. They may be described as heirs of the Bullion Report. They claimed that there was a close connection between the volume of coin and notes in circulation and the general level of prices. Thence they deduced that an unfavourable balance of payments, indicated by an outflow of Bank gold, could easily be corrected by the contraction of the note issue. Provided that this was not done with excessive suddenness, they thought lightly of the evil consequences involved. A major weakness was their failure to realise the significance of bank deposits and other forms of credit.

The Banking School were in many ways the heirs to the opposition to the Bullionists: their leading representatives were Thomas Tooke, J. Fullarton and J. W. Gilbart. Like their opponents, they believed in unitary issues and attacked the conduct of the Bank. They accepted their rivals' theory of the relation between prices and the exchanges and admitted some link between the quantity of money and prices. They held, however, that this link was remote and emphasised—sometimes to an exaggerated extent—the time-lags and difficulties involved in securing a reduction of prices through a contraction of the quantity of money. They exposed their opponents' ignorance on the question of deposits and rightly pointed out that not all outflows of Bank bullion called for the remedy of contraction.

While both Schools denied the anti-bullionist doctrine that an inconvertible paper currency would not be issued to excess, the Currency School went further. They maintained that even a convertible paper currency could be issued to excess—not permanently, but for periods long enough to run the risk of a second suspension and to generate financial crises. Moreover, Overstone had maintained before the 1840 Committee both that competitive banking made for over-issue and that not even a single bank of issue would manage its issues properly in the absence of adequate safeguards.(46)

The foremost objective of the Currency School was that the value of the monetary unit, or the level of prices, should be the same under a mixed currency as it would be under a wholly metallic currency. To this end they advocated that fluctuations in the volume of bank notes should correspond to the fluctuations which would occur in the volume of specie under a purely metallic currency—either assuming that the velocity of circulation of bank notes and of specie would be identical or failing to appreciate the necessity for such an assumption.(47) The doctrine undoubtedly owed its origin to the philosophy of the bullionists—namely that an inconvertible paper currency should be made to operate as would a convertible currency.

At the root of the controversy, and crucial to the success of the Currency School's proposals, was a basic conflict on the correct interpretation of money and credit. The Currency School contended that there was a close and quickly-operating connection between what they regarded as money —Bank of England notes and coin—and the various money substitutes. If there was such a close connection—which the Banking School denied—then the control of Bank notes must have its effect on activity and prices. Thus they maintained that, to prevent over-issue, a drain of gold—whatever the cause—had to be matched by an equivalent contraction, pound for pound, in Bank of England notes; when it was not so matched, by definition a state of over-issue existed.

The Banking School denied that there was any such close connection between the Bank's note-issue and other forms of credit, at least within any reasonable period. They pointed to the great volume of country notes, bills of exchange, deposits and cheques and the machinery of the bankers' clearing house; how could this enormous volume of purchasing power be sensitive, they asked, to small changes in a Bank of England note issue of only about £20 million *in toto*? They were undeniably right in stressing the importance of other forms of bank credit, although on occasion they overstated their case. Unfortunately, in their prescription they had little to offer for the correct regulation of the currency; they held that, so long as notes were convertible, over-issue was impossible since the value of the currency could not diverge from its legal value in terms of gold. This was their guarantee of the currency's value; as long as this was maintained, the measure of the correct amount of currency was simply the needs of the public. In their enunciation of the Banking Principle, therefore, the Banking School concluded that a convertible currency, issued by private banks in the ordinary process of competitive banking and not by the government, could never be subject to over-issue. The doctrine in many ways bore an unfortunate resemblance to the 'wants of trade' doctrine espoused by the Directors of the Bank of England before the Bullion Committee.

7. Proposals for reform

The Currency School, in their criticism of the Palmer Rule, had maintained that the circulation of the country ought to behave exactly as if it were purely metallic. 'The rule ought to be that variations in the amount of circulation shall correspond to variations in the amount of bullion'.(48)

This became the major premise of the idea, developed first by Overstone and later by Torrens, of dividing the Bank into two departments; one department was to issue notes against a fixed amount of government securities, and then exchange notes for gold and *vice versa,* while the other was to carry on normal banking business. 'The principles upon which these two branches of business ought to be conducted are perfectly distinct, and never can be reduced to one and the same rule.'(49) The notion of the separation of the departments appears to have been originally derived from Ricardo's posthumously published *Plan for the Establishment of a National Bank.* The idea became increasingly popular from 1837—the year in which it was taken up by Overstone—and during the following year it was discussed inside the Bank. Its advocates argued that the issue of notes and the granting of accommodation to commerce would be set apart and the issuing body thereby saved from the temptation of catering for the fickle moods of speculation.

According to the evidence of the 1840 Committee the rules by which the Bank had in 1832 claimed to be guided were not observed in practice. The Bank did not hold its securities constant; nor did it maintain a normal cash ratio of one-third of its liabilities to the public. More serious still, the note circulation did not vary in accord with movements in the reserve. In fact 'the result of the action of the Bank was to keep their circulation even and to let their deposits, securities, and bullion vary'.(50)

The general lack of any satisfactory policy contributed to the crisis of 1839, although in the end the difficulties of the Bank arose from the course of the trade cycle in Great Britain and the United States and in particular the depression which followed the boom of 1836-7. Nonetheless it was fair comment that the Bank had contributed to its own difficulties in 1839 by its previous pursuit of too lax a credit policy, not least towards the Anglo-American finance houses and certain Irish and British banks which found themselves in difficulties. Without the assistance of French finance the entire cash reserve of the Bank would have disappeared that year, a fact which did not commend itself to patriotic feeling at home. The existence of many independent sources of issue enabled defenders of the Bank who were versed in the Banking School's theories to argue, however, that it was useless for the Bank to contract its issues if, at the same time, the country banks increased theirs. If this was the case, their critics rejoined, then the only solution was to unite issues, either in the hands of the Bank or some other central authority.

According to Clapham, on 2nd February 1844, William Cotton and J.B. Heath, Governor and Deputy Governor of the Bank, presented to Peel an outline of their own proposals, having been invited by Peel the previous month to confer with him.(51) Their February memorandum is revealed as containing almost all the essential features of the 1844 Act, even to including a proposal that extensions of the fiduciary issue should be permitted if and when the need arose. It has been shown that Peel voted against the Horner Resolutions in 1811 (i.e. the adoption of the Bullion Report), spoke for the Bullionist principles in 1819 and was converted to the Currency Theory some time after 1833.(52)

The evidence suggests that at the January conference a ready rapport must have been struck by Peel and the leaders of the Bank, the former finding that his opinions coincided with those of the Governor and his deputy. The Act itself, therefore, took shape 'not as a framework imposed from outside, but as an attempt by the Bank to find for itself a short-cut to currency management'.(53) It is not surprising that Tooke, writing in 1857, remarked on the 'cordial approbation and co-operation' accorded to Peel's scheme by the Bank.(54) It seems that by 1844 the Bank, after searching for more than a generation for a simple and automatic method of monetary management, must have accepted the doctrine advocated by Lord Overstone (then S. J. Lloyd) that the failure of the Palmer Rule was due to its being inappropriate to an institution engaged in deposit banking as well as in note-issue. Hence the only solution was to separate these functions.

8. The Bank Charter Act of 1844

Apart from the restrictions on other banks of issue, the Act provided for the division of the Bank of England into two Departments. The Issue Department was to issue notes against securities to the value of £14 million and thereafter against any bullion which it might hold, provided that the amount of silver should never be more than one-fifth of the total bullion. It was also obliged to buy gold bullion at £3 17s 9d per ounce of standard fineness and to redeem its notes on demand in sovereigns. Provision was made for an increase in the fiduciary issue of two-thirds of the issues of other banks which forfeited their right of issue. Accounts were to be published weekly and the Banking Department was left free to conduct its business in the same way as any other joint-stock bank.

Ricardo had long since explained how a useful economy might be obtained by substituting credit money for gold to a certain amount and how this could be compatible with a gold standard system. In 1832 Palmer had conceived a constant level of securities held against both notes and deposits; the adoption by the Currency School of the Ricardian belief that deposits might be ignored, however, led inevitably to the association of the fixed level of securities with the note-issue of £14 million, any issue beyond that being backed by the fluctuating bullion reserve. Thus the fiduciary issue of 1844 was no more than a step from the Palmer Rule of 1832.(55) Both proposals incorporated a fixed volume of securities and both conceived that the Bank would passively receive and issue gold, pound for pound, against notes issued in excess of this limit. In effect this main principle of the 1844 Act may be described as 'the application of the Currency Theory to the Palmer Rule',[56] bearing in mind, however, that it represented, in Gregory's phrase, 'an attempted solution of certain definite difficulties, and not a mere application of an *a priori* theory'.[57]

Even if deposits were not money, as the Currency School believed, Tooke pointed out that it was impossible for the Issue Department to remain nominally solvent if the Banking Department was threatened with insolvency through the approaching exhaustion of its reserves. A suspension of the latter would have been almost as serious as the suspension of convertibility and it was an occurrence which the Directors were now obliged to prevent by just the same means, and under the same circumstances, as had previously been the case in the struggle to maintain convertibility.

The 1844 Act is usually credited with the establishment of the Bank of England's status as the national central bank, largely because of an identification of central banking with a monopoly of note-issue. If by central banking is meant the exercise by a single authority of a discretionary control over money and credit (such as had occurred in 1783 and 1795-6), however, then it should be noted that, on the one hand, the Act intended that the control of currency should be purely automatic and, on the other hand, that no special responsibilities were to be attached to the Bank in its banking business—in other words, responsibility for the control of non-monetary credit was ignored. In fact, in its banking business the Bank was expected to behave very much as any other large joint-stock bank. Under such influence and the admonitions of no less a person than Peel, it is not altogether surprising that in its development as a central bank, the practice of the Bank regressed in the decades immediately after the 1844 Act.

The Court of the Bank, mindful of their long search for 'an easy escape from the unwanted burden of monetary management, which their eighteenth century predecessors knew could not exist',[58] felt that at last they possessed a formula which would ensure an automatic solution to their difficulties. This retrenched attitude of the Bank was to shift yet again, however, as a result of the post-1844 crises and a re-enlightened Court was to turn away from the notion 'that responsibilities of the Bank began and ended with the observance of the rules governing the Issue Department'.[59] A renewed awareness of the Bank's need and duty to regulate credit conditions beyond the mere manipulation of the note-issue grew up; with it came new measures which were developed to implement and strengthen its control over other members of the market. The Bank could no longer directly control the total volume of notes but it could control the amount in the hands of the public by varying the reserve of the Banking Department. Furthermore, the Banking Department's reserve was responsive to exactly the same factors as had formerly influenced the gold reserve; an adequate protection of the one, as of the other, entailed a close watch on the foreign exchanges and other factors affecting the balance of payments. In fact, both the powers and the responsibilities of the Bank remained very much as they had been before, although the Act 'by device of accountancy transferred the seeming point of danger'.[60]

The effectiveness of Bank powers, however, was continually being qualified by factors beyond its control. Emerging out of a series of isolated local money markets was a much more closely-knit structure as joint-stock branch banks and bill-brokers, together with the rapidly-improving communications system, combined to produce a giant national money market. Eventually based on London, working to keener rates and finer turns on a much larger turnover, the market was becoming more susceptible to credit control by the Bank and corresponding movements in the monetary temperature. Until 1914 the Bank Charter Act remained unchanged even though the principles which lay behind its conception had been discarded long before. The essential fact, however, was that the freedom which the Act left to the Bank in the management of its banking business 'included the freedom to conduct it as a central bank'.[(61)]

9. The Bank of England and the money market

The evolution of central banking theory and practice, as far as the Bank of England was concerned, had suffered a severe setback with the passing of the Bank Charter Act. Granted that the doctrine had had a sporadic and uneven growth, yet in acting as lender of last resort in 1810 and 1825 the Bank had recognised national responsibilities beyond those owed to its own stockholders. In 1845, however, it was far less of a central bank than it had been twenty years before; even after the 1847 crisis its official attitude, as represented by William Cotton, was that 'the Bank of England should be conducted upon the same principle as any other bank is conducted'.[(62)] The recurrence of economic crises in 1857 and 1866, however, together with the teaching of Walter Bagehot, served to remind the Bank of its discarded duty.

The severity of these crises brought to the fore the question of the 'relaxing power'. The 1844 Act had made no allowance for abandoning the rigid requirements of the fiduciary issue in time of crisis; this had been left to the *ad hoc* discretion of the government. The lack of any formal provision and the risk of transgressing the specifications of its Charter may well have been responsible for the Bank's reluctance to accept the burden of ultimate provider of credit. The government's subsequent readiness to breach the law on behalf of the market in these crises provided the Bank with the assurance that it could act as lender of last resort and exceed, if necessary, the limits of the 1844 fiduciary issue. At the same time the accumulation of experience on these three occasions may well have given the Bank the confidence with which to adopt as a consistent policy what had hitherto been thought of as an on-the-spot solution. Increasingly after 1848 the issue raised was not simply whether the Bank should act as lender of last resort but whether it should proclaim in advance a readiness to do so—to cash any good security at a moment's notice at some price, instead of simply supporting the market *ex post*.[(63)] The difference in effect upon business confidence was considerable.

In 1860 Bagehot became editor of *The Economist*. He noted the existence of a single reserve system by which bankers—and particularly London bankers—concentrated their banking reserves in the Bank of England as a matter of convenience and profit to themselves. In 1861 he proclaimed of the Bank:

> They have a national function. They keep the sole bullion reserve in the country. The ultimate interest of the proprietors of the Bank, we believe, will be best advanced by the most complete discharge of the Bank's duty to the nation.[(64)]

Bagehot continued to preach the same doctrine throughout the 1860s, although there was no further widespread discussion of the problem until after the Overend-Gurney crisis of 1866 and the third authorisation to suspend the Bank Act.

In that crisis the Bank had lent freely but still gave no assurance that it would do the same in another crisis. At the end of the year G. W. Norman, a former Governor, wrote from the Bank to *The Economist:* 'That the Bank of England should keep the whole unused reserve of the country seems to me an arrangement at once impracticable, and unsound in principle.'(65) Thomson Hankey, at about the same time, censured *The Economist* for its editor's views. Undaunted, Bagehot continued to develop his argument that although it was considered not 'natural' to have a single reserve system, nonetheless it was wise for the country to accept it.

In *Lombard Street,* in 1873, Bagehot again reminded his readers that the Bank of England was the holder of the country's ultimate reserve, and wrote that:

> Theory suggests, and experience proves, that in a panic the holders of the ultimate Bank reserve (whether one bank or many) should lend to all that bring good securities quickly, freely and readily. By that policy they allay a panic; by every other policy they intensify it.(66)

By the middle of the 1870s the principle was no longer in doubt: 'The Bank of England as lender of last resort was, like the gold standard and the freedom of deposit banking, accepted as the foundation of monetary and banking orthodoxy.'(67)

As guardian of the gold standard, the prime ambition of the Bank, working under the conditions laid down by the Bank Charter Act, was necessarily that of maintaining an adequate reserve in the Banking Department. Emerging as its chief instrument of policy was Bank rate, whose deterrent effect had been gaining recognition over a number of years although, according to Weguelin's evidence in 1857, restraint upon the term of bills was still very much in favour.(68) Between the 1844 Act and the crisis of 1857, however, there were no less than fifty changes in the rate, of which just under half occurred in the final three years. By the introduction of a high Bank rate, gold was released from circulation (and hoards), attracted from country bank reserves and from foreigners who were induced to remit funds to the London market or to keep their existing stock there. Exchange rates would harden in favour of sterling, while domestic industrial and commercial activity would be restrained and inflationary tendencies checked.

The state of the reserve therefore determined Bank policy towards the market, while the state of the latter was itself influenced by a number of factors, all of which would be taken into account and allowed for by the Directors in their assessment of the need to trim the sails of the market. Movements in the reserve could be expected from the receipt and payment of government funds; Bank power over the market was thus at its strongest in the first quarter of the year, when government revenue increased. Similar movements could be expected as a result of seasonal fluctuations in the domestic circulation—including the half-yearly demand for gold from Scotland—and of seasonal changes in the volume of foreign trade. Between July and November of any year, these factors generally combined to depress the reserve and to reduce potential Bank control. Their influence upon Bank policy, gauged to a sufficient degree, would in turn depend on the expectation or realisation of other extraordinary factors—abnormal imports of corn, changes in foreign interest rates, wars and crises—whose coincidence would in all probability bring about a change in Bank rate.

For Bank rate to achieve its purpose, it was essential that a rise in it should be followed by a rise in market rates, without which correlation the former would be ineffective. The adequate fulfilment of this had been affected, however, as Bagehot had demonstrated, by certain developments in the London and national money market. The London money market was far from being simply a fusion of purely national—much less London—interests. Since the 1830s there had been a growth in the international bill acceptance business, originally with American firms but by the 1850s with many other foreign countries as well. By this means a large part of the world's trade was financed and London had become a form of clearing house for international payments. This in turn was largely responsible for the development of London as an international banking centre, as foreign houses began to realise the advantages to them of clearing their international payments and receipts, and keeping a deposit, in London.

Moreover, Britain was free from the disturbances which were alarming the Continent and were shortly to divide the United States. 'Hot money' began to flow in with the American Civil War and Bagehot in *Lombard Street* mentions the growth of foreign deposits after the Franco-Prussian war. International capital movements were in fact to become a feature of growing importance.[69] Long-term loans to foreign states had been known since the early years of the century; it was understood that a low domestic rate of interest tended to stimulate such transactions while a high rate checked them. Movements of short-term money, however, were not important until the 1850s, becoming much more so with the development of the telegraph: by the 1870s, comparative rates between London and other centres were being quoted in the daily press. The volatile nature of foreign deposits was such that prudent bankers would often hold an unusually high proportion of liquid assets against them—thereby indirectly affecting the market. Furthermore, London's position as the centre of the international gold market made the Bank's reserve liable to considerable fluctuations arising from changes in the commodity demand for the metal. The fact that most of the gold absorbed between 1858 and 1871 was taken into circulation also meant that a vastly increased trade was being conducted on the basis of an only slightly increased central reserve in the hands of the Bank of England. The result of these changes was that the London money market and the Bank of England became much more sensitive to conditions abroad so as, in Bagehot's view, to increase considerably the need for a larger reserve.

The boom in foreign business was not the least of the benefits which persuaded the joint-stock banks to come into London in the closing years of the century. Long before this, however, the growing strength of the joint-stock banks had exerted a significant change upon the domestic banking structure, thereby rendering the effect of Bank of England control a good deal more precarious. The deposits of the joint-stock banks were growing rapidly and as a whole were increasing much faster than those of the Bank of England. Vigorous competition amongst the joint-stock banks

—reflected in keen interest rates on deposits—and the need to employ deposits to the full led to a pronounced tendency to work to lower cash reserves and an offsetting increase in holdings of liquid assets—that is, money at call (usually with bill brokers) and bills of exchange. Thus a greater proportion of banking resources was seeking employment in the discount market, in which from the 1850s external bills were replacing inland bills and a greater amount of credit was being raised on a given cash base.(70) The funds employed by the Bank in the market, directly or indirectly, were therefore coming to represent a smaller and smaller proportion of the resources of the market as a whole.

At the beginning of the nineteenth century, the Bank had supplied the overwhelming bulk of the resources of the market by means of its discounts; apart from advances to the government, these were in fact the sole outlet for Bank finance. A reduction in the resources of the Bank would thus lead naturally to a reduction in the resources of the market, so that even if Bank (discount) rate remained unchanged discount facilities were curbed. In the 1850s, however, partly as a result of this growth in other sources of funds for the market, the volume of Bank discounts fell, and by the 1870s Bank predominance in the discount market was markedly diminished except for the period of the first quarter of the year when government revenue was being collected. The market was becoming more sensitive and—because of the nature and scale of some of the changes already described—was much less prone to the solitary influence of Bank rate. As early as the 1857 crisis, when Bank rate was raised by successive stages to 10 per cent, 'it had become manifest that the deterrent was insufficient',(71) although this was for the decade an exceptional circumstance. It was not until the 1870s, however, that the difficulty of making Bank rate effective became acute, probably because although in absolute terms the Bank still employed a large amount of money in the market this was a decreasing proportion of the market's whole resources.(72) At the beginning of this decade appeared the first wide gap between Bank rate and market rate which was later to become so pronounced.

The fact that the resources of the market were normally very intensively used accords with Bagehot's observation that a change in the discount policy of the Bank might make the difference between ease and stringency. The Bank could create an artificial tightness of money by drawing funds from the market, thereby obliging market rate to conform with Bank rate. This was a not uncommon ambition of Bank policy, particularly after 1890, when the Bank began to borrow directly from public authorities and, eventually, from the clearing banks themselves. Bank credit policy was beginning to depend upon auxiliary means of support for Bank rate.

Established methods of control open to the Court with which they could bolster Bank rate had included either selling securities or 'borrowing on stock'—that is, selling for cash and buying back for the account. From 1844 to 1890 'borrowing on Consols' was all that the Bank allowed itself in the way of what would now be called an open-market policy.(73) Both methods, however, were extremely expensive and would have to be carried to considerable lengths before they proved effective. The introduction of Treasury Bills in 1877 enabled the Bank to improve its control of the market, however; money which had formerly been taken from the Bank by means of deficiency bills could now be raised in the market. Even so, by and large, existing techniques were either uncertain or costly; in consequence the Bank turned to experimenting with new techniques, particularly in the last decade of the nineteenth century.

The amalgamation movement in banking had been proceeding throughout the century; it was not until the 1890s, however, that the scale of amalgamations increased so as to revolutionise the whole structure of the banking system and, at the same time, to modify the relations between the commercial banking system and the central bank. The decline of the inland bill was greatly accelerated for reasons already described; with the consolidation of the amalgamation process in the 1890s, the discount market had become insignificant in the finance of purely domestic industry. Although its power was radically diminished, the discount market nevertheless remained of unique importance in determining movements of short-term capital. Funds were provided partly by foreign, colonial and private firms; most important, however, were the resources of the joint-stock banks. These were the most sensitive to open-market operations, and it was generally agreed that the Bank's power over the market lay ultimately in its power over bankers' balances and on the joint-stock banks' reaction to a diminution in their cash balances—particularly the influence of this upon the bankers' short-term lending. Nevertheless the use of bankers' balances was a precarious method of controlling the market. Market operations were usually effective for a while, as the banks called in short loans, but very often the market soon fell away again as bankers redistributed their assets.(74) Market operations were therefore regarded solely as an emergency policy; the Bank itself was clearly aware of the defects of control through bankers' balances, since it developed other control measures.

Under William Lidderdale's governorship, in 1890 the Bank entered into an arrangement with Hampshire County Council, the latter agreeing to keep its balances with the Bank and that any amount over £20,000 should be lent, under the Bank's guarantee, to the market. Following this, similar arrangements were made with a number of public bodies, including the India Council; as a result, the rate for short loans, and then discount rates, were pushed up to Bank rate. Bank strength was further enhanced by the transfer of Russian balances from Baring's following the latter's disgrace in 1890. In the early years of the twentieth century the Bank also initiated a more active gold policy, undertaking direct operations in the gold market.

Apart from the object of making Bank rate effective, other motives were increasingly leading the Bank to experiment in other ways of protecting the reserve towards the end of the century. The Bank was becoming conscious of the fact that the rates charged for commercial advances throughout the country were coming to depend more and more on Bank rate, at once reflecting and enhancing Bank influence. Walter Leaf, writing in 1926, observed that 'the rate for bank loans is, with very few exceptions, based upon bank rate'.(75) The imposition of a penal rate to check an external outflow of gold could have serious effects on domestic industry and trade, as business became less willing to buy or to hold stocks on borrowed money. This was especially the case because loans and overdrafts—now the favoured means of business finance in place of inland bills, following the spread of joint-stock branch banking—could be expected to be more sensitive than bills to the rate of interest.(76) A rise in Bank rate was unnecessary, however, if market rates could be forced above it by the Bank either refusing to operate at its minimum rate or by charging a higher rate for advances than for discounts—a practice which was common in the 1890s.

The Bank's task was eased considerably by the fact that whereas in the third quarter of the nineteenth century Britain had been a debtor on short-term account, now she had become a creditor. It was therefore only necessary to bring about a rise in short-term interest rates sufficient to check new borrowing in order to secure an automatic inflow of gold as existing overseas assets matured. The success of the Bank's new techniques was nevertheless limited; the only cure for a major outflow of gold remained an effective rise in Bank rate.

The problem of making Bank rate effective was, therefore, as important as ever, and the period up to the outbreak of the first World War saw continuing changes in Bank market technique. The US Monetary Commission in 1908 noted that the Bank now rarely bought and sold securities for cash, nor did it sell stock for cash and buy it back for the account.(77) Instead, securities were pledged to brokers as collateral, these securities being then deducted from the assets of the Banking Department. After 1902, the influence of government borrowing in the market in ordinary times was greatly increased and, with it, the power of the Bank as its traditional financial agent. The Bank also fostered its dependence upon borrowing from public bodies like the County Councils and the India Council and in December 1905 borrowed directly from the clearing banks themselves.(78)

The Baring crisis of 1890 had been the turning point in the development of co-operation between the Bank and the joint-stock banks—traces of mutual jealousy and suspicion were now few. Such co-operation was crucial to the effective application of Bank control. Not only did the Bank depend on the clearing banks keeping balances with it, adjusting their liabilities in response to a change in these balances; it relied also on their readiness to accept its lead without the need to resort to coercion. For itself, the Bank had learned the art of adapting its reserve policy to the exigencies of the Bank Charter Act, not by the acquisition of vast reserves but by a management of its securities so as to make Bank rate effective. The ability to maintain the reserve at the level considered normally desirable had been assisted by the growing sensitivity of the international money market to changes in British Bank rate and by the enormous strength of the London market's credit and prestige. In this Backwell, Child, Glyn and even Lord Overstone would surely have accorded due tribute to the part played by the joint-stock banks.

REFERENCES

1. G. Harberler, *The theory of international trade*, translated by A. Stonier and F. Benham, William Hodge, London 1936, p. 31.

2. W. Boyd, *A letter to William Pitt*, 2nd ed., London 1801, p. xxxl.

3. J. K. Horsefield, 'The Duties of a Banker, II: The effects of inconvertibility'. Reprinted from *Economica*, May 1944, in *Papers in English Monetary History*, Ed. T. S. Ashton and R. S. Sayers, Clarendon Press, Oxford 1953, p. 30; see also F. W. Fetter, *The Development of British Monetary Orthodoxy 1797-1875*, Cambridge, Mass. 1965, pp. 39-40.

4. A. E. Feaveryear, *The Pound Sterling,* Oxford 1931, pp. 64-5.
5. J. H. Horsefield, 'The Duties of a Banker, I: The Eighteenth-Century View'. Reprinted from *Economica,* February 1941, in *Papers in English Monetary History,* p. 14.
6. *Ibid.,* p. 15.
7. Edwin Cannan, *The Paper Pound of 1797-1821: a Reprint of the Bullion Report,* London, 1919.
8. *Ibid.,* p. 50.
9. *Ibid.*
10. Report of the House of Lords Committee of Secrecy, 1797. Quoted by J. Viner, *Studies in the Theory of International Trade,* Allen and Unwin, London 1937, p. 149.
11. Viner, *op. cit.,* p. 159.
12. *Ibid.,* p. 160.
13. N. J. Silberling, 'Financial and Monetary policy of Great Britain during the Napoleonic Wars', *Quarterly Journal of Economics,* XXXVIII (1924), pp. 425-7; see also J. W. Angell, *The theory of international prices—history, criticism and restatement,* Cambridge, Mass. 1926, p. 486.
14. E. V. Morgan, *The Theory and Practice of Central Banking, 1797-1913,* Cambridge University Press, London 1943, p. 34.
15. Angell, *op. cit.,* Appx. A, p. 498.
16. Viner, *op. cit.,* p. 169.
17. Sir John Clapham, *The Bank of England,* Cambridge University Press, London 1944, Vol. II, p. 21.
18. Boyd, *op. cit.,* 1st ed. 1801, p. 20.
19. Silberling, *op. cit.,* p. 399.
20. J. Lowe, *The present state of England in regard to agriculture, trade and finance,* 2nd. ed. 1823, Appendix, p. 20. Quoted by Viner, *op. cit.,* p. 159.
21. Viner, *op. cit.,* p. 159.
22. J. Wheatley, *Remarks on Currency and Commerce,* London 1803, p. 186.
23. Morgan, *op. cit.,* p. 60.
24. Wheatley, *op. cit.,* p. 219. See also Horsefield, 'The Duties of the Banker, II', *op. cit.,* p. 35.
25. Horsefield, *ibid.,* p. 35.
26. H. Thornton, *An enquiry into the nature and effects of the paper credit of Great Britain,* London 1802, pp. 65-7.
27. Thornton, *ibid.,* p. 333.
28. R. G. Hawtrey, *Currency and Credit,* Longmans Green and Co., 4th ed., London 1950, p. 290.
29. Clapham, *op. cit.,* p. 20.

30. *Ibid.*, p. 21.
31. *Ibid.*, p. 26.
32. Fetter, *op. cit.*, p. 61.
33. *Ibid.*, p. 61.
34. Morgan, *op. cit.*, p. 48.
35. Hudson Gurney in the House of Commons, 18th May 1818.
36. 1 Hansard XXVI, 1178, July 9 1813.
37. Morgan, *op. cit.*, p. 48.
38. J. K. Horsefield, 'The Origins of the Bank Charter Act 1844', Reprinted from *Economica*, 1944, in *Papers in English Monetary History*, p. 113.
39. D. Ricardo, *Proposals for an Economical and Secure Currency*, Section IV.
40. J. Pennington, Memorandum (privately printed), London 1827.
41. Viner, *op. cit.*, pp. 225-6.
42. T. E. Gregory, *British Banking statutes and Reports*, Oxford University Press, London 1929, Vol. I, p. xl.
43. *Ibid.*, pp. 15-18.
44. Fetter, *op. cit.*, pp. 177-180.
45. See Morgan, *op. cit.*, Ch. 6, for an excellent summary of the controversy.
46. Gregory, *op. cit.*, Vol. I, p. 50.
47. Viner, *op. cit.*, p. 221.
48. Lord Overstone, *Further reflections on the state of the currency and the action of the Bank of England*, London 1837, p. 31.
49. *Tracts and other publications on metallic and paper currency*, London 1857, p. 63.
50. Gregory, *op. cit.*, Vol. I, p. xviii.
51. Clapham, *op. cit.*, Vol. II, pp. 178-9.
52. Macleod, *Theory and Practice of Banking* (3rd ed.), Vol. II, p. 338.
53. Horsefield, 'The Origins of the Bank Charter Act 1844', *op. cit.*, p. 111.
54. T. Tooke, *History of Prices*, London 1857, Vol. V, p. 529.
55. Horsefield, 'The Origins of the Bank Charter Act 1844', *op cit.*, p. 115.
56. *Ibid.*, p. 115.
57. Gregory, *op. cit.*, Vol. I, p. xvii.
58. Horsefield, 'The Origins of the Bank Charter Act 1844', *op. cit.*, p. 115.
59. P. Barret Whale, 'A Retrospective view of the Bank Charter Act of 1844', reprinted from *Economica*, August 1944, in *Papers in English Monetary History*, p. 127.
60. Morgan, *op. cit.*, p. 119.

61. Barret Whale, *op. cit.*, p. 127.
62. Quoted by Fetter, *op. cit.*, p. 261, from evidence before the Commons Committee of 1848.
63. Fetter, *op. cit.*, p. 267.
64. *The Economist*, September 14th 1861, p. 1009.
65. *Ibid.*, 22nd December 1866, p. 1488.
66. W. Bagehot, *Lombard Street*, p. 173.
67. Fetter, *op. cit.*, p. 275.
68. *Ibid.*, p. 267.
69. See Morgan, *op. cit.*, Ch. 9.
70. *Ibid.*, p. 168.
71. R. G. Hawtrey, *A Century of Bank Rate*, Longmans Green and Co., 4th ed., London 1950, p. 26.
72. Morgan, *op. cit.*, p. 173.
73. Hawtrey, *op. cit.*, p. 69.
74. Morgan, *op. cit.*, p. 214.
75. W. Leaf, *Banking*, Rev. by Ernest Sykes, 4th ed. Oxford University Press, London 1943, pp. 176-7.
76. Hawtrey, *op. cit.*, p. 61.
77. Morgan, *op. cit.*, p. 217.
78. See account in E. T. Powell, *The Evolution of the London Money Market, 1385-1915*, Cass, London 1966, p. 650.

PART II

THE MACMILLAN ERA (1918–1951)

CHAPTER SIX

The Growth of Deposits

1. The volume of deposits

In the preceding discussion of the development of joint-stock banking note was taken of the virtual displacement of the internal bill of exchange by banking facilities—the overdraft and loan, cheques and current accounts; by the end of World War I joint-stock banking was fully established in Britain. Growth and operation on the scale which had been attained by the clearing banks would merit detailed attention for any industry. Banks, however, occupy a special position in that they trade in and manufacture a commodity—money—which has the special quality of being able to acquire and dispose of all other goods and services. Because of this, banking assumes an importance in modern society beyond that accorded to any other industry.

In any developed economy there will be at least three magnitudes expressible in monetary terms which can be compared with each other: the stock of money, the flow of incomes and—since not all payments generate final income—the total volume of transactions. Virtually all transactions are settled in money; hence if the authorities wish to influence the flow of spending—to inflate the economy, as was the main concern of the Macmillan Committee reporting in 1931, or in the case of the Radcliffe Committee reporting in 1959, to restrain inflationary forces—an obvious instrument to use, broadly interpreted, is monetary policy. In the preceding chapter something of the early attempts to control the stock of money by regulation of Bank of England and private bank notes was noted. The significance attached to the note-issue, however, gradually disappeared with the decline of private note-issues and the recognition of the growing importance of the volume of bank deposits. The restrictions of private note-issues, indeed, stimulated the development of an alternative form of money in the shape of bank deposits just as, in more recent times, restrictions on bank deposits have stimulated the development of alternative forms of credit. Most payments, however, are still conducted through cash or by cheque in a developed economy, and bank deposits constitute the major form of money.

With the disappearance of private note-issues (except in Scotland) the primary business of the joint-stock banks had become the receipt, transfer and encashment of deposits—i.e. 'receiving money on deposit under various arrangements as to time for repayment and as to interest'. This is the essence of the modern joint-stock banker's business, as explained before the Macmillan Committee: 'We employ the money deposited with us in a variety of ways and in such a manner as will enable us to fulfil our obligations.' (1)

Bank deposits represent debts incurred by a bank to the general public; they correspond to assets people or institutions have offered to the bank in exchange for deposit claims against it. The essence of deposit creation is an exchange of claims; in its simplest form, the process can consist of an exchange of Bank of England notes, or coin, in return for a claim upon the bank concerned—that is, a bank deposit. An essentially similar exchange occurs when a bank, in return for a claim upon itself to a specified amount, accepts as an asset a mere promise to repay from a customer (in return, naturally, for due consideration). Thus an overdraft or loan facility creates a bank deposit which represents part of the supply of money; it can be used by borrowers to buy goods and services. The significance of this exchange of claims lies in the fact that the overdraft facility represents a debt incurred by the bank—a debt which did not previously exist—which is covered by no more than a promise (although usually with security) and can be used as an addition to general purchasing power.

The bank itself creates a deposit—that is, enters on its books a credit balance in favour of a customer—in return for any asset it is prepared to accept, whether this asset be cash, a government security or, if it makes an advance, the promise of a customer to repay. By its policy of acquiring assets and, in particular, by its lending policy, an individual bank can determine the level of its liabilities to the public—i.e. the level of its deposits. Hence the deposit liabilities of the banks to the public are determined by the action of the banks in acquiring assets, although in practice the process of expansion of assets and liabilities will result in various drains upon the liquid assets of the banks. This latter point is important because the acquisition of assets, and therefore the creation of deposits, is regulated by the banks with an eye not only to their profitability but also to the state of their liquidity. Originally this would have meant their cash reserves, held in the form of cash in hand and balances with the Bank of England; in recent times, however, it has involved their general liquidity position, as indicated by the overall ratio of liquid assets (cash, balances with the Bank of England, money at call and short notice and bills discounted) to deposits. Today, many would hold that it is this overall liquidity ratio—and not the cash ratio itself—which is the effective restraint upon the deposit-creating activities of the banks.

Traditionally, however, the banks' ability to create deposits was regarded as being subject to the restraint of the cash reserve within their overall liquid assets. The Macmillan Committee concluded that:

> If the different banks made a point of maintaining a constant ratio between their deposits and their cash reserves (whatever that ratio may be) then the additional lending capacity of a single bank, due to a greater proportion of the aggregate cash reserves passing to it in consequence of favourable clearing balances, will be offset by the smaller lending capacity of all those banks which have been losing cash to it through the clearing. (2)

In accepting cash, whether directly from a member of the public or through a favourable balance at the Clearing House, a bank is acting in a passive manner: there is usually a corresponding loss of cash by other banks and a corresponding reduction in their deposits, so that no increase in total bank deposits occurs. Similarly, and assuming no abnormal liquidity, a net increase in advances by the banks will not increase total deposits if the banks have sold off some of their investments to the general public in order to make way for the additional loans. (3) On the other hand, while a net acquisition of earning assets will increase the deposits of the banks it will not *ipso facto* supply them with an increased stock of coin, notes or balances at the Bank of England. Such a net acquisition can be undertaken by the banks, individually or as a whole, only if they possess surplus liquidity—in other words, only if there exists excess capacity arising from the fact that their ratios of cash and liquid assets to deposits are above the conventional or required minimum. By contrast, if they are fully loaned up, with cash and liquid assets ratios at the minimum acceptable level, they could increase deposits only at the cost of reducing their cash and liquid-asset ratios to an unacceptable level.

How then is the aggregate of deposits increased or decreased, especially if the banks have no excess capacity? One possibility is that the general public may reduce its holdings of cash, opting to hold less cash and more bank deposits and thereby placing cash at the disposal of the banks and increasing their reserves. If the public is accustomed to holding large amounts of notes as a store of value and if savings deposits—an alternative store of value—are important in the banking system, substantial variations in the total of bank deposits can occur independently of any initiative on the part of the banks. An example of this could be found in the post-war shrinkage of black markets, the operators in which, of course, preferred notes. On the other hand, aggregate deposits will fall if the public withdraws cash from the banks, holding a larger proportion of its liquid assets in the form of currency and a smaller proportion in the form of deposits.

British experience reveals considerable fluctuations in the public demand for notes *vis-à-vis* other forms of money. As may be seen from Chart I, notes and coin in circulation rose sharply in relation to bank deposits in both World Wars; after the first World War the decline was almost continuous, but, although there was another sharp relative drop between 1945 and 1948 notes and coin once more gained relative popularity in the early 1950s. In relation to the national income, on the other hand, the pattern has been more of a modest upward drift broken only by the sharp and temporary upsurge between 1941 and 1946. (4)

A second possible cause of an increase in aggregate bank deposits is the purchase by the Bank of England of securities, foreign exchange, or gold from the private sector. The Bank of England cheques received in payment will be placed by members of the general public to the credit of their accounts with the commercial banks; the latter will then find their balances at the Bank of England increased accordingly. On the strength of this addition to their cash reserve—and provided that this increase has not occurred at the expense of an identical decrease in their other liquid assets—the banks are able to add to their assets in more or less direct proportion to the increase in their cash, whether by the purchase of bonds or bills or by advances to customers. The opposite process will occur if the Bank of England sells securities, foreign exchange or gold to the general public or if the public makes net tax or other payments into the Bank of England accounts of government departments. In short, the Bank of England, by its operations in the money market, can influence the cash holdings of the commercial banking system and thereby aggregate bank deposits in the country.

It follows from all this that the volume of the deposit liabilities of the commercial banks depends broadly upon the policies and actions of the 'authorities' (the Bank of England and the Treasury), upon the reaction of the banks to changes induced by the authorities in their cash and overall liquidity position and upon their own actions in acquiring or disposing of

CHART 1

Currency as a % of National Income and L.C.B. Deposits 1905–1955

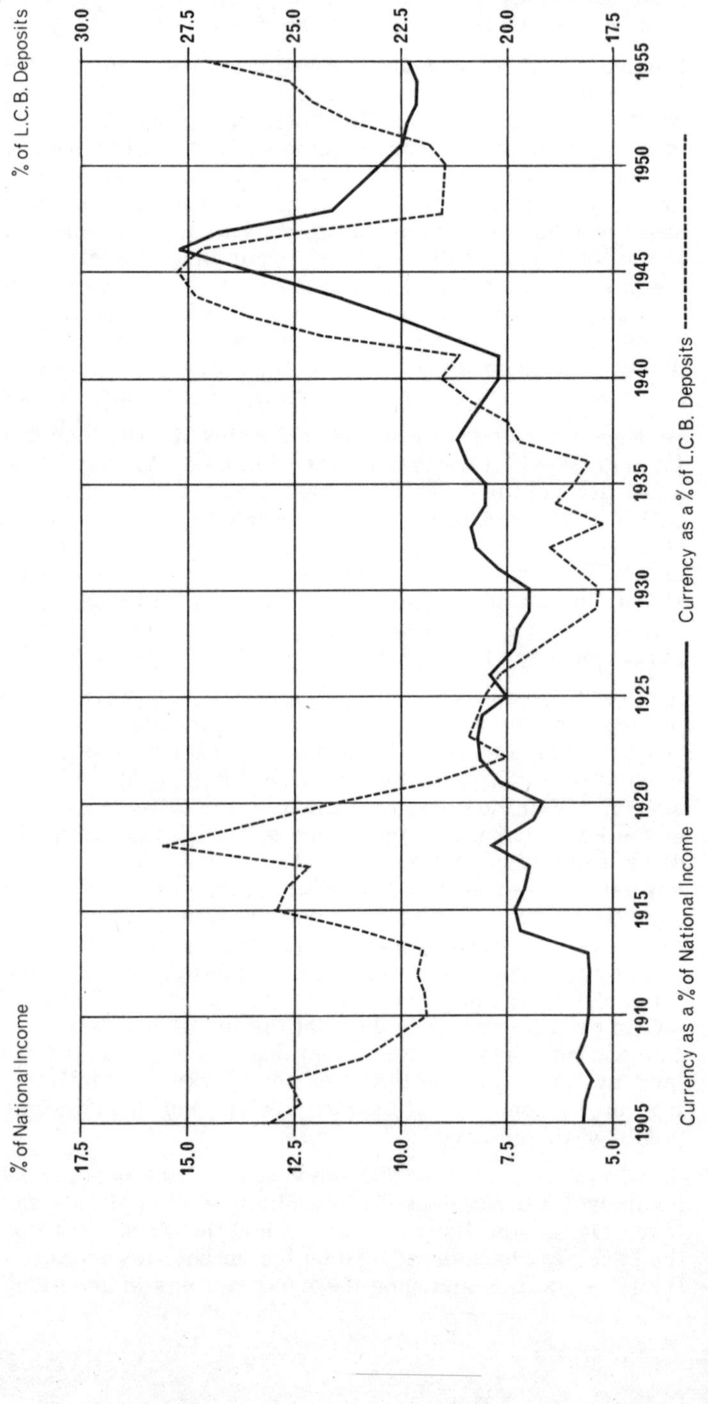

earning assets. Further, the banks are dependent on the general public's inclination to hold bank deposits rather than currency and upon the actions of the public in acquiring or disposing of earning assets—and, in particular, the general public's disposition to place funds with other financial institutions, notably those within the government sector, such as the Post Office Savings Bank, which may involve the banks in a loss of deposits and liquid assets, either directly by a straight transfer from the private to the public sector, or indirectly by the transfer of deposits to a private financial intermediary whose asset policy involves net purchases of new government debt.

Various other factors affect the policy and action of all parties. Among these may be included the volume of business and the state of public confidence, the lending opportunities open to the banks—including the credit standards they require of potential borrowers—the supply of liquid assets to the banks, their assessment of future movements in the bond market and conventions governing the ratios of cash and liquid assets to deposits. Also to be taken into account will be the country's budgetary and balance of payments position and the influence which these other factors will have upon government policy, especially the willingness of the authorities to countenance an expansion in the volume of credit.

2. Current accounts and deposit accounts

Bank deposits are 'money' to a degree exhibited by no assets other than notes and coin. The nature of bank deposits, and in particular of current accounts, makes them peculiarly significant from the point of view of both economic policy and the banks' own commercial policies—that is, their attitudes towards the acquisition or disposition of assets. At this point, however, it is necessary to examine the distinction between the two main forms of bank deposit. It is possible in the first place to differentiate between deposits which are constantly being turned over in settlement of debts arising out of current transactions and, on the other hand, savings deposits which are held as part of the total stock of wealth which individuals wish to hold as capital rather than as a convenient vehicle for recurring expenditures and receipts. Such savings deposits are regarded by their owners as liquid assets, either as a preparation for or an alternative to investment in less liquid form—equities, bonds, National Savings Certificates, real estate, and so on. Savings deposits, as such, are not usually turned over through current payments by cheque; they are essentially idle balances or hoards.

In Britain it is usual to associate the distinction between cash deposits and savings deposits with that between current accounts and deposit accounts; in the United States and elsewhere the corresponding distinction is that between demand (or sight) deposits and time (or notice) deposits. This is no more than an approximation, since a degree of overlapping exists which often blurs the distinction. Thus the Macmillan Report accepted that

> there is no universally recognised line of division between the two... but as far as possible current accounts are taken as sums payable on demand and deposit accounts as sums payable after date of notice.(5)

Current accounts are, of course, subject to transfer or encashment by cheque at sight; hence it is usual for banks to charge for the service of administering such accounts, either on the basis of total turnover or on the number of cheques negotiated. An agreement is often made, however, particularly with the larger customers, by which a minimum balance, although on current account, becomes a savings deposit earning free bank services in lieu of interest. Further, when interest rates offered by the banks on deposit accounts are low (as was the case from the 1930s until the 1950s, when the rate of interest on deposit accounts was down to ½ per cent) people are inclined to hold inactive balances in excess of their normal working requirements on current account; the low rate of interest is not considered worth the bother of re-transfer or the slight inconvenience of the small loss of liquidity involved in the notice required for withdrawal from a deposit account.

Balances on deposit account in Britain, and time or notice deposits in the United States, are nominally exchangeable only after some notice has been given and interest is paid on these accounts. In fact banks often waive the right to demand the full period of notice of withdrawal, thereby according current account privileges to a deposit account.

In evidence before the Macmillan Committee, the chairman of one major clearing bank remarked that 'even those deposits that are fixed for a period may be payable on demand by arrangement with depositors'.[(6)] Similarly, the Economic Adviser to the Midland Bank observed in 1933 that

> the distinction between the two groups is one of bank accountancy rather than of inherent quality; many current accounts bear interest, sometimes at higher rates even than London deposit accounts; the use of cheques is not confined absolutely to current accounts, and in practice it is possible to draw off a deposit account balance without notice.[(7)]

The Radcliffe Committee also confirmed that although they may sometimes speak of deposit accounts as being more stable than current accounts, in practice bankers appear to lump all their deposit liabilities together 'and to treat them as in effect repayable on demand'.[(8)]

The distribution of bank deposits between current accounts and deposit accounts can nevertheless provide a useful index of business activity. When the proportion of current accounts is high, business is usually good and money is circulating rapidly; when it is low, demand is falling off and trade tends to be depressed. During World War I and the post-war years of inflation, current accounts as a proportion of total accounts rose to high levels, and in 1923 they comprised about 60 per cent of the total. As may be seen from Chart II, however,[(9)] thereafter the proportion declined almost continuously, falling below 50 per cent in the worst depression year of 1932; by 1938, when business had recovered, it was up to about 55 per cent. The Second World War produced another rapid increase, to over 66 per cent; the postwar policy of ultra-cheap money, plus more or less continuous prosperity, made the subsequent decline a much slower and more gradual one.

3. Cheques and clearings

With the virtual displacement of the inland bill of exchange by the development of branch bank facilities, the larger transactions in the ordinary

CHART 2

London Clearing Banks — Current Accounts as a % of total liabilities 1921–1955

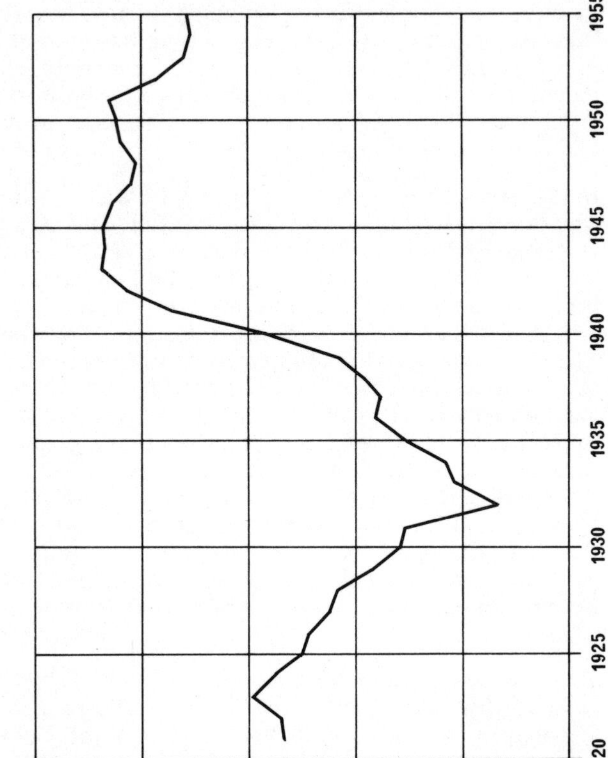

business of the country, and many of the smaller transactions, are settled by transfer of deposits by cheque, banker's order or credit clearing. Today all businesses and an increasing proportion of private individuals find it essential to hold deposits for these purposes. Their importance to the banks lies in the fact that deposits on current account do not generally involve the payment of interest and that a bank can rely on the maintenance of a large total of balances related in a broad way to the money value of the national income. As the Radcliffe Committee were to observe, 'Individual balances go up and down, depositors come and depositors go, but the total on current account goes on for ever.'(10) At the same time, the larger are these balances, particularly those on current account, both absolutely and in relation to the national income, the more freely can the general public spend on goods and services. Their total and velocity of circulation are therefore highly relevant to the pressure of aggregate demand.

The principal means of transfer of current account balances is payment by cheque. Cheques drawn on and paid into the same bank are cleared internally but the settlement of cheques between different banks is organised through London and provincial clearings. Just as total bank deposits can be regarded as one measure of potential purchasing power, so the volume of cheques drawn on current account provides an indication of realised expenditures and of the current level of economic activity.

In the period before the second World War the London Clearing House was divided into three sections: (a) the Town Clearing, (b) the Metropolitan Clearing and (c) the Country Clearing. Participants in the Town Clearing comprised the head offices of the clearing banks and such of their branches as were within five minutes' walk of the Clearing House—about 120 in all—the claims settled being mainly of a purely financial nature. The Metropolitan Clearing consisted of some 600 branches in the London area beyond the Town Clearing boundaries, while the Country Clearing handled cheques drawn on provincial branches or on non-clearing banks in England and Wales for which the clearing banks acted as agents. The Country Clearing would not handle cheques which were cleared through the Metropolitan or the Town Clearing or which were dealt with locally or by provincial clearing houses. At the beginning of the second World War the Town Clearing was modified (and was again in 1960) while the Metropolitan and Country Clearings were combined into a new General Clearing which handles the whole of England and Wales outside the new Town Clearing.(11)

Town Clearing figures rose from around £1, 500 million per month in 1919-20, fell back slightly in the 1920s, increased to over £3, 500 million a month in the boom of 1929-31, and then fell below £1, 900 million in the depression years of 1932-3. In 1934, however, they regained the £3, 000 million monthly level. Metropolitan Clearing figures fluctuated between £120 million and £190 million a month in the twenty years after the first World War while the total of Country Clearing cheques ranged between £210 million and £370 million per month. Total Provincial Clearings—of which Liverpool, Manchester and Birmingham accounted for just over two-thirds—had risen to nearly £300 million a month in the early 1920s but settled around £150 million in the later 1920s, falling to around £100 million a month in the depressed years of the early 1930s; even by 1937 they had recovered to no more than £110 million to £130 million a month.

As may be seen from Chart III,[12] the growth in the overall volume of bank clearings has been immense during the present century, only the generally depressed inter-war period interrupting its otherwise continuous ascent. In relation to the national income, however, the record has been a good deal more chequered. The first World War, with its marked expansion of the currency supply, was a period of positive retreat, and the crisis years of 1929-1932 produced a similar check; the second World War was over before the effects of the slump of the 1930s had been fully overcome. In relation to gross national product, indeed, it was not until 1962 that total bank clearings regained the importance they had attained in 1928.

4. The demand for bank deposits

The acceptability of bank deposits as money in the eyes of the general public depends on their convenience and safety, in the sense that they are usually transferable on demand, possess immunity from risk (other than erosion through inflation) and are of a form which is convenient to hold. On average most people have a positive holding of money because it is generally advantageous to hold some money either as cash or as a deposit at a bank, to deal with current payments—the transactions demand in Keynesian terminology. Similar in some respects, but by no means identical, is the holding of money against unforeseen contingencies—the Keynesian precautionary motive. Although this element of demand may be particularly volatile in times of national crisis—witness the high cash holdings of the second World War—in everyday life it involves no more than the sums which individuals and businesses set aside for unforeseen expenditures whose timing is, by definition, unpredictable. The precautionary demand differs from the transactions demand in that the latter may generally be regarded as varying in direct proportion to the value of transactions occurring at a given time, so that it is reasonable to assume that the demand for transactions balances will be primarily dependent on the level of national income, whereas the precautionary demand is influenced by the state of uncertainty as well as by the level of current expenditure.

The sums of money held under both these headings may be small, as in the case of weekly wage-earners, or large, as in the case of business and professional men whose balances may be as great as their annual income. An Oxford survey conducted in 1953 showed that the average deposit of those who earned more than £1, 000 gross a year was nearly £1, 200, although this figure was reduced to £660 when farmers' bank deposits were excluded. Balances of this size, however, are much bigger than most individuals need for purely transactions or precautionary purposes.

To explain the remainder, therefore, it is necessary to have recourse to the third element of the Keynesian analysis—the speculative demand. Whereas the transactions and precautionary motives may be described generally as a function of the level of national income, the speculative motive is essentially related to interest rates and expectations about their future levels. Speculative holdings arise because potential bond-holders think that the current rate of interest is significantly below the level they expect to prevail in the foreseeable future. By holding cash, interest income is foregone but it is anticipated that a greater capital loss will be avoided; in other words, the holder of speculative balances seeks to maintain capital values and possibly to increase future income by buying bonds after their price has fallen. A striking illustration of this motive in action

CHART 3

Bank Clearings 1900—1955

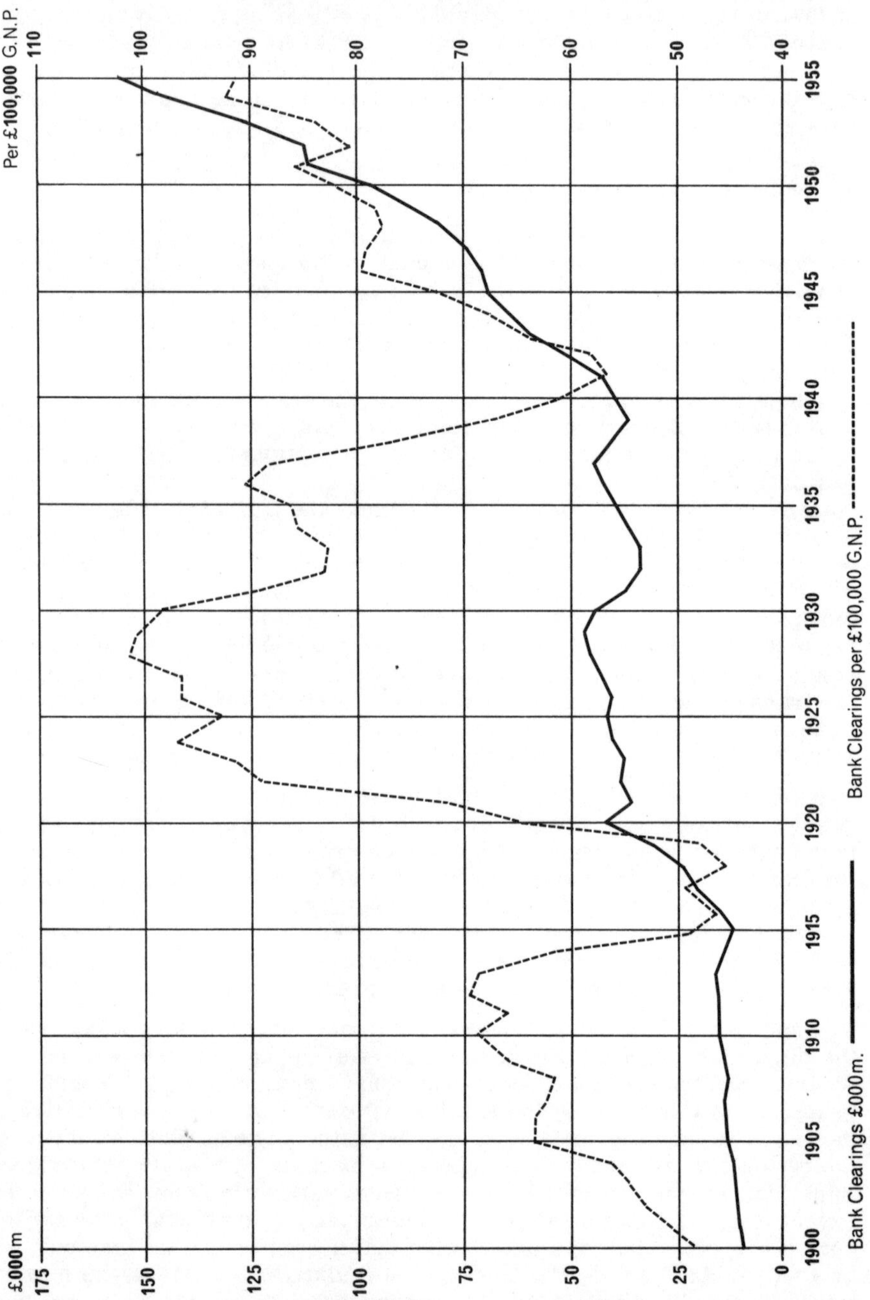

occurred in Britain after the second World War, when the authorities attempted—for a time successfully—to force down the long-term rate of interest. The market, however, believed that in the long run the rate would be higher than the induced 2½ per cent on Consols and that the latter would eventually move upwards, with corresponding falls in bond prices. Hence there arose a pronounced movement out of bonds into cash, with large holdings of speculative balances. The expectations which people entertain concerning future interest rates, and the degree of certainty with which they expect a change to take place, are inevitably related to the absolute level of interest rates. When rates have fallen to low levels, fears of a small rise in the rate of interest will cause widespread reluctance to hold bonds and a strong preference for cash if only because the rate never falls to zero and the next move is thought more likely to be upward; at the same time, the lower the rate of interest, the less is the income lost by holding cash.

Obviously the transactions and precautionary motives are of most relevance to ordinary current accounts, given their high degree of liquidity; the speculative demand, on the other hand, can also be satisfied through deposits with financial institutions other than banks. With the introduction of a cheap money policy such as that of the 1930s, a speculative drift out of securities into cash (bank deposits) is to be expected; although a movement out of securities may occur, however, it appears that the main recipients of such funds may increasingly be financial institutions other than the banks.

5. Deposits and the rate of interest

By the end of the nineteenth century, competition amongst the joint-stock banks had largely given way to oligopoly; rivalry expressed through interest rate charges had been replaced by fixed rates, the tendency being towards attracting custom by means of competition in services. Until 1886 interest rates paid by the London banks on deposit accounts had been on average one per cent below Bank rate, this being reduced to 1½ per cent below Bank rate until 1920. From the 1920s onwards, in accordance with agreed policy, the rate was fixed at two per cent below Bank rate, although provincial banks paid higher rates. Current account deposits sometimes still earned interest, and although the practice was slowly declining it was still common in many provincial districts; where interest was paid on balances on current account, however, a commission was charged for keeping the account.(13) This charge, based on either the average turnover of the account or the number of cheques collected, varied according to the standing of the customer and the competitive position between the banks. In London, where current accounts no longer carried interest, charges were not usually levied for keeping accounts, although the banks would recoup themselves by requiring that an adequate credit balance should be kept, the minimum size being subject to negotiation and, on occasion, to competitive bidding.(14)

From June 1932 to November 1951, except for a few weeks at the outbreak of the second World War, traditional monetary policy was largely set aside and Bank rate remained at two per cent. Correspondingly interest rates which were conventionally determined by Bank rate—those on deposits, bills, call money and advances (the latter subject to a minimum of 5 per cent)—were also at a low level. Rates on gilt-edged securities were also low—the average yield on 2½ per cent Consols fell from around 4.6 per cent in the late 1920s to less than 3 per cent in 1935-36—and relatively stable, while the average dividend yield on 50 equities included in the Moodies index fell from 8.0 per cent in 1931 to about 4.6 per cent during 1934-36. Throughout the 1930s and, indeed, up to 1951, the rate paid on London deposit accounts was only ½ per cent, although more (usually one per cent) was often paid on country deposits until 1945. Although bank deposits continued to increase, their growth was slower than might otherwise have been the case owing to the increase in deposits of other financial institutions. As will be seen, this was certainly a consequence of the low rates of interest paid by the banks on their deposits.

Even so, as may be seen from Chart IV, over the period 1920-51 as a whole there was a large-scale expansion of total bank deposits, both absolutely and (up to 1948) relatively to the national income. In absolute terms, deposits had increased by about 200 per cent between 1905 and 1920; for the following twelve years they remained virtually stable, but between 1932 and 1948 (the cheap-money period) they more than trebled again, entering then a period of only gradual expansion until 1956, when another sustained increase began. Over the whole period 1920-51 deposits grew by some 240 per cent. The ratio of deposits to national product, on the other hand, has behaved more erratically; between 1920 and 1922 it rose sharply from 27 to 40 per cent, but it was not until 1945 that it rose above 50 per cent, reaching a peak of just under 60 per cent in 1947. Since that year the ratio has continually declined, falling to less than 30 per cent by the early 1960s.

Within this general rise in deposits, as was observed earlier, there was first a switch from current to deposit accounts and then a long-sustained reversal of this movement between 1932 and 1943, the ratio of current accounts to total liabilities rising from the 55 per cent level characteristic of the 1920s and later 1930s to something over 65 per cent between 1943 and 1951. As will be noted later, this massive increase in deposits was associated with a corresponding increase in the liquidity of the assets of the banking system.(15)

6. Public liquidity and competition for deposits

Over the 'Macmillan era', liquid assets other than bank deposits became increasingly important as a means of wealth-holding by the personal and business sector, a development which was to attract considerable attention in due course from the Radcliffe Committee. The first World War brought relatively little change in the importance of such liquid assets in relationship to either the ownership of property or income, but the sharp deflation of the early 1920s, followed by the inauguration of cheap money in 1932 resulted in a significant increase in the relative importance of liquid assets which was carried a great deal further during the second World War.(16)

A large part of this increase reflected the growth in the volume of currency and bank deposits, but the banks' share of this augmented liquidity declined from about 60 per cent in 1914 to about 50 per cent in 1934 and 40 per cent in 1946; subsequently their share has sagged at just under that level. Financial institutions other than the clearing banks were meantime emerging as large-scale deposit-takers, reducing the amount available to

CHART 4

L.C.B. Gross Deposits (£M) and as a % of G.N.P.

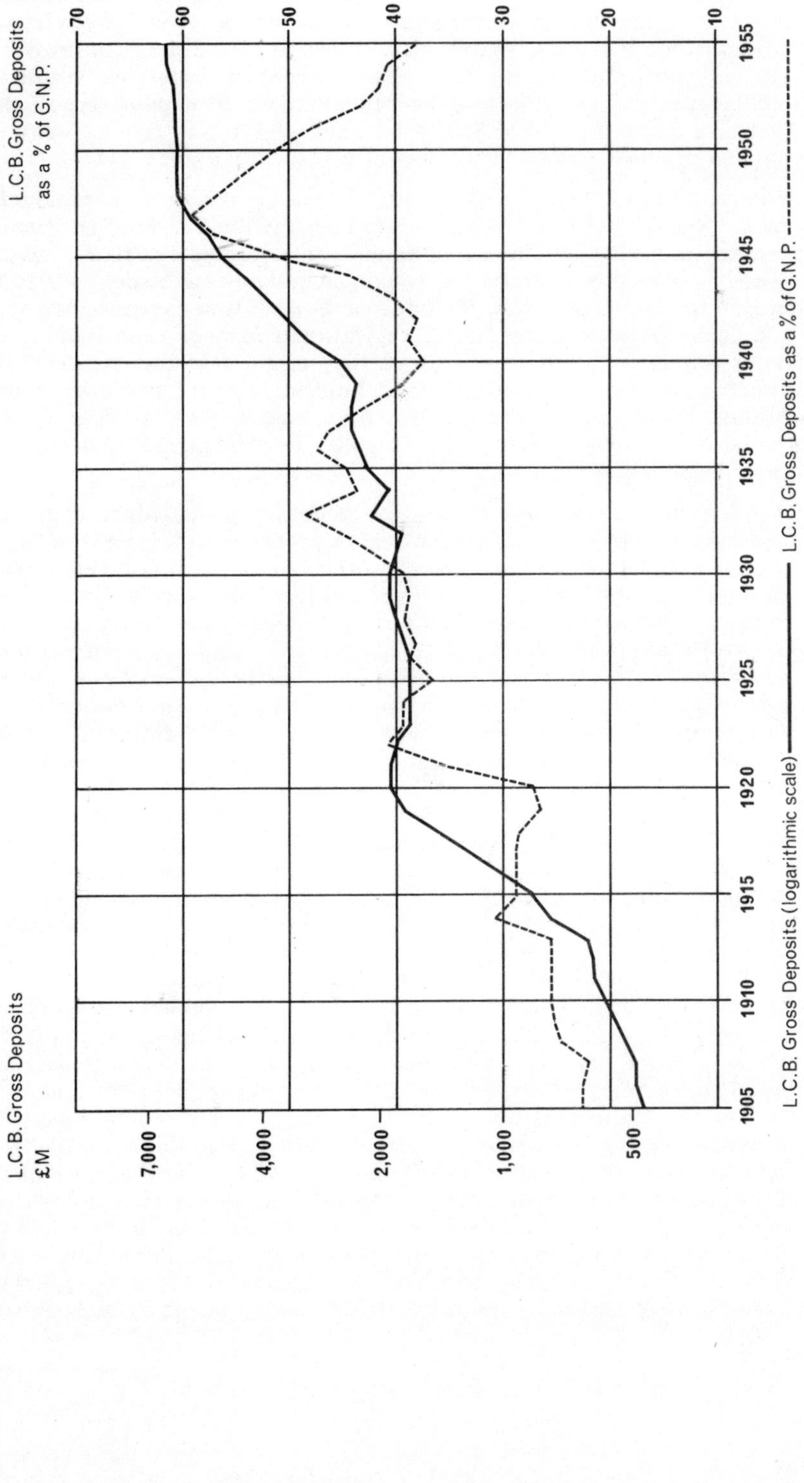

the joint-stock banks. Similar trends have been apparent in the history of American banking; while American commercial banks have grown in size, and are still that country's leading financial intermediaries, their growth has not kept pace with that of other deposit-type financial institutions. Thus, although over the twenty years since the end of the second World War total deposits in American commercial banks rose about 120 per cent, those of mutual savings banks more than tripled, those of savings and loan associations increased more than twelve-fold and those of credit unions, although still small in absolute size, increased some twenty-fold. The commercial banks' share of the resources of all deposit-type financial institutions in the United States dropped as a result from 86 per cent at the end of 1964 to about 65 per cent at the end of 1969.(17)

The liquidity of these rival assets is usually less than that associated with bank deposits but in most cases the risk involved is not significantly greater than that attached to a deposit in a joint-stock bank. Apart from deposits with the commercial banks, such non-bank assets would include, in Britain, balances in the Trustee or Post Office Savings Banks, shares and deposits in Building Societies, National Savings Certificates and Defence Bonds; in more recent times they might also include securities, whether commercial or gilt-edged, held through the medium of unit trusts. Almost all, of course, are lacking to various degrees in complete liquidity; the last-mentioned, indirect holdings of securities, may indeed carry considerable risk of loss.

It is a common but somewhat naive assumption that, since bank deposits are the only non-cash financial assets accepted in payment of debts, a transfer of deposits from banks to other financial institutions will be cancelled out as the latter pay these funds into their own accounts with the banks so that overall bank deposits are unchanged. Apart from the possibility of a drain of deposits into cash in circulation, such an assumption would ignore the fact that the competing institution may not bank with a private sector bank. This in fact is the case with the Post Office and Trustee Savings Banks which have at times been significant competitors for funds. Deposits transferred by private individuals or corporations from a commercial bank to such institutions are paid directly into an account at the Bank of England—indirectly in the case of the Special Department of the Trustee Savings Banks when purchasing newly-issued government debt. The banks, in such a situation, suffer a primary loss of deposits. Further, while a transfer of funds from the banks into non-government financial institutions—e.g. building societies or insurance companies—will not directly result in a net loss of deposits, it may do so indirectly if the institutions concerned, instead of leaving the funds in their account with the banks, invest part or all of them in government securities which would not otherwise have found their way into the hands of the private sector. The possibility and extent of such a secondary drain of deposits will depend on the reserve and investment policies of the financial institutions concerned. These, like the joint-stock banks themselves, need to hold reserves, part of which usually comprise holdings of government debt. Similarly, if lending opportunities, whether on mortgage or other private investment outlets, tend to be inadequate or unattractive—as in the 1930s—government securities may be a relatively attractive investment in their own right. There may therefore be an additional incentive for these financial intermediaries to invest in government debt beyond the extent required by their reserve ratios, to the ultimate detriment of the growth of bank deposits if the overall result is to increase the volume of public debt held by the private sector.

After 1951, and particularly after 1958, several factors appeared to mitigate the detrimental effects of competition from the financial intermediaries on the growth of bank deposits. These included the stagnation and comparative decline in importance of the official Savings Banks, the associated declining attractiveness of government debt and the corresponding increased popularity of and opportunity for private sector investment, and the growth and inauguration of new non-government financial intermediaries attracted more to these than to public debt holding. Both primary and secondary losses of deposits were therefore reduced; it is arguable, as will be seen later, that the net effect of competition has in fact been beneficial to the level of bank deposits. This was not the case, however, for the inter-war years and in particular the 1930s.

The most important source of new personal saving throughout the Macmillan generation was, and still is, that represented by insurance premiums and funds placed with building societies; large amounts have been re-lent in turn by these institutions to British industry through the new issue market and elsewhere. The purchase of annuities provided a profitable outlet for funds in the early 1930s when yields on securities were low. To this extent the insurance companies—together with the Post Office and Trustee Savings Banks and building societies, whose yields remained relatively high—competed, albeit passively, to attract funds away from the gilt-edged market at the expense of the growth of commercial bank deposits. If these outlets had not been offered to investors it is arguable that a continuous deflationary pressure would have been exerted by the accumulation of savings deposits in the banking system, a pressure which the banks could not have offset without quite fundamental changes in their operating policies. Deposits in the clearing banks, which in 1921 had amounted to about 60 per cent of the total liquid assets of the private sector, had by 1938 fallen to just over 49 per cent of that total, despite their steady growth in absolute terms.

A major cause of this was the fact that joint-stock bank rates on deposit accounts fell with the yields prevailing in the securities markets, whereas the rates paid by institutions such as the Post Office and Trustee Savings Banks and building societies and on insurance annuities were more sticky for reasons discussed later; they thus provided a higher yield and greater attraction than deposit accounts with the commercial banks. A second reason was probably the diffidence shown by the joint-stock banks with respect to cultivating the small saver. This became especially evident when the demands by the state for wartime finance generated an official policy of providing liquid assets for the so-called 'small saver' with strong appeal to patriotism. As a result, during the second World War, when incomes were high and consumption artificially restricted, Post Office and Trustee Savings Bank deposits, Savings Certificates and Defence Bonds together rose by more than £4, 000 million, or 308 per cent, while clearing bank deposits rose a mere £2, 850 million, or 127 per cent.

There is ample evidence that in peace as well as war investors are attracted to assets which are liquid but which at the same time carry a modest rate of interest. Although they have always had many small accounts, however, historically the great British banks have relied little on the attraction of small savings although these have been 'the object of competitive attractions of banks' in other countries.[18] Even in recent times, as the Radcliffe Committee noted, the clearing banks have broadly stood aside as a matter of deliberate and concerted policy while small savings have fed the development of building societies, official savings banks and other specialised financial intermediaries.[19] In their evidence to the Radcliffe Committee the banks confirmed their adherence to this policy.

During the 1930s and 1940s, however, other institutions which, unlike the clearing banks, had not reduced their interest payments were taking their share of the increase in liquidity. The Post Office and Trustee Savings Banks felt that a constant interest rate was appropriate to their policy of encouraging small savings; in the case of the building societies it was felt that a reduction of interest rates might have resulted in a withdrawal of the quasi-permanent funds which the long-term nature of the societies' assets made essential. As a result of these institutional rigidities there arose an interest-rate differential of which many important investors—by no means all in the 'small savings' category—appear to have taken advantage.[20] The relative advance of building society shares and deposits, however, came to an end with the outbreak of war in 1939—for fairly obvious reasons—and resumed from 1946 onwards.

Much of the inflow into non-bank deposits after 1932, therefore, consisted not so much of an increase in small savings as of a switch of funds attracted out of security holdings by the fall in interest rates; the margin between the yield on such deposits, which carried virtually no capital risk, and on Consols, which carried a great deal, was such that it would have been surprising if many investors had not thought it less than worthwhile to hold securities. It is probable that throughout the 1930s funds which would normally have been invested in the securities market were instead placed on deposit, under the spur of high capital values and relatively low interest rates, as security holders took capital gains offered by the effects of cheap money in the gilt-edged market and placed a substantial part of the proceeds in the hands of financial intermediaries. Investors were prepared to take advantage of the differential between institutional and joint-stock bank rates, sacrificing the greater liquidity of bank deposits in return for the higher yields accruing from deposits with other financial intermediaries.[21]

During the 1920s clearing bank deposits averaged about 37 per cent of the gross national product; during the 1930s the ratio rose to 44 per cent and in the 1940s to 48 per cent.[22] The political and economic uncertainties of the 1930s, together with the inflow of large sums of continental money into deposits in London, undoubtedly contributed to this increased desire for liquidity, but another major influence was undoubtedly the low level of interest rates resulting from the official policy of cheap money and the increased importance of speculative, as well as precautionary, holdings of money. A direct result after the early 1930s was the distinct tendency for interest rates on long-term securities to fall relatively to rates on advances; the latter were constrained by a minimum level below which the banks would not go. It therefore became more worthwhile to sell holdings of long-term securities (or to issue new ones) rather than to rely on bank loans; similarly, fluctuations in transactions needs were more conveniently and economically satisfied by varying balances on deposit than by running an overdraft up and down.

Yet another factor in the increased desire for liquidity during the 1930s was the fact that Treasury Bill rates fell to no more than the level which the banks were willing to pay on deposits. In the 1920s the Treasury bill rate had usually been about 1½ per cent above the bank deposit rate, but in the nineteen-year period after 1932 the average Treasury Bill rate exceeded 1¼ per cent only in 1939; in 13 years it was well below one per cent. As a result, large firms which preferred to hold Treasury Bills in the 1920s found bank or other deposit accounts a preferable asset.[(23)] The increased importance of speculative and precautionary balances in the 1930s and 1940s might have been expected to have increased the proportion held on deposit as compared with current account; that this did not occur was probably due to the low rate of interest (½ per cent) carried on deposit accounts from the 1930s onwards.[(24)] The effects of these low deposit rates on the joint-stock banks' relative share of the increased liquidity have already been noted; it would also appear that about three-quarters of the increase which did occur in bank deposits was taken up by increased holdings on current account.

7. Foreign deposits

The problems of monetary management in the 1930s—as indeed in more recent years—were aggravated by flows of foreign money into and out of deposits in London. 'Hot money' had been known in the City at least since the Franco-Prussian War, but the acquaintance was to be more than usually close in the years after the collapse of the international gold standard. Under a non-metallic currency movements of foreign capital have effects identical to those of shifts in the liquidity preference of an unchanged group of resident investors.[(25)] An inflow of foreign funds represents in effect a redistribution of the stock of domestic money, the bank deposits received by foreigners in return for gold or foreign exchange being given up by a domestic holder, while an outflow of funds would result in the reverse process. Assuming that an official stabilisation fund is operating in the foreign exchange market so as to eliminate fluctuations in the exchange rate, the effect of an inflow of funds on domestic credit thus depends on the reactions of the authorities to this change in the demand for money and on the use to which the foreign investor puts his newly-acquired bank deposit. If it was held as a stock of idle cash, the effect would be the same as if investors in a closed economy had suddenly raised their preference for holding cash: assuming no increase in the quantity of money, interest rates would rise. If the foreign funds were used to buy short-term securities, the effect would be the same as a rise in the demand for short-term securities, in a closed economy, the effect on interest rates depending on the way in which the purchase of foreign exchange by the Exchange Equalisation Account was financed.[(26)]

Although it is impossible to discover the precise disposition of foreign-owned resources in Britain, it is likely that during the 1930s they were concentrated primarily on bank deposits and short-term gilt-edged securities, little interest being shown in equities. Paish has shown that the net inflow of funds between March 1932 and March 1938 amounted to some £400 million; against this some £60 million Treasury Bills had been issued to the public and about £20 million had been financed by tap bills and Ways and Means Advances (i.e. in effect by credit creation).[(27)] The remaining £320 million must therefore have been financed by the issue of long-term securities and this figure corresponds fairly closely with the rise in the volume of national debt quoted on the London Stock Exchange. These increases in the supply of assets—bills rising by £60 million and long-term securities by £410 million—were the combined effect of the operations of the Exchange Equalisation Account and the official policy of funding the national debt. In fact the statistics confirm that in financing the purchase of gold as foreign capital flowed into London, no serious attempt was made by the authorities to adjust the supply of assets in order to prevent repercussions on the domestic credit structure.(28)

Deposits of 'hot money' during the 1930s originated from two main categories. In the first were the funds of private investors fearing political upsets in their own countries or a devaluation of their currency. In the second category were banking funds which flowed into London partly as a result of interest arbitrage (often encouraged by the deliberate policy of central banks which established an interest differential between their own country and London) and partly as a result of foreign exchange speculation; the latter, by creating discrepancies between 'spot' and 'forward' foreign exchange rates, enabled bankers to undertake profitable counter-operations without foreign exchange risk.

In 1936-7 some of the clearing banks engaged in intense competition for large deposits, mainly of foreign origin. Special concessions were made, including the granting of rates of interest normally given only to fixed deposits at long term and the waiving of the right to refuse to repay at short notice. Anything up to 1½ per cent was paid on foreign deposits at a time when the banks' lending rate in the money market was ½ per cent and the bill rate was oscillating between about ¼ per cent and 1 per cent. According to some authorities it was mainly on prestige grounds that the banks indulged in such competition.(29) Its result, apart from the adverse strains upon the balance of payments, was further complications for domestic monetary management by the introduction of relatively high rates of interest for transitory funds.

8. Wartime and after

During the second World War the techniques of cheap money, learnt somewhat inadvertently from 1932 onwards, were perfected and operated despite the pressures of open or suppressed inflation. Throughout the 1940s the authorities made no attempt to employ the traditional mechanisms of Bank rate and open-market operations to control the activities of the financial sector; instead priority was given to the maintenance of low interest rates —to make it a '3½ per cent war'—and the use of resources was subjected to physical controls plus reliance on direct requests to the banks to secure the provision of a financial flow consistent with them. Bank rate was maintained at 2 per cent throughout the period and the interest rates which were traditionally tied to it were thus held steady. The Banks continued, as in the 1930s, to give ½ per cent interest on deposit accounts.

Public liquidity remained high as a direct consequence of an expansion of the cash basis of the banking system in order to generate whatever money supply the public wished to hold at the low level of interest rates determined upon; this excess liquidity was not unnatural in wartime conditions, but it continued high long after the conclusion of hostilities. This is reflected in the high ratio of bank deposits to the national product; in 1950 this was well over 50 per cent compared with less than 40 per cent in 1939.

In 1947, however, as has already been noted, the ratio had approached 60 per cent, largely because of the marked expansion of the money supply associated with the Dalton policy of extremely low long-term interest rates.

In 1951 the ratio of current accounts to total deposits was still above the 66 per cent level, some 20 per cent higher than in 1938, although it would not have been unnatural to expect that the abnormally large balances resulting from the wartime suppression of normal expenditures would have been held on deposit account. The rise in the proportion of current accounts, however, may partly reflect the reduction in interest rates paid on country deposit accounts. Certainly in the ensuing years there was a gradual increase in the proportion of deposit accounts, partly as a result of the increase in rates paid on deposit accounts following the change in monetary policy in November 1951 and the abandonment of the longstanding 2 per cent Bank Rate.

By 1954 the ratio of total bank deposits to national income was down by more than 30 per cent in comparison with 1947 as a result of the running down of abnormal wartime and postwar cash holdings and the normal liquidity-preference effect of higher interest rates, so that it was much the same as it had been before the war. On this basis the fall in the liquidity of the personal sector since 1946, and even since 1951, had been spectacular but the loss of the abnormal 'bank-type' liquidity takes no account of the development of the 'near money' substitutes for bank deposits; when these other assets are taken into account 'personal liquidity' in 1954 was still well above the 1938 level.

In a real sense, then, the decades of the 1930s and 1940s had been a kind of twilight period for the London clearing banks. The 1920s were, in retrospect, the last decade for a very long time in which they were to play the role so painfully evolved during the nineteenth century and in the golden era preceding the first World War—loans and advances to private industry and commerce still represented the overwhelming bulk of their assets and despite the wartime expansion of the currency supply and 'small savings' securities by the government, the share of the clearing banks in the stock of public liquidity was as high in 1929 as it had been in 1905.

Different though the ensuing twenty years were to be in most senses—violent depression followed by hesitant recovery, then total war, and then postwar inflation—they possessed a striking similarity so far as the clearing banks were concerned, having in their context several characteristics in common. The first was, of course, the relative eclipse of the private lending function of the banks. Generated initially by the decline in demand as a result of industrial depression, it was continued thereafter by the reliance on physical controls during the war and early postwar years and by the easy availability of alternative sources of finance for such expenditures as were permitted.

Secondly, and arising from this, the period witnessed an almost continuous expansion in the dependence of the banking system on public rather than private debt. This was to have profound effects on the operation of monetary policy in Britain when its use was ultimately attempted again after 1951. On the one hand, it made the banks peculiarly vulnerable to the repercussions of credit policy on the gilt-edged market. On the other, insofar as the banks had become repositories of much of the floating debt their traditional relationships with the Bank of England underwent a gradual erosion; the latter, being the manager of the public debt, was in effect forced to adopt an attitude to the clearing banks which possessed attributes of partnership rather than the conventional master-and-servant relationship adumbrated by the Cunliffe Committee. As the Radcliffe Committee was to stress so heavily, this drastically qualified—if, indeed, it did not destroy—the strategic position of the cash ratio in British banking.

All this could lead expert observers to conclude, in 1950 or 1951, that the role of the clearing banks had permanently changed; from being the primary dispensers of short and medium-term credit to the private sector (the role which the bankers themselves accepted), they had become mere managers of the money supply—precisely the function which the Bank Charter Act of 1844 had sought to deny them. The conclusion would have been incontestable had it not been for a third characteristic of those two decades, the significance of which had not even then, perhaps, been appreciated. This was the steady growth throughout the period of instruments and institutions providing quite close substitutes for bank deposits: in 1920 the clearing banks could claim to account for 60 per cent of the economy's liquid assets but by 1950, on the most conservative basis of assessment, this was down to 42 per cent. And unlike the other two characteristics of the era, this trend was to be positively accelerated in the years which followed.

Each of these matters will require more detailed investigation in the chapters which follow. For the present it is enough to summarise the era by saying that after the evolutionary struggles of its formative era, the clearing banks had reached a plateau during the first decade of the Macmillan era before undergoing what could be seen in hindsight as a long period of unobtrusive but significant relative decline in their traditional role.

REFERENCES

1. Committee on Finance and Industry, *Minutes of Evidence*, HMSO, London 1931, Vol. I, Qu. 478.
2. *Report of the Committee on Finance and Industry* (Macmillan Report), Cmd. 3897, HMSO, London 1931, para. 22.
3. W. Manning Dacey, *Money Under Review*, London 1960, p. 47.
4. Based on data shown in Table 1, Statistical Appendix.
5. *Macmillan Report*, p. 283.
6. Macmillan, *Minutes of Evidence*, Vol. I, Hyde, Qu. 866-70.
7. W. F. Crick: address on 'Monetary policy and banking practice', delivered on 4th May 1933 before the Marshall Society, Cambridge.
8. *Report of the Committee on the Working of the Monetary System*, Cmnd. 827 (Radcliffe Report), HMSO, London 1959, para. 131, p. 44.
9. Based on Statistical Appendix, Table 2, col. 6.
10. *Radcliffe Report*, para. 128, p. 43.

11. For a full discussion see R. S. Sayers, *Modern Banking*, 7th ed., Oxford University Press, London 1967, Appx. 1.
12. Based on Statistical Appendix, Table 1, cols. 8-9.
13. B. Ellinger, *The City*, London 1940.
14. Macmillan, *Minutes of Evidence*, Vol. I, Hyde, Qu. 1071-82.
15. H. G. Johnson, 'Some Implications of secular changes in bank assets and liabilities in Great Britain', *Economic Journal*, Vol. LXI, September 1951, pp. 544-561.
16. E. V. Morgan, 'The National Debt and Monetary Policy', *Lloyds Bank Review*, No. 31, July 1955. See also Statistical Appendix, Table 4.
17. *National Banking Review and Federal Reserve Bulletin.*
18. *Radcliffe Report*, para. 132, p. 44.
19. *Ibid.*
20. E. T. Nevin, *The Mechanism of Cheap Money*, University of Wales Press, Cardiff 1955, Chap. IX, pp. 323-4.
21. *Ibid.*, Chap VII, pp. 256-60.
22. See Statistical Appendix, Table 1, col. (6). The comparison is slightly distorted (but to only some 1.5 per cent) by the inclusion of the District Bank in total deposits from 1939 onwards.
23. A. C. L. Day, *Outline of monetary economics*, Oxford University Press, London 1957, Chap 14, p. 189.
24. *Ibid.*, p. 196.
25. E. T. Nevin, *op. cit.*, Chap. IV, p. 144.
26. *Ibid.*, pp. 144-7.
27. F. W. Paish, *The post-war financial problem and other essays*, Macmillan, London 1950, p. 215-6.
28. See D. S. Lees, 'The technique of monetary insulation, December 1932 to December 1937', *Economica* (New Series), Vol. XX, No. 80, November 1953, pp. 341-55.
29. T. Balogh, *Studies in financial organisation*, National Institute of Economic and Social Research, Cambridge University Press, London 1947, Chap. 6, pp. 97-100.

CHAPTER SEVEN

Liquidity

1. Introduction

The ability to meet financial commitments is a natural cause of concern for most people (and even for governments) although this need is more often related to a period rather than to an individual moment. The possession of immediate spending power is an advantage to all institutions and persons but nowhere is it so significant a consideration as in the realm of banking. Bankers are dealers in borrowed money; their liabilities are financial assets to their customers and, representing spending power to a high degree, are subject to a high and fluctuating rate of turnover. The foremost responsibility of the banker, as the custodian of deposits belonging to his customers, has therefore always been to ensure that those deposits can be turned into cash as and when his customer dictates. This requirement necessarily governs the structure of bank assets; these must be regulated to ensure, first and foremost, that the bank has in hand at any given time a sufficiency of cash in the form of currency or balances at the Bank of England immediately convertible into currency. Secondly, in the disposition of earning assets the banker must ensure 'a constant reinforcement of cash through automatic repayment or immediate realisability'. (1)

Liquidity, therefore, implies for a banker the possession of cash sufficient to meet immediate commitments plus the ability to convert a proportion of other assets into cash at short notice and without loss. Hence, from the beginnings of commercial banking, in lending, buying securities or taking up bills the banker has had to pay a keen regard to the prime essential of liquidity; it was this which over the course of time was to lead to the evolution of standard ratios between various groups of assets and liabilities. Initially, the role of these ratios was restricted to one of guidance, being indicators rather than strict regulators of assets; certain ratios, however—and notably the liquid assets ratio—were to shift decidedly towards the latter basis with the change in monetary policy in 1951.

2. The cash ratio

The growth of large branch banks in Britain during the nineteenth century resulted in much greater *finesse* in the art of determining the minimum quantity of cash and liquid assets with which business could be carried out without the risk of insolvency, although the reserves remained very much a matter for the individual banker. No universally recognised ratio of cash to liabilities could be said to have applied during the nineteenth century and a small private banker in the provinces would feel it necessary to keep a level of reserves very different from that of his branch rivals, especially if the latter were at all large. London bankers, in turn, had different views on the desirable level of liquidity; much would depend not only upon seasonal influences but on different forms of banking business. A small bank with a few large industrial customers, for example, would take a different view of its desirable reserves from that of a similar bank with a great many small depositors.

By the end of the nineteenth century, however, the amalgamation movement had created a few large branch banks concerned primarily with deposits rather than private note-issues; greater uniformity in banking practice was thus bound to occur, especially in the matter of bank reserves. The campaigns of Goschen, following the Baring crisis, spurred bankers to become more conscious of the exact ratio of their cash to total liabilities; the cash ratio became a matter of importance to bankers, especially as their book-keeping methods improved to the extent that they were able to secure regular statements of their exact cash position. By the time of the Macmillan Report the cash ratio had come to dominate policy just as some thirty years later the implications of the liquidity ratio were to occupy the close attention of the Radcliffe Committee.

The cash position not only came to determine the policy of commercial banks but also to constitute a highly significant aggregate from the point of central bank control. Full balance sheets were and still are not drawn up every day; should a sudden inflow in cash occur, therefore, more elaborate and less easily reversible adjustments cannot be undertaken until it is known whether or not the increase in resources is likely to be permanent. Then and only then can the bank concerned decide whether it is appropriate to increase its lending or to buy long-term investments. Similarly, in the event of a loss of cash, sufficient assets (i.e. money at call or bills) usually mature automatically to permit the necessary adjustment. A bank can restore its cash position by not relending the amounts acquired from maturing assets or by declining the least desirable element of the demand for new advances. Fluctuations considered to be of a temporary nature, however, can be accommodated by allowing ratios to fluctuate rather than by a sudden restriction or promotion of advances. Continuity in advances policy is regarded as essential; a bank's customers plan their operations well ahead and the banks are more or less committed to help them. Variations in the day-to-day cash position have therefore always been more usually set off by corresponding adjustments in other liquid assets—money at call and short notice and bills discounted—but also, in the event of a recognised long-term trend, by adjusting holdings of gilt-edged securities. Known future demands for cash are taken care of mainly through the bill portfolio, while money at call and short notice is used to meet unforeseen demands. (2)

The proportion of cash held against deposits in the British banking system seems to have remained remarkably stable throughout the present century, subject to one important qualification. Until 1946, the published cash ratios of individual banks emerged from statements referring to selected 'make-up' days occurring once a month except at the ends of each half year. These figures were not necessarily representative of the banks' actual day-to-day positions and were certainly subject to further distortion by the banks themselves by manipulation of their asset structure—described in the following section—in order to present a favourable, but artificial, cash position. Further, it is practically certain that until 1919 the item today described as 'balances with other British banks and cheques in course of collection' was included by the majority of banks under the heading of cash. Although such balances might eventually provide an accession of cash for one particular bank, this was obviously not the case for the overall system; such balances simply inflate the balance-sheets of the banking system as a whole. End-year estimates for this item range from 3.1 per cent of liabilities in 1920 to 3.9 per cent in 1938. (3)

In order to attempt a comparison of cash reserves during the periods before and after the first World War it is thus advisable to compare the pre-1914 cash ratio with the post-war ratio of cash *plus* balances and cheques in the course of collection. Since a number of banks did not differentiate between cash and money at call and short notice before 1914, the pre-war figure has to be the average for 20 banks which did in fact make this distinction in their balance sheets. On this basis, it has been shown that the published cash ratios of these banks hardly declined at all between 1913 and 1938, remaining in the range of 16.3 to 16.8 between 1913 and 1929 and falling to a little over 15 per cent in the late 1930s. (4)

For the period after 1918, the figures for the cash ratio proper (i.e. excluding balances and cheques in course of collection) ranged around 12 per cent in the early 1920s, settling to between 10 and 11 per cent after 1926 in consequence of the Midland Bank's reduction in its cash ratio. Ratios still varied somewhat from bank to bank: at the end of 1938, for example, Barclays Bank showed the largest cash ratio (12.3 per cent) and Lloyds the lowest (10.2 per cent). The Macmillan Committee had held that uniformity in cash ratios was desirable since:

> . . . the power of the Bank of England to control the aggregate volume of credit in the country by means of open market operations and other measures essentially depends on the rigidity of this ratio. (5)

It would certainly seem that by 1931 the tradition of keeping a fixed ratio of cash against deposits was considered as binding; the impression created in the evidence before the Macmillan Committee was that a ratio of between 10 and 11 per cent had to be considered as a 'bedrock'. Subject to this minimum (although artificial) figure, individual ratios were said to be 'a matter of experience and judgement according to the nature of the deposits and the class of people one is dealing with and the way they are occupied and so forth'. (6) An unusually high proportion of short-term foreign deposits, for example, especially in the period after the collapse of the international gold standard, would oblige a cautious banker to increase his cash ratio accordingly.

It appears that the figure of 10 to 11 per cent was regarded by the banks as not only a minimum but also, circumstances permitting, a maximum ratio; in other words, the banks increased as well as decreased their assets so that their total liabilities maintained the accepted relationship to cash reserves. By the 1930s, however, the importance of the cash ratio was at times being affected by what would now be described as the 'secondary liquidity ratio'—that is, the ratio of cash, money at call and short notice and bills to deposits. Hence there were occasions, as will be shown later, when cash reserves rose above the conventional level but when a proportionately greater decline in other liquid items inhibited the banks from expanding credit until the desired combination of assets was restored. It is evident from the temporary surpluses in individual bank cash ratios, in fact, that their cash reserves were frequently treated as a residual item when difficulty was experienced in finding other assets of satisfactory liquidity.

Bank cash reserves are divided between balances with the Bank of England and till money needed for the conduct of everyday business. The proportion of till money to total cash reserves appears to have varied between 46.2 and 49.3 per cent throughout most of the 1930s, whereas before 1931 it was considerably higher than this. Until 1931 the banks did not report changes in the ratio of till money to total cash reserves at frequent intervals; hence the Bank of England could calculate the true state of the banks' till money holdings only once every half-year, possessing no accurate knowledge of the state of the total cash reserves of the banking system for the rest of the year beyond the bankers' deposits on its own books. This was often misleading and fluctuations in the ratio of till money to total cash reserves could create considerable difficulties for central monetary management.

The Macmillan Committee recommended the lowering of the proportion of till money from about 6 per cent of deposits to some 4 per cent, and the maintenance of the total cash ratio at about 10 per cent.[(7)] This implied a corresponding increase in bankers' deposits with the Bank of England. By changing bankers' deposits into till money or vice versa, the clearing banks had been able to vary the banknote reserve of the Banking Department of the Bank of England; in the days before the 1928 and 1939 Currency and Bank Notes Acts, they could—at least in theory, although in practice it was unthinkable—force the Bank to change its policy or to apply to the government for a suspension of the Bank Charter Act.[(8)] The Macmillan Committee, however, declined to recommend the American practice of the exclusion of till money from the cash ratio. After 1931 the clearing banks began the practice of informing the Bank of the state of their till money holdings; they also adopted the Macmillan Committee's recommendation that the till money ratio should be lowered. Following the Currency and Bank Notes Act of 1939 sufficient flexibility was provided in the management of the volume of note issue to obviate the problem of fluctuations in the volume of till money.

3. Window-dressing and the Treasury bill

The deficiencies in bank statistics on cash ratios referred to earlier were aggravated by a practice, common to all but one of the major clearing banks, of manipulating their asset structure so as to present a deceptively favourable figure for the cash ratio. The practice was undoubtedly a legacy from the dark days of Overend-Gurney and arose from the presumed need to assure depositors of the safety of the banks. The published cash ratio is the average of figures attained on one 'make-up' day per week and cannot accurately represent the daily position of each bank throughout the month. It was never the figure on the basis of which the clearing banks' policy was in fact determined. Until 1946 the 'Big Five' made up their weekly position on different days—Barclays on Mondays, Lloyds on Tuesdays, the Midland on Wednesdays, and the National Provincial and the Westminster on Thursdays.[(9)] This arrangement was conducive to the practice of 'window-dressing', an operation in which the banks appear to have indulged at the expense of a deterioration in the accuracy of British banking statistics.[(10)] When make-up day came round, each bank in turn could call in from the market rather more cash than usual; the other banks would allow their cash ratios to fall as the market in turn borrowed from them. The fact that make-up days differed made this a simple and cheap operation: each bank could arrange to attract cash from the other banks via the money market, thereby temporarily raising their individual cash reserves with the purpose of being able to show a higher cash ratio than they usually carried. If they had all made up on the same day, of course, their efforts in this direction would have mutually cancelled out.[11]

All each bank needed to do was to let part of its call money loans mature and postpone its normal re-lending activities for a day so as to increase its cash reserves by the temporary transfer of non-cash assets to the other banks, from whom the bill brokers borrowed in order to repay the bank concerned. The latter would in turn re-lend the cash the following morning in time for the next big bank to call in money-market loans for its making-up day. In the words of the Macmillan Committee,

> . . . . a certain part of the published reserves of the clearing banks in the shape of deposits with the Bank of England is like a stage army, the same liquid resources doing duty four times over in the course of each week.[12]

The cash ratio revealed in the bank's monthly statements was therefore a fictitious one, the Macmillan Committee estimating the average size of 'the stage army' at something of the order of £17 to £19 million for the years 1929-30; the true cash ratio was therefore only about 9½ per cent of deposits against the published figure of nearly 11 per cent.

At half-year ends the situation was different since all the banks drew up a balance-sheet relating to the same day; the normal procedure for window-dressing had therefore to be abandoned, resort being had instead to forcing the money market to borrow from the Bank of England. The banks would accordingly decrease their bill portfolio and allow the discount market to carry a higher proportion of bills in the month before the end of the half-year so as to ensure that the conversion of call money into cash should not distort the usual pattern of their balance sheets. Alternatively they were able to arrange their purchases of Treasury Bills, either directly through the tender or, after 1934, via the discount market, so as to have a large volume maturing at the end of each half-year, so helping to provide themselves with the extra cash required. At the end of the calendar year, when the Treasury also was short of cash, it too was obliged to borrow from the Bank of England; in effect the banks were putting the Treasury into the Bank rather than 'calling from the market'.[13] In comparison with the monthly statements, the half-year balance sheets tended to show lower bills, somewhat more call money and considerably more cash, the cash ratio being higher in fact than the average monthly figure, inflated as was the latter through the monthly window-dressing. In 1938, for example, the annual average cash ratio of the banks, calculated from their monthly statements, amounted to 10.6 per cent, while the ratios shown in the year-end statements averaged 11.2 per cent.[14]

The dangers of window-dressing, from the point of view of monetary management, stemmed largely from the fact that its extent was not constant and that the actual cash ratio could be calculated only twice a year—and even then not accurately. Following the publication in 1931 of statistics on 'till money', however, it became possible to estimate the extent of window-dressing. 'True cash' could be estimated by adding bankers' deposits at the Bank of England, as shown in the Bank's weekly return, and the amount of till money held by the clearing banks; 'declared cash' could be discovered from the average cash reserves published in the clearing banks' monthly statements. The accuracy of this method (from the point of view of the public) was unfortunately still limited by the fact that the

Bankers' Deposits published in the Bank of England returns included the balances of banks other than the London clearing banks.

Considerable variations occurred from year to year in the extent of window-dressing as revealed by a comparison of these two totals. From a maximum of over £40 million in June 1929, it fell to a minimum of £1 million in 1934. In the late 1930s it averaged about £20 million, slightly higher than the average for the years 1929-30 as estimated by the Macmillan Committee. Substantial variations were experienced within any one year; in 1939, for example, it ranged from £2 million in January to £29 million in December.

Shortly after the end of the second World War, the banks agreed to abandon the practice of window-dressing; as from 1946 a figure of 8 per cent was adopted as a true operational cash ratio by the commercial banks; from what has been said, it will be clear that this probably represented little, if any, real decline from the declared 10 to 11 per cent of the 1930s.

4. The significance of the cash ratio

The Macmillan Committee condemned the practice of window-dressing outright, but it has been argued that this condemnation was unmerited except for the possibility that the banks might be able temporarily to counteract the policy of the Bank of England.(15) Window-dressing did allow the banks to overcome purely temporary fluctuations in their deposits at the Bank of England arising from the Bank's role as government banker, a function which was by no means always compatible with its function as the central monetary authority, especially in the period after 1931 with its Exchange Equalisation Funds and violent international short-term capital movements. There were times when the Bank was unable immediately to offset sudden changes in the volume and quality of its assets and hence in the volume of bankers' cash. In such circumstances window-dressing enabled the banks to avoid unnecessary disturbance of their asset structures and the corresponding threat of compromise of their credit policies, by maintaining stability in their published cash ratios. Moreover, with regular communication to the Bank of England of data concerning their till money holdings, the potentially harmful effects of window-dressing on monetary control were considerably curtailed.

The Macmillan Committee nevertheless displayed a pre-occupation with the cash ratios of the banking system even to the extent of stating (with some subsequent qualification) that

> . . . since the banks as a whole maintain a cash proportion to deposits of from 10 to 11 per cent, they are in fact able to increase their deposits by some ten times the cash created by the Bank of England.(16)

Throughout the Macmillan era, however, it was unlikely that a loss of cash reserves would always bring about an automatic reaction by the commercial banks; the 10 per cent published ratio was not always regarded as a rigid rule and, as has been noted, changes in the true cash ratio could be concealed by window-dressing. Moreover, the fact that any commercial bank could restore its cash ratio immediately and without significant cost by recalling loans to the discount market or by letting bills mature meant that the ratio was of less significance than had often been thought. This was particularly evident with the beginning of the 'open back-door' policy inaugurated by the Bank of England in the late 1930s and continuing on a much greater scale through the 1940s. By this term is meant that the Bank indicated its willingness to buy Treasury bills from the market at market rates of interest and at the market's initiative, which implied that if the banks were well supplied with Treasury bills there was no effective limitation on their cash reserves or, therefore, on their ability to create credit.

The Committee's analysis under-estimated the importance of the banks' desire for liquid assets in their portfolios and the significance of assets such as bills, money at call and short notice and possibly investments through which an automatic realisation of cash could often be secured for an individual bank. With the Bank of England long established as lender of last resort, the banks were beginning to consider the ratio of their highly liquid assets to deposits as almost as important as the cash ratio itself; hence their readiness to expand credit on the basis of increased cash could be checked by a scarcity of these liquid assets. Instead of there being a simple ten-fold multiplier for the expansion of bank deposits, the creation of credit by any individual bank rested in fact not only on the cash ratio itself but also on the wider base of cash plus liquid assets convertible into cash amounting to roughly 25 to 35 per cent of their deposit liabilities. The multiplier underlying the creation of bank credit could therefore be smaller than the Macmillan Committee appears to have imagined.

It is essential to remember, however, that the ability to secure cash without significant cost through a reduction of call loans or commercial bill portfolios could be exercised only by an individual bank which, in effect, withdrew cash from other commercial banks. Only when the liquid assets in question were liabilities of the public sector—so that redemption involved a cheque drawn on the Bank of England—could the banking system *as a whole* reinforce its cash without forcing the money market to borrow at the Bank of England at penal cost—a process which would not be lightly undertaken nor easily prolonged. Much subsequent discussion of the liquidity ratio went seriously astray because this essential distinction between public and private sector assets was lost to sight.

It follows from this last point that bank holdings of government floating debt—i.e. Treasury bills, which in the early 1930s had largely replaced commercial bills of exchange—were of particular importance. The Macmillan report had noted this trend between 1919 and 1930; the proportion was to rise considerably in the next five years, however, as economic crises swept away the commercial bill as the mainstay of traders and bankers alike. This was to lead the Radcliffe Committee to conclude eventually—not perhaps entirely wisely—that the effective base of bank credit had become the total of liquid assets (based on the availability of Treasury bills) instead of the supply of cash.(17), (18)

5. The liquidity ratio

From the beginning, liquid assets had been important to the banks precisely by virtue of their liquidity. Rough and ready liquidity principles began to find a fuller development as soon as the developing money market, together with the Bank of England, provided facilities for the holding and adjustment of 'near cash' assets as the means of both protecting and economising cash.[19] Bagehot, in *Lombard Street*, confirmed the practice of the banks of putting 'reserves' to work; they were no longer predominantly held as balances at the Bank of England but kept as to 'a main part ..... on deposit with the bill-broker or in good and convertible interest bearing securities. From these they (the banks) obtain a large income.'[20] Fifteen years later, George Rae in *The Country Banker* had explicitly discussed the possibility of operating a bank with a reserve ratio of one-third, of which about two-thirds was held in cash and money at call and short notice and the remainder in Consols. The reason for the rather surprising inclusion of the latter was that, according to Rae,

> Consols stand unrivalled and alone in the supreme quality of convertibility. They are the one security which you can, with absolute certainty, turn into cash at any hour of any business day in the worst throes of panic.[21]

Consols, however, had experienced a marked loss of popularity after the severe drop in their capital value during the first decade of the twentieth century; as a result, their place in the banks' holdings of liquid assets was taken by bills (mainly trade) whose supply had temporarily increased.

Liquidity, of course, can be said to reflect a frame of mind: it consists in the confidence with which an asset *is regarded* as convertible quickly and without loss into cash. In establishing or assessing liquidity much depended, as it still does, on the attitudes of the Bank of England, especially in relation to the discount market. Liquidity, in other words, is largely concerned with the so-called 'shiftability' of assets on to the central bank via the Bank's accepted role of lender-of-last-resort. Assets which were deemed to possess the highest or automatic liquidity, other than cash, were, and are, primarily those eligible for rediscount with the central bank—such as prime bills—and which are taken as collateral against loans to the discount market. By virtue of this quality, liquidity confidence in such assets can be complete. Commercial bills, in other words, owe their liquidity not so much to the fact that they are of short maturity or of so-called 'self-liquidating' character—since for the banking system as a whole such criteria are largely illusory—but to their acceptability by the central bank as collateral or for re-discount.

Investments, on the other hand, have never been so acceptable by the Bank and could not be said to possess automatic liquidity except when near to maturity. From the fact of marketability alone, they could be said to be liquid to some degree—unlike advances—but their liquidity is inevitably more vulnerable than that of money market assets; except when close to maturity, they carry considerable risk of capital loss. Thus although bankers would often 'take a view' of their investment liquidity, such 'liquidity' had far more of a subjective quality than that of assets acceptable to the Bank of England. Liquidity confidence here depended largely on market outlook.

As regards the desirable proportion of liquid assets, as opposed to their content, some sort of rule of thumb was undoubtedly present by the 1920s, but almost certainly there was no universally recognised minimum liquidity ratio at this time other than that (at least nominally) applied to the cash reserve. Perhaps the most positive evidence on the operation of such ratios was that recorded by the Midland Bank in 1934, which implies that they had been in existence for some time:

> The banks, in order to maintain liquidity, work to *well established* ratios between their holdings of cash and other eminently liquid assets and the amount of their deposits. They do not create more money, in the form of bank deposits, than their holdings of cash and other liquid assets will support. (22)

The supposedly ancient, if not mythical, ancestry of the 30 per cent liquidity ratio was echoed nearly thirty years later by Lord Cromer, Governor of the Bank of England:

> A minimum level of 30 per cent for the liquidity ratio is historical; it was *the agreed minimum level of liquidity* which prudent bankers in their wisdom and experience had found appropriate to the circumstance of their business. (23)

On this basis it is of some interest to examine at what stage in their history the banks began to employ the 30 per cent ratio of cash, bills and call money to deposits as 'the agreed minimum level of liquidity', the issue being, of course, whether the banks contracted deposits when the agreed minimum ratio was threatened. In fact the evidence suggests that such a figure was not adhered to as a rigid minimum until after the requirement was officially imposed by the authorities in the 1950s.

From the 1920s onwards, however, the banks were undoubtedly looking more carefully at their ratios, largely because of the pervasive influence of the monthly statements whose publication had been resumed in 1921 in more comprehensive form—although the figures contained still lacked consistency in definition and composition as between the banks. The ratio with which the banks were most concerned was still that relating to their cash reserve, while their secondary reserves, although important, held to no uniform figure or component.

Before the Macmillan Committee the representatives of the Midland Bank had emphasised the importance attached by the banks to an asset structure of a definite pattern. Other banks, however, while broadly adhering to similar policies, did not accept the pattern described by the Midland Bank. Statistics for the clearing banks' liquid assets (cash, bills and call money) in the 1920s reveal a range between 37.9 and 31.6 per cent with a decennial average of 33.6 per cent, although individual ratios could of course have oscillated around 38 per cent in the case of one bank and 28 per cent in the case of another. Although it appears that each bank kept more or less faithfully to its own pattern for long periods, marked differences in fact existed between the various 'liquidity ratios' of individual banks, no doubt reflecting the varying nature of their respective liabilities and assets.

It has been argued that such figures as may accurately represent clearing bank liquidity ratios for the 1920s indicate that a downward trend in liquidity extending over a few months generally had important repercussions upon investments policy, even, in many instances, when the trend was plainly seasonal. (24) Bank investment holdings were likely to be varied in the event of liquidity pressure because of the difficulty of making any quick adjustment in advances. Thus between 1923 and 1930 the banks' investment holdings declined during the months of falling liquid assets (including cash) but only occasionally fell by more than the rise in advances. It would have been natural for the banks to have regard for their liquidity position in a decade when advances were generally high and expanding; it would be considered prudent to sell or redeem securities in order to make way for an expansion of advances and vice-versa, so that a 'scissors movement' between advances and investments was considered a normal feature of banking practice. [25] But there is no evidence that in the 1920s the banks regulated their asset policies on the basis of a common and constant minimum ratio of liquid assets (as opposed to cash) below which they sold investments or restricted advances.

> We say that we want to keep about 11 per cent of cash ...
> Then we come to our second line, and our second line primarily is the money that we have at call and short notice in the London money market ... We aim at keeping about 7 per cent of our assets in that form. Then our next line is our bills ... we keep about 15 per cent of our assets in bills. The next item is investments ... we aim at keeping about 12 per cent of our assets in the form of investments ... [26]

It is important to recognise the distinction between the practice by the banks of a rule-of-thumb liquidity principle involving individual and divergent ratios—containing as they did items included by one bank and disregarded by another—and a definite commitment to maintain a common and constant minimum ratio of liquid assets as is the contemporary practice. At least as late as the Macmillan Committee's enquiry some bankers appeared to have regarded investments as 'eminently liquid'; it was not until well on in the following decade that public attention could fairly be drawn to the possible existence of a common liquidity ratio of 30 per cent with a standard content of cash, bills and money at call and short notice. During most of what is called here the 'Macmillan era', however, it is apparent that apart from their cash ratio, the banks kept an eye on the ratio of advances (and investments) to total deposits, albeit in a rather flexible and informal way. [27] Truptil commented in 1936 on the 'striking reciprocal variations' between advances and investments, and on the 'very remarkable tendency for the total of advances and investments to remain in the neighbourhood of 70 per cent of the deposits'. [28] This tendency originated primarily in the conviction that the proper business of British banking lay in loans and advances, not in holding securities: the latter were simply a fill-in when any deficiency of quality or quantity existed in the demand for loans and overdrafts. Obviously the advances-investments ratio would vary in inverse proportion with the ratio of liquid assets (including cash) but it is probable that the banks did not concern themselves unduly with the proportion and composition of the latter in any direct sense, save only for their cash position. Cash was still the ultimate factor in determining the quantity of bank assets and the amount of cash available for the banks was in turn controlled by the Bank of England. Each bank had a pattern of assets which may have differed from that of others but was itself broadly stable; it was this stability which was the basis of all banking management. [29]

In the 1930s, however, certain changes were enforced in both the volume and nature of the banks' liquid assets and their investments, and as the so-called 'bill-famine' developed they began to pay greater attention to the exact ratio of their liquid assets to total deposits. It was not long before attention was drawn to the fact that there were few occasions when the common ratio of these assets to deposits fell much below 30 per cent, and that prior to the bill famine such instances had invariably arisen in the first quarter of the year—the season of peak government revenue inflow.[30] From this emerged the argument that although the conventional cash reserve provided a bank with adequate protection against foreseeable demands for cash, a secondary reserve of assets which could quickly provide cash through maturity or sale was required to meet any unexpectedly large or prolonged drain on cash. According to the *Midland Bank Review*,

> the recognised cash ratio is based on the assumption that behind the cash holding is an adequate supply of bills, guaranteeing a steady daily inflow of cash. Bills provide a reinforcement of cash holdings, and unless an adequate supply is available the banks, who must at all times have first regard to liquidity, are unable to increase their holdings of investments to the full extent made possible by their cash holdings considered alone.[31]

Even so, the practice of the banks in this connection was distinctly less sharply defined than the primary liquidity rule involving cash reserves, and the widespread discussion of it in the 1930s and subsequent years lacked unanimity.[32] Before entering into detailed discussion of the significance of the secondary reserve, however, it is worthwile examining the consequences of the changes in the supply and nature of the banks' liquid assets.

6. Bank liquidity and the supply of bills

Between June 1933 and March 1934, a fall in bank deposits occurred which did not reflect any change in cash reserves. On the basis of the 10 per cent cash ratio the banks had sufficient surplus cash in 1934 to have expanded deposits to a total some 14 per cent greater than the actual average level existing in that year. Again, a fall in deposits between June 1938 and March 1939 was associated with *increased* cash reserves. In fact the banks were holding the volume of credit below the maximum made possible by their cash reserves considered alone, apparently as a result of the contraction in the supply of bills; this reduced their supply of liquid assets both directly and indirectly through the fall in loans to the money market.

As far as the banks were concerned, this contraction had three causes: first, the decline in the overall supply of commercial bills, secondly, the reduction in the volume of market Treasury Bills and thirdly, the increased competition for both types of bills from holders of foreign funds moving into London in these years.[33] The decline in the importance of the London bill of exchange as an instrument for financing trade had been a process continuing, as has been seen, from the late nineteenth century. Accentuating this was the general decline in the importance of London as a financial centre and the overall decline in international trade itself during the 1930s; both were responsible for a further contraction in the volume of commercial bills seeking discount in London.

It has been estimated that the volume of commercial bills in circulation in London fell from about £470 million in 1930 to less than £250 million in 1933, remaining under £300 million throughout the remaining years of the decade. The volume of tender Treasury bills, on the other hand, increased between 1930 and 1933 from £460 million to £580 million, but this was not enough to offset the decline in commercial bills.[34] As a result, the total volume of bills circulating in the London market fell during these years by about £100 million, falling a further £80 million or so during 1934-5 and recovering again during 1936-8 to about the 1933 level. The decline in the total supply of bills was serious enough for the various institutions dealing in them, but the situation was worsened for the British clearing banks because outside competition for bills significantly reduced the proportion available for their own portfolios. During 1931 and 1932 the large outflows of foreign capital from London had reduced the competition for bills in the market; with the return of foreign capital to London, however, the banks' share was markedly reduced; during 1937-8, despite the fact that total deposits had increased by nearly 20 per cent, clearing bank holdings of bills had increased on average by less than 5 per cent.

It is reasonably clear that it was the fall in the supply of Treasury Bills to the banks, both absolutely and relatively, which was the fundamental cause of the problem during the 1930s.[35] After 1931, when a considerable reduction in advances took place, the continued shortage of bills made an expansion of short-term assets impossible and the banks were hard put to find suitable earning assets. When Bank of England open-market operations in connection with the conversion of 5 per cent War Loan increased their cash reserves in 1932, therefore, the banks were obliged to expand their holdings of securities, and between February 1932 and October 1935 investment portfolios rose from £264 million to £616 million.[36] Although investments (usually meaning Consols) had been regarded as highly liquid assets in the nineteenth century, with the turn of the century their sharp fall in price, together with the increased supply of bills, had cost them their place among the banks' liquid assets. Even so in the early years of the century the banks continued to regard then as reasonable reinforcements to their liquidity position. By 1934, however, they were holding twice as many securities as bills and a direct consequence of this massive proportionate increase was that the banks were obliged to adjust their attitude towards the liquidity of investments.[37]

The concept of liquidity is an ambiguous one: as has been stressed, it entails the belief in the ability to convert assets into cash without delay. It also requires the separate ability to do so *in full*; if depositors' claims are to be fully satisfied, therefore, bank assets must be convertible into cash without loss.[38] Undoubtedly gilt-edged securities can be sold quickly but the amount of cash which can be so obtained depends upon the market price at the moment of sale; this could involve the banks in losses which even the amount of their secret reserves might not incline them to take. Only by waiting until the maturity date, if any, could the face value of a security be certainly obtained; to sell before then, especially when the banks held a large share of the total long-term national debt, carried the risk of considerable capital loss. As a result, a growing caution was observed in the banks' investment policies. As for investments, the *Midland Bank Review* recorded in early 1934:

> ... the banks' holdings seem now to have reached the limit of discretion, having regard to the primary necessity of maintaining liquidity and safety of capital.[39]

Much would depend on the demand for advances. Signs of a revival would indicate to the banks not only the chance of more profitable business—so that they might be able to afford to sell investments even at some loss—but also a general business revival which would ease the burden of frozen loans or bad debts. Thus a more favourable view could be taken of the overall liquidity position. Throughout most of the 1930s, however, the demand for advances was declining or static and bank investments correspondingly remained at high levels. A keen watch had therefore to be kept on the banks' existing liquidity reserves; with investments more generally regarded as risk assets along with advances, the secondary liquidity ratio of about 30 per cent began to assume importance as a (riskless) liquidity buffer against not only the known risk of advances but also that now embodied in the greatly increased portfolio of securities.

Had the banks been operating a rigid secondary ratio they could offset the decline in their holdings of liquid assets (i.e. bills—since money at call and short notice, being employed largely in the discount of bills, tends to vary closely with bills discounted) either by increasing their primary reserve (i.e. cash) or by decreasing the amount of their total liabilities until the primary and secondary reserve ratios together had risen sufficiently. During the 1930s, however, the banks could not control the absolute magnitude of their cash reserves, which were determined by Bank of England policy; if there were a reduction in the supply of liquid assets below the level thought necessary, therefore, the banks could refrain from replacing them with risk assets or could reduce such assets until the secondary ratio was restored.

As has already been made clear, however, the statistics suggest that the attitude of the banks towards their secondary liquidity reserves was by no means unequivocal; there is no evidence of the secondary ratio operating in a quasi-automatic fashion. As may be seen from Chart V, during the 'hey-day' of the 1920s there was no obvious pattern of liquidity ratio, with annual averages varying from 31.6 to 37.5 per cent and the statistics of individual bank ratios showing a similar variation with the banks as a whole.(40) During the 1930s the annual averages for the clearing banks as a whole ranged from 34.2 per cent in 1933 to 28.8 per cent in 1939. Between 1925 and 1939 not one of the Big Five maintained a ratio close to 30 per cent, the actual ratios for the whole period taken together ranging from 34.0 per cent in the case of the National Provincial to 37.1 per cent in the case of the Westminster. The range of ratios becomes even wider when the remaining clearing banks are considered: Martins and the National, for example, maintained average liquidity ratios consistently below 30 per cent, the annual average falling below 25 per cent in four years with Martins and in five years in the case of the National. Glyn Mills, on the other hand, maintained an average of 35 per cent over the period as a whole and kept an average ratio of more than 40 per cent during two years. The absolute level of ratios is of less importance than their constancy, of course, but in this respect no really constant ratio whatever can be said to have existed for the several banks, either in common or individually.

Of greater importance than the question of any precise statistical ratio, however, is that of whether the banks contracted credit when liquid assets were declining as some commentators believed to be the case almost regardless of the level from which the fall began.(41) The evidence does not lend support to this view. It would be natural to expect that if the banks were operating a fairly rigid secondary ratio they would refrain

CHART 5

Total Liquid Assets of the London Clearing Banks 1921–1955

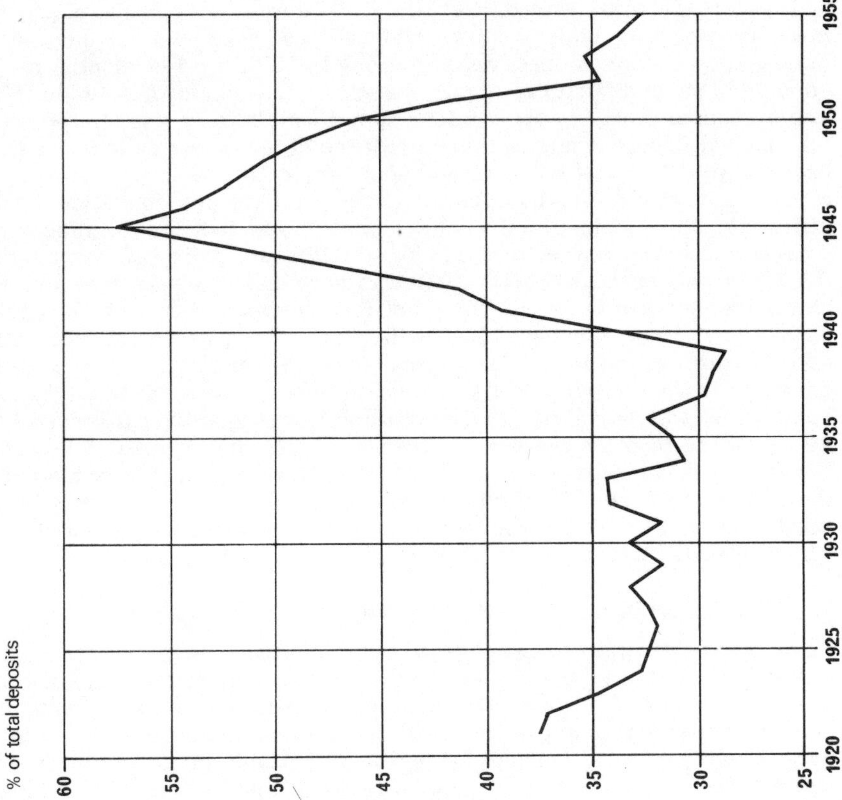

from increasing risk assets during those months when the secondary ratio was falling near or below the minimum. Between 1934 and 1939 there was only one year (1936) in which the secondary ratio was at 30 per cent; in the other five years the ratio was below this level. In only one year, however, were 'risk assets' reduced when liquidity fell, and then only by £2 million: in all other cases risk assets were actually increased by substantial amounts, despite, in four years, months with a secondary ratio of less than 29 per cent, and even (in 1939) a ratio of little more than 26 per cent.(42)

It might be argued, of course, that a secondary rule of 30 per cent would not be enforced during months of merely seasonal pressure on liquidity. Even so, looking at months other than the seasonal low point of March, there were 23 months between 1934 and the end of 1939 in which the liquidity ratio fell below 30 per cent, and on several of these occasions risk assets were increased. Certainly there was no evidence of a systematic tendency for deposits to be reduced *pari passu* with liquid assets; indeed, they moved in opposite directions in 52 of the 120 months involved.(43) It is difficult to argue, therefore, that during the 1930s there was a general tendency for a fall in liquid assets to be associated with a fall in total deposits, nor is there evidence of any great sensitivity apparent amongst the banks to a fixed secondary ratio. With the outbreak of war in 1939, of course, the question ceased to have any operational significance. The emphasis on a 'cheap money' war led to an immense expansion of short-term borrowing and a deliberate policy of ensuring that the banks possessed whatever cash was necessary to guarantee that the expanded debt was taken up—the chief means being, of course, the ability of the banks to re-discount bills at the Bank of England at current rates on their own initiative. Whatever problems the outbreak of war may have created for the clearing banks, the attainment of technical liquidity requirements was certainly not one of them. The liquidity ratio rose from 34 in 1940 to over 57 per cent in 1945 and remained over 40 per cent until the restoration of monetary 'orthodoxy' in November 1951. Indeed, it is the transformation of the liquidity position of the banking system which marks the point at which the 'Macmillan era' can be said to end and at which the new 'Radcliffe era' begins.

7. The importance of the environment

Reverting to the inter-war years, it would appear that the reaction of the banks to a decline in liquid assets varied according to the circumstances of the time. In other words, the importance attached to the secondary reserve depended on prevailing trade conditions and general economic outlook and hence the opportunities for the suitable employment of resources set free as a result of the decline in liquid assets. The banks might well have been said to be 'faced with a perennial conflict between liquidity and profitability, but not with a hard and fast line between liquid and illiquid assets'.(44) Thus a very short bond, say with only a month to maturity, is as liquid as a bill; similarly, some advances, particularly of the 'self-liquidating' kind, are much more liquid than others. In other words, bankers pay attention to the whole range of assets, and not merely to their division among a few rather arbitrary categories. This being the case, the level of liquid assets thought necessary would depend partly on the liquidity of assets outside that category; a banker whose investments comprised mostly very short bonds might be content to hold fewer bills and *vice versa*. In all probability the state of secret reserves would also have some influence; the penalty of illiquidity being possible capital losses, the stronger the inner reserves, the more of this risk a banker would feel justified in taking. In effect the liquidity ratio rested on a rational evaluation of the pros and cons of different forms of banking asset and the obvious flexibility of the supposedly traditional 30 per cent rule would reflect factors such as fluctuations in confidence in the gilt-edged market or the feelings with which the banks viewed their advances. The formulation of standard ratios between the various groups of bank assets and deposit liabilities was, in fact, fundamentally 'for guidance rather than strict regulation'.(45)

Although trade conditions were on the whole improving after 1933 the recovery was gradual and did not check the long-continued decline in advances. During the 1920s the ratio of advances to GNP had crept steadily upwards from about 16 per cent in 1921 to nearly 22 per cent in 1931; for the succeeding three years they fell absolutely as well as relatively to GNP, but even by 1939 clearing bank advances were less than 18 per cent of GNP. Partly because of this, and partly because of the shortage of bills in the market, the banks adopted a competitive cutting of discount rates at the weekly Treasury bill tender in an attempt to increase their holdings of bills. Given the inelasticity of supply, this led to a redistribution of bills away from the discount market and towards the banks and a consequent reduction of loans to the discount market. The net gain to the banks' overall liquidity reserve was therefore limited and secured only at the cost of threatening the survival of the discount market. With the continuing decline in the volume of advances and the shortage of bills, the banks could maintain their level of earning assets only by increasing their holdings of government securities. Despite the need to replace the decline of £153 million in other earning assets between June 1933 and March 1934, however, the banks increased their investments by only £3 million.

The reason for this failure to expand further into securities may be found in the misgivings with which the banks were beginning to view their greatly enlarged security portfolios; as *The Economist* observed, 'If they increased their holdings they might be exposing themselves too much to the vicissitudes of the gilt-edged market'.(46) A similar development occurred between June 1938 and March 1939 when the liquidity of securities was again considered suspect—on this occasion because of the general political outlook rather than current economic conditions. The banks' secondary reserves were then declining, as were advances, but instead of offsetting the decline in the latter by increased purchases of gilt-edged securities, the banks actually sold securities on a falling market in order to prevent a further decline in the ratio of their liquid assets to total liabilities.

At other times, as has been shown, a decline in the secondary ratio did not prevent banks from adding to what they regarded as their risk assets, investments as well as advances. In March and April of 1935, for example, with the secondary ratio below 29 per cent, the banks partly offset a decline of £76 million in liquid assets by an increase of £19 million in advances and of £12 million in investments. Again, two years later, between March and November of 1937, with the secondary ratio averaging 29.4 per cent, the banks offset a decline of £16 million in call money and bills by a net rise of £46 million in 'risk' assets, selling £37 million of investments but increasing advances by no less than £83 million.(47)

The explanation of the differences in behaviour during these periods is to be found in the state of economic activity. When the outlook seemed favourable the banks were willing and able to expand advances even though by so doing they prevented a rise in, or even further reduced, a secondary ratio which was below 30 per cent; when a low secondary ratio appears to have been associated with a reduction in bank credit, on the other hand, a decline in the volume of advances was apparent, the trend being generally visible before the decline in the liquidity ratio. Throughout the Macmillan period, in other words, the criterion of adequacy in the level of liquid assets fluctuated according to the general state of the economy and, especially, according to the availability of suitable alternative assets in which surplus funds could be employed. Such a flexibility was by no means abnormal even with reference to the conventionally rigid cash ratios; by varying the amount of 'window-dressing' in which they indulged, the banks could significantly alter the actual cash reserve on which they were operating, relaxing their requirements in times of buoyant expectations and tightening them in times when the economic outlook was less favourable.(48) Hence during the recession of 1931-2 a reduction occurred in window-dressing from an average of about 11.5 per cent of true cash in 1931 to one of about 6.6 per cent in 1934. With the revival of economic expansion, the average rose again to more than 10 per cent in 1937, reaching 15.8 per cent in November of that year when the liquid assets ratio was down to 27.5 per cent. In 1938-9 the deteriorating political atmosphere, together with economic recession, led to another reduction, the average level of window-dressing falling well below 5 per cent in the third quarter of 1939.

In general, like the extent of window-dressing, the importance attached to the secondary ratio varied with prevailing economic conditions. One important point should be noticed. A decline in window-dressing was generally a sign of increasing caution on the part of the banks—of a desire to have true cash reserves more closely approximating to the published ratios. A closer regard to the secondary ratio, on the other hand, although originating in the same general feeling, might be particularly related to the difficulty of replacing liquid assets except with securities—that is, to a lack of opportunity to increase or maintain advances to borrowers of a sufficiently satisfactory credit-worthiness.

8. Wartime policy and the postwar aftermath

During the 1940s no attempt was made to use the mechanisms of Bank rate and open-market operations in order to limit the amount of lending by the commercial banks. The policy of the authorities was to maintain low and stable short-term interest rates and to allow the commercial banks to create whatever amount of deposits the public chose to hold at those interest rates. Both were achieved by the Bank's readiness to buy Treasury bills from the discount market or the commercial banks on their own initiative and at prices corresponding to market rates of interest. This 'open back-door' policy of the Bank was thus in direct contrast to the traditional front-door operation which involved purchases of, or lending against, prime bills to assist the market only at 'penal rates'.

The rapid expansion in the banks' holdings of Treasury bills during the early months of the war corresponded to a rapid expansion in the tender bill issue; the further expansion to June 1940, on the other hand, greatly exceeded the small contemporary rise in the tender total, the difference being probably attributable to the issue of bills to the banks direct through 'the tap'.[49] After mid-1940, however, the government's floating debt requirements from the banking system were met mainly by the issue of Treasury Deposit Receipts. These were introduced as an 'emergency' measure so as to enable the Treasury to call money for 5, 6, or 7 month periods from the London clearing and Scottish banks (plus two overseas banks), the amount called from each bank being in strict proportion to its deposits. Treasury Deposit Receipts were not transferable, but it was informally agreed that the Bank of England would buy them (at a discount equal to the current Bank rate) in the event of an emergency. Until 1945 they earned 1⅛ per cent interest; in 1946 this was reduced to ⅝ per cent.

Despite their higher earning power in comparison with Treasury bills, Treasury Deposit Receipts were never popular with the banks—partly because they could not be sold freely, partly because they were compulsory and partly, no doubt, because they were an 'artificial' emergency innovation. Nevertheless, by the end of the war they amounted to over £2,000 million and accounted for nearly 40 per cent of the banks' total assets. By 1950, however, most of them had been replaced by Treasury bills whose supply was greatly expanded in the post-war period; in 1952 they were abandoned.

Between June 1940 and June 1945 the banks' discounts of Treasury bills fell by more than half, despite the near doubling of the tender total. The decline was largely explained by the growth of the share in the weekly tenders taken by 'outside' (domestic and foreign) demand. Indeed, the evidence suggests that throughout the 1930s and 1940s the banks were becoming the residual holders of tender Treasury bills, as well as other bills; their share in the Treasury bill total tender fell from between 30 to 40 per cent in the 1930s to less than 10 per cent of tender bills outstanding and less than 4 per cent of the total issue in 1944-45.[50] From June 1945, however, bank holdings of Treasury bills increased rapidly, largely because of, on the one hand, the beginnings of the switch from Treasury Deposit Receipts to Treasury bills and, on the other, the requirements of the 'cheaper money' policy pursued by the authorities during 1946-47. By the end of 1950 bank holdings of Treasury bills had increased to about 20 per cent of deposit liabilities compared with 4 per cent in 1944-45, while holdings of commercial bills amounted to another 2 per cent. At the end of that year, therefore, bank cash stood at 8.2 per cent (8 per cent having become the agreed minimum for cash ratios in 1946), money at call or short notice at 9 per cent and bills discounted at 22.7 per cent. Hence clearing bank liquid assets (excluding TDRs which stood at 7.6 per cent of deposits) amounted to 39.9 per cent of total deposits, compared with 29 per cent at the end of 1938—the last 'normal' year—the chief difference being in the banks' discounts, which in 1950 were double the 1938 figure. In comparison with the pre-war situation, therefore, the banks were excessively liquid and in practice their liquidity had been further increased by the Bank of England's open-back-door policy of rediscounting bills at market rates.

Under such circumstances it was obvious that any worries the banks might have about their liquidity ratios would be far less than their concern for their advances ratio; in 1950, despite the post-war recovery, the latter was still under half its level in the 1920s. For the authorities, on the other hand, the excessive liquidity of the banks seemed likely to frustrate any attempt to return to traditional monetary policy as an instrument for correcting disequilibrium in the economy. The traditional mechanisms of Bank rate and open-market operations had rested upon the constraint of the banks' cash ratios. The advent of the Exchange Equalisation Account, the increase in the supply of Treasury Bills, the greater interchangeability between cash and Treasury bills and the gradual establishment among the London clearing banks of somewhat firmer conventions as to the proportion of assets to be held in the most liquid forms—all these were to lead the Radcliffe Committee to conclude that the liquidity ratio had become more important for credit control than the cash ratio. The process had been permitted and encouraged from the beginning by the readiness of the Bank of England to act as lender of last resort and, on occasion, to absorb surplus cash by selling bills and had been vastly advanced by the introduction of the open-back-door policy. Hence it became clear that a banking system generously endowed with Treasury bills was in a position to ignore customary monetary techniques by simply not renewing holdings of such bills as they matured and using the cash so acquired as a basis for advances.

In order to regain control over the banks' willingness and ability to lend, therefore, the authorities took steps to make a secondary liquidity ratio effective. These occurred in 1951 with the compulsory conversion or funding of a large part of the banks' holdings of Treasury bills into holdings of medium-dated securities with one, two and three years to run to maturity. This automatically increased the ratio of investments in the banks' balance sheets and reduced their liquid assets ratio to 32 per cent, while certain individual ratios fell close to 30 per cent. At the same time an 'informal understanding'—a somewhat euphemistic expression much favoured in the City—had been achieved between the Bank of England and the London clearing banks concerning the observance of a minimum liquidity ratio; the Governor of the Bank of England indicated to the banks that a liquidity ratio of from 32 to 28 per cent would be regarded as normal and that it would be undesirable for the ratio to fall below 25 per cent as an extreme limit.

By the early 1950s, therefore, the somewhat doubtful 30 per cent ratio of the inter-war years had become a minimum acceptable level, a fall below which would bring down on an erring bank the 'remonstrations' of the Governor of the Bank of England, despite the fact that bankers generally considered such a level to be in excess of the normal requirements of banking prudence. The effect was that the banks ran a risk of reducing their liquid assets below the acceptable minimum if, to expand advances, they obtained cash by calling loans from the discount market or by running down their Treasury bills. It seemed to the authorities—and others—that the liquid assets ratio had been made potentially effective.

It must be repeated, however, that liquidity is far from being a rigid concept. It is essentially subjective, a function of prevailing attitudes and expectations of investors rather than inherent in the nature of an asset. To the authorities the measure of bank liquidity had come to be indentified with holdings of 'official' liquid assets—i.e. cash, money at call and short notice and Treasury and other bills shiftable on to the central bank—

although the category continues to be adjusted marginally from time to time so as to include a wide range of assets—for example, some foreign currencies, short-term loans to British (non-clearing) banks as well as to the discount houses, stock-brokers and jobbers, overseas Treasury bills, the banks' own holdings of Tax Reserve Certificates and, after 1961, re-financeable export credits.[51]

To the banks, however, liquidity can be more flexible. From their point of view, liquid assets can comprise not only cash but also a range of other supporting assets which would include not only those already listed—the secondary reserve—but a variety of short bonds and even short-term advances of the self-liquidating kind. Although shiftability on to the central bank remains the hallmark of the liquidity of a banker's assets, to an individual bank liquidity may effectively include assets lacking any such official attribute. Until 1951 short bonds maturing within 12 months had been included among bills discounted by some London clearing banks. Despite their subsequent exclusion as a component of the banks' 'official' liquid assets they remain an attractive asset and one whose liquidity is good enough for the average banker; they are usually marketable speedily and with little risk of loss on the market or at par on maturity.

One effect of the introduction of an official liquidity ratio, therefore, was to force the banks to take more heed of the distribution of their investment portfolios in order to protect themselves from undue restraints imposed by the minimum ratio; the authorities, in turn, were obliged to become more discriminating in their debt policy. A corresponding feature which developed in the years after the Radcliffe Report was the alteration in the composition of the banks' official liquid-asset portfolios owing to the substantial revival in popularity of the commercial bill. The discount market's holdings of commercial bills had grown from relative insignificance during the post-war years and early 1950s until by March 1965 they had become the market's second largest asset after bonds which—especially short-dated stocks—had pre-empted the position held by the Treasury bill for some thirty years. Such bills had always been accepted by the banks as collateral for loans to the market, of course, and bonds were also so accepted after the second World War; both were included in the bank's direct purchases from the market. The cost attraction of commercial bills to prospective borrowers was matched by the willingness of the banks to acquire highly liquid assets acceptable to the Bank of England and less subject to the vagaries of official control. The experience of the post-1951 era was to show, in fact, that the reliance on a rigid secondary ratio implicitly *but not explicitly* based on the supply of Treasury bills took no account of the extent to which the banks might hold—and indeed stimulate the supply of—other assets of comparable liquidity in order to boost their liquidity reserves speedily and without loss. The minimum liquidity ratio, in other words, was to prove a doubtful basis for monetary control precisely because of the vital respect in which it differed from the conventional cash basis—its composition of assets whose supply lay partly within the control of the banks themselves.

REFERENCES

1. *Midland Bank Review*, September, 1934, p. 2.

2. T. Balogh, *Studies in Financial Organisation*, Cambridge University Press, London 1950, Chap. 5, p. 37.
3. *Ibid.*, p. 44.
4. *Ibid.*, p. 45.
5. *Report of the Committee on Finance and Industry* (Macmillan Report), Cmd. 3897 HMSO, London 1931, paras. 79-81, pp. 36-7, and paras. 358-370, pp. 153-161.
6. *Minutes of Evidence*, Macmillan Committee, Qu. 485, Goodenough.
7. *Macmillan Report*, paras. 341-6, pp. 146-7, and para. 368, pp. 156-7.
8. Balogh, *op. cit.*, p. 42.
9. R. J. Truptil, *British Banks and the London Money Market*, Jonathan Cape, London 1936, p. 93.
10. It appears that the practice was continued after the war by some banks, but to a very greatly reduced extent. See E. T. Nevin, 'Window-Dressing in Minor Key', *The Banker*, Vol. CVII, No. 372, January 1957.
11. See also 'The Truth about Cash', *The Banker*, January 1947, and Balogh, *op. cit.*, pp. 45-6.
12. *Macmillan Report*, p. 156.
13. Balogh, *op. cit.*, p. 50.
14. *Ibid.*, p. 49.
15. *Ibid.*, p. 55.
16. *Macmillan Report*, para. 371.
17. *Report of the Committee on the Working of the Monetary system*, 1959 (Radcliffe Report), para. 367.
18. This 'cash or liquidity' debate is discussed further in Chap. 13 below.
19. W. T. C. King, 'Should Liquidity Ratios Be Prescribed?', *The Banker*, Vol. CVI, No. 364, April 1956.
20. W. Bagehot, *Lombard Street*, London 1870, 14th ed., pp. 240-1.
21. G. Rae, *The Country Banker*, London 1885, pp. 211-5.
22. *Midland Bank Review*, February-March 1934, p. 3.
23. Speech of Governor of Bank of England, Lord Mayor's Banquet, 16th Oct. 1963, reported in Bank of England *Quarterly Bulletin*, Vol. III, No. 4, December 1963.
24. W. T. C. King, *The Banker*, January 1952.
25. W. Manning Dacey, *The British Banking Mechanism*, Hutchinson, London 1951, p. 95.
26. *Minutes of Evidence*, Macmillan Committee, Qu. 871.
27. *Macmillan Report*, para. 84, p. 38.
28. Truptil, *op. cit.*, p. 105.
29. W. T. C. King, 'Should Liquidity Ratios be Prescribed?', *The Banker*, April 1936.

30. See, inter alia, *Midland Bank Review*, September 1934 and 1939, and F. W. Paish, 'British Floating Debt Policy', *Economica*, 1940.

31. *Midland Bank Review*, September 1934, p. 2.

32. See discussions in *Bulletin of the Oxford University Institute of Statistics*, Vol. 14, 1952, and W. T. C. King, *The Banker*, Vol. 98, 1952.

33. *Midland Bank Review*, February-March 1934, p. 5.

34. E. T. Nevin, *The Mechanism of Cheap Money*, University of Wales Press, Cardiff 1955, Chap. IV.

35. *Ibid.*

36. H. G. Johnson, 'Clearing bank holdings of public debt, 1930-1950', *London and Cambridge Economic Bulletin*, Vol. 29, No. 4, Nov. 1951, pp. 102-9. Also *Midland Bank Review*, March-April, 1934, p. 5.

37. Johnson, *op. cit.*

38. R. S. Sayers, *Modern Banking*, 7th ed., Oxford University Press, London 1967, Chap 8, pp. 178-81, and Bank of England *Quarterly Bulletin*, Vol. II, No. 4, December 1962.

39. *Midland Bank Review*, February-March 1934, p. 5.

40. E. T. Nevin in 'Monetary Policy Again', *Bulletin of the Oxford University Institute of Statistics*, Vol. 14, August 1952, p. 287-90.

41. W. T. C. King, *The Banker*, January 1952.

42. Nevin, *The Mechanism of Cheap Money*, pp. 128-9.

43. *Ibid.*, p. 130.

44. E. V. Morgan in 'Monetary Policy Again', *Bulletin of the Oxford Institute of Statistics*, Vol. 14, August 1952, pp. 273-7.

45. *Midland Bank Review*, September 1934, p. 2.

46. *The Economist*, July 21st 1934, p. 119.

47. Nevin, *op. cit.*, pp. 155-6. In fact it appears that it was because of pressure upon their cash position that the banks sold investments to make way for advances.

48. Nevin, *op. cit.*, p. 139. See also A. H. Brown, 'The liquidity preference schedules of the London clearing banks', *Oxford Economic Papers* (Old Series), Vol. I, No. 1, October 1938, pp. 49-82 and R. M. Goodwin, 'The supply of bank money in England and Wales, 1920-38', *Ibid.*, No. 5, June 1941, pp. 1-29.

49. Johnson, *op. cit.*, p. 104.

50. *Ibid.*

51. See Bank of England *Quarterly Bulletin*, Vol. II, No. 4, December, 1962.

CHAPTER EIGHT

Investments

1. Bank investment portfolios

While the banks' attitudes towards their advances and liquid assets have long been regarded as more or less unequivocal—being functions of a known demand for profit or liquidity—their attitude towards investments has shown a more uncertain development; it is in this context, indeed, that the banks' dichotomy of interest as between profitability and liquidity is most clearly illustrated. Until 1900 bankers were fortunate in being able to regard their investments as both liquid and profitable; this view had prevailed for a century, if not longer, and was to some extent to linger into the present century. The experience of the twentieth century, however, has been one of considerable shifts in such attitudes; one the one hand, there has been an increasing tendency to regard investments as risk assets liable to significant fluctuation in capital values; on the other hand, it has also been recognised that, when appropriately distributed, they can be valuable supports to a bank's liquidity position.

Long before Bagehot's day the banks had been accustomed to buying negotiable securities. The growth of the market in bills of exchange during the nineteenth century has already been discussed, but apart from this there had always been a keen demand for bonds and stocks of various denominations, ranging from the debt or equity of associated banks to investments in industrial or government securities. Amongst the latter, investment—or rather speculation—in decidedly doubtful railway ventures had been popular in the 1840s, although many of these schemes advanced no further than the drawing boards. 'Stagging' profits, as much as high yields, were the attraction, regardless of the risk involved. Public securities, on the other hand, could include not only the highly respectable Consols but also securities of colonial and overseas governments whose acquisition was frequently something of a gamble.

Foreign stocks had played a prominent part in the financial crisis of 1825 and had also featured noticeably in the Baring crisis of 1890. Of course there were always good stocks, but hard experience contrived to teach the banks the wisdom of caution in their portfolio selection and the virtues of confining themselves to 'old faithfuls'—particularly issues of British government stock—and to the bill of exchange, a highly suitable bank asset. For the riskier side of portfolio investment a specialised knowledge rapidly became essential, given the increasing complexity and sophistication of the markets. The joint-stock banks preferred to concentrate on providing their industrial customers with floating capital by overdraft and loan, leaving other financial agents—amongst them some of their erstwhile private rivals in the City now turned merchant bankers—to concern themselves with raising fixed capital for industry and foreign governments. According to *The Economist Banking Supplement*, in 1890 joint-stock bank investment holdings amounted to £82 million, some 17.8 per cent of their total assets.(1) In the ensuing decade, however, Goschen and Palgrave launched their campaign for increased bank liquidity, a campaign whose progress was advanced by the increase in the supply of commercial bills.

A major factor influencing the policy of the banks was the behaviour of the market and the reversal of the long-term trend in bond prices. The nineteenth-century pattern of long-term interest rates had been one of almost steady decline and consequent capital appreciation; the investor of 1900 would have considered it worthwhile to buy government Funds in spite of their low yield because he was virtually sure of a handsome capital gain. By 1896, however, Consols had in fact reached their all-time high—113⅞—a price which they were not to regain even during the later 1930s and the era of even cheaper money during the later 1940s. Between 1897 and 1920 the price of Consols fell by 70¼ points, or 62 per cent—the largest price decline in their history until 1961—the bulk of the decline occurring in the first decade of the twentieth century. At the same time bill rates, as represented by the open market rate of discount, began to rise, averaging 3.16 per cent for the first decade of the twentieth century compared with only 2.79 per cent on Consols.

It was not surprising, therefore, that in the period just before the first World War, when the supply of commercial bills was approaching what was to prove a peak of £500 million, investment holdings had fallen to 15 per cent of total assets—in absolute terms to £121 million. The big banks, however, had reduced their investment holdings much more.(2) Barclays investment portfolio, which in 1895 amounted to 29.8 per cent of total assets, had fallen to 16.8 per cent in 1913; during the same period, securities held by Lloyds fell from 22.2 to 9.8 per cent of total assets, those of the National and Provincial from 32.8 to 17.5 per cent and of the Midland from 13.6 per cent in 1890 to 7.2 per cent in 1913. (The Westminster, by contrast, had increased its investment holdings from 14.3 per cent of total assets in 1895 to 18.4 per cent in 1913, possibly because it considered its asset structure sufficiently liquid.) For the joint-stock banks as a whole, investments were becoming predominantly holdings of public debt and especially those of the British Government. Despite the decline in capital values, however, the importance of gilt-edged securities to the banks was to increase considerably with the expansion of the national debt in the first World War and in succeeding years, a subject which is the main concern of this chapter.

In the period with which the present discussion is mainly concerned, from 1920 to the 1950s, 'Investments' comprised British government and government guaranteed securities as well as 'other securities', the latter being almost exclusively those of Dominion and Colonial Governments, British public boards and municipal corporations. 'Trade Investments' would also be included, although both these and 'other securities' varied over the period between 9.8 and 3.7 per cent of the total, standing at about 5.3 per cent of total investments at the end of 1950.(3) Their total was insignificant, therefore, in relation to British government and government-guaranteed securities. Other public debt holdings of the banks were, of course, Treasury bills and, during and immediately after the second World War, Treasury Deposit Receipts. Unofficial estimates of direct bank holdings inevitably under-emphasise the extent of the change in the importance of public debt in bank assets, since banks also lend to financial institutions which use their funds to acquire holdings of public debt.(4) Thus 'money at call and short notice', nominally representing short-term loans to the discount market and members of the stock exchange, contains a significant addition to (indirect) bank lending to the government arising from the replacement of the trade bill by its government counterpart. As well as the greatly increased proportion of Treasury Bills in the total supply of bills, short-term gilt-edged securities began to find a market with the discount houses in the immediate pre-war years and dealings in gilt-edged were also featuring to an increasing extent on the Stock Exchange. It is probable, in fact, that over most of this period money at call and short notice consisted almost entirely of indirect holdings of government debt. The banks' cash reserves also represent indirect holdings of public debt, of course, since they comprise liabilities of the Bank of England which in turn are secured almost exclusively by holdings of public debt. Taken all in all, by 1950 the banks' total holdings of government debt, direct and indirect, probably amounted to about two-thirds of total bank deposits.

This chapter is primarily concerned with gilt-edged investments, although the significance of the Treasury bill in Government debt policy and administration is vital for an understanding of the banks' attitude towards their gilt-edged investments. At this stage, therefore, it is important to say something about the growth of the national debt; changes in its nature and volume, together with independent changes in the volume of commercial bills as well as advances, were to shape the investment policy of the banks.

2. The growth of the national debt

The extraordinary growth of the national debt may be seen from Table 3. At the beginning of the century its nominal value was just under £640 million, of which over £500 million was in $2\frac{3}{4}$ per cent Consols and a mere £16 million in Treasury bills. On the eve of the first World War it had grown to somewhat over £700 million. Consols were then being quoted well below par; the debt's market value was in fact only about £500 million. Some £180 million of the nominal debt was held by government departments, including the savings banks, while the commercial banks, including Scottish and Irish banks, held £190 million at their own balance-sheet valuation. Of the remainder, persons and institutions other than banks accounted for something over £250 million nominal, or somewhat less than £200 million at current market prices.

As may be seen from Table 3, the first World War increased the nominal value of the debt by nearly ten times; by March 1925 it amounted to £6,525 million. Of this, approximately £740 million consisted of floating debt, with a further £1,020 million maturing within five years. Long-term securities, on the other hand, included £3,500 million with final redemption dates more than twenty years ahead. As regards the distribution of the debt, government departments (including the Currency Notes Redemption Account and the Savings Banks) now held about £1,000 million, while the holdings of the Bank of England, the commercial banks and the discount market had increased to approximately £750 million. Further, there had been a remarkable increase in the popularity of government securities among both individuals and institutions.

The introduction of cheap money in 1932 was accompanied by important changes in the structure of the debt and in its management but there was comparatively little change in its total volume. The second World War,

TABLE 3

The structure of the UK National Debt, 1900-1968

(£ million as at March 31st each year)

	1900	1914	1918	1928	1938	1948	1958	1968
1. Floating debt	16	13	1,166	689	842	6,542	4,848	5,732
2. Quoted securities with a maximum life of:								
i. less than 5 years	—	21	376	570	100	2,023	3,773	6,699
ii. 5 to 15 years	—	—	733	396	972	2,160	4,971	3,496
iii. 15 to 25 years	—	6	52	2,406	614	3,093	1,818	3,814
iv. Over 25 years	—	—	2,054	728	817	1,361	971	2,522
3. Redeemable only by government option	539	573	304	1,336	3,351	3,888	3,755	3,559
4. Other internal debt	84	93	241	493	539	5,253	5,257	6,070
5. External debt	—	—	995	1,095	1,032	1,555	2,163	2,301
TOTAL	639	706	5,921	7,714	8,267	25,874	27,556	34,193

Source: 1900-58, Pember and Boyle, *British Government Securities in the Twentieth Century,* 2nd edition, London, June 1950 and Supplements, October 1952-August 1963. 1968: *Annual Abstract of Statistics* No. 105, HMSO, London 1968, Table 318. Figures for this last year are not strictly comparable with those for earlier years since they exclude bonds tendered for death duties and held by the National Debt Commissioners. Small discrepancies in totals due to rounding.

however, brought a four-fold increase in the debt, so that its nominal value was nearly £26,000 million in 1948. Ten years later, in March 1958, it stood at £27,556 million, of which over £15,000 million represented securities quoted on the London Stock Exchange. Government departmental holdings had risen to something over £3,500 million, the (now nationalised) Bank of England held over £2,000 million and an unknown amount—probably several thousand million—was held by foreign persons or institutions.

The floating debt had been reduced during the1920s, with difficulty, to under 8 per cent of the total internal debt by 1931/32; as a result of the second World War, however, it rose to 27 per cent of the internal debt in 1945/46 and by 1952/55 was holding fairly steady at about 18 per cent. The share of total interest payments accounted for by the floating debt rose from less than 3 to nearly 18 per cent of total charges over the course of the first World War and the second World War witnessed a similar rise from less than 2 per cent to 13 per cent of the total. Until 1952 well over half the interest payments on the floating debt accrued to official or banking holders. The major change was the increase in the share going to the government itself, from less than 20 per cent of the total in 1930-31 to 30 per cent in 1951-2.(5) The share of the banking system was largely unchanged between 1930 and 1950 at about a third of the total, although the funding operation of November 1951 was responsible for a sharp decline in 1951-52. As regards the rest of the debt, the 'under 3 year' and '3 to 10 year' securities—the investments in which the banking system is today mainly interested—comprised about 9 per cent of the total capital value in 1929, fell to less than 6 per cent in 1933 and by the mid-1950s were running at about 19 per cent. Undated stocks and dated stocks with more than twenty years to final redemption date formed 28 per cent of the debt in 1929, rose to as much as 55 per cent in the middle 1930s but by the mid-1950s had fallen to about 20 per cent. A single issue—five per cent War Loan—amounted to £2,000 million of the quoted debt during the 1920s; until its conversion to a 3½ per cent coupon in 1932 it represented a severe burden to the Exchequer as well as a check to a policy of cheap money.

The effects of the scarcity of short-term assets in the 1930s upon the banks' investment policies have already been noted; later in the course of this chapter, however, it will be relevant to examine more fully the extent to which the scarcity of short-term assets—bills and bonds of less than ten years' maturity—obliged the banks to commit themselves in the 1930s to investment in the longer-dated stocks.

3. The banks and the national debt

The financing of the first World War encouraged a speedy expansion of bank investments, both absolutely and relatively, as the banks were called upon to guarantee the success of the war loans, both by direct purchases on their own part and by lending to customers for the same purpose. By 1918, aggregate bank investments, amounting to nearly £350 million, had increased to form 22 per cent of their total assets. After the war, funding operations initiated by the Treasury in an attempt to reduce the volume of the floating debt appear to have been responsible for an increase in aggregate bank investments from an average of around 18 per cent of total assets in 1921 to a maximum of 23 per cent in August 1922. The supply of commercial bills, on the other hand, had not kept pace with the expansion of bank deposits. After a serious collapse in the course of the war to less than £300 million in 1917-18, the commercial bill circulation in London did not expand—even in the post-war boom of 1920-1—to more than a little over £600 million, an increase of 20 per cent over the £500 million of 1913 compared with a 100 per cent expansion of bank deposit liabilities over the same period.

The supply of Treasury Bills, however, had increased enormously—to as much as £1,200 million in June 1921. In subsequent years the action of the Treasury in reducing the total volume of Treasury bills outstanding depressed the banks' bill portfolios, increasingly dependent as they now were on the supply of Treasury bills. It was in fact no longer possible for the banks to rely upon commercial bills to increase the ratio of their 'quick' or liquid assets, especially as the demand for bills outside the clearing bank system had increased sharply. Moreover, with the collapse of the post-war inflation in 1922 not only was the supply of commercial bills reduced but the level of bank advances fell in addition, the annual average falling from £833 million in 1921 to £750 million in 1922. As a consequence of this, when Treasury funding operations caused bank bill holdings to be reduced, contrary to the usual seasonal pattern, by more than £50 million between March and August of 1922, the banks were able to offset this fall only by buying securities.

In subsequent years the gradual recovery of the economy enabled the banks to expand their advances from £750 million in 1922 to £991 million in 1929, a process which was financed to a substantial degree by a fall of some £130 million in investments as the banks appear to have felt that they could not much reduce their liquid assets. (In fact, as will be seen, clearing bank investments are largely a residual dependent upon the demand for advances on the one hand and their liquidity position on the other.) The turn of the decade and the spread of the world depression to Britain brought a halt to the liquidation of bank investments, since the purchase of gilt-edged securities then provided the only major outlet for bank funds. Treasury funding operations further reduced the volume of floating debt outstanding, thereby restricting one of the safest and most convenient outlets for banking funds at a time when trade depression was considerably reducing the volume of advances and commercial bills. The decisive change in the bankers' attitude to investments occurred after Britain went off the gold standard.(6) Primarily as a means of reducing the level of budgetary expenditure, the Treasury and the Bank of England reserve of the banking system was increased rapidly to ensure the success of the operation. From a low of about £170 million in February 1932, bank cash rose to £188 million in June and £203 million in December 1932. The continuing bill shortage meant that expansion through this type of asset was impossible, while an expansion of advances was not only difficult at the time but also appeared a highly unlikely prospect for the foreseeable future. When Bank of England open-market operations increased their cash reserves, therefore, the banks were obliged to increase their investment portfolio to make any sort of profit at all.(7)

An expansion of approximately £60 million in bank holdings of government and government-guaranteed securities in the first half of 1932, stimulated by the increase in the cash base of the banking system and the simultaneous decline in advances, contributed to the buoyancy in the gilt-edged market which made the 5 per cent War Loan Conversion feasible.(8) By June 1933 the banks had expanded their holdings of gilt-edged securities by over £200 million, a signal contribution to the success of the conversion operation. By 1935, the clearing banks, through their own direct holdings of national debt (including their Treasury Bills) together with indirect financing of purchases of government debt through call money and advances, were effectively lending to the government around 50 per cent of their deposits. Already concern was being expressed that banking was taking on more of the nature of an investment business. After the War Loan conversion operation, the reduction in interest rates created by it was itself elevated into a 'policy' of cheap money aimed at economic recovery rather than mere budgetary relief. Under the influence of this policy, and of the contracted demand for advances, the banks' holdings continued to expand until December 1936, although more slowly and with some checks. One of these, in the first half of 1934, was due to the banks' caution in the face of high gilt-edged prices and their own heavy commitment; another, in the second half of 1935, was due to the alternative opportunities offered by an increase in 'tender' Treasury bills.(9) From December 1936 until June 1939 the banks' gilt-edged holdings declined gradually with the recovery of business and an increasing demand for advances, reflecting also the influence of fluctuations in the supply of Treasury bills and the working of the 'secondary liquidity' factor. It is probable that this decline was partly responsible for the gradual retreat from the 'cheap money' level of gilt-edged prices.

The increase in bank holdings of gilt-edged over the period 1931-39 was largely the effect (and part of the mechanism) of cheap money; it was also in part a logical corollary of official debt funding policy, the increased holdings of gilt-edged replacing the decreased holdings of Treasury bills. Behind this overall increase in the banks' share of total gilt-edged securities lay an important shift in the attitude of the banks towards their investments. Aggregate bank investment holdings had risen from £264 million in February 1932 to an average of £615 million in 1935. An increase of this magnitude, almost entirely in the form of gilt-edged securities, was accompanied by and responsible for a significant development in the standing of securities in the eyes of the banks, a process carried still further by the experience of the gilt-edged market after the second World War.

General, and even complacent, confidence in the safety of government stocks had been rudely shaken by the collapse of the gilt-edged market at the time of the Boer War, but with the recovery of the market after 1920 it seemed that this confidence had been largely restored. By the time of the Macmillan Committee bank opinion seems to have held investments to be nearly as liquid as bills, although this view was no doubt subject to periodic revision by the banks depending on market outlook. The marked expansion of the banks' investment portfolios during the 1930s, however, raised their gilt-edged holdings to a level where a separate element of liquidity—the freedom from risk of fluctuation in capital values—was as vital a concern as ready convertibility into cash. Although government securities were theoretically still highly marketable assets, the banks now held so considerable a share of the quoted national debt—and particularly of its long-term stocks—that the sale of any appreciable percentage of their holding could be undertaken only with difficulty and with the near-certainty of engendering a substantial drop in their capital value.

Between 1932 and 1935 the banks bought investments at prices ranging between 13 and 30 per cent over those which they had paid in 1931. If prices had fallen back to the 1931 level, and if the banks had been obliged to dispose of their newly-acquired investments, or to write down their capital values, they could have been faced with a loss of some £70 million, a far greater amount than they would have needed to find in a slump if the increase in assets had taken the form of loans and advances.[10] Some indication of the risks of price fluctuation is afforded by $2\frac{1}{2}$ per cent Consols; these stood at $54\frac{1}{2}$ at the end of 1928, had risen above 94 in January 1933 but had fallen to $77\frac{1}{2}$ in February 1937. The 1931-2 fall in the gilt-edged market had required the clearing banks to write off over £9 million out of their published reserves in order to meet part of the depreciation of about £15 million in the value of their investments. Although these reserves were gradually replenished between 1932 and 1935, they were still £3 million less at the end of that year than they had been in 1931.[11] As a result, from about 1934 investments were increasingly regarded as 'risk assets' along with advances, and the 'secondary' liquidity reserve became a significant factor in influencing bank investment policy. In other words, the important risk to a banker was ceasing to be the risk of default on debts and was becoming instead the risk of a rise in the market rate of interest and the resulting book-losses on the capital value of gilt-edged holdings.[12] Capital risks, rather than credit risks, had become of major concern to bankers; for them the continuance of cheap money and the stabilisation of the gilt-edged market by official intervention had become very much a matter of interest.[13]

It can be argued that the danger of capital loss was no more than a 'paper tiger'; there could be no *real* loss unless the banks had to realise securities before maturity and were thus forced to take a lower price for them than that originally paid.[14] Certainly in the phase of excessive endowment with Treasury Bills and an increased supply of short-dated bonds the banks possessed more than enough liquidity to enable them to hold securities until maturity. On the other hand, throughout the 1930s—as in more recent years—periods occurred when the banks were not excessively liquid and, as in the years of the bill famine or the late 1950s, felt obliged to sell investments either to restore liquidity (or cash) ratios or to expand advances, the source of greatest profit. Funding operations, moreover—especially if undertaken on the scale experienced in 1951—could not only mop up surplus bank liquidity but could oblige the banking sector to run a risk of real loss if they were forced to sell securities to maintain liquidity.

Of obvious importance here is the question of whether the banks could afford to hold securities until maturity, especially in periods such as the 1930s when they were far from possessing surplus liquidity. Essentially this depends on the distribution of their investment portfolios, and unfortunately information on this subject is very scant. It was not until the early 1950s that the 'Big Five' clearing banks began to give some indication of the composition of their investment portfolios in their bi-annual statements. Previously information had been given, if at all, only in the chairmen's annual speeches. All the evidence suggests, however, that the pre-war distribution of bank securities was distinctly longer than that known to exist after the war. A plausible assumption seems to be that for the years 1930 to 1938 the banks held 10 per cent of their portfolios in securities maturing within five years, 60 per cent in securities having a life of between five and fifteen years and 30 per cent in securities having a life of fifteen to twenty-five years.[15] It would be well to include in the latter proportion a certain percentage of undated stocks.

4. Official funding operations

As has been noted, fluctuations in the supply of Treasury bills, together with the decline in commercial bills and advances, had seriously reduced the volume of short-term assets available to the banks. At the same time, although investment in gilt-edged securities remained open to them, the range of securities available was itself curtailed by the effects of official funding operations. Of these by far the most important was the 1932 conversion of the 5 per cent War Loan.[16] On 30th June 1932 the Chancellor of the Exchequer announced that 5 per cent War Loan, 1929-47, was to be repaid between then and December 1st and replaced by a 3½ per cent War Loan repayable at the option of the government in or after 1952. This was by far the largest conversion operation in the history of the National Debt; the outstanding War Loan at the end of March 1932 amounted to £2,085 million, comprising 27 per cent of the total debt and 38 per cent of the British Government securities quoted on the London Stock Exchange. A significant reduction in the long-term gilt-edged rate was impossible so long as War Loan remained outstanding on a 5 per cent basis and the whole operation was therefore of first importance if interest rates generally were to be reduced. Conversion was required, however, rather than cash repayment, and in order to attain this end holders of 5 per cent War Loan were encouraged by a bonus of £1 for every £100 exchanged to take their capital repayment in the form of the new 3½ per cent stock. In the event no less than £1,921 million, or 92 per cent of the old War Loan, was converted into the new 3½ per cent security; only £164 million was repaid in cash.

Crucial to the success of the operation was the state of business and financial confidence. Current opinion in these circles expected interest rates to fall as a result of the trade depression, the general view, as expressed by one observer, being that 'with industry depressed, money which would otherwise be required for trade purposes must be steadily diverted into gilt-edged'.[17] A further element during the first half of 1932 had been the improvement in both domestic and foreign confidence in the soundness and stability of the pound sterling. By the eve of the conversion announcement the gilt-edged market had been bid up to something very like a 3½ per cent basis under the impact of various psychological but highly practical considerations. Even before the conversion announcement security prices were standing at levels such that 5 per cent was obtainable only by moving into securities whose credit-rating was distinctly below that of government securities. Within a week of the announcement such a yield was rare even among high-class industrial securities and unobtainable on fixed-interest industrial debentures.[18] After adjustment for the greater uncertainty attending expectations as to future earnings on private sector assets, most investors, the banks included, had little choice but to take up the conversion offer. The new War Loan, giving a return of 3½ per cent per annum for more than twenty years, was the best investment of its kind available at that time.[19]

For the banks, as for other investors, therefore, the result of the official policy of the 1930s was a contraction in the supply of liquid assets and a lengthening of the average life of available gilt-edged securities, despite the increase in the nominal value of the gold reserves and the concomitant rise in the demand for liquid assets. In 1930-1, 32 per cent of the total national debt had taken the form of securities of over 25 years; by 1938-9 the proportion in the over-25 year range had risen to 40 per cent.(20) Throughout the decade, therefore, the gilt-edged securities in which the banking system could be said to be primarily interested—those of under 15 years' maturity—never comprised more than 13 per cent of the total national debt, and even this figure included a proportion of securities which modern bankers would view with decided distrust. As a result of three separate funding loans by the Government between March 1932 and March 1938, the outstanding volume of short-term securities—i.e. those having a maximum life of five years—fell from £494 million to £100 million. By 1938, therefore, even if the banks had held every such security in existence, they could not have held more than 17 per cent of their total investment portfolio in this form,(21) whereas by 1950 the banks were probably holding about 40 per cent of their portfolios in securities maturing within five years.

The effect of government policy in the 1930s, therefore, was not only to reduce the supply of tender Treasury bills but also that of securities which were a reasonably close substitute for them.(22) The scope of the banks' ability to keep short was thus highly restricted, while on the other hand there was no shortage of long-term bonds. Under such circumstances, it was hardly surprising that the banks committed themselves to the longer and riskier end of the gilt-edged market. In so doing, naturally enough, they appear to have become increasingly conscious of the importance of their overall liquidity position, viewing their liquid assets not only as a buffer to their existing reserves but as a guarantee of some freedom of manoeuvre. The banks' share of gilt-edged securities, expressed as a percentage of the total outstanding at year-ends, rose from just under 4.4 to 7.3 per cent during 1932; it increased further to a peak of 9.5 per cent at the end of 1936, subsequently declining to just under 8.5 per cent at the end of 1939.

The outbreak of war accentuated these trends sharply, and the wartime period is, in this context, no more than a continuance of the cheap money era ushered in during 1932. By the end of 1941, however, the share of the banking system in the gilt-edged market had climbed back to a peak of almost 11.4 per cent, falling back under 9.3 per cent at the end of 1945. The banks' security holdings more than doubled in absolute terms between 1939 and 1946 under the combined impact of the wartime cheap money policy, the fiscal needs of the government and the severe wartime contraction of advances to the private sector. In the first wartime year the relatively small increase of bank investments suggest that the banks played little part in supporting the market during the brief period of official minimum prices for gilt-edged stocks while the slackening of the rate of growth in them during 1943 and 1944 reflected the improving efficiency of war finance and controls. Bank gilt-edged holdings in fact fell sharply throughout 1944 and the first half of 1945 as a result of the urge to increase liquidity, the banks being unwilling to reduce their small discount portfolios.(23)

5. Postwar monetary policy

In 1945-46 gilt-edged prices rose sharply as a result of the end of hostilities and of the announced policy of the new Labour government to force down the long-term market rate of interest even further. Although the rising bond prices instigated by the Chancellor of the Exchequer, Dr Dalton, in 1946 were not altogether to the liking of City opinion, Consols were forced up from $81\frac{1}{2}$—a yield basis of 3.06 per cent—in 1945 to a high of $99\frac{5}{8}$ (or 2.51 per cent); they had not reached par since 1900 and did not quite do so in 1946. The government floated a new issue of $2\frac{1}{2}$ per cent undated Treasury stock (henceforth known as 'Daltons') which the Chancellor held to be preferable to Consols because they could not be redeemed until 1975. Between June 1945 and June 1947 estimated gilt-edged holdings by the banks show an increase of about a third; this reflects the boost to existing portfolio values arising from the rise in long-term gilt-edged prices as well as the increased purchases of such stock 'forced' upon the banks.

The increase was less striking, however, when expressed as a share of total outstanding gilt-edged securities or as a percentage of total bank deposits; in neither respect does it compare with that experienced in 1931-2 or even 1939-41. In June 1945, bank holdings of British Government and Government guaranteed securities had amounted to £1,067 million; a year later they had risen to £1,316 million, although it is uncertain to what extent these figures understate the actual increase in market value of portfolios because of the banks' practice of valuing securities at whichever is the lower of purchase price or market price. By June 1947 the banks' gilt-edged goldings had risen to £1,401 million, although it was evident that the banks were becoming increasingly cautious in the face of rising bond prices and the general market suspicion of Daltonian policy. Just as other investors increased their speculative holdings of cash throughout 1946-47 so the banks' own operation of the speculative motive may be partly responsible for their increased holdings of Treasury bills in this period.

The Dalton experiment of ultra-cheap money through a combination of large-scale official purchases of gilt-edged, expansion of bank deposits and what can only be described as official ballyhoo collapsed at the end of 1947 as a result of increasing and invincible public scepticism concerning its chances of permanent success in the face of postwar recovery. From 1948 onwards a long-term decline began in the gilt-edged market, although the continuing formal policy of cheap money was reflected in low short-term rates and sporadic attempts by the authorities to support the gilt-edged market. Notable amongst the latter was the intervention of the Government broker in November 1949. The long-term market in government securities was in a demoralised state when on November 11th the government broker entered the floor of the stock exchange and enquired of the jobbers the price at which they would sell long-term gilt-edged. It appears that not much stock was bought, but the action was nevertheless enough to revive market morale and temporarily check the fall in gilt-edged prices.

In general, however, government bonds were of declining interest to postwar investors—the banks included—particularly without the attraction of either potential capital gains or the high yields enjoyed after the first World War. After the abandonment of Daltonian cheap money, Consols declined further to around 65 to yield 3.84 per cent. Although there was some recovery in 1950 and 1951, by the latter year Consols were down to a little over 60, to yield 4.16 per cent. It is evident that both the collapse of the Daltonian market and the fall of the pound sterling in 1949 had hit the banks hard, although to an extent which it is only possible to conjecture. As a result of the Dalton experiment, bank holdings of gilt-edged had increased to 10.8 per cent of the total outstanding at the end of 1947 but they had fallen to just over 9.6 per cent at the end of 1950. As a percentage of total deposits bank investments had risen to about 26 per cent during 1946 but thereafter declined slightly to maintain a level of about 25 per cent until the funding operations of 1951-2.

The postwar changes had been strongly influenced by, amongst other factors, the growth of the gilt-edged market resulting from the various nationalisation issues, the switch from Treasury Deposit Receipts to Treasury bills and the reviving demand for bank advances. It would not have been unnatural to have expected a much greater contraction in the ratio of bank investments to deposits, given the dismal experience of the post-war gilt-edged market. It must be remembered, however, that although the falls in security prices, and particularly in those of long-term stocks, implied substantial paper losses for the banks, these losses were actually realised only to the extent that the banks sold securities. There was therefore an incentive to the banks to hold on to their longer-dated securities at times when their prices were weak. In any event, the banks were obliged to look to their investments in order to make up their profits, given the fact that the postwar recovery in advances showed no signs of approaching the proportions of the 1920s and, in addition, that the yield on Treasury bills and Treasury Deposit Receipts was barely above ½ per cent.

The revival of monetary orthodoxy from November 1951 was marked by the re-introduction—at least in theory—of a penal Bank Rate and by the large-scale funding operation by the authorities to which reference was made in the previous chapter. These changes heaped a new and larger depreciation of gilt-edged on to the not inconsiderable fall which had occurred in the preceding years, creating an immediate and large impact on the market value of the banks' investment portfolios. Over 1951 as a whole the longest-dated stocks had shown falls of fully 18 per cent, a fall experienced by 'Daltons' although not by Consols. In general, stocks with a maximum life of more than ten years at the year-end showed losses of 9 to 14 per cent, although it should be noted that most of these stocks had in fact a maximum life of at least fifteen years. The shortest stocks—those having a maturity of three years or under—fell by 2 per cent or less.

A natural consequence of these sharp movements was the fear that the banks might be unable to provide out of their inner reserves the whole amount required to write down their portfolios to market value, since bank reserves were known to have been seriously depleted by the decline of the gilt-edged market in 1949. Under these circumstances there was some expectation that the banks would follow the precedent of 1931, when almost all the big banks made good the depreciation in their investments partly by transferring substantial sums from published reserves. Before the funding operation of 1951 the aggregate investments of the clearing banks stood at £1,555 million, so that an average fall of no more than one per cent would have represented over £15 million. The secrecy maintained by the banks concerning their portfolio distributions made it impossible to be precise about the actual fall in their market value. According to *The Banker* it was unlikely to have approached five per cent in any bank while, on the other hand, it would have required a very cautious policy 'pursued over a lengthy period' to have held it below 3 per cent.[24] The aggregate book loss, according to Lloyd's Chairman, 'must have amounted to tens of millions'. Even so, in the event the banks were able to avoid transfers from their published reserves, although in that year they all returned the whole of their undiminished profits to inner reserves under the heading of 'contingencies', most of them augmenting these transfers by running down the profit balance carried forward.

The fact that the banks were able to avoid drafts on published reserves in this way reflects not only their internal strength but also the increasing caution which had been observed in their investment policies. Nor should it be forgotten that the funding operations, while reducing liquidity and threatening bank reserves, also increased the proportion of the more remunerative assets in the overall asset-structure of the banks; together with higher rates on advances, this increased bank profits so that they could better afford to write down book losses. The interest cost of their deposits rose to a lesser degree, of course, owing to the substantial proportion of interest-free current accounts. Nevertheless it is evident that, even without the experience of the massive funding operations of 1951-2, the lessons of 1947 and 1949 had been well learnt; the banks had been losing no opportunity to shorten the average life of their portfolios. Adverse market experiences, coupled with a reviving demand for advances and an ample supply of bills and short-term bonds, were combining to lessen the banks' interest in long-dated gilt-edged and the experience of 1951-2 was the last straw.

The speeches of the bank chairmen suggest that by 1952-3 the banks were well on the way to the successful completion of their efforts to sell or redeem the longest of their securities and to switch into relatively short-term stock. Their statements imply that maturities of five years or under had probably come to represent at least 50 per cent of the banks' holdings of gilt-edged, the remainder consisting of ten- or perhaps fifteen-year maturities. According to the Radcliffe Report, the joint-stock banks and the accepting houses had 'without any evident discomfort' held as much in the over-five-year bracket as in the under-five-year bracket, although as regards the former category the Committee noted that the banks confined themselves mostly to ten-year maturities.[25]

6. The attitude to gilt-edged

The banks' ability to switch into short-term securities had arisen from the tendency in the postwar period towards a shorter maturity in the quoted national debt. The war-time demand for debt had been entirely abnormal: it was in the main a demand for assets which would be quickly available for conversion into spending-power after the war. In going out to meet that demand as fully as possible—in the sense of providing debt issues in the short-term forms most wanted—the authorities were able to channel the flow of war finance without compromising their policy of maintaining low interest rates. This necessarily implied a heavy succession of post-war maturities and necessarily added to the opportunities available to the banks—as indeed to the general public—to increase their liquidity by not renewing maturing bonds or by switching into shorter stocks.

After the end of the war the nature of the demand for the national debt inevitably changed. Many holders—and particularly the banks—began to attach importance to the option to sell securities without appreciable loss at almost any time, whereas traditionally it had been more usual for the banks to hold securities until maturity. This change in the demand for debt was satisfied by the increased availability of short-term securities, meeting the banks' preference for bonds which could be marketed at any time without great capital loss—exemplified by the slight falls of 2 per cent or less sustained on stock of under three years' maturity at the end of 1951—a safeguard which could be maximised by holding a portfolio with a range of maturities evenly spread over a period of, say, ten years or less. The penalty restraints on the liquidity of gilt-edged, in other words, were far less in the case of short-dated stock—conventionally taken to mean those maturing within five years; the shorter the time to maturity the less the loss sustained if a bank did sell and, conversely, the less any delay in regaining its face value through maturity. Moreover, the liquidity of the banking system had been considerably increased by the growth of the market in short-term bonds and through the official recognition, by both the Bank of England and the commercial banks, of the eligibility of such bonds as collateral against loans to the discount market.

This shift in the banks' attitudes reflected not only a changing market outlook but also a reaction to the introduction of an official minimum liquidity ratio—and especially the relatively high level of 30 per cent required from 1957. Historically, the concept of adequacy in liquidity reserves had evolved informally as a matter of banking prudence. When a minimum secondary ratio became, by official request, as vital a line of defence as the old cash ratio, it inevitably implied a need for the banks to support their liquidity ratios by some additional buffer, just as their liquid assets had traditionally reinforced their cash ratio. The only alternative to the sacrifice of income involved in increased holdings of bills, call money or cash was the resort to skilled investment management. The ease with which the banks could relieve pressure on their liquidity ratios in the short run, in other words, was governed largely by the extent and maturity of their security holdings and, in particular, by their holdings of stocks with maturities of five years or less.

As long as the banks have a steady and substantial annual stream of maturities in their bond portfolios, no normal manipulation of interest rates can impose a penalty on banks wishing to achieve a gradual expansion of advances by running down investments. Suppose that a bank's investments amount to 35 per cent of its total deposits, and its advances to around 25 per cent of deposits, proportions which in fact obtained for the clearing banks as a whole during 1954. If its portfolio contains securities of approximately half this amount in evenly-staggered maturities within a five-year range, it can count on redeeming some $3\frac{1}{2}$ per cent of its investments each year at no capital loss whatever; it could therefore use the cash so obtained to permit an increase of the order of 10 per cent a year in its advances. The practical application of such a policy would obviously depend on the demand for advances—and in the event of interest-rate action by the authorities, on a price-inelastic demand at that—as well as a possible official resort to other controls. Furthermore, no bank would wish to 'denude itself entirely of the nearest maturities'; a rapid and sustained expansion of advances would thus imply that the banks would also seek to unload some of their longer stocks, which would necessarily bring them within the scope of interest rate action by the authorities. Nonetheless the distribution of bank investments throughout the 1950s—and particularly the large proportion of holdings of short bonds which acted as a substantial cushion to the restraints which the authorities sought to impose through the minimum liquidity ratio—clearly militated against the effectiveness of conventional measures of control by the monetary authorities.

In other words, the 'Roosa effect'—that is, the 'locking-in' of banks as a result of a decline in the market value of securities which prevents sales of securities to finance advances—could hardly be said to have been acting as a deterrent, at least for the London clearing banks in the late 1950s. The fact that by then the banks were holding relatively short maturities, and these 'in echelon', meant that they could not only count on a considerable proportion of their securities maturing each year, but could contemplate selling beyond this in order to meet an expanding demand for advances, as in 1958 onwards; the possible loss in capital values was certainly smaller than would have been sustained on longer stocks. Moreover, since the banks are classed as 'dealers' in securities, capital gains and losses are treated as income for tax purposes; consequently, all losses on sales of gilt-edged would be automatically reduced by about a half.

After 1958 the banks sold investments on a large scale in order to finance an increase in advances of nearly £1, 500 million between 1958 and 1961. Over these years they sold off more than a half of their total investments, bringing the investment ratio down from 32 to 15 per cent, at the same time correspondingly raising their advances ratio to 45 per cent. This had the effect of restoring a distribution of bank assets essentially similar to that of the early 1920s, and of reducing the investment ratio to a level close to the (apparently) minimum level acceptable to the banks. Although in this respect no rigid conventions seem to apply, a certain level of investments is as important to the banks as the liquidity ratio itself. It is probable that the banks would be reluctant to see their investment ratios fall much below 10 per cent of total deposits, depending, of course, on the relative proportions of their assets as well as on other factors. This in itself puts a finite, if undefined, limit on the extent to which investments and advances can be substituted for one another. Other things being equal, this approach to a minimum level would have brought the banks within the scope of market operations by the authorities. In the event, however, other things never are equal; in particular, the ability of the authorities to manipulate the gilt-edged market decisively in support of monetary policy has been continuously compromised in recent years by the continued growth of the national debt and by the conflicting conviction, on the official side, of the existence of a need to maintain a stable market in order to maintain the demand for government paper. This is an issue to which the discussion will need to revert in a later chapter.

REFERENCES

1. *The Economist Banking Supplement,* 1890.
2. T. Balogh, *Studies in Financial Organisation,* Cambridge University Press, London 1950, p. 71.
3. H. G. Johnson, 'Some implications of secular changes in bank assets and liabilities in Great Britain', *Economic Journal,* Vol. LXI, No. 2431, September 1951, p. 548.
4. *Ibid.*

5. E.T.Nevin, *The Problem of the National Debt,* University of Wales Press, Cardiff 1954, p. 39.

6. Balogh, *op. cit.,* p. 63.

7. *Ibid.,* p. 72.

8. H.G.Johnson, 'Clearing bank holdings of public debt, 1930-1950', *London and Cambridge Economic Service Bulletin,* Vol. 29, No. 4, November 1951, p. 106.

9. *Ibid.*

10. E.B.Ellinger, *The City,* P.S.King, London 1940, p. 162.

11. *Ibid.*

12. Johnson, 'Some implications of secular changes', etc... *op. cit.,* pp. 550-551.

13. *Ibid.*

14. *Ibid.*

15. Nevin, *op. cit.,* p. 47.

16. E.T.Nevin, *The Mechanism of Cheap Money,* p. 99.

17. *Investors' Chronicle,* 14th May 1932, p. 94.

18. Nevin, *The Mechanism of Cheap Money,* p. 99.

19. *Ibid.*

20. Nevin, *The Problem of the National Debt,* p. 43.

21. *Ibid.,* p. 47.

22. Nevin, *The Mechanism of Cheap Money,* p. 147.

23. Johnson, 'Clearing bank holdings of public debt, 1930-50', *op. cit.,* p. 106.

24. See 'The Banks and their reserves', *The Banker,* August 1952, pp. 65-76.

25. *Report of the Committee on the Working of the Monetary System,* Cmd 827, HMSO, London 1959, paras. 542, 548.

CHAPTER NINE

Advances

1. The pattern and supply of bank lending

Of the several ways in which the banks employ the deposits of their customers their advances, in the form of loans and overdrafts, undoubtedly constitute the item in the banks' business which attracts the greatest public attention. It is to advances that the banker looks for his highest rate of profit and it is in connection with them that he has on occasion to meet the strongest competition of rivals. Indirectly these assets are also important to the banks because of the possibility that an overdraft in case of need may help to attract depositors into the bank. The banks are naturally aware of this and out of concern for the goodwill of their customers, as well as for their own profits, they try to arrange their other assets so that they will always be able to accommodate reasonable demands for bank finance. Within the framework of monetary control, also, advances are endowed with the highest significance since for most companies and individuals bank loans are the most accessible and convenient form of borrowing. Regulation of bank advances, whether it takes the form of mandatory restraints upon supply or of deterrents to demand, may thus have an important effect upon the credit position of the economy.

Bank lending can of course take the form of bill finance and in the nineteenth century this was in fact a favoured way of making advances. The decline of the bill of exchange and its subsequent partial recovery has already been mentioned. The recovery, in recent years, has been partly due to the fact that in the post-1951 period, with Bank rate set loose from its long-established 2 per cent, bills could be a cheaper form of borrowing than overdrafts or loans tied to a rising Bank rate; hence they were increasingly favoured by large industrialists as well as export-import merchants. More to the point, perhaps, has been their popularity with the banks themselves; they provide a highly liquid asset which at the same time allows the banks to satisfy customer requirements at times when direct advances by loan or overdraft are being subjected to restraint by the authorities.

Despite its steady increase during the 1960s, however, the volume of trade bills held by the clearing banks amounted at the end of 1968 to only about 10 per cent of the sums advanced on loan and overdraft, and in the 1930s the proportion was decidedly less. Hence it remains substantially true to say that advances by the clearing banks are granted predominantly in the form of loans and overdrafts. Loans are made for fixed periods and for fixed amounts; they are credited to the current account of the borrower, who is at once debited with the full amount of the loan even if he uses only part of the credit. On the one hand, the banks' liabilities are increased, since the loan is immediately credited to the account of the borrower, thereby swelling its deposits. On the other hand, a corresponding increase occurs in the banks' assets as the borrower is debited with the total sum in a loan or advance account. In the case of overdrafts, however—that is, permission to draw on the bank up to a fixed maximum amount, but not necessarily for a fixed period—the borrower is debited only with the amount by which he overdraws his account and it is only by this amount that bank deposits are increased. The practice of lending on loans was the usual one in London in the early years of the century, while overdrafts were used mainly in the provinces; by the 1930s, however, the latter system was largely replacing the London practice of granting advances by loan.(1) Since then, following the recommendations of the Radcliffe Committee, the loan concept has come back into vogue with the introduction of term loans along the lines set by American banks. As yet, however, the proportion of loans to overdrafts remains small.

In the period after the first World War the rate for bank advances on average security was generally 'one per cent over Bank rate varying'.(2) In addition the banks tended to protect themselves by enforcing a minimum below which Bank rate would not normally be followed. With the introduction of cheap money in the 1930s the rates charged on bank advances fell only slowly in comparison with the sharp decline in market rates of interest. Throughout the decade the normal minimum was kept at 5 per cent, although it appears that the fall in the market rates produced a decline in bank advance rates from between 5 and 6 per cent in 1931 to between 4½ and 5½ per cent in the mid-1930s. The rate charged would vary, of course, according to the credit and standing of the customer and the nature of the loan and the collateral offered.

From the 1950s until 1969 the general pattern for clearing bank customers seems to have been that the nationalised industries and a few other favoured borrowers obtain overdrafts at Bank rate itself; for other fairly large or medium-sized businesses the rate would vary between ½ and 1 per cent over Bank rate; most personal or small business borrowers would be charged 1½ to 2 per cent over Bank rate. It must be emphasised, however, that these are generalisations; much depends on the nature of the advance required and the collateral offered. No precise statistics are available for the inter-war years, but in this matter practice certainly varied widely from bank to bank.(3) Some large industrial bank customers of undoubted security were apparently able to squeeze the rate they paid on their bank advances to under 5 per cent, a reflection of the eagerness of the banks to obtain this sort of business in those years. Such habits, however, were not ones which the banks would advertise to their rivals: price competition continued to be taboo, at any rate in public. The stickiness of advances rates reflected, on the one hand, the oligopolistic nature of British joint-stock banking and, on the other, the high proportion of its overhead costs. Price-cutting on any public scale would necessarily have forced competitors to follow suit, thereby depriving the prime mover of his original relative advantage; at the same time the high proportion of overhead costs would make such competition distinctly risky, even if the first factor did not make it largely pointless.(4) According to the Chairman of the Midland Bank in 1934, a reduction of 1 per cent in the rate charged on advances by that bank would have entailed either a one-third cut in salaries or an almost complete suspension of dividend payments.(5) Under the circumstances it seems idle to speculate as to whether or not in those years the banks regarded the demand for advances as being inelastic with respect to interest rates.

Surveys conducted by Oxford economists prior to the second World War and subsequently supported by other empirical evidence appeared to show that the rate of interest was not as significant an item in business decisions as had been commonly thought; borrowers, it was suggested, placed greater emphasis on the availability of credit and were relatively indifferent to any likely degree of variation in cost. In other words, the availability of credit itself, varying via the application of adjustable bank lending standards, appeared to be a more significant factor than the traditional deterrent (cum incentive) of the interest rate mechanism. Monetary policy, working through Bank rate and open-market operations, affected not only interest rates but commercial bank credit standards as well; from the point of view of the borrower as well as the banks, it was the latter which was the crucial factor.(6) For a generation after the great depression, however, any such constraints upon the supply side were very much subordinate to deficiencies in demand. In the mid-1930s the Chairman of Lloyds Bank was lamenting that 'In my memory there has never been a time when we have been less critical on purely theoretical grounds as to the merits of applications for advances.'(7)

In granting a loan or overdraft, banks look primarily to the safety of the loan and the profit to be made on it. Although it is usual to associate an increased profitability of advances with periods of high Bank rate—because of the high proportion of deposits on which no interest is paid—their relative profitability to the banks is in fact enhanced in periods of low Bank rate, when yields on money market assets tend to be particularly low. Since the second World War, of course, and particularly after 1951, yields on money market assets have been relatively high.

Partially offsetting, as well as reflecting, the higher yields on advances are the increased risks of bad debts. Concern for an increase in such risks was apparent at an early date—certainly by the 1920s—from the watch kept by the banks on the ratio of advances to total deposits. As has been seen, this ratio probably meant at least as much to the banks as their liquidity ratio, certainly until the years of the bill famine. Fluctuations in the desired ratio would reflect shifts in bank attitudes and standards as well as variations in demand and in the 1920s, the banks' experience of a substantial proportion of 'locked in' loans resulted in an enforced upwards revision of it. By the time of the Macmillan Committee the ratio considered compatible with safety and profit, as stated by the representatives of the Big Five, ranged from 50 to 60 per cent, with an average of just under 55 per cent, compared with the 50 per cent considered to be the conventional maximum before the first World War.(8) By 1932 bank advances had begun to feel the effects of the world-wide depression and advances entered a long-term decline which was not fully reversed until late in the 1950s. Throughout these years, however, bankers tended to retain their traditional concepts concerning the optimum ratio for advances, although it was not until after 1958 that the pre-depression distribution of assets was in general restored.

2. Maturity preference and the supply of bank loans

As regards the theoretical approach to lending, the traditional preference of the London clearing banks had generally been for the short-term advance, a reflection of the short-term nature of their deposit liabilities. The classic example of such maturity preference in bank lending has generally been the self-liquidating advance—that is to say, the advance which itself provides the means of its repayment as, for instance, when a shopkeeper borrows in order to finance extra stock for Christmas or the January sales. Of such a type was the seasonal advance, usually of six months' duration, which was a mainstay of bank lending in the 1920s and before. Even today this is still an important and cherished element of bank lending. Especially favoured would be the advance concerned with the customers' 'in and out business'—not borrowing for fixed capital expenditure but temporary accommodation which would in the course of a few weeks or months liquidate itself. Where overdrafts were prolonged too long it was frequently because a customer had not fulfilled a promise to obtain long-term capital or to fund his debt by means of a mortgage—perhaps because he found it cheaper to use bank finance—and had not been pressed hard enough for repayment. Such a situation, however, was anathema to the orthodox banker for whom the cardinal criterion of lending policy was, and remains, that 'there must be no lock-up of capital'.(9)

In itself the standard justification of the self-liquidating loan is a false one; although the sale of a finished product puts a borrower in funds within a reasonable period, the only way in which he can in fact liquidate his bank debt is by surrendering all or part of the proceeds in discharge of the loan.(10) In other words, the withdrawal of the loan or overdraft facilities could entail a reduction or suspension of the borrower's business activities. Equally it would be reflected in a parallel decline in both the bank's deposit liabilities and its advances. Moreover, if all banks were following the same policy, their individual cash reserves would be but little improved, while the cut in spending occasioned by a more rigorous lending policy would tend in normal circumstances to set in train a deflationary spiral which would destroy the 'self-liquidating' quality of the transaction being financed. The real justification of this type of loan, as argued by Sayers and subsequently echoed by the Radcliffe Committee, is simply that it limits the range of judgement required in the average bank manager, whose training is not generally such as to enable him confidently to assess long-term profitability.(11)

Although rare in British deposit banking, a lengthy commitment of funds in the finance of fixed capital formation has long been a relatively common practice on the continent. There the pace of industrial development was often too rapid—and the antipathy of entrepreneurs to public participation too ingrained—for such capital needs to be accommodated in the somewhat haphazard fashion in which British industry had traditionally obtained its long-term capital. Hence at a fairly early stage it became the habit of the banks, particularly in Germany, to mobilise funds for the finance of new enterprises, providing fixed as well as working capital. The banks, with staffs of skilled experts, consider requests from industrialists of good standing with a view to sharing in the finance of a new venture. A company would then be formed in which the bank takes shares—even perhaps a controlling interest—and one or more of the directors of the bank take seats on the board of the new enterprise. The new enterprise can be operated until it proves successful, whereupon, at an auspicious moment, the bank debt can be extinguished, although the bank might continue to retain some financial interest in the company.

It appears, in fact, that the German banks would not risk their capital unless they were able to exercise some influence in its application; their assistance is thus inevitably bound up with control. In Britain, with fears of a 'money-trust' arising with the culmination of the amalgamation movement and the appointment of the Cunliffe Committee in 1918, it is probable, as Leaf points out, that public opinion would not have tolerated the control of industry by a few banks.[12] Further, by the nature of their background, their liabilities and their staff training, this was not business which the clearing banks felt competent to undertake. The current account deposits of the German banks were proportionately much less than the British clearing banks, owing to the fact that the use of the cheque was not so highly developed. In addition, the pre-existing channels of long-term industrial finance were much more highly developed in Britain than on the continent: the Stock Exchange, issuing houses and merchant banks to some extent pre-empted interference by the banks in this field even if the latter had been willing to attempt it. The London merchant bankers in particular, dealing in their own capital and with only a small proportion of public deposits, were better equipped to conduct such business, even if on a smaller scale. Continental bankers thus became involved in the fortunes of particular industrial firms to an extent unknown to their British brethren, a practice for which they paid the penalty in times of depression, especially in 1929 and the early 1930s. The success of British banks in withstanding the world economic crisis naturally encouraged a reversion to the more orthodox (British) attitudes and the subsequent tendency throughout Western Europe has been for commercial banks to confine themselves more strictly to short-term lending.[13]

Even so, despite this tradition and inclination in British banking, the course of nineteenth-century bank history in Britain had shown the folly of making large advances to individual customers, especially to those engaged in heavy industries subject to cyclical fluctuations. Through such transactions bank resources were locked up in long-term and risky loans and at the cost of the sacrifice of a proper degree of liquidity. A salutary reminder of this fact was provided by the deflation of the early 1920s when the evidence suggests that several banks were saddled with a large proportion of 'frozen' loans. In the boom immediately following the first World War many banks appear to have advanced credit unwisely and subsequently found their advances locked in by the depression in precisely those industries which had received most help from the banks—textiles and steel.[14] They were then faced with the possibilities of either writing off these loans or forcing their debtors into the bankruptcy court—a solution which would in any case have lost them the bulk of their money. Accordingly the banks felt obliged to maintain their customers—and, indeed, to extend further assistance where necessary to this end. Although subject to criticism at the time, in the event this approach was in general justified by the eventual recovery which took place when Britain abandoned the gold standard.

All this, however, confirmed British banks in their traditional preference for short-term advances, heightening the awareness, evident today, of the risk to which any bank exposes itself if it cannot turn its assets quickly into cash to meet sudden demands from depositors. The preference is highly relevant today, even if—as has been suggested—its justification lies only in the fact that it limits the range of judgement required in the lending banker. As the Radcliffe Committee noted, the great majority of overdraft agreements made by the banks

> must be based, at least in large part, on the judgement of the branch manager, and these managers may reasonably be expected to assess

the capacity of a borrower to repay in a short time, although they could have no assurance in estimating long-term profitability.[15]

Large customers, wishing to stretch a point in the matter of maturity, have to place their hope, under the system of bank lending controls, in the attention of the bank's head office.

British bankers, therefore, retain their traditional view that their proper business is the finance of working capital—particularly of the 'seed-time to harvest' nature—the provision of bridging loans and (within cautious limits) the temporary finance of fixed capital development pending the raising of long-term finance through other channels. Nevertheless, it would be wrong to imply that there was ever a single universal doctrine rigidly held by all British bankers, even at the time of the Macmillan Committee. Many banks would probably have welcomed the chance of profitable business in those depressed years, even if the nature of the advances concerned might hardly have merited the description of liquid, and this was especially the case after the long-term decline in advances had set in.

In the early 1930s the British banking system entered a phase in which advances were falling while total deposits were simultaneously rising as a consequence of an expansionary monetary policy. Since that time the tendency in British banking—as distinct from continental practice—has been gradually to widen the concepts and scope of the traditional lending activities of the banks. In 1932, for example, Lloyds Bank granted an advance of £3 million to the steel company of Stewart and Lloyds for an indefinite period, contrary to all British deposit banking traditions, in order to facilitate the development of the Corby scheme. It was three years before debentures were issued on the capital market to repay this advance.[16] Although a particularly striking case, it was to appear less remarkable in succeeding years with the shift of bank attitudes towards a longer maturity distribution in bank assets.

One consequence of the amalgamation movement in British banking which culminated in 1918 had been a more restricted, if more uniform, range of lending activities. Partly because of this, but also because of other developments in business life—for example, industrial integration and the increased adoption of cash payments in retail trade—the growth of the importance of bank lending in relation to national income had been slowing down in the late 1920s.[17] As may be seen from Table 3A of the Statistical Appendix, advances by the London Clearing Banks reached a peak of just under 22 per cent of GNP in 1931, a relative level which was never regained; since the outbreak of World War II, in fact, it has not been even remotely approached. The economic collapse throughout the world in the great crisis reduced the traditional outlets for profitable lending even further so that, even with the recovery of trade after 1934, the British banks found their advances substantially below what they regarded as the desired levels. This was a situation which was to endure for some twenty years and even with the post-war recovery in advances the traditional optimum ratio of advances to deposits was not restored until well into the 1960s.

A not unnatural consequence of the chronic shortage of profitable lending outlets was the development of somewhat more flexible attitudes on the part of the banks as to what was and what was not proper banking business.

With the 'underlent' position of the banks having effects even on their internal organisation, bank eagerness to lend was reflected in the disappearance of the 'unsatisfied fringe' of borrowers.(18) Tradition or unduly doctrinaire maxims now tended to be set aside in deference to opportunities which seemed reasonably safe. By the late 1950s, this trend had shown considerable progress, certainly to the extent of the acceptance of the provision of temporary loans for fixed capital purposes and of lending on property mortgages or life assurance policies.

3. The demand for bank credit

With the general recovery of the British economy in the mid-1930s, many firms hit by the depression were able to repay bank debt by liquidating inventories of physical or financial assets, by accumulating profits or by being able to apply once more to the long-term capital market. At the same time the level of new advances did not rise proportionately in the subsequent recovery of the economy. It appeared that a secular tendency towards a declining demand for advances had set in; indeed, many observers thought that this would have been clearly visible in the 1920s had it not been masked by the phenomenon of high but illiquid advances during some of those years.(19) The ratio of advances to total deposits fell from 55 per cent in 1929 to around 43 per cent in 1938 and to a low of 16.4 per cent in 1945. As a proportion of GNP, advances by the clearing banks had averaged about 21 per cent in 1926-9 but had fallen to a little over 18 per cent in 1936-9, despite the addition of the District Bank to the clearing bank list during the latter period. To have maintained the ratio of advances to deposits characteristic of the 1920s would probably have been impossible; it would have required a large rise of advances in relation to national income whereas in fact the tendency of the time was in the opposite direction.(20)

This experience was by no means confined to Britain, declining bank advances being a feature common to most countries; in France between 1929 and 1934 they declined by some 20 per cent, in Holland by 40 per cent, in Belgium and Italy by a half and by more than half in Germany and the United States.(21) Attention was first drawn to the possibility of a secular contraction in the demand for bank loans by Sayers in 1938, although bankers and business commentators had been worried about the state of advances for some years previously.(22) According to the Chairman of the Westminster Bank in 1935,

> The fact that we are underlent comes from lack of demand, for never before were the banks more competitive in their desire to provide accommodation within the appropriate limits of banking facilities.(23)

The causes of this decline in the demand for bank advances included changes in the organisation of industry (for example, mergers and a tendency towards increased unit size), in sources of finance (for example, the growth of agricultural mortgage institutions and increased reliance on retained profits) and in commercial practice such as the decline in the importance of credit accounts at shops. Even in 1935 and 1936, when bank advances showed temporary signs of recovery, only about a third of the increase in the Midland Banks' lending was due to the demands of industry and commerce.(24) For the clearing banks as a whole, industrial and commercial borrowing accounted for around 55 per cent of total borrowing in 1929-30 whereas by 1936 it amounted to only some 47 per cent.

From the industrial viewpoint increasing integration would certainly be a major factor tending to eliminate one mainstay of bank lending—the seasonal credit requirement to pay for raw materials or for semi-manufactured goods. Within an integrated unit seasonal drains and surpluses of cash could be matched up, thereby avoiding the need for temporary bank cover.(25) Moreover, if the volume of overall working capital did not fluctuate seasonally its finance would not result in a loss of interest over part of the year through the need to hold idle funds. Yet another consequence of integration could be a fall in the average cost of investing surplus funds—for example, by justifying the establishment of an investment department as the size of the industry increased. Similarly, the larger a firm, in general, the greater the ease with which access to long-term capital can be obtained on the open market. As the interest margin on which clearing banks work is substantial, with rates on advances subject to a minimum of around 5 per cent, a large firm might well find it profitable to obtain working capital through long-term finance.

The finance of investment through new capital issues undoubtedly gave a great impetus to the downward trend of bank advances during the 1930s. According to an analysis made by the Midland Bank—albeit from a relatively small sample—the two main causes of the decline in their advances had been, on the one hand, the floating of new issues by companies and the consequent reduction of bank debt and, on the other, amalgamations into larger units with greater facility for internal finance.(26) This and other evidence lends support to the view that these two factors were responsible for a substantial part of the relative decline in the demand for bank advances during the 1930s. The statistics of sums owed by a sample of companies in the form of bank debt or on mortgage during this period show a general reduction of indebtedness as recovery proceeded, total debt under these two headings running during 1936-9 at only about 55-60 per cent of the 1930 level. (27) In the case of bank debt the process was uneven, possibly because of the common habit of financing investment in its initial stages by bank overdrafts prior to a new issue on the capital market.

Thus a rise in bank debt during 1932-3 and its relapse afterwards was accompanied by a sharp rise in the debenture debt of the companies concerned of £9.5 million in 1933-4, while a rise of bank debt in 1935 and a fall in 1936, followed by relative stability, was matched by a rise of debenture debt during 1936, after which the volume of outstanding debentures remained constant.(28)

Cheap money itself, with its effects on the pattern of interest rates and on the relationship between the capital market and the volume of bank advances, was also a factor of considerable importance. Analysis of company issues for the early 1930s shows that for the companies analysed 25 per cent of new issues were devoted to the reduction of bank debt, so that the replacement of bank debt by 'cheap and permanent capital' was, according to one observer, an important cause of the failure of bank advances to rise before 1936; another attributed to the cheap money policy the fact that many undertakings had been able to consolidate their floating indebtedness.(29) The major reason for the increased popularity of capital market finance was of course the fact that when interest rates on long-term securities fell relatively to advances rates, it became cheaper to issue long-term securities—or realise capital gains on existing holdings of long-term securities—and use the proceeds to replace more expensive bank finance. It is evident from fluctuations in corporate security holdings that the introduction of cheap money in 1932 was responsible for a large-scale realisation of industrial holdings of securities to be used in direct or indirect finance of investment. The banks themselves, by their heavy purchases of gilt-edged, had helped bid up security prices to the point where firms could sell their holdings at a profit, using the proceeds to provide working capital. Fluctuations in transaction needs could be met by varying holdings of cash, instead of by running an overdraft up and down. Not surprisingly firms preferred to sell securities yielding only about 3 per cent rather than pledge them as collateral against bank loans on which the minimum rate was usually not less than 5 per cent.(30) Thus the banks were, in fact, financing industry not through advances but indirectly through their purchases of securities.(31)

During the second World War further constraints upon the volume of advances reflected, on the supply side, a series of requests to banks to limit advances as well as the continuing decline in demand. The ratio of advances to deposits fell from 43 per cent in 1938 to a low of 16 per cent in 1945. The demand for industrial bank credit, in which some recovery might have been expected under conditions of rising defence expenditure, was in fact much reduced by the system of advance and progress payments to contractors from government departments. New advances to the reviving agricultural sector were probably more than offset by repayments of long-standing pre-war debts, while advances to customers other than those engaged on essential production were discouraged by the authorities. Commercial bill finance also dwindled away as the finance of imports and exports passed increasingly into the hands of the various ministries.(32)

After 1945, while advances showed some recovery from their low wartime level they still remained at abnormally low levels in relation to both deposits and national income. Although the retention of directives concerning bank lending certainly played a part in this, as did the maintenance of an overall budget surplus, the significant factor continued to be the stagnation of demand for bank loans. Of relevance here, especially after the war, was the comparative decline in the private sector of the economy. The government had become a more important economic power than ever before and the nationalised industries, while still using bank advances, were probably less dependent on them than their private predecessors.

With the growth in the national debt, by 1951 the government had become easily the most important borrower from the banking system and the banks appeared to have become far less important as financial intermediaries than had been the case for several generations. Perhaps the most important influence upon the post-war demand for advances was the abnormally high liquidity which had accumulated in the private sector primarily as a result of war-time policies and scarcities. By 1946, the liquid assets of the private sector—as measured in Table 4 of the Statistical Appendix—had risen to no less than 144 per cent of GNP compared with less than 81 per cent in 1940. This build-up of liquidity—some 40 per cent of which consisted of deposits in the banking system—would in itself have had the effect of reducing the advances ratio, even if advances had remained constant or increased slightly in aggregate terms. Many firms and individuals possessing large holdings of cash and other liquid assets which they had been virtually compelled to accumulate during the war, when severe restrictions were imposed on the purchase of goods and equipment, inevitably had less need than usual for bank finance when spending restrictions were gradually lifted.

As a result of increased liquidity, on the one hand, and the decline in the private demand for bank finance, on the other, at the end of the 1940s the banks were in the position of doing far less private lending than they would have liked. Although as a percentage of deposits advances had begun to recover after the war, by 1950 the ratio was still slightly less than half of the 55 per cent which in the 1920s had been regarded as the optimum ratio—and this despite the liberalisation of bank lending policy with respect to both consumer loans and the provision of medium-term capital for industry. As a percentage of GNP, advances had fallen from over 21 per cent in 1929 to 8 per cent in 1945, rising only to less than 14 per cent in 1950. Apart from obviously bad credit risks, the banks were tending to satisfy all demands for finance: it appeared to some observers that, for all practical purposes, the volume of bank advances could now be regarded as demand determined.(33)

In the early 1950s, of course, the demand for bank credit was still subject to the high degree of post-war personal and corporate liquidity. It is clear, however, that from 1951 onwards, the vagaries of official monetary policy and mechanisms also played their part in keeping down the volume of advances—if not by damping down demand through the interest rate mechanism, then certainly by affecting conditions of supply, not least in relation to bank credit requirements. A not unnatural legacy of the long years of stagnation, followed by some frustration of the demand for bank finance, was therefore the uncertainty displayed by bank representatives before the Radcliffe Committee as to the desirable ratio of advances to deposits.

In July 1958, however, with advances still abnormally low in relation to both deposits and current income levels, the banks were 'liberated' from official restrictions. Between 1958 and 1961, bank advances almost doubled; the ratio of advances to deposits rose from 29 per cent in 1958 to 45 per cent in 1961. The bulk of this increase was financed by sales of securities and the remainder by a rise in deposits, the banks' investment ratio falling from 32 per cent to 15 per cent over the same period. Within the space of three years, therefore, the banks found themselves largely returning to their traditional position of lending a substantial proportion of their resources to the private sector and to a much closer approximation to their pre-1930 distribution of assets. A radical arrest of the long-term trend had at last occurred, although in fact bank loans in the aggregate still remained smaller in relation to national income than in the 1920s.

4. The distribution of bank advances

The provision of working capital has always been the British banker's traditional role. Between two World Wars, however, and particularly in the 1920s, the London clearing banks were heavily involved—at considerable cost—in the provision of reconstruction capital for industries such as cotton and steel. Although working capital remained the mainstay of banking business, since the 1930s there has occurred a radical movement

TABLE 4

London Clearing Banks' Classification of Advances.[1]

(% of total)

		1929-30[2]	1936[3]	1968[3]
1.	Textiles (Cotton, Wool, Linen, Jute)	8.3	4.6	4.1
2.	Heavy Industries: Iron/Steel, Engineering and Shipbuilding	6.4	4.7	16.4
3.	Agriculture and Fishing	7.0	6.6	8.5
4.	Mining and Quarrying	3.0	2.1	0.3
5.	Food, Drink and Tobacco	6.4	3.4	4.1
6.	Leather, Rubber and Chemicals	2.2	1.4	2.1
7.	Shipping and Transport (incl. Railways)	2.5	2.6	2.2
8.	Building Trades	4.8	7.1	6.0
9.	Miscellaneous and Retail Trades	14.7	14.7	28.5
	TOTAL, INDUSTRIAL AND COMMERCIAL	55.3	47.2	72.2
10.	Local Authorities & Public Utilities	5.3	5.8	2.4
11.	Amusements, Clubs, Churches, Charities	2.7	4.7	n.a.
12.	Financial (including Banks and Building Societies)	14.4	12.6	9.3
13.	Other Advances	22.1	29.7	16.1
	TOTAL	100	100	100

1. Excludes money at call and short notice
2. Ten banks
3. Eleven banks (District included)

away from the classical addiction to the 'self-liquidating loan' and towards the provision of medium-term capital formation. This was, of course, a natural result of the pressures imposed upon the banks to expand their business in other ways as a result of the decline in traditional-type advances.

Information on the distribution of bank lending between the wars is unfortunately very scant. Statistics were compiled and published by the Macmillan Committee for the year 1929-30, but despite recommendations by the Committee that similar statements should be published annually, this was not done until 1936, and then for that year only, when details for eleven banks were published in the Bank of England's *Statistical Summary*. Table 4 above shows how comparatively small a percentage of total advances went directly into industry. Textiles, heavy industries, mining, leather, rubber and chemicals, shipping as well as agriculture and building between them accounted for less than a third of total bank advances, compared with over 50 per cent in the early 1960s.

Lending to agriculture, in particular, had been traditionally a major outlet for bank resources, recognised well before Stuckey's time, and need not be stressed. The Macmillan Committee's figures show that 7 per cent of bank advances went to agriculture and fishing, compared with an average of about 11 per cent in the late 1950s, of which about a third was estimated to be unsecured. The Radcliffe Committee noted that the joint-stock banks were still the principal institutional source of agricultural credit, whether short-term (that is, seed-time to harvest), medium-term for the purchase of livestock and machinery or long-term for the purchase or improvement of land and buildings; nowadays lending to agriculture still accounts for some 10 per cent of total advances.(34) From the point of view of medium-term and long-term agricultural finance particular problems emerged, although the Radcliffe Committee generally rejected criticism of the adequacy of bank lending. The question of the suitability of bank methods of finance, however, is which can be validly raised in relation to the whole range of bank lending; it is one which is discussed below.

5. The finance of small businesses

One of the matters which particularly concerned the Macmillan Committee was the adequacy or otherwise of financing facilities for small and medium-sized enterprises in Britain. It was the opinion of the Committee that there was a real danger that the growth of some small firms might be impeded because they lacked some of the sources open to larger companies for obtaining capital.(35) In the 1930s, as well as in the Radcliffe years, the main source of long-term funds for small businesses and private companies would be their own accumulated reserves. Under normal circumstances such companies would not need to use outside funds: if they did, and if they were large enough, then the new issue market was the logical fulfilment of their requirements. But in the early 1930s many large firms, and *a fortiori* small concerns, were in fact experiencing severe depletion of their reserves and the question of external finance was therefore of great importance to them. Moreover, it is as true today as it was then that it was the more enterprising and rapidly-growing firm which was most likely to be in need of funds. Although hire-purchase finance and trade credit might be available, a limit necessarily exists to the amount of long-term capital obtainable by the use of such funds and it tends in any case to be an expensive and risky way of doing business. Furthermore, the supply of such finance was on a much more limited scale in the 1930s than it has proved to be since the war.

During the twenty years or so following the Macmillan Committee's report, considerable progress was made towards the solution of these difficulties although, as the Radcliffe Committee noted, there was still scope for further improvement. In 1934 the Charterhouse Investment Trust, with the co-operation of the Prudential Assurance Company, Lloyds Bank and the Midland Bank, set up the Charterhouse Industrial Development Company, an institution designed to assist the financing of small enterprises. In the same year United Dominions Trust extended its credit activities in direct response to recommendations of the Macmillan Committee by establishing a subsidiary company, Credit for Industry Ltd., whose object was to grant loans ranging from £100 to £50,000 to small businesses. Finally, immediately after the second World War the British banks, with the token co-operation of the Bank of England, set up the Industrial and

Commercial Finance Corporation to provide medium-term or long-term finance for smaller industrial or commercial enterprises.

The banks themselves were, of course, directly and willingly involved in the provision of credit to small businesses and through their branch networks were able to maintain close liaison with their smaller customers. Their credit, as the Radcliffe Committee notes, often extended to the provision of medium-term and sometimes long-term capital. But the difficulty from the point of view of both industry and agriculture was the very informality and unreliability of bank loans. Bank lending is most commonly by overdrafts which are still legally repayable on demand and in practice subject to annual review. The British joint-stock banks, certainly, have always displayed a reluctance to depart formally from this principle, although in practice considerable leeway is applied. It was clear from the evidence of the London Clearing Bankers before the Radcliffe Committee that when the banks allow customers to overdraw for medium-term or long-term purposes they look, in normal circumstances, for regular annual reductions in the overdraft over an agreed period.(36) According to the Committee's evidence, however, they never make formal arrangements for the annual reduction of an overdraft, and in certain circumstances (for example, after a bad harvest) will readily renew an overdraft from one year to another without reduction.(37)

The Scottish banks, on the other hand, have traditionally been more willing than their English counterparts to acknowledge the long-term nature of some of their advances and have not been reluctant to act accordingly.(38) This was particularly the case with agriculture and with small businesses, where the bank concerned automatically gave up its right to call for repayment at any time. (On occasion, of course, such a relaxation has cost a bank dear.) Thus greater flexibility may well have had its origins in the old cash-credit system practised by the Scots banks in their earliest years, a system of lending on character backed by personal guarantee.(39)

The Radcliffe Committee felt that it was not unreasonable for farmers, and indeed for other borrowers, to look for some assurance that credit which they sought for medium-term purposes would not be prematurely recalled. This being the case, the Committee recommended that the banks should either give firmer assurances that such loans would not be prematurely recalled, or adopt the American practice of formal term loans whereby credit could be granted for fixed periods repayable by regular instalments and not recallable before the agreed term.(40) In reaction to the Radcliffe Committee's proposals, some of the banks announced schemes for term loans of up to 20 years' duration with a normal rate of interest of 2 per cent over Bank rate and a minimum of 6 per cent. These facilities do not seem to have been extensively used so far, probably because of their high cost.

Despite the appearance of specialist intermediaries, then, the 'Macmillan gap' had not entirely disappeared even by the late 1950s. One area in which this was particularly noticeable, so the Radcliffe Committee felt, was in export finance. Although much progress had been made in the provision of insurance protection by the Export Credits Guarantee Department (ECGD) set up by the government, as late as 1959 there remained difficulty in finding willing holders for private debt of between about 8 and 12 years' maturity. The banks themselves had been ready to do such business, even in excess of 5 years' maturity, as long as their advances/

deposits ratio was still below their optimum level. With a general tendency towards lengthening commitments, however, the banks had become reluctant to accept further business of this kind and special arrangements were made under ECGD cover to share out very large transactions with other financial institutions, notably the insurance companies, who took on the longer end of the business.

With the expansion of bank lending in 1958-9 and the restoration of their advances ratio to something like their pre-1930 level, the banks were less willing to undertake commitments of this nature. To do so, they argued, would have tied up funds for some considerable time ahead at the risk of future illiquidity which could prevent them from meeting the normal working demands of their ordinary customers. The difficulty was partly met, as far as exports were concerned, by the decision in February 1961 to allow the banks to re-finance with the Bank of England part of their lending for certain defined export business. (The part eligible for Bank re-finance comprised instalments repayable by the buyer within 18 months.) At the same time, all such re-financeable export credits were to be regarded by the Bank of England as counting towards the banks' official liquid assets. Thus the banks could rely on the fact that a percentage of their actual advances to exporters (as much as 30 per cent) would count as an increase in their liquid assets. The effect was such as considerably to minimise the illiquidity dangers inherent in bank export finance.

6. Consumer finance

The extension of new concepts in bank lending, particularly as far as the consumer was concerned, had to wait until 1958. Despite the example of the American banks, British banks were reluctant to embark on new methods of doing business. Enterprise was to an extent muted by the post-war anti-inflationary policies intended to keep down the pressure of consumer demand for goods and services. Other specialist intermediaries, however, were developing their business, especially in the supply of hire-purchase credit to consumers. In the 1930s, consumer finance had provided a major growth-point—virtually the only one, apart from loans to house builders—for bank advances when demand from industry and trade was generally depressed. Clearing bank attitudes on the subject of consumer credit, however, were traditionally conservative, although less so than is sometimes realised. As for other borrowers, the banks would need to know the purpose of the loan, its duration, the source from which repayment was to come, the security offered and the character of the customer. During the inter-war years the banks had been prepared to provide finance for a wide range of purposes, even—if somewhat surreptitiously—for house-purchase, especially where the borrower had been able to repay in a fairly short period of time. In November 1936 Barclays Bank, for example, had some 34 per cent of its advances in loans to personal and professional borrowers, and 10 per cent of these outstanding advances were for the purchase of land and/or houses, although most were in fact probably no more than bridging loans.

Nevertheless, even well after the war, credit for consumer durables along the lines established by US banks continued to be considered somewhat improper banking business in Britain. In 1958, however, the government lifted the restrictions on lending with which the banks had been beleaguered for much of the decade. The relaxation prompted the banks into a sudden expansion of this growing area of business. Several of the banks acquired interests in hire-purchase subsidiaries and channelled funds to consumers through this medium; at the same time they introduced personal loans for identical financing purposes, with agreed repayment by instalments. With this new expansion of consumer credit, the authorities permitting, the banks could rely on business with sufficient growth potential to maintain a buoyant overall demand for advances.

For the ordinary individual it is easy enough to exaggerate the part played by the banks in the provision of credit; the word 'borrowing' readily brings to mind the image of a visit to the bank manager. Popular associations of this kind, however, while emphasising the apparent dominance in the public eye of the banks as lenders to the personal sector, do not accurately represent the importance of the banks in the provision of overall credit to the economy. At least forty years previously Leaf had drawn attention to the fact that the bulk of credit was independent of the banks altogether: 'the banks deal in fact only with the bare fringe of this great mass of credit'.

7. The financial intermediaries

In relation to the total flow of credit in Britain, financial intermediaries other than the banks had actively expanded their resources into British industry and commerce, although it is unlikely that by the end of the 1950s the insurance companies or hire purchase companies presented a real threat to the volume of bank advances. To an extent they were competing in different markets from the banks; despite their eagerness to boost their advances ratio, the clearing banks were still far from ready for an expansion of credit for many of the purposes which are now familiar to modern bankers.

The market for credit, it has been stated, is a single market.[(41)] While fundamentally correct, the interpretation is a general one and not strictly accurate as a description of the market mechanism, especially before the second World War. The credit market consisted of a series of interconnected and imperfectly competing sub-markets—for small loans, large loans, short and long-term credit, for varied purposes and on widely differing security. Together these might be said to comprise a single market, but liquidity and other preferences of the institutional investors would tend to introduce some rigidities—clotting, as it were—into the credit system, with the result that smooth switches of funds on any large scale from one part of the market to the other were not normally to be expected. The building societies and insurance companies specialised, obviously, in their own particular fields—usually marked by the long-term nature of their finance; hire-purchase companies, on the other hand, while competing with the banks in the short end of the loans market, were prepared to lend in ways to which the banks were not accustomed and, despite changing pressures, were slow to recognise as legitimate business of their own.

Of the external sources of finance, the most serious threat to the bankers' market was probably the growth in trade credit. Although it is obvious that trade and industry cannot indefinitely generate additional net credit out of the dealings of one business with another, nonetheless it remains true that accommodation can be provided for the illiquid firm by the liquid firm out of the latter's own savings at the expense of potential bank borrowing. If the running-down of physical inventories by a creditor is excluded, then such accommodation can be provided through the realisation of liquid assets, whether securities, positive bank balances or, for that matter, by varying bank overdrafts. From the monetary point of view, trade credit introduces elasticity into the system. As far as the banks are concerned their advances suffer from this inter-company switching of liquid assets, and particularly from the substitution effect in times of national credit stringency.

The Radcliffe Report estimated that net credit for quoted companies in manufacturing, building and distribution had increased from £210 million in 1949 to £590 million in 1957, while their use of bank credit fell short of £500 million.(42) The evidence suggested that trade credit was more important to small firms than to large, and that small firms—especially young, rapidly-growing enterprises—were generally more likely to be net receivers of credit. As they became larger such firms were able to secure access to the new issue market, often becoming net donors of credit. Table 5 provides some indication of the magnitude of trade credit *vis-à-vis* bank credit during 1949-1957.

Some controversy was aired before the Radcliffe Committee on the question of whether or not net donor firms tended to provide credit partly financed by bank overdrafts which more insignificant firms, especially in credit squeezes, were not able to obtain.(43) Statistical evidence produced in 1959 has shown that bank advances had more-than-average importance

TABLE 5

Quoted Companies: Manufacturing, Building and Distribution: Trade Credit, Bank Credit and Stocks, 1949-1957-

(£ million)

	Outstanding net trade credit given by companies	Change in net trade credit given by companies	Change in bank advances to companies	Change of liabilities to trade creditors	Change in value of stocks and work in progress
1949	210	37	14	76	134
1950	270	63	35	159	286
1951	290	19	111	266	655
1952	350	63	–36	–1	23
1953	385	35	–43	65	–12
1954	485	37	22	181	225
1955	550	63	60	237	372
1956	560	10	72	159	343
1957	590	30	40	170	240

Source: Report of the Committee on the working of the monetary system, Cmd 827, HMSO, London 1959, Table 19, p. 105.

for those companies which gave relatively large amounts of trade credit,[44] while other commentators have argued that with trade credit forming so large a part of manufacturers' short-term assets, it is likely that bank credit does finance a large part of big firms' net grants of trade credit—particularly of the relevant net grants which are not financed by reduced investment stocks.[45] The real threat to bank advances, however, came from the growth and extension of corporate and personal liquidity, enabling liquid firms (and individuals) to channel credit to illiquid firms. The readiness of large firms to grant accommodation reflects the overall growth of corporate liquidity and the consequent independence of the corporate sector of such external means of finance as the new issue market, the banks and other financial or trade intermediaries.

From the evidence submitted to them, the Radcliffe Committee concluded that, of total available funds, retained earnings have been the most important source of capital for industrial expansion since the second World War, while sums set aside for eventual capital replacement have been even larger.[46] Bank finance has played a subordinate part. Investigations into the balance sheets of 3, 000 quoted companies by the National Institute for Economic and Social Research reveal that nearly half showed no bank overdraft on any of their balance sheets between 1949 and 1953 and that, as a group, these companies held several times as much in cash in 1953 as they owed to the banks on overdraft. Allowing for the possibility that the post-war liquidity bulge may have accounted for part of this, these facts serve as a reminder of the limited role of the banks in relation to the total supply of industrial and commercial credit.

Statistics for the period 1952-1965 published by the Bank of England show that of total funds available for industrial and commercial companies, internal funds—comprising gross trading profits (less stock appreciation) and other current domestic and foreign income—accounted for more than 75 per cent of the total over the period.[47] More recently, from 1959 onwards, the importance of external finance—for example, capital issues, borrowing from banks and other financial institutions—has increased, but it is still small in relation to total funds available. As a proportion of funds from all sources, internal funds have fallen from 93 per cent in 1952-58 to 85 per cent in 1959-65. Correspondingly, the increase in external funds reflects greater recourse to market finance—more borrowing on capital issues and from banks and other financial institutions, and the running down of certain liquid assets. Over the whole period, just under a half of total borrowing (some 22 per cent of total capital requirements) was on capital issues; in the last seven years, however, the emphasis on bank borrowing increased to form nearly a half of total borrowing, representing 12 per cent of total capital expenditure.

As a group, the London clearing banks are still predominant among British financial intermediaries; their importance is based chiefly on the short end of the credit market, but from the 1930s it has extended into the market for capital with loans of five or more years. Future developments in the latter sphere, however, appear under present conditions unlikely on anything but a limited scale except when channelled through their subsidiaries; almost certainly it will be largely confined to certain sectors, such as agriculture and exports, and to a few other favoured borrowers. With their advances averaging over 50 per cent of deposits in the mid-1960s, the banks were within close reach of their optimum ratio, and given the importance of their investments as a secondary and profitable reserve, it appeared doubtful whether the banks would be prepared to allow their investment ratios to sink much below the remaining 10 to 12 per cent of deposits. Old fears about the possible secular decline of advances had been displaced; on the other hand, an increasing worry was to become the economic condition of the country itself and the introduction of controls upon bank lending. The imposition of restrictions on bank advances obliges the banks to be more fussy about their lending business than they have been accustomed to being for three decades, and to concentrate their credit, with the given exceptions, more or less upon the traditional outlets. After a generation of adaptation to shifts in demand the banks were to find themselves obliged to mark time—not because of factors on the demand side but, rather, because of restrictions imposed on the supply side by official policy measures stimulated by the overall state of the economy.

REFERENCES

1. T. Balogh, *Studies in Financial Organisation*, Cambridge University Press, London 1950, p. 74.
2. W. Leaf, *Banking* (4th edition), Home University Library, University Press, London 1943, p. 177.
3. *The Economist Banking Supplement*, 12th May 1934, p. 5.
4. E. T. Nevin, *The Mechanism of Cheap Money*, University of Wales Press, Cardiff 1955, p. 315.
5. Rt. Hon. R. McKenna's Address to shareholders, *Midland Bank Review*, Jan-Feb. 1934, p. 5.
6. Nevin, *op. cit.*, pp. 315-8.
7. Mr B. Pease, A.G.M. Lloyds Bank 1936, quoted by B. Ellinger, *The City*, London 1940, p. 159.
8. W. J. Thorne, *Banking*, Home University Library, Oxford University Press, London 1948.
9. Leaf, *op. cit.*, p. 157.
10. W. Manning Dacey, *The British Banking Mechanism*, Hutchinson, London 1967, pp. 86-87.
11. R. S. Sayers, *Modern Banking* (7th edition), Oxford University Press, London 1967, p. 186.
12. Leaf, *op. cit.*, p. 160.
13. Sayers, *op. cit.*, pp. 188-9.
14. Balogh, *op. cit.*, p. 78.
15. *Committee on the Working of the Monetary System*, Cmnd. 827 (Radcliffe Report), HMSO; London 1959, para. 136.
16. R. J. Truptil, *British Banks and the London Money Market*, Cape, London 1936, p. 105.
17. Sayers, *op. cit.*, p. 189.

18. *Ibid.*, p. 190.

19. Balogh, *op. cit.*, p. 78.

20. A. C. Day, *Outline of Monetary Economics*, Oxford University Press, London 1957, p. 189.

21. Ellinger, *op. cit.*, p. 15 7.

22. Sayers, *op. cit.*, pp. 188-90.

23. Truptil, *op. cit.*, p. 306.

24. McKenna, Annual General Meeting of the Midland Bank, 1937.

25. Truptil, *op. cit.*, p. 307.

26. Ellinger, *op. cit.*, p. 159.

27. Nevin, *op. cit.*, pp. 248-51.

28. *Ibid.*, p. 226.

29. A. M. Allen, *The Banker*, April, 1936, p. 18 and P. Einzig, *The Banker*, August, 1936.

30. H. Parkinson, 'The Outlook for gilt-edged stock', *The Banker*, May 1935, p. 107.

31. Allen, *op. cit.*

32. Thorne, *op. cit.*, p. 56.

33. H. G. Johnson, 'Some implications of secular changes in bank assets and liabilities in Great Britain', *Economic Journal*, September 1951, p. 550.

34. *Bank of England Statistical Summary.*

35. *Radcliffe Report*, para. 913.

36. *Ibid.*, para 920.

37. *Ibid.*

38. Radcliffe Committee, *Minutes of Evidence*, Qu. 4801-5 and 4810-13.

39. Maxwell Gaskin, *The Scottish Banks*, Glasgow University Press, pp. 143-5 and 149.

40. *Radcliffe Report*, para. 920.

41. *Ibid.* para. 125.

42. *Ibid.*, para. 305.

43. *Ibid.*, para. 311.

44. R. F. Henderson, 'Trade Credit', Tew and Henderson, *Studies in Company Finance*, Cambridge University Press, London 1959, pp. 103-6.

45. W. H. White, 'Trade Credit and Monetary Policy: A Reconciliation', *Economic Journal*, Vol. LXXIV, No. 296, December 1964, p. 943.

46. *Radcliffe Report*, para. 318.

47. *Bank of England Quarterly Bulletin*, March 1967.

PART III

COMPETITION AND CONCENTRATION (1951–)

CHAPTER TEN

Organisation and Management

1. Introduction

It would be broadly true to say that for half a century the organisation and structure of the British joint-stock banks remained within the pattern described by the Colwyn Committee in 1918. The Committee had observed that the larger British banks considered it necessary to match each important merger by another, sooner or later, in order to preserve an approximate balance of resources and competitive power. Although the dangers of monopoly in the banking sphere were not considered by the Committee to be particularly serious, nonetheless it felt that in view of the strategic importance to the economy of the banking sector some measure of government intervention was essential.(1) The resort to legislation proved to be unnecessary, however, when the banks gave an undertaking that they would submit any proposed future mergers for official approval.

Given this constraint the banks were obliged to pursue growth through an active policy of branch expansion and, also, through one of deposit attraction based on such expansion or on other forms of non-price competition. Since price competition had been more less suspended, the provision of more attractive services was in fact virtually the only method left by which the banks could compete with one another, including in this term the growing emphasis placed upon competition through the provision of ancillary services, especially after the introduction of Trustee and Overseas Departments and foreign branches before and after the first World War. This laid the foundation of the pattern of British joint-stock banking as the Radcliffe Committee was to find it some forty years later. Even by 1958 there had been little fundamental change in the general approach to banking or in its organisation—monetary control excepted—although by the time of the somewhat unexpected scrutiny of the system by the National Board for Prices and Incomes in 1967, pressures incipient at the time of the Radcliffe Report had emerged and revealed a banking world in the process of transition.

The cue for the 1968 bank mergers came, of course, from the bonus reference by the Prices and Incomes Board to the possibility of further mergers among the Big Five themselves. The authorities, it was stated,

> would not obstruct some further amalgamation if the banks were willing to contemplate such a development, and we think that a further reduction in the number of independent banking units would not necessarily affect very significantly the degree of competition.(2)

This opinion—which was to cause some embarrassment to the authorities in the light of subsequent events—has to be considered in the light of the clearing banks' cartel on interest rates, which the PIB felt to be the main deterrent to a more competitive banking system. The retention of this practice, it was suggested, prevented any significant improvement in the competitive ability of British banks. A further reduction of banking units, however, although in itself doing little to promote competition, might at least reduce some of the excesses of non-price competition to which any oligopolistic industry is prone.

The traditional interpretation of the official attitude had therefore to be revised; within months of the publication of the PIB report extensive changes were initiated. In January 1968 the merger of the National Provincial and Westminster Bank was announced, to be followed soon afterwards by the news of an amalgamation between the Three Banks Group (Royal Bank of Scotland, Glyn Mills and Williams Deacons) and the National Commercial Bank of Scotland, itself a product of the 1959 merger between the National Bank of Scotland and the Commercial Bank of Scotland. Both decisions appear to have been the product of some months' consideration, although the same cannot be claimed for that proposed between Barclays, Lloyds and Martins. Martins had been the last independent regional bank after the acquisition by the National Provincial of the District Bank in 1961, a merger which in itself could be regarded as following the natural line of evolution in the absorption or coalescing of the regional banks and thereby falling within the tenets prescribed for proposed amalgamations by the Colwyn Committee. The same justification could almost be applied to the Scottish bank groups, or even the National Provincial and Westminster, which dovetailed together regionally and in customer distribution.

The proposed merger of Barclays, Lloyds and Martins, however, would have created a mammoth bank handling nearly 50 per cent of total clearing bank deposits and supplying approximately 25 per cent of all call money to the discount market, as well as involving a reduction in the number of independent suppliers of credit. The amalgamation of such large banking units, and the reduction of the Big Five to three, inevitably raised questions of public interest. The Board of Trade accordingly referred the triple merger of Barclays, Lloyds and Martins to the Monopolies Commission for investigation. The Commission concluded, by a majority verdict, that the suggested benefits to the public interest were little more than marginal and would be offset by the risks arising from the reduction in the number of sources of finance for medium-sized and small businesses, particularly in so far as fast-growing, innovating companies were concerned.[3] Further competition among the clearing banks was in the public interest, and such competition was likely to be keener with four large clearing banks of roughly comparable size than with three banks with one as large as the other two combined.

In accordance with the Commission's majority report the government refused to allow the proposed merger between Barclays and Lloyds, although no objection was raised to the former's takeover of Martins. In the official announcement, particular emphasis was placed upon the danger of instability in the post-merger situation. A disturbance of market equilibrium, it was felt, could eventually lead to the absorption of the Midland Bank and the development of a banking duopoly. Both the Treasury and the Bank of England had held the view that this was inevitable: in this all members of the Monopolies Commission disagreed, although the risk appears to have weighed heavily in the government's final decision.

The Monopolies Commission looked—as had the Prices and Incomes Board and others before them—for a different approach by the banks to competition if Britain was to secure a better banking system. Any such approach was inevitably associated with the adoption of price competition and a readiness to engage in new areas and techniques of credit rather than a continued reliance on the traditional approach of service competition via branches; the latter, it was argued, was an 'expensive and not very effective' form of competition.[4] The present chapter examines the organisation and management of the clearing banks within the existing competitive environment, leaving until chapters 11 and 12 the respective backgrounds of competition in price or in new areas of credit.

2. Organisation and management

Since the nineteenth century almost all of the British clearing banks have maintained their head offices in London, the two exceptions being Williams Deacons and Martins. In general—and with the single exception of Barclays Bank—they have maintained a policy of centralisation, so that branch control has been within the jurisdiction of head offices. Although the other banks possess regional offices or district committees, until the mid-1960s only Barclays had pursued an active programme of decentralisation. In 1965, however, the Westminster Bank embarked on a similar policy and there were indications that other large banks were thinking along similar lines, especially as a result of the development of computer services for banking, while the process received an additional boost with the merger of the National Provincial and Westminster Banks.

The introduction of the computer into banking administration can not only reduce much of the routine work in branches and provide information required for management 'on line' to head office, but as a result of present developments could provide similar information at places other than the originating branch and put it 'on line' as certain branches are at present. Decentralisation of management thus becomes possible for those activities—for example, control of branch advances and staff—not directly required to be conducted in the City of London itself. Considerable saving on real estate could thus be secured, bearing in mind the exceedingly high cost of suitable office space in London.

Management itself has always been in the hands of professional bankers who are usually recruited from within the bank; 'working directors' (other than the chairman), such as those to be found in the old private banks or in the present merchant banks, are not a characteristic of the British joint-stock banks. The larger banks have boards of up to 25 members embodying a spread of contacts and interests in banking and business, their main function being to approve policy submitted to them from the management and perhaps sometimes to initiate it—and to exercise a general watch over the profitability of the bank. The effective administration and control of the banks is normally the responsibility of a Chief General Manager and on normal line-management patterns passes downwards through General Managers and Assistant General Managers to heads of bank departments—for example, Accountancy, Registrar, Foreign Department, Trustee and Executor Departments, O & M Communications and Computer, Intelligence, Staff and so on. Finally, perhaps via regional managers where applicable, it would filter down to management staff at branch level.

The day-to-day running of a large joint-stock bank is therefore carried out primarily by a team of six or seven people consisting of a chief general manager, perhaps a deputy chief general manager, and four or five other senior officers variously described by the banks as joint general managers and general managers.[5] These are often assigned a regional role, assuming responsibility for development, representation and staffing of the bank within a certain area of the country. In addition, or as an alternative, a joint general manager, or assistant general manager in a smaller bank, may be responsible for the administration of specific functions, such as general staff policy, premises development and expenditure, O & M computer and automated data-processing procedures, economic intelligence, export finance, credit cards or other services which a bank may want to emphasise. These staff make up a General Managers' committee, with the Chief General Manager as chairman; this meets as often as is required, but in most banks there is usually a daily meeting in one form or another. At this, discussions are held concerning not only problems relating to the current affairs of the bank but also future lines of policy, including those which require the approval of the board. At a lower, but still important, level the branch managers themselves are of course responsible for the local administration of bank policy. In most of the joint-stock banks local managers have discretionary limits for lending beyond which requests are usually dealt with by branch superintendents having their own discretionary limits or, if they exceed those limits, by Assistant General Managers. Propositions involving particularly large sums of money are usually referred to the General Managers' Committee itself.

Management skill is difficult to assess in any industry but this is especially so in banking. The banks, for reasons discussed more fully later, do not compete directly in price, until recently concealing their true profits and, with their special place in the monetary system, the least efficient tend to be cushioned from the full effects of competition by official restraints upon aggressive deposit creation. It is easy enough to make an arbitrary judgement of efficiency based on the volume of individual bank deposits, but deposits and costs per branch are almost as important as the aggregate volume of deposits. The position is further confused by the transition process currently affecting British banking. In recent years the relative position of the banks in the overall financial sector has been weakened by the growth of other financial intermediaries, which might suggest grounds for an indictment of joint-stock bank efficiency. Here again, however, special considerations apply and some of these are the subject of the following chapter. Prudence, perhaps, dictates no more than a few broad generalisations on this point.

By and large it is probably true to say that the banks have only recently appreciated the value of a scientific approach to management. While 'rule of thumb' techniques may have worked well for the merchant banks, for example, the latter, comprising as they do only one or two offices, are so much smaller in comparison that a close control can be fairly easily maintained over costs and activities. For the large joint-stock bank a more sophisticated approach to management is nowadays essential. The traditional attitude to bank management, apparent even today, is to some extent a legacy of the image of banking as a 'profession'—and thus distinct, in some genteel fashion, from the more vulgar occupations of industry and commerce—and epitomised by the attitude that 'the banker knows best' in some vague and unspecified manner when it comes to money and finance. In some banks such a frame of mind may have tended to foster their marked inclination to an innate conservatism. One example may be seen in the reluctance until recently to bring in specialist or other staff from outside and in the virtually complete reliance on internal promotion.

From about the 1950s the banks have ventured into the field of management and computer services—for example, through the creation of O & M departments or economics departments—although one bank, the Midland, has had an economics department since the 1930s. Even here, however, it is to be noted that the full potential of such services and specialists is far from being realised in these fields. There is some reason for suspecting that many of these innovations were originally introduced merely from a concern for public 'image' and a wish to keep up with the industrial Joneses. Although this was certainly superseded, if not accompanied, by a recognition of the inherent value of such information services for both customers and management, there was for long a tendency to regard them as no more than a modern version of the bank's intelligence or other departments, not to mention a marked reluctance to employ them in an active O and M programme.

It is scarcely deniable that in most industries the larger the unit the greater the need for a scientific approach to management. For banking the arrival of the computer in particular has prompted moves in this direction not least, perhaps, because of the need to avoid the much higher cost of mistakes which they can involve. Further, the success of the large units resulting from bank mergers could well depend on advanced applications of management science, particularly in the case of computer systems. While the banks have readily appreciated the savings in costs made possible by the automatic processing of accounts and so on, the more valuable function of the computer in the long run lies in its ability to provide not only comprehensive and immediate information for management but to employ simulation models to programme decisions as well. Beyond the piecemeal application of management science as a separate operation lies the ultimate target of the 'total system'—that is, an organisation in which all the ends are drawn together into a single system holding all available information and possessing the ability to manipulate it for the benefit of all participants, including management, staff and customers. [6]

3. Staffing

Branch banking has always been a good example of a labour intensive industry. This remains true today with 70 per cent of joint-stock bank operating costs attributable to salaries and labour on-costs. Until the 1950s not much change had occurred in the calibre of the supply of bank staff and bank recruiting was aimed at two types of staff—clerical and management material. Full employment and the development of grant-aided university education, however, have tended to reduce not only the supply of 16- and 18-year-old school leavers to the banks, in a quantitative sense, by attracting them to more glamorous occupations or to universities but have also skimmed off the best of potential entrants in terms of quality.

Under conditions of full employment the old, persisting image of banks as providers of a secure but humdrum employment has tended to be less attractive. Far more serious, however, has been the erosion of the differential between bank earnings and those of similar staff in national and local government and in the nationalised industries; this has operated to the detriment of bank labour recruitment over a period when the demand for staff has been expanding. To meet much of their demand for clerical labour the banks have been obliged to use more female staff and have also sought to improve their public image by advertising, particularly by placing emphasis on the one-in-two prospects of management for male staff. By the end of the 1950s, however, the general programmes of diversification, the development of specialised services, and the process of general modernisation had together emphasised the need for higher calibre staff. The banks' reaction was to step up their emphasis on graduate recruitment by offering special salary scales and stressing career prospects. Nevertheless most, if not all, banks retain a preference for the home-bred product; recruitment at middle and senior management levels continues to occur almost invariably from within a bank—only too often according to an age scale or on a seniority basis.

At the end of 1948 the London clearing banks employed 85, 000 people of which 60, 000 were men and 25, 000 women. By the end of 1969 bank staff had risen to 180, 000 comprising 82, 000 men, 90, 000 women and 8, 000 non-clerical workers. Between 1963 and 1969, the number of staff employed by the clearing banks increased by 41 per cent, reflecting both the continued programme of branch expansion and the move towards more diverse and specialised banking services. Over the longer period the proportion of female clerical employees rose from 30 per cent of the total to 52 per cent.(7)

One of the inevitable consequences of the banks' long-sustained policy of competition through branch expansion has been the great number of relatively small sites occupied by their branches. This has meant that each branch office tends to be just too small to absorb the business of another which could then close down. For the same reason it has also often proved virtually impossible to build bigger offices on existing sites. In the past the only solution appeared to be to open more and more new branches, thereby increasing the number of staff required. The development of computer-based communications, with accounts linked via branch terminals at the central computer base, however, could radically affect costs, quite apart from bank mergers and the potentialities of branch rationalisation inherent in them. If the banks can produce a viable programme for their new computers which obviates the need for their big turnover in female machine operators, they may well find an answer to one of their worst staff problems.(8) So far, despite heavy investment in computers, labour recruitment has continued to rise. This by no means necessarily implies deteriorating bank efficiency, of course, since the volume of work performed has undoubtedly increased although it is difficult to find any satisfactory measure of bank productivity.

4. Labour relations and collective bargaining

Because of the relative decline in banking salaries and professional prestige *vis-à-vis* other industries since the second World War, dissatisfaction amongst employees was almost bound to occur at some stage. Apart from the erosion of the differential in their pay in comparison with that of workers in similar occupations, bank employees had also suffered a narrowing of their hours differential; employees in other industries had been establishing a five-day week, but until recently bank employees have still been required to work a six-day week, although admittedly on a rota basis. Employees' unrest has probably been increased by the low degree of mobility of highly-qualified labour in the banking world, not only between banking and other sectors of the economy but within the clearing bank network itself. In the past the banks have never encouraged interbank movement, although for the lower clerical grades and certain specialist staff exceptions occasionally occur. It is still virtually unheard of for staff on 'general manager' appointments—for example, accountants or branch managers—to switch from one clearing bank to another.

For these reasons bank staff have become increasingly union-minded although until recently the channels for official complaint and negotiation have been on a strictly bilateral basis between an individual bank and its staff association. These associations were set up at the instigation of the banks after the first World War in order to counter the appeal of trade unionism among bank staffs and, in particular, of its practical expressions in the form of the Bank Officers' Guild established in 1918 and the Scottish Bankers' Association founded in 1919. In 1946 these two bodies merged to form the National Union of Bank Employees which continued the long struggle to win national recognition. Barclays Bank was for long the only bank to come to terms with the 'unofficial' union, having recognised the old Bank Officers' Guild in 1941. During the 1960s, however, various banks agreed to receive representatives from NUBE and in 1963 the Cameron Enquiry, set up by the government in response to a complaint by NUBE, urged that the remaining banks should receive representatives from NUBE and that attempts should be made to establish national negotiating machinery. The situation was still exacerbated, however, by the bitter rivalry between the NUBE and the staff associations, a rivalry which eventually succeeded in convincing at least two of the Big Five—the Midland and the National Provincial—of the wisdom of abandoning their bilateral structure in favour of multilateral national machinery. Until this was set up there would be no single body dealing with the banks, staff associations and NUBE to which common grievances could be referred.

In 1967 NUBE members took unprecedented strike action in support of their claim for recognition and power of negotiation as well as in protest over pay and hours. As a result of the action NUBE membership increased from 57, 000 to some 65, 000, although this latter figure was still less than staff association membership. Later in the same year, representatives of the union met representatives of the Committee of London Clearing Bankers for the first time. Nine of the eleven clearing banks agreed to recognise the union, the Midland and Coutts remaining aloof until the following year, when a Joint Negotiating Council for Banking was established. The eventual aim of NUBE is clearly—and naturally—to swallow up the staff associations; for the present, however, it has to adjust its policies in order to achieve a consensus, the chances of success for the new national machinery otherwise being slight. The bank mergers in themselves will make the staff associations of the merged banks larger and more powerful and will also simplify the problem of decision-making by the Council of Bank Staff Associations.

5. Costs and non-price competition

Labour costs are by far the most important item in bank operating costs, arising directly in the form of wages and salaries and indirectly in the form of pensions or contributions to pension funds or fringe benefits such as cheap loans for housing and other purposes. Other operating costs include rent, rates, repairs, printing, stationery and advertising, but none of these amounts to more than a small percentage of total operating cost. (Owing to the variations in bank accounting methods estimation of the trends and components of bank costs can only be approximate.) Over 70 per cent ot total bank operating costs in 1965 consisted of labour on-costs, excluding Selective Employment Tax. According to a special survey prepared for the National Board for Prices and Incomes, savings of 12 per cent in total clerical staff costs were possible even before the burst of amalgamations or full computer development, a figure which in the light of subsequent comments seems unlikely to have been far wrong.(9) With the introduction of electronic calculators, cheque sorters and so on, however, the relative importance of direct labour costs has been declining, while indirect labour costs, including SET and National Insurance contributions, have been rising more steeply, so that total labour costs continue to be about two-thirds of total operating costs.

In terms of output, the main work of the banks consists of providing facilities for making payments and it is through the clerical labour involved in this that their chief operating costs are incurred. Such facilities, of course, together with a wide range of ancillary services, are supplied through the banks' branches. By providing well-placed and attractive branches the banks have sought to make their services more readily available to the public and, at the same time, to create a prominent advertisement for the parent bank. By this means both deposits and lending opportunities are promoted. Since 1918 especially, the banks have relied upon branch expansion, with their associated range of bank services, as the main vehicle of inter-bank competition. As the Prices and Incomes Board noted, however, unrestricted branch expansion imposes costs—not only upon the bank but also upon the community—by using up resources in the construction and maintenance of an excessive number of buildings.(10) In the United Kingdom at the present time there is one branch to about 3, 900 people, compared with one for every 6, 250 persons in the United States.

The Prices and Incomes Board investigation into branch networks scrutinised bank attitudes towards the opening of new branches.(11) Although the banks consider branch expansion (or contraction) in the context of their network as a whole, each individual branch is required to maintain its own profit and loss account, usually on a half-yearly basis. In this account the operating costs of the branch are taken to consist of its running expenses—including notional or actual rental—and a contribution to Head Office expenses, together with the interest paid to its depositors. They would also include an imputed interest payment (at rates lower than the current rate on advances and higher than that on deposits) on funds which it may have had to 'borrow' from Head Office or elsewhere within the system in order to meet its own lending requirements. Its income, on the other hand, is taken to include commissions, interest receipts on loans and advances and interest imputed to any surplus deposits which the branch, after making advances to its own customers, had remitted to Head Office to be used elsewhere. The rates imputed on such surplus funds are lower than the current rate on advances but are higher for deposit account surpluses than for current account surpluses. By altering the imputed rate of interest paid on surplus funds lent to Head Office or charged on funds borrowed from it, the bank is able to influence the attitudes of its branch managers to advances and so exercise a further measure of discipline over them.

On this basis, the banks expect most new branches to be profitable within three to five years. Rigorous comparison of branches on a profitability basis is not possible, however, given the interdependence of individual branches in the network and the mutual benefits accruing from their geographical dispersion. Deposit-collecting branches in non-industrial areas, for example, are likely to appear less profitable than 'lending' branches in industrial areas, but in fact the latter depend heavily on the former for the supply of 'excess' deposits. Other relevant factors would also include estimates of the potential of the locality where the branch was situated, the existence or otherwise of alternative branches of the bank with the area, possible actions by competitors and so on.

In the minds of many bankers a call for deposit expansion is still regarded as synonymous with branch expansion; in 1960, for example, the Westminster Bank embarked upon an aggressive policy of branch-openings in order to counter a deteriorating competitive position. There is, naturally, a fairly strong correlation between branch growth and deposit growth, but the difficulty arises in estimating the point of diminishing marginal productivity or, conversely, the optimum number of branches per bank. Table 6 illustrates the difference between per-branch deposit figures in Great Britain and in the USA. Extreme caution must be adopted in any such comparison because of differing business conditions and so on, but it is not

TABLE 6

Average profits and deposits per branch, UK & US banks, 1966

Bank	No. of Branches		Profits/ Branch £	Deposits/ Branch (£000)
	Domestic	Foreign		
Bank of America	902	43	42,700	6,204
First National City Bank of New York	164	195	104,350	21,756[1]
Chase Manhattan	140	44	191,450	29,357[1]
Manufacturers Hanover	140	2	140,650	15,664[1]
Chemical Bank	136	2	144,700	15,891
UK Clearing banks	12,000[2]	—	15,400[3]	792

1. Domestic branches only
2. Approximate
3. Source: Estimate by 'Phaedra', 'London Banks' Profits, 1966', *The Bankers' Magazine*, Vol. CCIV, August 1967, pp. 74-6.

Source: J. R. Harrold, 'Why not two clearers?', *The Bankers' Magazine*, Vol. CCVI, No. 1494, September 1968, p. 140.

without interest that the largest US bank in terms of deposits also possesses the largest number of branches, although in this case the number is much less than those of the big UK clearing banks. This has been mainly due to legal restraints upon US banks but also, to a lesser extent, to factors such as geographical and financial conditions—for example, the growth, in the United States, of concentrated shopping areas with drive-in bank branches offering cash dispensing services, or the expansion of credit cards and other cash substitutes—many of which have tended to reduce the need for a large number of branches providing a comprehensive range of services.

Given the current environment of British banking, with alternative forms of competition not fully within its own discretion, some care must be exercised before expressing criticism of the zeal with which banks have extended their branch systems. This is illustrated by the disagreements to be discovered in the analyses contained in the reports of the National Board for Prices and Incomes and the Monopolies Commission respectively. In the case of the former the statement may be found that 'in the competitive environment in which they operate, the banks' management of their networks is rational', [(12)] followed in the subsequent paragraph by the assertion that the banks

> compete strongly with each other, imposing costs upon one another through the competitive duplication of branches and upon the community... and through neglect of economies of scale to be derived from operating larger branches. [(13)]

The Monopolies Commission, on the other hand, took a somewhat different line:

> Each bank has attempted to win the greater share of the business... through an increase in the number of outlets. This has led to the widely accepted theory that the country is overbanked. But the evidence on this point is inconclusive. [(14)]

In view of this inadequacy of empirical evidence, it is perhaps surprising to find the Commission nevertheless taking a rather more positive line in the statement that: 'Nevertheless, competition through branch networks has remained the main, but expensive and not very effective, form of competition.'[(15)]

The argument that economies of scale can be attained in banking appears plausible but again lacks adequate empirical support, depending in Britain at least upon a statistical survey of 302 branches conducted by the National Board for Prices and Incomes which suggests an optimum of between three to four thousand accounts. [(16)] The Monopolies Commission, however, held that 'No firm conclusion can be drawn about the presence or absence of economies of scale in British banking.'[(17)] Altogether it would not be unreasonable to conclude that so far as the London clearing banks are concerned allegations of overbanking rest rather more on intuition than on empirical evidence. While it seems not implausible that there is some *a priori* ground for suspecting the existence of overbanking, particularly in smaller towns, [(18)] and the existence of economies of scale (at least as far as routine services are concerned) over a size of three thousand accounts per branch, categorical assertions on these matters are clearly unjustified in the present state of knowledge.

As far as the 1968 mergers are concerned, it is difficult to assess what consequential economies in branches might be expected. Scottish experience, as provided by the 1959 merger, indicates that some economies could be achieved, although the PIB survey suggests that Scotland has been relatively more overbanked than England and Wales.[19] Between 1959 and 1967, however, the National Commercial Bank closed fifty-eight branches and opened only thirteen, achieving an overall saving of five per cent of branch running costs and ten per cent on administration and specialist services while similar economies are being achieved following its merger with the Royal Bank of Scotland. Even after the abandonment of the proposed merger of Barclays and Lloyds, significant economies in branch expansion by the former to counter the loss of migrating customers were made possible by the absorption of Martins Bank. Similarly, the amalgamation of the National Provincial and District Banks with the Westminster provided a more even geographical distribution of branches and thereby reduced the need for expansion into areas where previously one or other had had inferior representation. The realisation of further economies depends, of course, on the readiness of the banks to weld themselves into a single unit, a step which the National Provincial and District Banks did not take—possibly because of regional patriotism—following their merger in 1961.

The difficulties inherent in the measurement of branch productivity constitute a particular example of the general problem of measuring and costing the services provided by banks. In their emphasis upon non-price, or service, competition the banks have in recent years multiplied the number of services they provide. Hence although output has undoubtedly increased as well as operating costs, it is exceedingly difficult to find any single measure of output against which such costs can be judged.

Table 7 summarises the attempt made by the National Board for Prices and Incomes to grapple with this problem. The number of clearings seems to be as close an approximation to an index of physical output as is possible for the purely 'transfer' aspects of the banking industry; precisely because it is a 'real' measure, however (and also a partial one), the extent to which it can be validly related to an index of total money costs is obviously limited. Subject to all this, it could be argued that a rate of increase of some 6.5 per cent a year in output over 1961-65 is *prima facie* not a bad record.

The services provided by the banks may be classified into three categories: first, transfer services, secondly, credit services and thirdly, ancillary services. The first two arise essentially from the banks' established business of remitting and lending funds, while the third is of more recent development, although a beginning had been made before the first World War with the introduction of Trustee and Overseas Departments.

Under transfer services can be grouped all those transactions connected with the payment and remittance of money, whether by cheque, credit transfer, direct debiting, and so on, or by credit or cheque cards. Some of these—especially the operation of current accounts involving the use of cheques and credit cards—are time-consuming and costly; others, such as the newer system of direct debiting or the exchange of magnetic tape through the medium of the inter-bank computer bureau, promise to eliminate much routine paperwork.

TABLE 7

Indices of total costs and activity

(1961 = 100)

	1962	1963	1964	1965
a. London Clearing Banks				
(1) No. of Debit and Credit Clearings	105	113	123	129
(2) Total Costs	110	117	132	144
(3) Number of Accounts	102	108	114	120
(4) Value of Advances	102	116	129	139
b. Scottish Banks				
(5) Total costs	108	114	126	141
(6) Number of Accounts	103	107	113	118
(7) Value of Advances	108	118	126	141

Source: National Board for Prices and Incomes, *Bank Charges*, Report No. 34, Cmd. 3292, HMSO, London 1967, p. 49, Table 7. 1.

Daily cheque clearings by the clearing banks are growing at a yearly rate of over 5 per cent, while the average number of cheques handled daily in the banks' verification and sorting centres has reached 2½ million, attaining a level of 6 million at times of peak pressure. Credit clearing, itself intended to reduce the pressure on cheques, includes standing orders, counter credits by companies and private customers' salary credits and traders' credits; these operations are growing at twice the speed of cheque clearings, approaching a 10 per cent annual growth with a daily movement of about 1½ million separate transactions. Although no precise costing information is yet available, a common estimate for the average costs of clearing a cheque in 1968 was about 4 N.P. Given the increasing shortage and cost of clerical staff and the high cost of office space—particularly in London—there has been every incentive for the banks to mechanise their transfer systems at branch terminals as well as at the clearing centres, so developing a system in which large volumes of information are processed without a single sheet of paperwork.

Apart from their remittance functions, the banks are also engaged in borrowing and lending and in the provision of ancillary services ranging from financial advice to travel information. One of the earliest such services—the banks' foreign departments—originally facilitated the overseas trading activities of clients through the provision of foreign exchange and acceptance facilities. With the growth of international trade and travel, particularly after the second World War, the activities of such departments have widened to include, on the one hand, advice and assistance to exporters and, on the other, travellers' cheques and travel-agent type advice to personal customers. Similarly, Executor and Trustee Departments began as a service to shareholders but in recent years have been extended to provide advice on various legal, tax and investment problems; more recently still, the introduction of bank unit trusts has been a logical extension of the activities of these departments. Economic Intelligence Departments, begun by the Midland Bank in the 1930s, really developed only in the 1950s; their function, as the name implies, is the provision of economic intelligence for the banks and their customers and also the publication of reviews and bulletins which act as an advertisement for the individual bank.

For all these services, as well as many others including a range of financial advice, a charge is often although not always made; when imposed, it is usually on an *ad hoc* basis, being related to the turnover of the account in question. From the evidence before it, the National Board for Prices and Incomes noted that often no separate costing was made of individual services and that, in estimating charges, banks would assess not only the present costs and benefits of handling an account but the potential attractiveness of the account to the bank.[20] It quoted one prominent banker as saying:

> ...let us not forget that it is the presence of these additional services that distinguishes us from our competitors in the money transfer field and the goodwill element flowing from these additional services must not be overlooked. Nor, indeed, must the way in which the goodwill frequently translates itself into deposits.[21]

Charges paid by a customer usually purchase a mix of services, the prices of which are not clearly stated in any tariff or schedule. It is apparent, however, that for their range of services the banks generally charge on commission something less than the cost of providing such services. Hence the opinion of the National Board for Prices and Incomes that the banks would be justified in basing their charges, both for handling current accounts and for other services, more closely upon the cost involved.[22] To do so, however, would involve the banks in the risk of reducing their competitive 'low-price' position *vis-à-vis* other financial institutions, particularly the Post Office giro. Some services—and particularly some of the banks' own giro transfer services—appear to be 'loss leaders' designed not only to meet the competition of the Post Office giro but, within the banking network, to switch customers away from traditional and wasteful remittance methods into (eventually) more economical ones.

A more rational assessment of the banks' branch activities could possibly be achieved by a positive attempt to isolate their main functions. All British bank branches sell two main products: first, their transfer and encashment services and secondly, their credit services. In terms of the demand for the latter alone, it is likely that the number of branches is excessive and that such services could be concentrated on a much smaller number of main branches. In the case of the other main function of the banks—providing transfer and encashment services—a reduction is less easily achievable, although still highly desirable. Economies could certainly be obtained by automatic cash dispensers, drive-in branches providing simple cash services and the development of credit cards. Progress in this direction has already begun, notably in the case of credit cards, but still remains fairly limited. There seems to be no reason why all but the simplest cash, transfer and deposit facilities could not be transferred to main branches of the banks, leaving routine cash facilities to be provided in what would be the equivalent of cash bars.

The national interest requires competition primarily in the provision of credit and in the attraction of deposits. It is questionable whether the public interest would be unduly harmed by a downwards extension of the clearing house principle to the branch level, perhaps based initially on the consolidation of the banks' computer systems and services under a joint services company,[23] even if this eventually involved a reduction of inter-bank competition in transfer services—which need not necessarily follow. The value of such competition is debatable and must certainly be weighed against the loss of public welfare involved by the existing or supposed state of overbanking; in any case, the loss of inter-bank competition would tend to be offset by the increased competition implied by the creation of a Post Office Giro. The merger of the National Provincial and Westminster Banks, for example, would allow a number of sub-optimum branches to be merged into communal cash bars, with savings in space and staff, particularly with regard to high-cost managerial employees. A more interesting, if speculative, possibility would be the establishment by all the banks of a joint services company, owned and administered by them on some common basis—perhaps with safeguards for customer secrecy—designed to deal with all routine current account services in conjunction with credit or cheque cards and with direct telephone links to main branch computer terminals. The demand for other facilities—credit facilities, the placing of large deposits, financial advice, trustee work, etc.—could then be confined to branches in county towns and other medium-to-large centres. Some division of labour is of course already practised, but the development (and cost) of the computer and of substitutes for ready cash suggest that more economies could be achieved, particularly in rural and suburban areas.

An alternative would naturally be for the banks to perfect their individual costing techniques and to adjust their charges where necessary so as to price services on a full-cost basis. This pre-supposes, however, that the banks would be prepared to accept the risk that the high cost of some services would divert demand elsewhere—for example, to the Post Office Giro—with consequent loss of deposits (in the form of positive balances and money in the course of collection). In the end it is certainly arguable that if the banks are unable to contain the increasing costs of their services it would be preferable for them to concentrate their efforts upon more profitable activities, both new and old, in association with direct competition in price. With full price competition it is likely that many branches would be seen to be unprofitable; on the other hand, it could also be argued that in the absence of restraints upon bank lending, many would be sufficiently profitable to subsidise their other services.[24] Here again questions of public interest are raised; there seems little doubt that under current conditions the balance of probabilities tend to weigh against the latter hypothesis.

6. Computer costs and services

It was in response to the need to contain the rising costs being incurred in the provision of both established and new services that the banks began to invest heavily in computers. According to the National Board for

Prices and Incomes, annual expenditure by the banks on capital equipment more than doubled between 1960 and 1965, rising to nearly £8 million in the latter year. By the early 1970s the banks expect to have completed their current computer programmes; in consequence, they will have both a greater ability and a greater incentive to perfect internal costing techniques, which to date can hardly be said to be a strong point of bank management. Total expenditure on computer hardware and software over the period 1958-1968 (including orders outstanding and long-term rentals but excluding capital expenditure on special premises designed for computers and staff) has probably been in the region of £90-£100 million, the bulk of which represents purchases by the old Big Five.

Such expenditure has naturally involved mistakes and the extra expense inevitably incurred in the introductory and experimental phase of an entirely new process. The process of computerisation is also bound to be affected as the newly-merged banks attempt to rationalise their computer systems which in some cases have been incompatible to a major degree. The banks must expect to write off most of this new equipment within five or seven years, which gives some indication of the sort of savings they hope to achieve in operational costs by the switch to computers. It is expected that within five years at the outside — less for the leaders — the substitution of computers for such routine activities as handling current accounts and share registrations would achieve its break-even point and possibly show a reasonable credit balance. In the longer term the benefits from the management organisation, information and research side are likely to be at least as important — probably considerably more so.

The advent of the computer has made possible fundamental improvements in money transfer methods which can be of benefit to both the banks and their customers. Large users of bank giro credits will be able to supply their banks with information on tape instead of on paper vouchers. With direct debiting, businesses will be able to supply their banks with tape recordings of the payments for which claims are being made, while firms issuing large numbers of cheques will be able to obtain similar tape recordings of cheques which have been debited to their account. On present trends it appears that most future developments in banking will have a computer base; indeed, the prospect of an almost cashless and chequeless society is no longer far-fetched. By reducing the amount of cash in the hands of the public the banks can of course hope for an increase in their deposits. If any pronounced improvement is achieved in the speed of payments transmission, however, they will be faced with a loss of the interest normally earned on money in the course of collection—which again raises the problem of the policy to be adopted by the banks in charging for their services.

7. Profits

Profits accrue to the banks partly from the charges levied for the various services which they provide but mainly from the difference between the interest which they earn on their assets and the interest which they pay on their deposits. In fact, commission income does not yield on average more than 10 per cent of the banks' total income.[25] Before 1970 British banks did not fully disclose their profits in their published accounts. From their overall gross profits they first made provision for taxation and then set aside an amount to their undisclosed or 'inner' reserves and to guard against bad debts and losses on investments. It was the amount of profits remaining after these provisions had been made which the banks disclosed to the public as their published profits. The origin of this procedure lay in the venerable fear of a 'run on the bank' or, to put it in its more sophisticated version, of a possible loss of public confidence in a bank in the event of the disclosure of substantial losses on investments or bad debts. To the extent that the banks now hold securities whose average maturity is much shorter than formerly, one need for these inner reserves had largely disappeared. The fact that for a century the Bank of England has acted as lender of last resort to the banks and in modern conditions would not allow a clearing bank to fail, was a further argument in favour of the abolition of the practice.

As the National Board for Prices and Incomes observed, however, the banks have been entering fields of activity involving new and to some extent unknown risks; the trend towards concentration in industry has also increased the average size of many deposits and many individual loans—and hence the risk involved.(26) Under such circumstances there might have been something to be said for the continuance of secret reserves. In theory, of course, the retention of undisclosed profits in the form of inner reserves can misrepresent not only the level but also the trend of profits as conveyed by the published figures, a fact which has long been a source of concern for financial journalists. In practice, however, the trend of profits over the last twenty years or so seems to have been faithfully represented by the banks' disclosed profits, although 'inner reserve' policy has enabled the banks to moderate the fluctuations in the absolute magnitude of their published profits from year to year.

Apart from commission income, the gross profits of the banks depend on the volume of their deposits and the proportionate distribution of their assets. Of the substantial increase in profits between 1956 and 1965, nearly a half can be attributed to the growth in deposits and therefore in assets, while the dramatic recovery in advances since 1958 has been the other main factor. A higher proportion of deposits employed in the form of advances tends to increase profits and vice-versa; on the other hand, a decline in the gilt-edged market may mean that the banks have to restore their inner reserves if their investments portfolios are substantial in relation to their reserve position.

Since the nineteenth century the rates paid on advances and deposits to or by the joint-stock banks have been tied to Bank rate. Owing to the abolition of interest on current accounts, however, a considerable proportion (currently over 50 per cent) of bank deposits are on an interest-free basis and are thus available to the banks at zero cost. The effect of an increase in Bank rate is therefore to widen the profit margin per unit of assets whose earning rates are affected by Bank rate (bills, call money and advances) and the share of such assets in the total normally exceeds the proportion of deposits on which interest payments—tied to Bank rate—are made. Offsetting this so-called 'endowment' effect of a rise in Bank rate, however, is the need to make extra provision for bad debts in times of credit stringency and for falls in the quoted prices of investments. There is also a tendency towards an increase in the proportion of deposit accounts on which interest has to be paid. A further offsetting factor since the war has been the official restrictions on bank lending which have usually been associated with increases in Bank rate. The PIB concluded, however, that during the 1956-1965 decade the beneficial effects on profit margins arising from the increased average level of Bank rate, and from the changed structure of bank assets and liabilities (shown by Table 8), had been greater than the adverse effects resulting from the upward movement in costs; consequently bank profit margins, on average, had widened over those ten years. (27)

TABLE 8

Assets and liabilities of the London Clearing Banks as % of total deposits

	31.12.56	15.12.65
Assets		
Cash in hand and balances with Bank of England	8.6	8.4
Money at call and short notice	7.6	10.8
Bills discounted	21.3	13.0
Total liquid assets	37.5	32.1
Investments at book value	29.7	12.5
Advances to customers and other accounts	28.7	48.3
Other*	4.1	7.1
	100.0	100.0
Liabilities†		
Current Accounts	64.2	53.1
Deposit and other Accounts	35.8	46.9
	100.0	100.0

* Inter-bank deposits and items in transit; investments in affiliated banks and subsidiary companies; bank premises.

† Excluding capital paid up, reserve funds, and contingent liabilities.

The bulk of bank costs, however, arises from its labour charges; these are independent of the level of Bank rate and their upward movement since the war has been detrimental to the banks' profit margins. So far, however, the banks have been cushioned against this upward pressure in operating costs by the endowment effect of a high average Bank rate. Under present circumstances the banks' operating costs exceed that part of their income not directly sensitive to Bank rate. An increase in operating costs per unit of gross assets, therefore, even if accompanied by an equal proportionate increase in commission income, would squeeze bank profit margins. The ability of the banks to increase their advances is limited, while in the view of the PIB the competitive environment in which the banks find themselves is likely to inhibit them from passing on increased costs to the consumer; hence the net effect has been such as to produce a tendency towards a contraction in bank profit margins.

The range of services provided by the banks involves a number of different markets—for large deposits, for small deposits, for large loans, for small loans and so on—and the conditions of competition differ in each. For example, personal deposit accounts with the banks face competition from the Post Office Savings Bank and the Trustee Savings Bank and, to a lesser degree—because they are less liquid—from building societies and hire purchase companies; for large corporate deposits, of course, competition has been sharpened considerably by the growth of the secondary markets and much the same is true of the 'loans' markets. Even the banks' safest activities, current account and remittance facilities, are threatened by developments such as the Giro. With the growing pressure on costs and profit margins since the second World War, therefore, the reaction of the banks to these pressures and the concomitant emphasis on size in finance as well as in industry almost inevitably took the form of the plunge into amalgamation.

This latter development was something of an irrelevance, however, so far as many observers were concerned. In their view, increased size was not necessarily the answer to the problems confronting banking, although given the pressures of postwar trends it inevitably constituted something of a temptation. The fundamental issue before all branch banks in this country is whether they can devise a more precise and rational system of costing and pricing for all their banking services. They need to achieve, the argument would run, a more positive demolition of the cartel which has shielded them from the full effects of cost increases and has delayed much longer-needed improvements in costing and the supply of services. If the banks were monopolistic suppliers of credit, or takers of deposits, the consequences of apathy would be less serious for them. But this has never been the case and since the second World War the situation has become increasingly complex as various other competitors have taken advantage of the gaps in the market. Failure by the banks to take more positive action necessarily condemns them to a continued erosion of their erstwhile dominant position in the economy.

REFERENCES

1. *Report of the Treasury Committee on Bank Amalgamations,* 11th March 1918, para. 8.

2. National Board for Prices and Incomes, *Bank Charges,* Report No. 34, Cmd. 3292, HMSO, London 1967, para. 154.

3. Monopolies Commission, *Barclays Bank Ltd., Lloyds Bank Ltd. and Martins Bank Ltd.,* HMSO, London 1968, para. 260.

4. *Ibid.* para 225.

5. See A. D. Chesterfield, 'Organisational Structure', *The future of British Banking,* Institute of Bankers Seminar, 1968, pp. 11-25.

6. R. Hindle, 'The Operational Significance of Mergers', *'The Bankers' Magazine,* April 1968, p. 224.
7. National Board for Prices and Incomes, *Pay in the London Clearing Banks,* Report No. 106, Cmd. 3943, HMSO, London 1969, p. 4.
8. C. Gwinner, 'The Industry's Structure after Mergers', *Financial Times Banking Supplement,* June 4th 1968, p. 20. According to the PIB report *Pay in the London Clearing Banks,* in the 18-23 years age group the wastage rate amongst females in 1968 was no less than 25 per cent. *Ibid.,* p. 5.
9. National Board for Prices and Incomes, *Bank Charges,* para. 144.
10. *Ibid.,* para. 149.
11. *Ibid.,* paras. 145-155.
12. National Board for Prices and Incomes, *Bank Charges,* para. 148.
13. *Ibid.,* para. 149.
14. Monopolies Commission, *op. cit.,* para. 222.
15. *Ibid.,* para. 225.
16. National Board for Prices and Incomes, *Bank Charges,* Appendix XI.
17. Monopolies Commission, *op. cit.,* para. 163.
18. National Board for Prices and Incomes, *Bank Charges,* Appendix XI.
19. *Ibid.,* Appendix XII.
20. *Ibid.,* para. 103.
21. L. C. Mather, 'Banker and Customers', *The future of British Banking,* p. 43.
22. National Board for Prices and Incomes, *Bank charges,* para. 125.
23. See H. G. Johnson, 'Observations on the bank merger proposals', *The Bankers' Magazine,* September 1968, p. 136.
24. L. C. Mather, *op. cit.,* p. 40.
25. National Board for Prices and Incomes, *Bank Charges,* para. 107.
26. *Ibid.,* para. 37.
27. *Ibid.,* para. 41.

CHAPTER ELEVEN

Competition in British Banking

1. The growth of the 'secondary system'

The financial institutions which came under the scrutiny of the Radcliffe Committee were much of the old order: the discount houses, accepting houses, building societies and insurance companies, the old-established British and foreign overseas banks, even the finance houses—all had been engaged for many years in the related but loosely knit markets ancillary to those which still remained the province of the joint-stock commercial banks. Within less than a decade, by the time of the Prices and Incomes Board Report of 1967, however, a very different scene was presented. Entirely new credit markets had appeared, although the institutions dealing in them were in most cases old-established city institutions which had grafted new types of business on to their earlier activities. In December 1951 clearing bank deposits had comprised nearly 80 per cent of total bank deposits in Britain; by the end of 1967 this share had dropped to 46 per cent—or 64 per cent when foreign currency deposits are excluded.

Within this context the Prices and Incomes Board noted that in their role of financial intermediaries the banks faced increasing competition from other institutions whose liabilities, from the point of view of the investor, were in varying degree almost as liquid as bank deposits—and had the added attraction of a higher return.(1) Between 1959 and 1965 joint-stock bank deposits had risen on average by just under 5 per cent, compared with an average annual growth of approximately 6 per cent a year in GNP. Deposits of UK residents with overseas banks had meanwhile grown by over 25 per cent a year, deposits with accepting houses by over 30 per cent a year, deposits with hire purchase companies by somewhat over 20 per cent a year and building societies' shares and deposits by just over 10 per cent a year. By contrast, the average annual rate of growth in deposits with the Trustee Savings Banks was only 9 per cent and that of Post Office Savings Banks deposits had been less than 2 per cent. Since the late 1940s London Clearing bank deposits had fallen rapidly in relation to GNP from nearly 60 per cent in 1947 to 34 per cent in 1956, a trend largely reflecting the decline of wartime and postwar excess liquidity; during the late 1950s, however, a levelling off in the decline was apparent, so that in 1961 they still amounted to something over 30 per cent of GNP at current prices.

Although during the 1950s as a whole bank turnover more than kept pace with the growth of GNP, the rate of growth of bank deposits lagged behind not only the growth of national income but also the expansion of other financial assets; as may be seen from Table 4 of the Statistical Appendix, between 1950 and 1960 the share of clearing bank deposits in the major categories of liquid assets in the United Kingdom fell from 42 to 38 per cent. The question raised by the Prices and Incomes Board was whether this relative loss of importance could be moderated by action on the part of the banks themselves and, in particular, by the abandonment of their conventions with regard to non-price competition. The Board concluded in fact that the banks could initiate an increase in their deposits, in contrast to the traditional view that the volume of bank deposits was solely determined by the authorities; the volume of deposits, it was argued, would depend in part upon the monetary authorities but would also vary with the preference of the public for liquid assets, and the most obvious way of influencing the latter would be the dissolution of the cartel agreement on rates.(2) Two years previously, indeed, in April 1963, at a banquet to commemorate Martins' 400th anniversary, no less a person than the Governor of the Bank of England had enquired 'whether the considerable rigidity in interest rates which has grown up in the banking world in the last 20 years or so is an encouragement to the growth of bank deposits'. Clearing bank reactions were generally hostile to any radical departure from their current practice, however. In this they were strongly supported by the Treasury, whose concern appears to have stemmed from acceptance of the bankers' arguments that direct price competition would raise the cost of credit, which was not considered to be in the best interests of the economy.

Of some relevance here is the history of the banks' attitude to price competition. Until 1945 the clearing banks had offered an agreed rate on seven-day-notice deposits but offered special rates for reasonably sized deposits placed for a fixed period—i.e. 'fixtures'. In October 1945, however, as part of Dr Dalton's cheap money policy, the authorities had insisted that the banks should cease the practice of making competitive bids for fixtures and should maintain only an agreed fourteen-day interest rate. At that time, and for some six or seven years afterwards, this probably had little effect on the competitive attractions of bank deposits, given the prevailing situation of excess liquidity and generally low interest rates. Treasury bills, for instance—a suitable outlet for large funds—carried rates of not more than $1/32$ per cent above the banks' deposit rate, although the rates offered by other institutions, notably the building societies and insurance companies, were higher; these latter institutions certainly continued to attract deposits, but even so there was no substantial differential between clearing bank deposit rates and other short-term money rates.

In 1951, however, the position was altered; the change in monetary policy in favour of the positive use of interest rates in that year provided the springboard for the subsequent development of other financial intermediaries.(3) Until that time most merchant banks, as well as the overseas and foreign banks in London, had followed the clearing bank interest-rate structure, but thereafter for the most part they offered and charged higher rates than the clearing banks for short money. As the clearing banks were abstaining from competition on rates, both between themselves and with other financial institutions, the way was open for the development of other competitors. Until 1958, however, commercial bidders for fixtures—such as hire-purchase companies, accepting houses and the foreign, overseas and Commonwealth banks—including funds deposited by overseas residents, expanded only relatively slowly; their deposits amounted to £573 million at the end of 1958 compared with £542 million at the end of 1951. Deposits with American banks, also including non-resident accounts, rose during the same period from £96 million to £130 million, while deposits with accepting houses rose from £136 million to £212 million. The main threat to bank deposits as liquid assets during these years came directly from the government sector in the form of Treasury bills, purchases of which by companies rose from £176 million to £602 million between 1953 and 1958, subsequently rising to well over £800 million in 1960.

In 1958, however, both hire-purchase undertakings and the banks themselves were set free from restrictions on lending and a swift expansion followed; at the same time exchange control requirements were relaxed in favour of external holders of current sterling. Three years before local authorities had also been driven to meet their borrowing needs by competing in the capital market, their freedom of access to the Public Works Loans Board having been severely limited. All these developments helped to make business undertakings, and the public generally, more keenly aware of yields and of alternative sources of finance, while the trend towards amalgamation and grouping amongst British companies encouraged a more profitable employment of their liquid resources. The stage was set, therefore, for a revolution in the financial markets as various 'takers of funds'—the overseas banks, accepting houses and other specialised institutions—began to bid higher rates for deposits which they were able to lend profitably to local authorities, hire purchase companies and so on, partly because they were not subject to any official liquidity ratio requirements.

If at this stage the clearing banks had been able and willing to bid for time deposits there might have been much to be said for it from their point of view. By reputation and habit the clearers, together perhaps with the Scottish banks, were still the only recognised first-class takers of large deposits; if they had bid competitive rates it would have been difficult for others to make rapid progress in the market. Indeed, some bankers at that time strongly supported such a course, but for a number of reasons the majority were opposed to it and it is probable that for some years the authorities would also have been opposed. The continuance of such opposition was apparent not only in the discussions of 1963 but in the evidence submitted to the Monopolies Commission not only by the banks but also by the Treasury and Bank of England representatives, their contention being that the present practice allowed for the provision of credit at lower rates than would otherwise have been possible.(4)

In these circumstances an extensive market in fixed deposits quickly grew up in which the volume of short-term funds employed came to exceed that in the long-established markets. These came to be known as 'parallel' or 'secondary' or sometimes 'unsecured' markets to distinguish their activities from the secure borrowing of the discount houses in the 'primary' markets.(5) Within this tangled and fluid network it is possible to distinguish three main sub-markets: one in short-term deposits, where the principal borrowers are local authorities and hire purchase finance houses, the second dealing in funds generally described as Euro-dollars and the third handling inter-bank transactions in sterling. The main institutions engaged in these markets comprise the accepting houses, overseas British and foreign bank offices and hire purchase finance companies who have grafted fresh activities on to old ones. When credit restrictions returned to hamper other 'traditional' financial activities, including those of the primary markets, the new markets gained further ground. Under pressure of competition they developed further and bid increasingly high rates, so that a significant differential was established between the clearing banks' seven-day deposit rate and the 'competitive' rate for fixtures. In addition, of course, there remained the established financial intermediaries—the Building Societies, insurance companies and the Post Office and Trustee Savings Banks—which in general restricted themselves to their traditional markets.

2. Clearing bank subsidiaries

Until 1958 the banks stood aside from the newer markets; as has been seen, these were still only just beginning. They preferred to maintain their cartel agreements on rates for borrowing and lending and to compete with one another, as well as with the financial intermediaries, through the provision of branches and associated services. In that year, however, a radical departure occurred when the clearing banks acquired control or part ownership of several hire-purchase companies. By this means they were beginning to participate in the growth potential of this expanding field of finance, a field which had been enjoying a considerable boom since the late 1950s, especially in consumer finance. Although the clearing banks are sure of a large volume of deposits as a result of the growth of national expenditure, there is no close and dependable relationship between deposits and transactions such as to ensure that the banks maintain their share in total lending and investment or in the total profits earned by financial institutions. Through their hire-purchase subsidiaries the banks therefore became able to channel funds into a form of lending which was highly profitable but which the banks themselves, for various reasons, preferred to keep distinct from their primary activities—for which preference they were subsequently to earn the censure of the National Board for Prices and Incomes.

Foremost among the reasons for the banks' instinct towards separation must have been the fact that hire-purchase companies were not subject to any official liquidity ratio and were therefore able to lend to an extent not always permissible for an ordinary clearing bank. An additional 'bonus' may be seen here in the opportunity open to a banking group of switching funds from the subsidiary to the parent bank at times of pressure on the latter's liquidity ratio. Further, finance houses were not bound by any of the cartel agreements on rates applying to the London clearing bankers. Through their subsidiaries, therefore, the banks were able to bid competitively for deposits and proceeded to do so, although only for large amounts and for fixed and longer periods than the usual seven-day notice on clearing bank deposit accounts. Apart from an initial setback, when the banks appear to have pumped more funds into their new associates than they could properly handle—a spate of unwise lending and bad debts occurring in 1958-9—the new subsidiaries made rapid progress.(6)

Meanwhile the other components of the secondary markets had also rapidly expanded their business, as may be seen from Table 9. The so-called secondary banks—i.e. accepting houses, British Overseas and Commonwealth banks, American banks and others—expanded their deposits by over 400 per cent between 1958 and 1966. Part of this growth in total deposits was accounted for by the arrival of new foreign banks, while the total was also increased by the presence of the deposits of overseas banking offices: nearly all the latter were deposits by overseas branches with the London head office in the case of overseas banks and of head office and non-UK branches with the London branch in the case of foreign banks. A further 'inflating' element was inter-bank deposits, both in sterling and other currencies.(7)

After excluding deposits held by overseas banking offices and inter-bank deposits, it still appears, according to reliable estimates, that the deposits of the British joint-stock banks were only three times as big as those of 'secondary' banks in 1966, whereas they had been 14 to 15 times their size

TABLE 9

Deposits of UK Secondary System Banks*

(£ million: end-year totals)

	1951	1958	1966	1967‡	1968
Accepting houses	136	212	1,135	1,464	1,877
British overseas and Commonwealth banks	542	573	1,811	2,300	2,744
American banks	96	130	2,215	3,283	5,301
Others†	(85)	460	1,646	2,551	3,669
Total	(859)	1,375	6,807	9,598	13,591
Deposit banks					
London clearing banks	6,333	7,199	9,501	10,262	10,736
Scottish banks	754	791	982	1,070	1,138
Northern Ireland banks	123	143	222	253	267
Total	7,210	8,133	10,705	11,585	12,141

* Including non-resident accounts, inter-bank deposits in sterling and other currencies, and (for 1968) negotiable sterling certificates of deposit.

† Comprises members of foreign banks and affiliates, other overseas banks and other banks. The last include some hire purchase finance houses, accepting houses, loosely described as merchant banks etc., not members of the Accepting houses Committee or the Overseas bank associations.

‡ Foreign currency items are affected by the devaluation of sterling on 18th November 1967.

Source: Bank of England Quarterly Bulletin.

in 1951.(8) Particularly rapid growth rates were recorded by the US banks, which were by far the largest single category of banks in the secondary system by 1966; the growth rate of their deposits was around 24 times from 1951 to 1966. This was partly due to the readiness of the larger US banks to continue providing banking services to their domestic corporate customers when these established branches or subsidiaries overseas; it is also partly due to the fact that a substantial proportion of US overseas direct investment has been directed towards Great Britain. According to the same estimates, something in the region of 75 per cent of the London sterling business of American banks is accounted for by British subsidiaries of US companies.(9) Yet another factor has been the restrictions imposed on the outflow of funds from the United States as a result of the US balance of payments problem; these have encouraged US bank branches in London to acquire their own deposits rather than simply rely on funds transmitted from their head offices, partly by aggressive bidding for deposits from British residents and partly by a successful tapping of the Euro-dollar market, in which field the American banks have become easily the most important operators in London.

It appears that the impact of such competition may nevertheless have been exaggerated. The resident sterling deposits of the American banks amounted to only £253 million at the end of 1968, excluding inter-bank deposits, out of an overall total of £5,301 million, and had grown only from the equivalent of 1 per cent of total deposits of the clearing banks at the end of 1964 to the equivalent of 2.4 per cent at the end of 1968. Even so, the proportion of sterling deposits taken from British-owned companies and others was certainly increasing, reflecting the attractive rates offered on deposits by American banks. The Monopolies Commission considered that it was in their sterling lending that the US banks were in more direct competition with the clearing banks, although even here 80 per cent of such business was with American and other foreign-owned customers.(10) In relation to the advances of the clearing banks, American bank lending to British borrowers had increased only from 0.6 to 0.9 per cent between 1964 and 1968. Their main role in London has in fact been in the Euro-currency and inter-bank markets, although any tightening of these markets could certainly result in an increased resort to domestic non-bank suppliers and takers of funds within Britain.

For the secondary banks as a whole, UK residents—mainly industrial and commercial companies but also investment trusts, finance houses and insurance companies—provided at end-1968 just under 65 per cent, or approximately £2,000 million, of their total sterling deposits excluding those by other banks; the secondary banks were in turn lending just over £1,200 million in sterling (£1,712 million if other currencies are included) to non-bank UK residents, as well as some £1,100 million in loans to British local authorities.

Clearing bank involvement in the secondary markets proper has been much more recent than the acquisition by the banks of hire-purchase subsidiaries in and around 1958, through which subsidiaries the banks dabbled on the side, although not very extensively, in the new markets. The success of others in the field, together with a growing concern at the effect this has had on clearing bank deposits, helped to push the clearing banks into the formation of their own secondary subsidiaries designed to re-enter the market for fixed deposits on a much larger scale. This was particularly so after the establishment of the Midland and International Bank in 1964 stimulated a surge of interest in this field. The newer subsidiaries differ considerably amongst themselves in form and in the range of their activities, although most are classified by the Bank of England under the heading of other banks and overseas banks. Many, in fact, were existing subsidiaries operating in international banking or hire purchase—for example, Barclays Bank (France) Ltd., Lloyds Bank (Europe) Ltd., the Midland Bank Finance Corporation and the County Bank etc.,—whose activities either readily lent themselves to, or were re-designed to take advantage of, the new markets. Other institutions, on the other hand, such as the National Provincial and Rothschilds (International) Ltd., were especially formed for the purpose.

By the end of 1967 these subsidiaries were known to control deposits well in excess of £500 million. Another estimate suggests that the banks' 'back-door deposits' held by all their subsidiaries (excluding Barclays DCO, BOLSA, the Standard Bank, etc.) in fact amounted to as much as

£1,200 million at the end of 1967, between one half and two thirds of this being probably in sterling and the rest in other currencies, mainly dollars. By mid-1968 the Bank of England, cautiously admitting the possibly deleterious effect on clearing bank deposits of secondary bank competition, was able to declare that 'the clearing banks now appear to have checked this trend by setting up subsidiaries offering higher rates for deposits'.(11) Another indication, if very approximate, of the growth of these 'bidding' subsidiaries is provided by the official category of 'other banks' in which most of these clearing bank subsidiaries appear. The remaining bidding subsidiaries, classified elsewhere, are, however, significantly important in terms of deposits although numerically very small. The 'other bank' clearing subsidiaries comprised in 1969 seventeen out of the thirty-one contributing members and analysis of the balance sheets of the remaining (non-clearing-bank subsidiary) members for 1968 and 1969 suggests that, for these years at least, deposits held by the clearers' subsidiaries amounted to about two-thirds of total deposits.

TABLE 10

Other Banks: Analysis of Deposits. End Year Figures (£ million)

	TOTAL	U.K. Banks		Other U.K. Residents		Overseas Residents	
		Sterling	Other Currencies	Sterling	Other Currencies	Sterling	Other Currencies
1965	317.6	40.8	39.1	143.1	0.6	35.2	58.8
1966	358.1	54.3	39.4	152.1	3.7	47.6	61.0
1967	879.3	133.4	144.5	351.7	19.5	56.9	173.3
1968	1544.1	302.2	214.6	630.3	13.6	59.6	323.8
1969	2509.6	455.5	527.9	769.5	27.9	73.2	655.6

3. Financial intermediaries and the volume of deposits

The National Board for Prices and Incomes contended that without jeopardising the broad economic aims of the monetary authorities the banks could achieve a larger volume of deposits if these were more attractive for the public to hold; the abandonment of the agreement on interest rates, it was argued, would produce this result.(12) The Board pointed out that although at the time of its investigation it could be said that the banks were under no compulsion to seek a greater volume of deposits in order to maintain their traditional business in the long run this might not continue to be the case; in any event, it was argued, failure to attract sufficient deposits was likely to inhibit the banks from more diversified lending policies. A similar point had been made by the Radcliffe Report in 1959 when it commented that:

> The banks' restrictive attitude in attracting deposits had been supposed to set corresponding limits on the kind of lending they could engage in; the truth is rather that it has limited their quantitative share of the total lending in the economy.(13)

Two years later, as a result of the boom in consumer credit, the banks found their advances ratios restored to a level not known for nearly thirty years. This massive expansion of their lending had been financed largely out of sales of investments, which were now severely reduced. In consequence the banks were faced with the fact that further expansion of their lending would increasingly depend on their ability to secure additional deposits. The two issues which are of most significance are, first, the banks' predisposition towards non-price competition and the effect this has on their deposits and, secondly, their attitude to new types of lending and the effect which their existing policies have on their share of total consumer credit. Both are necessarily interdependent and closely linked, but the former is the main topic in this chapter; a detailed discussion of the banks' relative position in the market for consumer credit is postponed until Chapter 12.

As far as the market for deposits is concerned, it may well be true that the clearing banks would have had a much larger share of the market in 1968 if different policy decisions had been taken ten years previously. It does not follow, of course, that it would be right simply on that account to reverse those decisions in the future. Although turnover on bank accounts has risen a good deal faster than national income, however, the fact remains that the community has greatly reduced its bank balances in relation to the payments being made—in other words, the velocity of circulation of bank deposits has greatly increased—although a good deal turns on the length of the time period taken into consideration, a factor which the Board did not discuss but which is examined in some detail in Chapter 13 below.

Public preference for bank deposits has undoubtedly been affected by the growth of financial intermediaries offering more attractive rates of interest on short-term deposits than the banks, despite the fact that, unlike bank deposits, balances with such intermediaries cannot be generally used for payments. The risk of 'leakages' of deposits incurred through the activities of these intermediaries has been greater in the periods of high and rising interest rates experienced since 1951 during which the velocity of circulation of cash (demand deposits) rises and the attraction of interest-bearing liquid assets increases *vis-à-vis* the zero return experienced on cash. A further factor underlying this switch, of course, may have been the effect of post-war full employment policies on expectations; diminished uncertainty may have led to a reduction in balances held for precautionary purposes while inflation—the by-product of full employment policies—has increased the real cost of holding idle cash. Under such circumstances the demand for bank deposits is dependent upon the cross-elasticities of demand with respect to other interest-bearing close substitutes. It should be noted, however, that there is no simple relationship between interest-rate differentials and the degree of substitution between bank deposits and such assets as building society shares and deposits or deposits in the Trustee and Post Office Savings Banks; the differentials have on occasion varied widely without any obvious movement of funds from one intermediary to the other.[14] Indeed, the demand for bank deposits would appear to be somewhat less responsive to interest rates than the demand for the liabilities of these particular financial intermediaries. This may not be entirely surprising, perhaps, in view of the usefulness of the current account as a means of making current payments—or even of the deposit account, as the closest adjunct to it; in other words, the liquidity aspect introduces some inelasticity into consumers' preferences.[15]

At the same time it can be shown that movements of funds within the group of non-bank financial intermediaries have undoubtedly occurred in response to interest rate differentials. It would appear, however, that their impact on the demand for both bank and non-bank financial liabilities, and on the velocity of circulation of bank deposits, has been dwarfed by the movement of funds into other assets as the public has sought to protect itself against inflation.[(16)] Obviously this does not exclude the possibility that such movements may be responsive to, amongst other factors, implied real interest-rate differentials on assets, which, despite a sacrifice of liquidity, carry a higher return than that to be derived from deposits with banks and other intermediaries. Despite their limitations, and the perplexities of public liquidity and asset preferences, the importance of interest-rate differentials cannot entirely be denied; their effect for the clearing banks is perhaps most readily apparent in the decline of corporate bank balances. Between December 1963 and December 1968, balances of companies with the deposit banks (Clearing, Scottish and Northern Ireland banks) rose by only £110 million to £2,146 million, whereas their balances with accepting houses, overseas and other banks rose from £496 million to £1,301 million. Over the same period, total balances with the deposit banks held by 'other' depositors—mainly personal—rose by nearly £2,300 million to £8,313 million.

Within the continued decline of clearing bank deposits in relation to GNP, the greatest slump has been experienced in current accounts, clearing bank deposit accounts declining only slightly in relative terms. It appears likely that the stagnation in the demand for corporate balances on deposit account has been to some extent offset by the growth of personal balances on deposit account and, of course, by an overall shift from current accounts to deposit accounts; expressed as a percentage of total clearing bank liabilities, current accounts fell from 62.8 per cent in 1955 to 51.1 per cent in 1968. Furthermore, whereas the differential between the zero yield on cash (including current accounts) and on interest-bearing liquid assets widened quite sharply after 1951, the cost of holding deposit accounts—as measured by the differential between clearing bank deposit account rates and that on other interest-bearing liquid assets—did not rise so much; deposit accounts, regarded in Britain as substantially repayable on demand, have thus tended, perhaps, to aquire part of the functions of current accounts.

In addition to causing this relative weakening in the demand for bank deposits, the growth of other deposit attracting institutions may impair the inherent ability of the clearing banks to create deposits. The simplest way in which this can happen is through primary losses of deposits directly transferred from the clearing banks into the government sector itself through official agencies such as the Savings Banks; these involve the clearing banks in a loss not only of deposits but an equal amount of cash as well, with a consequent reduction in their credit-creative power. On the other hand, transfers to bodies which maintain accounts with the joint-stock banks, although involving no direct and immediate loss, may also have an effect on deposits if these institutions deploy part of their acquired resources in a liquidity reserve composed of Treasury bills or other gilt-edged securities.

The most direct form of competition which the banks face, in other words, is that from the central government itself and its range of securities of varying liquidity. In so far as it is able to borrow directly from the public the government can avoid borrowing from the banks, which are thereby deprived of the cash and liquid assets necessary for deposit expansion. The eventual result of a sustained denial of cash to the banks—still the largest lenders in the economy—would of course be deflationary. In the end the government is obliged to provide the cash and liquidity base for an adequate level of bank deposits, although this action could be postponed by the presence of other lenders in the economy whose provision of credit in substitution of bank advances introduces a lag into the process. At this point it is important to examine in some detail the manner in which the existence of other intermediaries in the private sector can affect the volume of bank deposits.

As a result of discontinuities in the credit market—for example, the banks' virtual abstention from instalment credit—there has been ample opportunity in recent years for new lending institutions to emerge in order to finance a growing proportion of these borrowing needs—partly by bidding for funds which would otherwise have remained in current or deposit accounts at the banks. In the course of circulation most of the deposits withdrawn from the banks will of course return to the banks as credits to other accounts—for example, those of dealers who have sold cars upon which the borrowing customers of the financial intermediary have spent their loans. The aggregate deposits of the banks will be reduced only to the extent of leakages into the government sector—for example, if the intermediary allocates part of its deposits to a reserve including government securities or if, at the end of circulation, funds are used to repay advances made by those banks or to buy other assets from them.[(17)] In the latter case, however, the reduction in deposits will usually be only temporary; the banks will normally re-expand their risk assets to take up the slack created in liquidity ratios—assuming, of course, that the authorities do not intervene.

Apart from these instances, therefore, there is no direct effect upon the volume of bank deposits. Since the movement of deposits is usually circular, with the banks acting as a catchment area, so to speak, it is often alleged that responsibility for the secular decline in the volume of bank deposits and bank lending relative to national output cannot be passed to the banks. The volume of bank deposits, it is argued, depends on the amount of liquid assets allowed into the banking system by the authorities; since deposits, however used, must eventually return to the banks—subject only to the possibility of the 'leakages' cited above—then the main effect of the growth of financial intermediaries is a reduced share of profitable lending outlets for the banks and the leaner profits which result. Such an analysis, however, postulates too passive a role for the authorities and neglects their significance as a counter-balance to situations continually altering as a result of changes in the private sector. Deposits transferred from a clearing bank to the intermediaries—for example, to finance houses—allow the latter to increase their lending, and to a proportionately greater extent than is possible for a clearing bank because of the latter's higher liquidity ratio. In effect there occurs a fall in the demand for idle cash balances and an increase in the supply of active balances, a shift which tends to drive down interest rates and to raise the level of spending—possibly with adverse effects on the balance of payments. In such circumstances the authorities might of course be forced to take counter-action (for example, the sale of bonds) which reduces the lending power of the clearing banks themselves.

The converse of this sequence is that if the banks, by bidding higher rates, 'gain' deposits from the non-bank financial intermediaries, the immediate effect will be a transfer of ownership within the banking system without any increase in total bank deposits or liquid assets. As a result of the intermediaries being denied a substantial part of their funds, however, an equivalent part of their lending activities will be stopped; this will tend to be reflected, in turn, in a reduced demand either for existing assets — stock exchange securities or fixed assets—or for newly-produced consumer or capital goods.(18) Thus initially there will be an upward pressure on interest rates due to the banks' bidding for deposits, a pressure which will gather greater momentum as a result of the reduction of 'outside' credit facilities. Further, the banks' deposits will remain the same while the volume of non-bank lending will have fallen; if they wish to maintain the given level of demand, therefore, the authorities will need to expand the credit base in order that bank lending and bank deposits can be increased.(19)

In such a situation the government may be expected sooner or later to counter deflationary tendencies by adopting policies rather more reflationary than would otherwise have been employed. Whether through fiscal measures or direct monetary expansion, therefore, the result is likely to be an injection of additional liquidity into the banking system and a consequent increase in deposits. Such measures might possibly include a reduction of the required liquidity ratio, so that banks would be able to expand their credit and fill the gap created by the fall in intermediaries' deposits and lending-power. When equilibrium has been restored, national income and output would be the same; the volume of bank deposits in relation to it would be larger, however, as might also be bank advances. The velocity of circulation of bank deposits would be less, as would be the business of financial intermediaries.(21)

By bidding for deposits the banks could hope not only to frustrate the lending activities of the finance houses and similar institutions but also to attract funds otherwise destined for new issues of government securities; these, even if automatically re-lent to the government via Treasury bills, would still provide an injection of liquid assets necessary for an expansion of deposits. Other funds potentially available to the banks include deposits with local authorities and cash in the form of notes and coin.(21) The first is in fact nearly equivalent to the denial of funds to a financial intermediary, except that a local authority would probably be able to switch its borrowing back to the Public Works Loan Board. The latter, being financed by the Treasury, would in turn acquire the required funds by borrowing newly-created deposits from the banks, thereby providing the banks with liquid assets necessary for deposit creation. On the other hand, if rates were sufficiently attractive, local authorities might attract additional deposits from overseas. There is certainly evidence that in the 1960s there was substantial switching of funds (often from the Euro-dollar market) into sterling by secondary banks in order to take advantage of favourable domestic UK rates. Such a net inflow of foreign currency would usually be sold to the Exchange Equalisation Account, so that once again a government agency might be obliged to borrow newly-created bank deposits —with the same consequences for the credit-creative powers of the banks.

Not least of the possibilities to be derived from a competitive bidding for deposits by the banks would be an attraction of funds previously held in the form of cash. Cash in circulation plus balances with the Post Office and Trustee Savings Banks together amount to about 75 per cent of total domestic bank deposits. If the banks were to be successful in reducing cash in circulation by a half, deposits could be increased on a once-for-all basis by about 15 per cent. The banks' traditional indifference to the small saver, however, has already been noted. It appears that this attitude is changing, especially since the early 1960s, with the introduction by the banks of publicity drives and various services (for example, budget accounts) designed to attract small deposits. Such deposits continue to be costly to process, however, and the banks apparently consider bidding for such funds to be an unnecessary addition to costs. In the case of the general public the banks may probably be able to rely on a hard core of deposits largely insensitive to interest rate movements. At present the main effect of price competition seems to be that the banks are failing to attract corporate rather than personal deposits; the latter have in fact risen nearly in step with GNP. For the personal depositor it is probably the development of facilities such as credit cards which will not only reduce drains of cash into circulation but also attract new (non-bank) customers into the banking system, a possibility discussed in the next chapter.

The relative position of the clearing banks is again being threatened by the Post Office Giro and by the development of a current account system by the Trustee Savings Banks. Deposits with these bodies will possess qualities hitherto confined to joint-stock bank deposits; they will serve as money rather than call for payment in some other form, such as currency. Moreover, bank deposits transferred to these institutions will be invested in government securities, with a consequential decline in clearing bank deposits and liquid assets. Hence these institutions will compete with the clearing banks in a way which other institutions at present do not. This would be especially true if, as the Monopolies Commission postulated, the Post Office Giro were to be developed into a full state bank in competition with the clearing banks. What is more, there is a distinct possibility that if the non-government intermediaries—for example, the accepting houses or American banks—continue to grow and develop services similar to those provided by the joint-stock banks (such as chequing or current account facilities or lending of a type hitherto largely confined to the joint-stock banks), the magnitude of effective leaks of both deposits and liquid assets will increase as deposits are circulated within the new network. On the other hand, such progress is likely to be associated with developments by which these institutions are brought more directly within the sphere of monetary control. One step in this direction was announced in June 1968—a special cash deposits scheme to be introduced when direct restrictions then being imposed on bank lending were lifted. This will in fact increase the extent of 'leakages', as bank deposits are passed on to the Bank of England rather than to other customers of the clearing banks.

The banks' reaction to mounting evidence of their competitive disadvantage was the formation of their own 'secondary' subsidiaries, as distinct from hire-purchase agencies. A response to outside competition in the form of direct across-the-counter price competition of their own—as recommended by the National Board for Prices and Incomes—rather than 'through the back door' remains an unpopular concept for the British clearing banker. Practical considerations undoubtedly dictate some caution and the reluctance of clearing bankers to break their deposit-rate cartel stems as much from the difficulty of containing and localising exceptions to the rule as from dislike of price competition itself. The clearing banks appear to feel that if they adopted the PIB recommendation—i.e. that they should experiment through their branches in a range of rates for fixtures of varying maturities—[22] there would be a danger of a switch of funds out of current accounts and into fixtures so that they would merely be paying more on deposits which they already possessed. For many banks in the secondary system, the minimum amount for a sterling deposit is £50,000; hardly any would consider the offer of a deposit of less than £10,000. From the point of view of low-cost processing, the size of deposits is at least as important as their maturity and, in the view of the banks, companies with large surplus funds could continue to be directed towards their subsidiaries in which rates appropriate to the amount and duration of a deposit could be offered.

Intimately connected with the issue of price competition for deposits is the question of the diversification of clearing bank lending activities. Clearing bankers have found themselves increasingly pushed in this direction, first by the Radcliffe Report and subsequently by the National Board for Prices and Incomes. In addition to the issue of price competition, then, there is the distinct but related question of the entry of the clearing banks into markets for lending traditionally regarded as not proper banking business. Most bankers argue that it would not be feasible for them to offer higher rates for deposits unless they were also able, in turn, to engage in new types of lending at higher rates—for example, hire purchase finance, factoring and so on. Such activities the banks feel to be sufficiently beyond their normal routine—and the training of their staff—to warrant their being hived off into specialist subsidiaries along with their deposit-bidding activities. It is in fact debatable, to put it no higher, whether fields of activity such as medium-term instalment credit involve any radical departure from established lending principles, although admittedly new skills might be required in order to assess long-term profitability. The secondary banks are low-cost institutions operating on narrow margins between borrowing and lending rates and 'matching' assets and liabilities in a way perhaps more suited to a small specialist concern. Moreover, the nature of their business—for example, takeover finance or speculative property deals—is regarded as being decidedly less interest-elastic than the demand for clearing bank credit; from this point of view the institutions involved can afford to outbid any rates which the banks could sensibly offer—without, that is, finding themselves in the position of paying much more for almost the same total of funds and thus being obliged to increase their rates for traditional business. If, on the other hand, the banks were successful in bidding deposits away from the financial intermediaries, with the effects which have already been noted, then in order to recoup the increased cost of their deposits, the banks would not only have to raise their normal advances rates but might be forced to undertake directly the more risky business to which they have traditionally been averse. The question of the banks' entry into these other areas of credit is dealt with more fully in the following chapter; for the moment it is enough to note that bank deposit and lending rates are usually below those prevailing elsewhere in the open market and have therefore been a contributing factor to the growth of other lending institutions so that it is probable that a substantial proportion of the additional lending opportunities which would be presented to the banks would not be very different from their customary business.[23] The apprehensions concerning the prospect of containing an increase in rates, together with a reluctance to contemplate direct involvement in other forms of credit, have nevertheless contributed to the banks' decision to compete in these fields only via their subsidiaries.

The most important single reason for this channelling of competition through the banks' subsidiaries, however, is probably to be found in the special position of the banks in the monetary sector. In the past, secondary bankers have not been required to keep 8 per cent of their assets in cash or a further 20 per cent in official liquid assets earning distinctly less than funds employed in the secondary or parallel markets. By working to comparatively low liquidity reserves, the secondary banks have been able to lend out a higher proportion of their deposits than was possible for the clearing banks and are likely to continue to do so. This is one reason why the secondary banks can afford to attract deposits by offering higher rates than those offered by the joint-stock banks and for the preference of the latter for concentrating their efforts at price competition on their subsidiaries. This constraint upon the clearing banks has been reinforced by the official requirement of a liquidity ratio which is substantially in excess of that considered by the banks themselves to be strictly necessary for normal working—still more so after the bank mergers—and is, at the same time, composed to a substantial extent of assets which involve a loss of deposits and cash in favour of the public sector. In a real sense, then, the legal reserve ratio acts as a tax upon the banks, taking approximately 25 per cent of any increase in deposits (cash, call money employed by the discount market for the purchase of Treasury bills, Treasury bills themselves and very short-term gilt-edged securities), although a partial offset to this is provided by the continued toleration by the authorities of the clearing banks' cartel on rates.[24]

The somewhat glib comparisons ventured by the National Board for Prices and Incomes between British banks and those of other countries largely ignored the significant differences in international banking and economic conditions, particularly the relative burdens of the national debt. In Germany, where interest rates have been freed from official control, the banks bid for time deposits in which they expanded medium and long-term credit. Bank lending rates, on the other hand, have been held down by means of a narrowing of their profit margins. They have enjoyed a compensating advantage over British banks, however, in that the liquidity reserve ratios required for time and savings deposits are much smaller than those required for sight deposits. In other words, German banks are able to lend a greater proportion of their fixed deposits than of their sight deposits, a factor which undoubtedly tends to offset their higher cost. Similarly, in the USA differential reserve requirements are applied to the banks' fixed and sight deposits; the result is that the former represent a significantly greater addition to lending capacity than do demand deposits. In Britain, of course, no distinction is made between current and deposit account liabilities in the assessment of liquidity requirements. British banks are thus at a disadvantage in this respect; their required liquidity ratio is generally at a higher average level than the ratios required against sight deposits in other countries—for example, Canada or the United States—and at a much higher level in comparison with the fixed deposit ratios required in countries such as Germany and the United States.

British banks themselves are partly to blame for this state of affairs because of their readiness to regard deposit accounts as virtually repayable on demand. American banks, by contrast, are more exacting in their requirements for withdrawals of time and savings deposits, often imposing penalty clauses which may be invoked in the case of premature withdrawals. To the extent that banks prefer a reduced velocity of deposit turnover in order to increase their long-term lending, a competitive bidding for deposits is not in itself necessarily the answer, since it could of course tend to have the opposite effect. More important could be an increased emphasis upon formal time and savings accounts in the deposit mix; such accounts might indeed need to be attracted by higher rates.

In this context American experience is highly relevant. Table 11 provides a comparison of the rates of growth of relevant financial deposits held in various US financial intermediaries between 1946 and 1966. During most of the 1950s US banks abstained from price competition and used demand deposits as their primary deposit input to expand credit—in other words, like British clearing banks at that time and even today, their competition was orientated around the service-based demand deposit. As interest rates generally rose in the 1950s, however, so did the relative attractiveness to the public of interest-bearing deposits or other forms of 'near money' as opposed to demand deposits. As the public learned to make do with smaller transactions balances in relation to GNP, so the deposit input flows to the banks increased at a slower rate than to the non-banks, a development which gave rise to considerable concern and a substantial volume of academic analysis.(25) In the 1960s, however, this pattern was entirely changed. Following the introduction of more favourable official reserve requirements, with ratios of only 4 per cent required for time deposits, by aggressively bidding up rates for time deposits the banks not only doubled time deposits between the second halves of the 1950s and the 1960s, but maintained their demand deposits at the rate of growth experienced in the 1950s. Total deposits, therefore, increased by nearly 300 per cent, while—and more significant—the increased emphasis on time deposits had not affected the growth of demand deposits.(26)

It is therefore possible that direct price competition could increase both the volume and the cost of British bank credit, although the dangers involved are open to debate and are most relevant from the point of view of the public debt. On the other hand, it is possible that, apart from a marginal hardening of lending rates and commission charges, the competitive environment would deter the banks from raising their lending rates. The present system, however, undoubtedly enables a subsidy to be paid by certain sectors of the economy (e.g. depositors) to the favoured areas of commerce and industry in so far as bank deposit and lending rates are held below 'equilibrium' levels in some sense.(27) The fact that the banks borrow and lend below the levels prevailing in the rest of the market has encouraged the growth of other intermediaries whose actions reduce the deposits of the banks themselves.

The retention of the inter-bank cartel has generally been held to have had a soporific effect upon the banks; in the opinion of the Monopolies Commission, so long as their rate agreements existed, no foreseeable change in the structure of the clearing bank system could greatly increase the degree of competition.(28) Certainly the authorities have for long tended to discourage any change in this matter and in their evidence

TABLE 11

Annual Growth Rates of Deposit-Type Assets held by the Public, USA, 1946-1966

(Compound annual rates of change, per cent)

	Commercial Banks			Non-banks				Total deposit-type holdings of public
Periods	Demand deposits Adj.*	Time deposits **	Total deposits	Mutual savings banks	Savings and loans associations	Credit Unions	Total Non-bank	
	1	2	3(1 + 2)	4	5	6	7(4 + 5+6)	8(3 + 7)
1946-50	2.2	1.9	2.2	4.4	13.3	15.8	7.7	3.3
1950-55	3.3	6.3	4.2	6.9	18.0	21.0	12.4	6.2
1955-60	0.9	8.0	3.3	5.2	14.1	15.8	10.6	5.6
1960-66	3.3	16.7	9.4	8.7	12.9	15.5	11.6	10.2

* Demand deposits at all commercial banks, other than those due to domestic commercial banks and the US Government, less cash items in process of collection and Federal Reserve float and foreign demand balances at Federal Reserve Banks.

** Time deposits at all commercial banks, other than those due to domestic commercial banks and the US Government. Data are for December 31st where available.

Source: Federal Reserve Bulletin, Flow of funds Accounts, E, Bloch, 'Changes in the structure of bank and non-bank competition in the United States', *Banca Nazionale del Lavoro Quarterly Review*, No. 84, March 1968, p. 25.

before the Monopolies Commission in 1968 representatives of the banks suggested that the fact of mergers would not in itself lead to the abandonment of the cartel.[29] There is little doubt that by adopting direct across-the-counter price competition the banks would increase not only their deposits but also their average cost, as well as alter the mix of their deposits by stimulating the transfer of funds from current to deposit account. It is possible, of course, that the more competitive environment would be reflected in a squeeze on bank profit margins rather than in an upward drift in lending rates. Under such circumstances there would presumably be increased pressure upon them to maximise their efficiency. On the other hand, there would be little incentive for them to initiate direct price competition—and more especially to diversify their lending along the lines suggested by their critics—unless measures were taken to increase the banks' credit multiplier, perhaps by the introduction of reduced reserve ratios in relation to funds on deposit account. A real deterrent to more aggressive competition—and this is a cause of the consequent emphasis upon competition 'via the back door'—undoubtedly comes from the fact that the position of the banks in the monetary sector has limited the extent to which they have been able to compete by employing their funds in different types of asset.[30]

4. Negotiable certificates of deposit

One credit instrument which the British clearing banks have recently begun to use in order to attract large deposits via their subsidiaries is the negotiable Certificate of Deposit, an American innovation resulting from efforts by New York banks to counter the pressures of a rising demand for advances without comparable deposit growth. The Certificate of Deposit was invented in order to provide a means of competing with other income-earning assets which would be attractive to the banks' corporate customers but less expensive than an across-the-board rise in all deposit rates. It takes the form of a fixed deposit for which a certificate is exchanged, the certificate being negotiable in law, so that holders can—where desired—redeem their deposits before maturity by selling to a third party. An obviously crucial element is thus the existence of an active market for such certificates. Introduced in 1961, by December 1968 the total volume of negotiable CDs issued by US banks had reached approximately $24 billion. The success of the US experience encouraged New York banks to issue dollar CDs in Britain and the example was followed by some of the UK clearing bank subsidiaries, amongst others, so that total issues amounted to $ 800 million by July 1968 and a substantial market developed for them in London.

In Britain the growth of the parallel credit markets, and the clearing banks' indirect dealings in them via their subsidiaries, tended to blunt any urgency which might otherwise have induced the banks to compete for funds, directly or indirectly, through Certificates of Deposit. Moreover, some concern was felt over the effect of the new instrument upon the whole range of bank deposit rates. On the initiative of the First National City Bank, however, in 1968 discussions were renewed concerning the possible issue of and market for sterling CDs. The experience already obtained from the existing markets for dollar CDs in London as well as New York, in addition to the success of the parallel markets and the intervention in them by the clearing-bank subsidiaries, had combined to overcome earlier opposition. Provisions were made in the 1968 Finance Bill to remove certain difficulties arising from the Exchange Control Act and from October 1968 banks in the UK were authorised to issue negotiable sterling CDs.

Sterling CDs are issued in a minimum denomination of £50,000 with maturities of not less than three months and not more than five years. Their issue—and the main market in them—is concentrated amongst the clearing bank subsidiaries, other banks and the discount houses; the purchasers comprise those institutions already active in the secondary credit markets. At the end of 1968 the market, mainly consisting of the discount houses, was quoting rates around 7-7⅛ per cent for three-month CDs compared with a discount rate of 6 9/16 per cent for three-month Treasury bills and 7 per cent for three month deposits in the local authority markets. It is expected that a part—possibly a large part—will find its home within the clearing bank system, either as discounted paper or as security against loans to the secondary market. The existence of a stable and orderly market depends very much on the presence of a liquidity 'prop'—in other words, the existence of an institution or institutions prepared to carry CDs when necessary, acting as lender-of-last resort in the way which the Bank of England is prepared to re-discount prime bills of exchange.[31] This function the clearing banks themselves have agreed to perform, although individual issuing banks are most unlikely to purchase, or lend against, their own certificates. By so doing a bank, or rather its subsidiary, would have increased its deposits and its liquid assets by an equal amount, consequently raising its liquidity ratio, and such a procedure would be unlikely to meet with the approval of the authorities. Nonetheless, for the clearing bank system as a whole, the machinery is available for the creation of liquidity.[32] Although CDs are not counted as official liquid assets, they are acceptable to the clearing banks themselves as well as their subsidiaries as security for short-term call loans which are, of course, 'official' liquid assets. An effective sanction in the form of a 'request' or directive is available to the authorities, however, in the event of any deliberate attempt to inflate liquidity by this means.

Deposits withdrawn from the clearing banks and placed in CDs may be assumed to be largely transferred to one or other of the clearing banks' subsidiaries which are issuing this sort of paper. The overall volume of clearing bank deposits are not reduced by them, therefore, while the attraction of outside deposits by the clearing bank subsidiaries should weaken the power of other deposit-bidding institutions to the ultimate benefit of the clearing bank system. (In its first month of operation there was already some evidence of funds being switched from the local authority market into CDs.) It is possible that CDs may attract a good deal of the resources previously being invested by the non-banking sector in Treasury bills; in other words, it could well reduce the outside demand for Treasury bills at the weekly tenders. This would be a development not without its attraction to the discount houses or the clearing banks, in that the government would be forced to borrow more from the clearing bank system; this takes no account, however, of eventual counter-action by the authorities.

US experience suggests that the introduction of CDs is likely to strengthen the tendency for money deposited with the banking system for fixed terms to increase relatively to amounts left on current account. This necessarily implies an increase in the average cost of deposits to the banks themselves and is precisely the sort of development of which British clearing banks have been afraid. Their support for the new venture rests to some extent upon the tacit assumption that any increase in deposit rates can be localised within the banks' subsidiaries. The subsidiaries' comparative freedom from monetary restraint, their ability to match assets and liabilities in a way requiring only a small liquidity reserve and the more profitable nature of their assets are together expected to offset the increased cost of their deposits. Whether any such pressure can be contained or, on the other hand, will spread to the whole range of deposit rates is open to debate, but it is clear that a shift has already occurred towards increased costs of deposits. This is partly due to the current era of comparatively high interest rates, which naturally increase the proportion left on deposit account; it is also due to more technical developments in the improvement and evolution of the payments machinery. Improved remittance facilities—for example, the giro system, computerised techniques for salaries, dividends and other payments, standing orders and so on indicate a movement towards not merely a cashless society but perhaps a chequeless society. In such circumstances, there would be a corresponding tendency for amounts left on idle balances to be reduced and shifted into income-earning liquid assets.[33]

5. The growth of overseas banking

It is important to consider the competitive position of the clearing banks in the wider context of developments in international, as well as domestic, banking. As early as 1905 an awareness of the growth potential of foreign business was evidenced by the establishment by the Midland Bank of a foreign exchange department. Other banks followed suit and after the establishment of a branch in Paris by Lloyds in 1911 and the inauguration of the Westminster Foreign Bank Ltd. with branches on the Continent, the pattern was set for an international extension of bank competition. The process was undoubtedly accelerated by the restraints on further amalgamations amongst the main commercial banks as a result of the recommendations of the Colwyn Committee.

After the first World War the British joint-stock banks entered the acceptance credit business, becoming formidable competitors of the acceptance houses. In 1918 and 1923 Lloyds acquired majority holdings in the London and River Plate Bank (Argentine) and the London and Brazilian Bank, both of which formed the basis for the subsequent formation of the Bank of London and South America.

Barclays also acquired substantial interests abroad by obtaining control of Cox & Co. (France) in 1921, subsequently converting it into Barclays Bank (France) Ltd., with fifteen branches in France and Algeria. After further expansion on the continent, a notable advance was made in 1925 with the formation of several non-European banks already controlled by Barclays into Barclays Bank (Dominion, Colonial and Overseas).

For nearly a generation British joint-stock banks remained, in terms of deposits, the largest in the world, and the international network of their subsidiaries dominated finance in many areas, especially, of course, in the British Dominions and Colonies. After the second World War the growth of international trade and business and, in particular, the extension of US overseas investment brought other competitors to the fore. The great American banks—Chase Manhattan, the Bank of America, the First National

City Bank and so on—restrained by US banking legislation from widespread branch expansion at home, emerged as active competitors in many overseas territories (and even within Britain) where the subsidiaries and affiliates of the British clearing banks had long enjoyed a privileged position.

6. Concentration in British banking

With the growing concentration of modern business and the rise of large international corporations, international banking competition increased considerably in the 1960s. At the same time development of the Euro-dollar and parallel markets attracted still more competitors, the number of overseas and foreign bank branches in London rising from 82 to 108 between 1962 and early 1968, while their share of net deposits with banks in the UK increased from 19 per cent to 34 per cent over the same period. The reaction of the British clearing banks was to strengthen the ties among themselves and at the same time with other overseas banks by correspondent relationships, participations and joint ventures. Links between the British clearing banks, Scottish banks, British Commonwealth and foreign banks had of course existed for some time; apart from direct interests in Scottish, Ulster, Commonwealth and overseas banks, however—for example, the Clydesdale Banks, the Standard Bank, National and Grindlays, BOLSA and so on—relationships with foreign banks were generally conducted on a correspondent basis, a method which has hardly been conducive to aggressive international competition.

In more recent years, the British clearing banks, Commonwealth and foreign banks have been brought into formal association with European and American banks in the joint establishment of specialised subsidiaries to meet the requirements of large international customers.(34) In 1967, for example, in addition to such existing subsidiaries as Midland and International Bank Ltd., four new joint ventures were established, involving Barclays twice, the Westminster once and the Midland once in co-operation with several European, British overseas and American banks. Altogether over 30 participations and joint ventures occurred in the four years up to June 1968, involving British clearing and merchant banks and a whole variety of overseas banks. This total does not include the clearing banks' directly owned hire-purchase and secondary subsidiaries of which over a dozen are presently in business nor, of course, the established connections between clearing banks, Scottish, Commonwealth and other overseas banks.

This movement towards vertical integration in the credit markets can be said to have begun in 1958 with the acquisition by the clearing banks of hire-purchase subsidiaries. Subsequently their response to competition in both its international and domestic aspects has been to strengthen their links not only with overseas banks but also domestic non-clearing banks by moving into vertically-organised banking of the merchant bank pattern.

Prominent examples here have been the Midland Bank's acquisition of a 30 per cent interest in Montagus, the National Provincial's joint venture with Rothschilds, and Westminster and Hambros Unit Trust Fund; an even earlier forerunner of these was the merchant bank National Commercial and Schroder, established in 1964 by the National Commercial Bank of Scotland, Lloyds and Scottish (a hire purchase company, 50 per cent of whose capital was owned by Lloyds Bank) and Schroder Wagg (merchant bank). Overall clearing bank interests have extended to include subsidiary or associated companies engaged in leasing, factoring, credit cards and the management of unit trusts, as well as their venture into hire purchase and the specialised activities of the secondary markets.

In 1968, however, came the shift to horizontal integration with the mergers amongst the clearing banks themselves. The 1968 mergers are nevertheless a random event in the history of British joint-stock banking: they are not, except perhaps for the acquisition of Martins Bank by Barclays, an inevitably logical result of the trends of the postwar years. Their importance to the observer lies in the publicity once again given to the main postwar problem of British banking—the need for measures to improve the efficiency and competitiveness of the banking industry consistently with the smooth implementation of monetary and other policies. The mergers themselves will do nothing to increase the total deposits of the banking system nor, perhaps, will they have much impact upon the individual banks' competitive ability. This is even more likely to be true if the banks are able to continue to rely upon the 'endowment effect' of a high average Bank rate to protect even the less efficient from the full effects of cost inflation. The abolition of rate agreements and restrictive lending policies would have a more stimulating effect, however, and it is here that the wider context of bank concentration—vertical integration with other financial intermediaries—is more interesting. Within their institutional environment the banks, with some noticeable success, have attempted to move in the direction so often canvassed by their critics. It is possible that the breach in some of their rivals' traditional markets may encourage the banks to seek further diversification in their lending activities, following a policy which might in time see the banks more or less completely recapturing the markets lost to, say, the finance houses and even perhaps engaged in volume in such areas as property mortgage. To the extent that the banks consolidate their various borrowing and lending activities within one unit, the authorities could hope to obtain an improved control over the entire monetary sector. Resort to such diversification by the banks—with the corresponding implication of direct price competition—is not fully within their discretion, however, nor is it particularly practicable given current constraints upon their earnings potential.

In its present form, therefore, the pricing of clearing bank services is inefficient and discriminates against depositors, involving both subsidies to and taxes upon various classes of bank borrowers.[(35)] The public interest, however, is involved not only with the existence of an efficient banking system but, as has been so often stressed, with the working of the overall monetary and fiscal mechanism. From the point of view of the central government, a major advantage of present bank pricing policy is the reduced budgetary cost of the national debt effected by the banks' exploitation of their depositors through sub-equilibrium rates on deposits, part of this gain being transferred directly or indirectly to the Treasury through bank holdings of cash and low-yielding official liquid assets. If the clearing banks were to compete directly in price there can be little doubt that their overall efficiency would improve; the budgetary cost of the national debt would probably also rise, however, with the result that a necessary offset would have to be sought in increased taxation in order to replace the present 'implicit taxation of bank depositors'.[(36)] Although it is true to say that before the second World War the authorities operated under conditions in which price competition of a type existed, the experience of those years is not really overwhelmingly relevant to the modern economy in which—to mention but one difference—the magnitude of the national debt is so much greater. The simultaneous attainment of a highly efficient banking system and the objectives of overall monetary policy represents an ideal which is not only somewhat remote from practical reality but depends, fundamentally perhaps, on a major reappraisal of the existing monetary and fiscal framework.

REFERENCES

1. National Board for Prices and Incomes, *Bank Charges*, Report No. 34, Cmd 3292, HMSO, London 1967, para. 12.
2. *Ibid.*, paras. 57-59.
3. See 'London's New Markets for Money', *Midland Bank Review*, August 1966, p. 3.
4. Monopolies Commission, *Barclays Bank Ltd., Lloyds Bank Ltd. and Martins Bank Ltd.*, HMSO, London 1968, para. 206.
5. *Midland Bank Review, loc. cit.*, p. 3.
6. *Scottish Bankers' Magazine*, February, 1963, pp. 227-31.
7. J. R. S. Revell, *Changes in British Banking*, Hill, Samuel Occasional Paper No. 3, pp. 10-14.
8. *Ibid.*, p. 13.
9. *Ibid.*
10. Monopolies Commission, *op. cit.*, para. 178
11. Bank of England *Quarterly Bulletin*, Vol. 8, No. 2, June 1968, p. 159.
12. *Bank Charges*, para. 59.
13. *Report of the Committee on the working of the monetary system*, Cmd 827, HMSO, London 1959, p. 44, para. 132.
14. N. J. Gibson, *Financial intermediaries and monetary policy*, Hobart Paper No. 39, Institute of Economic Affairs, London 1967, p. 21.
15. A. A. Walters, *Money in boom and slump*, Hobart Paper No. 40, Institute of Economic Affairs, London 1969, p. 20.
16. Gibson, *op. cit.*, p. 22.
17. W. T. C. King, 'Should the banks bid for deposits?' *The Banker*, December 1962, p. 767.
18. *Ibid.*
19. *Ibid.* See also *Bank Charges*, para. 59 and F. W. L. Paish, 'Deposit Rates After Mr Jones', *The Banker*, Vol. 117, October 1967, pp. 845-9.
20. W. T. C. King, *op. cit.*
21. *Ibid.*
22. *Bank Charges*, para. 66.
23. W. T. C. King, *op. cit.*

24. H. G. Johnson, 'The Report on Bank Charges—II', *The Bankers' Magazine,* August 1967, p. 61.

25. See, for example, J. G. Gurley and E. S. Shaw, *Money in a theory of finance,* Brookings Institution, Washington 1960.

26. E. Bloch, 'Changes in the structure of bank and nonbank competition in the United States', *Banca Nazionale del Lavoro Quarterly Review,* No. 84, March 1968, p. 26.

27. Artis, 'The Monopolies Commission report', *The Bankers' Magazine,* September 1968, p. 128.

28. Monopolies Commission, *op. cit.,* para. 220.

29. *Ibid.,* para. 205.

30. *Ibid.,* para. 221.

31. Allen, Harvey and Ross Ltd., *Report of conference on sterling CDs,* London, July 1968.

32. See P. Bareau in Allen, Harvey and Ross Ltd., *op. cit.,* p. 14.

33. *Ibid.,* p. 13.

34. J. R. S. Revell, *op. cit.*

35. H. G. Johnson, 'Observations on the bank merger proposals', *The Bankers' Magazine,* September 1968, p. 136.

36. *Ibid.,* p. 137.

CHAPTER TWELVE

The New Look in Credit

1. Introduction

Up to this point the examination of bank attitudes to competition has concentrated mainly on the significance of price and non-price competition. As was observed in the previous chapter, however, the question of the clearing banks' readiness to engage in new methods of extending credit—and, indeed, to embark upon entirely new areas of credit—is of at least equal importance. Although the arena of competition has been widening, the markets in which the banks have been prepared to lend directly have been tending to contract as a result of restrictions imposed by both the banks themselves and the monetary authorities. As a result, substitutes have become available for the clearing bank overdraft—both for corporate and personal borrowers—and for the remission and simple current account services which were previously the unique function of the clearing banks.

Although the attractions of the clearing bank overdraft are still considerable, cheap and flexible in use as it is, it appears that its virtues were stronger in past periods of easy credit than they are today when bank customers may be willing to pay a premium for certainty. This is not to deny the undoubted merits of the overdraft system, the benefits of which are beginning to be realised by banks and their customers in other countries; the whole notion of credit cards is also completely akin to the principle of the overdraft, involving only a difference of technicalities. The dominance of the overdraft as a means of clearing bank finance, however, has tended to exclude other forms of lending which may be better suited to meet special requirements. The finance of corporate fixed capital formation, for example, is less amenable to the overdraft, normally repayable on demand and certainly entailing limits subject to periodic review, than that of simple working capital requirements. In such circumstances the clearing bank overdraft has come to be regarded as a residual or marginal item by many borrowers, an increasing proportion of their requirements being provided in the form of fixed loan finance by other lenders.

An exhortation towards greater diversification of lending is nothing new, however, in the annals of banking history. Before the first World War the spate of bank mergers had prompted opinions (by no means rigorously established) that the reduction in the number of banks had narrowed the areas of credit in which the clearing bank system was prepared to engage.(1) The Macmillan Committee had also been concerned with the question of gaps in the finance of industry. Although the problem of the 'Macmillan Gap' seems to have been largely solved by the time of the Radcliffe Committee, nevertheless discussion once again centred on the clearing banks' traditional lending attitudes and was then revived by the criticisms of the National Board for Prices and Incomes. By the time of this latter investigation, however, concern was being expressed more at the effects on the banks' own relative position than over the needs of borrowers who were increasingly able to find other sources of credit.

Since the appearance of the Radcliffe Report substantial modifications have undoubtedly occurred in traditional clearing bank attitudes, and some remarkable new ventures have been organised both within the banks themselves and through their subsidiaries. These, together with the implications of new forms of credit are the subject of this chapter.

2. Hire-purchase and term loans

With the relaxation of credit controls in 1958 and the consequent upsurge in the demand for bank finance the banks had again become eager, and even aggressive, lenders for the first time in some twenty years. The Radcliffe Committee's evidence, however, related to the circumstances of the mid-1950s when bank advances were still below what bankers considered to be their optimum ratio. In this environment it had not been unreasonable for the Radcliffe Committee to recommend a departure not only from traditional lending methods but from traditional concepts as well. Even before the promptings of the Radcliffe Committee, and as a result of the opportunities provided by the 1958 credit relaxation, the banks had begun to respond to the demand for more diverse credit facilities. In and after 1958 the banks had ventured into instalment lending through the purchase and formation of their own hire-purchase subsidiaries. In addition, two of the banks—the Midland and the Westminster—announced new schemes for personal loans which were intended to secure a direct, if modest, share in the lucrative business of instalment credit. Their example was soon followed by other British banks, although the National Provincial and Lloyds stood aloof, preferring to utilise their existing lending practices.

Not long afterwards, and in response to the proposals of the Radcliffe Report, some of the banks introduced term loans for their industrial customers. The personal loan was in fact also a term loan, with provision for the repayment of capital and interest on a monthly basis as in conventional hire-purchase finance, although differing from the latter in that there was usually no security other than the character and standing of the borrower. Since interest was to be calculated on the original sum for the whole period, the effective rate of interest was about 50 per cent higher than the nominal rate; the business was consequently highly profitable from the point of view of the banks.

The publicity attached to these new schemes had an immediate effect; even so, it appears that much the largest part of the resultant increase in lending to personal borrowers consisted of advances of the traditional kind. This was true not only for personal loans but for their industrial counterpart. At the end of 1958 aggregate new personal loans outstanding were probably a good deal less than £20 million, whereas over the full year total advances had risen by £364 million to a new peak of £2,245 million.[(2)] By 1961 the advances ratio had been restored almost to the levels typical of the 1920s, a fact which was almost entirely due to the upsurge in consumer demand. At this point, therefore, the further extension of bank lending rested essentially on the ability of the banks to increase deposits, a fact which implied dependence not only upon the policy of the authorities but also upon the methods of competition adopted by the banks themselves.

The 1965 report of the National Board for Prices and Incomes once again raised the question of the traditional reliance by the banks on the 'self-liquidating' loan, a tradition which, it was recognised, stemmed from the banks' dependence upon short-term liabilities.(3) Even so, according to the Board, there was nothing in the nature of banking as such which prevented the British banks from following the example of banks in other countries—notably the United States—in the development of mortgage loans and instalment credit.(4) The argument begs a number of issues; in particular it neglects the differences in the reserve requirements enforced in other countries and the implications for official policies on money rates. Even so, there would still appear to be no intrinsic reason why British banks should not enter such areas of credit—as indeed has already happened, although on a limited scale. Despite its limitations, international banking experience is still relevant in that it provides examples of certain types of credit which modern deposit banks can successfully supply. The main qualification is, of course, that conditions in other countries approximate in certain aspects more closely to free markets in which British banking no longer operates.

Statistics gathered from about 150 of the largest banks in the United States for the period 1967-8 indicate that more than 45 per cent of their outstanding commercial and industrial loans were made under agreements which provide the borrower with credit for more than a year—up to seven or eight years in many cases.(5) So far as American practice is concerned, an ordinary term loan is a business loan with an original maturity of more than one year. It may be repayable in a lump sum or in periodic instalments (a serial term loan), the terms of the loan agreement being tailored to the specific needs of the borrower and varying greatly. Repayment schedules range from monthly to annual and the amount to be repaid can vary over the life of the loan. The general preference of the banks themselves is for the self-amortising term loan which provides for a substantial annual inflow of cash available to meet continuing demand. Interest rates are usually fixed but are sometimes arranged to escalate with a ceiling and a floor, usually not more than one per cent apart; at the same time the lending bank usually insists on its customer maintaining a compensating credit balance of between 10 and 20 per cent, which is neither interest-bearing nor available for set-off.

Term loans are well suited to the finance of capital expenditures which can be recouped from the borrower's earnings and depreciation allowance in 5 to 8 years. They have been extended primarily to large American companies in extractive industries and transport utilities, where operating units are large and demand for credit is not purely seasonal, often to finance equipment purchases. One- or two-year credits may also be used to provide interim or bridging finance in the early stages of plant construction, or equipment purchases which will eventually be funded through a security issue. This type of advance is, of course, well known in Britain, differing perhaps only in the formality and terms with which the interim credit is arranged.

In the case of medium to long-term credit, however, British experience differs, both in extent—being less than the 45 per cent suggested by American experience—and also in the nature of the advance. The bulk of British clearing bank lending over five years is in fact usually provided to exporters and ship-builders under ECGD guarantee and, of course, provides the banks with a useful offset in the form of an officially recognised liquid asset. There is no doubt that this form of lending requires staff well trained in credit analysis and investment techniques working in co-operation with credit bureaux and intelligence agencies which are more highly developed in the United States than in Britain. On the other hand, although a lack of trained staff was identified by the Radcliffe Committee as an important deterrent to British bank enterprise, it is difficult to believe that such activities are beyond the scope of British banks a decade later.

3. Instalment lending and the international setting

Although hire purchase facilities are available in Britain from the banks' hire-purchase subsidiaries, it is still not usual to associate the London clearing banks with such finance, the bulk of their lending to date having continued to be by means of the traditional overdraft. The larger American banks, however, undertake every type of instalment loan and most of the small banks will do so for cars, yachts, swimming pools, household goods and improvements or education. Vigorous competition takes place with the finance companies, particularly in car finance. In the case of consumer durable finance it is usual for an American bank to take security, unlike British banks whose only security would be that of the individual's credit standing, perhaps supported by collateral in the form of liquid assets or insurance policies.

Relevant transatlantic experience can be discovered not only in the United States but in Canada as well, where banking conditions more closely resemble those of Britain. Once again it suggests that hire-purchase finance is a suitable and profitable field for bank expansion. When the Canadian chartered banks made an aggressive entry into instalment credit in the later 1950s, their intervention was reflected in a rise in their share of total consumer credit from 15 per cent in 1956 to 29 per cent by 1964 at the expense of the finance companies whose share dropped from 26 per cent to 17 per cent. Recent legislation has allowed the Canadian banks limited debenture-issuing powers and has also introduced different reserve ratios for demand and time deposits which on average gives a reduced minimum reserve ratio of around 6½ per cent;(6) it has also given the banks the right to make conventional mortgage loans and has made provision for the removal of the interest-rate ceiling on bank loans, including that on mortgages.(7) As a result of these changes the banks developed into the fastest-growing industry in Canada, their assets increasing by 16.7 per cent in the 14 months following the introduction of the new Bank Act. Amongst these assets was a total of $165 million placed in mortgages.

In Germany the freeing of interest rates from official control, and the subsequent squeezing of bank profit margins, virtually obliged the commercial banks to diversify their lending activities. On the strength of their increased fixed deposits, German commercial banks moved further into the granting of medium and long-term credits. Most noticeable in this connection was the drive to capture part of the mortgage market in which the banks, backed by heavy advertising, offered private householders first, second and even third mortgages on their homes. It is not always appreciated that British banks are themselves directly involved in mortgage credit, although to an extent which is minute when compared with the assets of the Building Societies. Evidence submitted to the Radcliffe Committee revealed that the banks had £132 million out in housing loans by early 1959, compared with £130 million in late 1951, rising to over £350 million in the first quarter of 1968; this accounted for over 30 per cent of total personal loans, a proportion unchanged since 1951. Apart from a relatively insignificant amount advanced on full term mortgages to their own staff, the bulk of the banks' housing loans would be short-term credit, especially bridging finance.

Pressure upon the clearing banks to diversify their asset policies, and essentially the nature of their lending, has existed for some years. Equally, or almost so, from the late 1950s onwards there developed a movement by the banks themselves towards a new look in bank credit. For most banks this has been very much a defensive action, reflecting a wish to counter the encroachments of other lenders or of innovators in their own ranks; in particular it reflects the need to retain customers by the provision of a complete range of financial services. There has been far less evidence of any deliberate policy of diversification of lending, partly because of the rigidities imposed on the banks by their institutional and economic environment but partly also because of a reluctance (natural to cartel-minded producers) to recognise the growth of substitutes or to initiate action which may incur too drastic a change in their traditional way of doing business. The alternative, however, could well be the erosion of their relative position amongst financial intermediaries, a fact of which the banks are increasingly becoming aware.

Contemporary bank thinking is in a state of flux; even so, traditional attitudes still tend to be prominent. To an extent these attitudes derive from structural rigidities but they are also rooted in an inherent caution which has perhaps inhibited the development of the clearing banker as the complete entrepreneur. The essence of 'traditional' bank attitudes may perhaps be summed up as follows. First, diversification would require a specially trained staff which would be expensive to obtain. Further, money would be locked up in illiquid advances, with the risk of a bank being unable to meet sudden but normal short-term demand. Thirdly, present methods are preferred by customers, particularly from the point of low-cost borrowing. What is more, profits would be diminished by reduced commission resulting from the smaller turnover on longer advances, and they might also be affected by long-term lending at fixed rates in a period of a secular rise in interest rates. Profits might also be less because of the fact that, unlike their competitors, the banks are required to keep a high minimum ratio of liquid assets.

It would not be particularly difficult to demonstrate the limitations of each ingredient in this argument. In the first place, there is clearly a danger of exaggerating the difference between various types of lending and the different degrees of skill required by each. Lending on hire-purchase, for example, can hardly be considered to be more difficult or even inherently different from any normal bank secured loan, let alone unsecured loans. The assessment of requests for long-term credit, on the other hand, might certainly be beyond the capacity of the average branch manager, but even in this case all British clearing banks now possess staff at head and regional offices capable of a rational assessment of long-term trends. There is of course no contesting the fact that if the banks are assumed to be operating with no excess capacity (ignoring for this purpose any spare capacity created by the action of the authorities) then expansion of their lending beyond the satisfaction of the 'normal' demand certainly depends upon their ability to attract deposits and the methods of competition they adopt. This is clearly an implication for the deposit-seeking policies of the banks rather than an immutable constraint on their lending policies.

It is probably accurate to say that British bank credit is cheaper on average than that available in other countries. This is particularly so if a direct comparison is made between, for example, the cost of a British overdraft facility and that of an American bank term loan, with its compensating balances and commitment charges. For British banks to lend on loan account—i.e. one requiring the borrower to keep a minimum compensating credit balance of between 10 and 20 per cent—would certainly be more profitable. Furthermore, US banks engaged in mortgage business commonly charge fees (usually 1 per cent) in addition to interest payments. As far as particular long-term markets are concerned, however, it is debatable whether under present conditions British banks would be able to capture a significant share of the mortgage market. Competition with the Building Societies—non-profit-making institutions enjoying a comparatively favourable tax and liquidity position—would be such that the banks' ability or inclination to match their lending rates would be severely limited. To the extent that the banks deprive building societies of deposits by competitive bidding, however, the latter's lending power would be reduced, allowing the banks to substitute their credit and thus exercise a stronger influence over mortgage rates. It is doubtful, however, whether the consequent equilibrium rate would be at a lower level than before. In the case of hire-purchase finance, bank intervention could well be more successful, probably resulting in an equilibrium rate equivalent to or lower than the present norm.

There is no doubt that bank profits might suffer as a result of 'unorthodox' lending policies unless the basis of bank lending charges was adapted to suit the new borrowing requirements. In the case of all demands for credit, for example, it might be necessary that commitment fees should be levied in instances where facilities are not drawn upon immediately, inasmuch as funds have to be set aside by the banks to provide for undrawn commitments and, of course, have an opportunity cost; to a limited extent, in fact, this is already being done. It might also prove necessary to ensure that appropriate safeguards are established against the banks being 'caught' by an upward drift in interest rates; this could be done by arrangements for the escalation of rates, subject to a certain percentage variation. From the point of view of the borrower, this would usually be preferable to the risk of having the loan called in.

Of wider significance generally is the basic question of the optimum return on bank lending, some of the implications of which have been discussed in the preceding chapter. The cost of bank credit appears to have been below market equilibrium levels in Britain during recent years, a fact which has encouraged the growth of other lenders. Not only is British bank credit cheap in relation to bank credit in other countries; it compares favourably with credit costs in other UK capital markets. A move to reduce this discrepancy—and to reduce the volume of 'chronic' overdrafts—was made in the autumn of 1969 when the margin between clearing bank deposit and advances rates was widened by a ½ per cent increase in the latter. Clearing bank lending rates now range within a 3 per cent band above Bank Rate. Thus 2½-3 per cent above Bank Rate will be charged for borrowers of average security including personal and professional borrowers, while one per cent above Bank Rate (the so-called blue-chip rate) is the usual charge to first-class borrowers of undoubted security—for example, local authorities, building societies, insurance companies and other first-class industrial and commercial borrowers. Local authority temporary borrowing in the three-month market, on the other hand, currently stands at just over $1\frac{1}{2}$ per cent over Bank Rate, while other short-term lending rates—for example, on loans by finance companies—are of course at substantially higher levels.

The presence of direct controls, and their effect on bank profits, has been largely responsible for the banks' diversion of most of their new activities into the hands of subsidiaries. The disadvantages of the present system of monetary controls, particularly the inhibitions inadvertently imposed upon bank competition, are well known. More emphasis needs to be placed on the way in which such controls can inhibit innovations in new forms of credit. The basic assumption underlying the system of direct controls imposed upon British clearing banks is that such banks are all doing a broadly similar kind of business and working to the same liquidity ratios, based on 'uniformly accepted definitions of what constitutes a liquid asset'.[8] This assumption of 'sameness', although true for past and even present circumstances, necessarily commits the banks to the risk of fossilisation in their present structure and a future as propitious as that of the dinosaurs. Virtually by definition, so it seems, individual clearing banks are precluded from direct diversification or from incorporating large new enterprises under one roof, largely because of the profits constraint instantly imposed upon them by official controls. If it is in the public interest for the banks to compete directly in the hire-purchase or mortgage markets, therefore, a case could be made for a downward reduction of the liquidity ratio against increases in such assets. Conversely, as in the case of the USA and Germany, a differential reserve requirement for term and sight deposits could at some future date be introduced, enabling the clearing banks to increase medium and long-term credit on the expansion of their fixed term deposits.

4. The significance of deposit and asset rates

Empirical and theoretical analysis of the structure and policies of the US banking system shows that a strong factor in favour of their competition with non-bank intermediaries is the banks' greater ability to squeeze the margin between deposit and asset rates. The advance portfolio of an individual US bank will contain a range of assets of varying maturity and category—for example, consumer credit, business term loans and residential or business mortgages plus a substantial share of short-term loans—each type carrying a different rate of return. The rates of return on credit extended will comprise declining interest costs to borrowers, reflecting a bank's ability to compete in price as well as in non-price terms. This gives the bank's sloped supply schedule of credit (AR), shown in Figure 1. Hence the bank can increase its credit—by extending along the AR line—only in so far as it is willing to take a reduced rate of income.

The AC curve, on the other hand, comprises the cost of attracting (or retaining) deposits from the public. This curve—together, of course, with the MC curve—reflects the bank's willingness to acquire or retain more demand or time deposits and it can be reasonably assumed that increased efforts to acquire deposits will bid up costs. The more deposits the bank acquires, however, the greater will be its volume of output. Conventional theory suggests that the firm will attain its optimum—that is, make maximum total profits—where the MC and MR schedules intersect. In the real

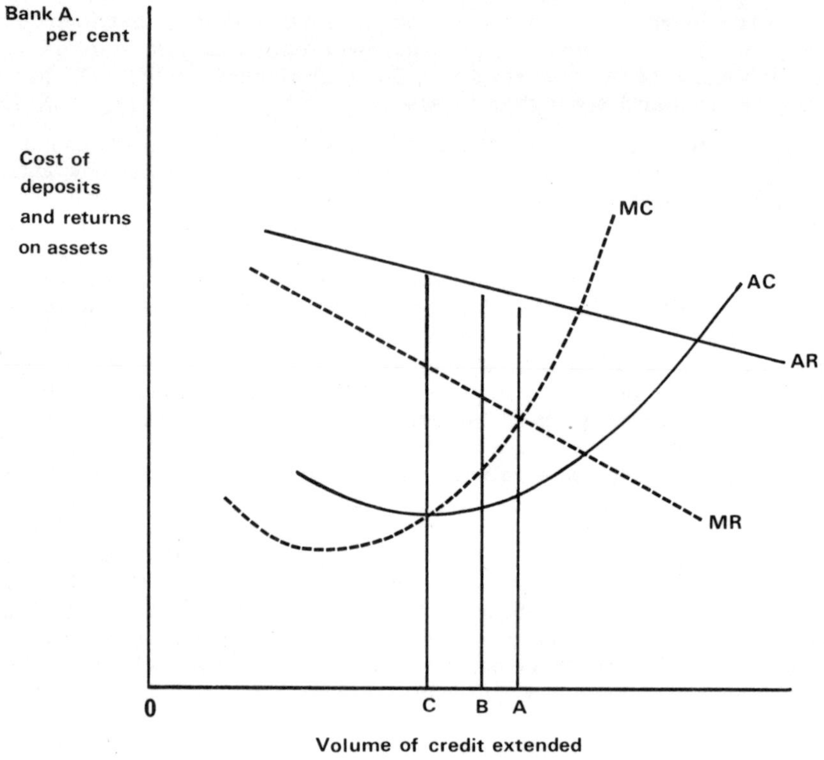

world, of course, the actual output position of the firm may not be at this optimum point, depending on a variety of factors—market conditions and policies, elasticities of demand for its product and supply of its inputs etc., and including government controls or even the political inexpediency of maximising profits; the output position of a bank will thus be below and to the left of its optimum point, somewhere between OA and OC where average cost is minimised. The liquidity reserve requirement enforced upon banks in most countries, including the USA and the UK, necessarily reduces the yield on their total asset structure by confining a proportion of their assets to sterile reserves. To the extent that banks hold bankers' balances with the central bank (or till money) in excess of clearance and transactions needs, therefore, some assets earn nothing at all, while others—in the case of British banks—receive less than their potential market value. Consequently banks cannot push to the profit-maximising point OA where MC = MR.

At the actual output point, under conditions of non-price competition, deposit inputs may include a relatively high ratio of demand deposits; with the differential reserve system under which US banks operate, a correspondingly high volume of 'required' reserves will be necessary. Under such circumstances, with a reduced ratio of earning assets, a higher profit per unit may have been desired by the banks. This at any rate appears to have been the actual position of US banks in the 1950s, and also of British clearing banks—with the notable difference that the latter continue in this position today.

Between 1958 and 1962, however, several reductions were made in the reserve requirements of US banks, so that after 1962 required reserves stood between 12 and 16½ per cent for demand deposits and at 4 per cent for time deposits. Consequently the banks were able to expand output nearer to their optimum point MC = MR, being able to hold an increased ratio of earning assets. Equally as important as the shift in the attitude of the authorities was the willingness of the banks to compete by cutting unit profits, accepting a rise in AC as rates were bid up on time deposits and a decline in AR due to the effect of the increased credit output. Hence as a result of price competition the new equilibrium position of US banks was shifted away from OC and towards OA, the actual output level depending on the compromise made between maximum profit per unit of output or maximum total profit.

For all deposit-taking intermediaries the interest rates paid to holders of time or deposit accounts (or in the case of demand or current accounts, compensating services) are, of course, a function of the rates of return earned on the deployment of their assets, with an appropriate margin for profit and risk taking. In a period of rising rates, however, a competitive advantage would tend to lie with the intermediary possessing the greatest adaptability built into its asset portfolio and willing to engage in price competition. The more responsive is the asset structure to rising rates, the greater is the capacity to pay for additional deposit inputs and hence for growth. In the context of the American environment this advantage lay with the banks. Unlike nonbank financial intermediaries, the banks could choose to increase competitive pressure because they operate in an output area where MR exceeds MC. Most banks can be regarded as 'maturity makers'—unlike, for example, the Savings and Loans Associations in the case of the United States or the Building Societies in Britain, who are better classed as 'maturity takers', being heavily committed by virtue of their main business to long-term assets such as mortgages with a slow rate of turnover. Although US bank lending has on average tended to lengthen, a large proportion is still at short term. As a result the banks can make the level of their AR for any year respond reasonably quickly to changes in interest rates and other market conditions. Their willingness to compete by paying rates on time deposits which were rising faster than revenues reflected their readiness to contract unit profit margins in order to raise total profits. The US Savings and Loans Associations, on the other hand, were inhibited from raising their own deposit rates to the extent required; because of the nature and yield of their asset distribution, their AR function was prevented from rising as fast as that of the banks. In a period of rapidly rising interest rates this necessarily placed them at a disadvantage by limiting the extent to which they could hold, let alone attract, price-elastic deposits.

What relevance does US experience have for British banking, given the substantial differences in market conditions between the two countries? At the moment British banks are at a disadvantage *vis-à-vis* other competitors in the deployment of their assets. Given the assumption that the appropriate incentives are provided by the authorities, however, there seems no reason for not supposing that an equivalent degree of success is possible for British banks, depending on the maturity structure of their rivals' assets. Here the building societies would be most vulnerable, the hire-purchase companies and secondary banks being vulnerable to a lesser extent. It is of course true that it would be perfectly possible for the building societies to provide short-term instalment credit for household durables, competing with the banks and by diversification improving their competitive ability. Generally however it seems plausible to expect a greater emphasis on market share in most aspects of credit from the banks, and probably a corresponding readiness on their part to cut profit margins in order to secure an expansion of output. Even in the absence of any official incentives such a trend seems to be already well on its way.

5. Initiatives in credit facilities

Despite their rooted caution in the face of new ideas, the phenomenon of outside competition has prompted British banks into a remarkable drive towards the promotion of new enterprise. While for British non-financial companies generally bank borrowing has increased in popularity from 1959 onwards, the proportion extended by the clearing banks has experienced a relative decline. With the absorption of post-war liquidity, the proportion of total capital expenditure financed by all bank loans has risen from less than 1.5 per cent in 1952-8 to nearly 12 per cent in 1959-65. Unfortunately, there are no statistics to show the contribution of the secondary banks to this sector before March 1963, although statistics on their sterling advances to UK residents show that these had increased on average by about 2½ times between the end of 1957 and the end of 1962. Between end-1962 and end-1968, however, it appears that the secondary banks have increased their share of the non-financial company business enormously; their advances to residents of the UK amounted to about 13 per cent of total clearing bank advances in 1962 but to over 31 per cent of that total at the end of 1968.(9) Included within these figures, of course, is the share obtained by the clearing banks' own subsidiaries who are members of the Accepting Houses Committee, the British Overseas and Commonwealth Bank Association, the Foreign Banks and Affiliates Association and Other banks. Particular publicity has attached to the role played by the American banks, whose share of the secondary banks' total credit to UK residents is the largest component.

The significance of this had been noted by the Monopolies Commission who noted that 80 per cent of their sterling lending was to American and other foreign-owned subsidiaries in this country.(10) Even allowing for the fact that their lending is a function of US direct investment in recent years, it seemed undeniable that the clearing banks had within a five-year period lost an appreciable amount of business to other lenders.

One reason for the increased popularity of secondary bank finance may have been a tendency on the part of non-financial companies to move away from the notion of securing an overdraft for general working capital purposes and towards securing loans for particular capital projects. Under these circumstances there has been a growing demand for medium-term finance—of three to five years or even seven years—which in the current British environment, dominated by the credit squeezes of the 1960s, suggests that companies may have acquired an increased preference for the greater certainty of a secondary-bank term loan compared with the cheaper but less secure clearing bank overdraft.(11)

The formality of the term loan also has its attractions for the clearing banks themselves. Their conspicuous difficulties in reducing overdrafts in response to official pressure in that direction has led many bankers to look with increasing favour on the contractual and more predictable nature of term-loan credit. Like the acceptor of a bill, the user of term loans has virtually no alternative but to reduce his indebtedness at the allotted time; under the overdraft system, on the other hand, the final repayment date can become a matter of relative bargaining positions (in which weakness is not necessarily disadvantageous) rather than of fixed, objective reality. Furthermore, the overdraft system involves the adoption of drawing facilities, the degree of usage of which has a disconcerting habit (from the bankers' point of view) of rising sharply precisely when, and because, a restrictive policy is being enforced by the authorities. It is probably fallacious to argue that the use of overdraft facilities involves a bank in holding idle resources as an insurance against the unexpected or undue use of those facilities; a borrower forced to take a term loan rather than an overdraft would almost certainly dispose of unused balances elsewhere in the banking system until required and would consequently subject the system as a whole to exactly the same sudden and unpredicted shocks as would be the case if he were calling on unused overdraft facilities. But even if the overall control of *deposits* would be unaffected by a switch from overdrafts to term loans, the bankers' control over their *advances* would be firmer, and if the authorities persist in enforcing policy changes through aggregate advances, rather than deposits, the switch could reduce the degree of neurosis induced in the clearing banker by his exposure to such policy changes.

This policy aspect apart, however, there has been little incentive for the clearing banks to emulate their rivals in this matter. Such ventures as they made into term loans did not meet with conspicuous success, largely because of the qualitative and quantitative controls officially imposed on clearing bank advances, restrictions which were tardily applied to other lenders and even then were by no means as rigorous. Prominent casualties included the suspension of personal loan schemes and term loans for farm purchase and improvement. Conversely, instalment credit at a fixed $5\frac{1}{2}$ per cent for ship-builders and exporters proved popular, although hardly to the benefit of the banks. It is not surprising, therefore, that the banks subsequently preferred to switch funds into subsidiaries where they could be more profitably employed. The question of whether this function is best carried out by the banks directly or through their subsidiaries has proved to be far less important than the fact that they were in the event developing new methods of lending and using money.

The most publicised of these new methods has probably been the banks' venture into credit cards. Once again the origin of the idea is to be found in transatlantic experience, notably Diners Club Ltd., American Express and the Bank of America Card. Although bank credit cards had been known in the USA since 1952 it was not until 1966 and 1967 that banks in America and Britain entered the credit card business in force. Their intervention reflected the widening acceptance of credit cards generally, the growing availability of efficient processing equipment and an increasing realisation that credit cards could be profitably provided. Although the National Provincial had previously introduced a card to be issued to selected customers, allowing them restricted cashing rights for their cheques at any branch, the first expansion into the credit card business proper in Britain came in late 1965 with the Westminster Bank's bid for, and subsequent acquisition of, a substantial holding of Diners Club. In 1966 Barclays introduced the Barclaycard with reciprocal arrangements with the Bank of

America Card. Although both cheque and credit cards provide some guarantee of the customer's financial standing, the latter goes much further. The cheque card, favoured by the majority of banks, does no more than ensure that a supplier of cash, goods or services will accept a cheque in payment. The credit card, on the other hand, dispenses with the need for a cheque altogether and supplies credit in that actual settlement of the account by the customer can be delayed without (direct) cost for up to about a month. The bank reimburses the retailer and allows the customer to borrow from the bank if necessary, the charge being borne by the retailer from whom the bank takes a set commission. To some extent credit cards may be regarded as consumers' bills of exchange in that, through their holders, they are accepted by the bank.[12]

Eventually the introduction of a credit card system operating within a fully automated transfer mechanism can be expected. A prototype of such an automated sales system is already being operated by one US bank in collaboration with a chain of retail shops. Before a sale takes place, the customer's card is inserted in a terminal device in the shop linked by telephone to the bank's computer. The computer immediately interrogates the account data stored in its magnetic files, calculates a credit rating based on the current state of the customer's account and transmits the information to the terminal device. Beyond this stage it would not be difficult to incorporate credit facilities for such transactions by suitable programming of the computer, so that although the retailer received immediate value, the customer would be debited later, as he is under the present card system.[13]

The introduction of credit cards represents one more stage in the keen competition for a larger share of the consumer credit business and also an attempt to reduce the high and growing cost of using cash. In the case of the former, the banks can expect a high per-unit gross income which is subject in the short run to heavy promotion and other fixed costs plus bad debts, but which in the long run promises attractive profits. The main long-run advantage of the credit card from the point of the participating banks will be found in a reduction in the volume of cheques and cash—both expensive to use—although in the short run, before economies of scale can be derived, credit cards increase the internal clearing problem. In the first instance a bank must process an even larger volume of paper, including the sales drafts which would normally be paid by cheque and those which replace former cash purchases. On the other hand, credit cards are particularly suited to cope with a large volume of small transactions with a minimum of decision-making for a bank, easily absorbing those functions whose processing costs are high relative to their return—a good example being small personal loans and overdrafts. The success of the scheme depends very much on a high volume of transactions and turnover.

It is possible that from the point of view of the retailer who bears the cost of the card, the problems as well as the potential inflationary characteristics have been exaggerated. For the banks concerned, on the other hand, probably more important is the question of credit control and the risk of a dramatic rise in an individual bank's proportion of bad debts, not least through the lack of regular banking relationships. Further, if an individual bank's credit cards are successful, then this implies that the credit policy of that bank is committed in relation to its total resources and this will affect other asset policies of the bank; the lines of credit assured by credit cards are unsecured and automatic and the bank may expose itself to unpredictable surges in credit demand which it must meet by adjusting its asset portfolio—probably investments in the case of UK banks.

An eventual attraction, first for the individual bank (e.g. Barclays) and in time for the banking system as a whole, may be the effects upon bank liquidity. It is possible to envisage a universal practice whereby, instead of being withdrawn in cash from the bank by the customer and then paid direct to the retailer (or for that matter transferred by cheque), money will be retailed by the bank at which the customer has an account, effectively as a loan paid for by the retailer until the latter receives payment. In practice the time lag before repayment should be very short, so that the banks will be able to operate with a lower cash ratio—provided that retailers do not require large cash repayments. In the event of the latter occurring, either directly or indirectly through the retailer's own bank, pressure would be placed upon the bank's cash position. Till money would have to be paid out with a lag occurring before a corresponding decrease in deposits.[14] This latter possibility, however, is much less likely than the former, given that the demand for cash by retailers derives from that for petty cash and wages which, as far as the former is concerned, will be actually reduced since credit cards do not require change. In so far as the public chooses to hold smaller cash balances, the banks can also look for a 'once-for-all' hoist in their liquidity reserves. For some banks, at least, this would appear to be a more attractive means of acquiring deposits than a resort to price competition. It would have the further advantage of a more stable aggregation of deposits which people of moderate income would keep with a bank in order to provide them with a convenient way of making payments.[15]

6. Insurance, unit trusts and investment management

Leaving aside developments in the markets for credit, it is important not to forget new ventures in other financial services perhaps most suitably attributed to the motive of deposit-retention rather than savings attraction. For many years it has not been unusual to find bank branch managers combining their main appointment with that of sub-agent for firms of insurance brokers or underwriters. The Westminster Bank took this a step further when it announced the establishment of its own head office broking department to which branches could apply on behalf of customers for quotations on life assurance, fire and motor insurance, while individual branches were empowered to issue cover notes. Whether or not this will become a common feature of bank practice is difficult to say; even more speculative is the question of whether the banks will go beyond this and actually engage in underwriting business.

Another facility in this category has been the introduction of bank investment trusts and unit trusts—basically an easy extension from their trustee departments; the former have been aimed at the institutional market while the latter—exemplified by the newer bank unit trusts such as the Westminster Hambros Unit Trust—have been slanted towards the retail market, appealing to the small investor through the issue of units of a sufficiently small size.

In accord with the movement to provide a fuller financial service for their clients, British clearing banks have widened their activities to include functions previously considered to be within the domain of the merchant banks and others. A notable innovation occurred in 1965, for example, with the entry of the Westminster Bank into the new issue market on behalf of one of its customers. For some years the banks had been providing a 'background' new issue and registrar service for their clients, stopping short, however, of actual flotation. The Westminster's direct placing was another indication that the 'traditional role' of the clearing banks was becoming very much a matter of debate.

More recent developments have included the provision by nearly all of the banks of leasing and factoring services for individual customers, although so far bank intervention has taken place through subsidiary or associated companies. At the moment it appears that banks will simply offer such facilities to their customers as another part of a financial package deal. The demand for lease finance is derived from the demand for credit to acquire fixed assets. Basically such leases are similar to secured term loans, usually having maturities of from three to eight years, the term depending on the nature of the equipment and the needs and qualifications of the borrower. If the equipment has an expected economic life of ten years, for example, and if the borrower was eligible for an amortised secured term loan with an eight-year maturity, then the lessor would probably grant an eight-year lease.

A factor, on the other hand, in return for a fixed service fee, purchases invoices from his customer, ledgers them, sends an account to the trade debtors, collects the debts and also assumes full responsibility for bad debts on all sales previously approved by the factor. At the same time the factor, as well as providing a comprehensive sales ledger service, agrees to pay the supplier, his customer, on a pre-determined date which is calculated on the overall average debt turnover in the supplier's own sales ledger prior to the factoring agreements.[16] Additional facilities include the provision of credit to the customer in advance of the agreed maturity date of the factored debts, up to a maximum of 80 per cent of the value of the invoices. This enables the customer to pay his own suppliers of raw materials more promptly, thereby securing discounts for cash payment which may to a large extent offset the cost of the service. The advantages from the point of view of the customer, particularly the small firm, include the concentration of creditor-debtor relationships, the elimination of the risk of bad debts and of the need for trained credit-control and collection staff.

The 1960s proved to be an era of change for many sectors of Britain's economy and especially for the clearing banks, large technological and structural changes occurring as well as significant developments in competition. The traditional 'Big Five' no longer exists, although it is questionable if this is as important as the emergence—even before the mergers—of large banking groups engaged in a range of diverse financial activities, including several which would have been unthought of a decade previously and with more than a hint of others still to come.

The extent of the new boldness in bank thinking was epitomised by the 1968 amendments to the memorandum of association of one of the leading banks. This provides for that bank the right

> to promote, effect, insure, guarantee, underwrite, secure the subscription or placing of, subscribe or tender for..., manage or carry out of any issue, public or private.... to carry on financial business and

> financial operations of all kinds, and in particular... to finance or assist in the financing of the sale of goods, articles or commodities of all and every kind whether by way of personal loan, hire purchase, instalment finance, deferred payments or otherwise, to acquire by assignment or otherwise debts due and owing to any person or company and to collect such debts and to constitute and to act as managers of unit trusts and investment trusts and to issue and transact business in respect of all types of bankers' cards and credit cards and to carry on all kinds of insurance business and generally to act as financiers, traders, factors, commission agents, insurance brokers or in any other capacity, and to import, export, buy, sell, barter, exchange, let on hire, pledge, make advances upon or otherwise deal in any property whether tangible or intangible.[17]

For industrial enterprises innovation is a basis for growth, but for British clearing banks it had been more nearly anathema for far too long. Since 1958 many innovations have occurred, some at the initiative of the banks themselves and others imposed upon them from outside. The transition phase in British banking is still far from complete and in any event involves so many unknown factors that it is difficult to forecast with accuracy an eventual equilibrium position. Technological change, increased outside competition, the renewed presence of monetary controls—all have combined to influence the direction of bank activity. These factors, above all, are the most important determinants of current and future developments in banking.

Technological innovations and the promise of a cashless society, or at least a 'less cheque' society, have the most profound potential implications for the clearing bank system. In conjunction with a widespread adoption of credit cards, automated procedures could provide a more efficient and less costly payments system as well as a sophisticated management information service. The comparative freedom from expensive routines which the banks could hope to achieve during the 1970s would allow them to divert both entrepreneurs and skilled labour to more rewarding functions—for example, the development of new fields of business. On the other hand, the prospect of a cashless society, however remote at the moment, presents the banks with problems. There could well develop a system which could be programmed 'so that for a given day's money payments no one had more or less in his account, taking into account inflows, than needed to cover outflows. If this were so, velocity would approach infinity and money supply zero.'[18] This sort of effect of automation on bank deposits (and assets) has to be considered seriously; in any foreseeable system it appears likely that there will exist the ability to maintain account balances not only on a daily but an hourly basis. This implies the eventual separation of the liquidity and transactions functions of the bank deposit so that its use could be reduced solely to the latter—that of a medium of exchange. No one, in other words, need be holding deposits as a store of value or as a liquidity reserve, so that money managers may be forced to become liquidity or near-money managers.[19] To the limited extent that bank deposits have ever been a medium for current savings, the movement towards fully automated procedures implies that the banks may need to attempt a more positive interception of real savings. For their own survival, therefore, they may need to become specialised managers of the country's near money—in conjunction, of course, with associated areas of finance.

This is a process which, as has been seen, has already been initiated but its inauguration has undoubtedly sprung primarily from the pressures of the competitive environment in which the banks have increasingly found themselves. During the post-war years the clearing banks have been regarded as joint-stock profit maximisers, by virtue of their cartel on interest rates. Some further distinction is possible, however, when one considers the two main functions of the clearing banks—on the one hand to provide facilities for making payments and, on the other, to supply credit. In their former function, as suppliers of remittance services, the banks could be more aptly described as sales maximisers. In the latter function, however, they are joint-profit maximisers, subject to a high liquidity or risk aversion constraint but correspondingly compensated by the endowment profits enjoyed through their cartel. Even in this connection, however, it appears that they are being pushed towards the adoption of sales maximisation policies—a tendency which will be accentuated if the cartel breaks down—with the provision of a complete range of credit services. Market share is becoming a matter of much greater consequence and—when circumstances permit—the banks are likely to show decreasing tolerance of other substitutes for their lending.

In recent years the clearing banks have moved a considerable way towards the diversification of their activities and structure. Given the continuance of this trend, the ultimate pattern of the banking system is unlikely to be settled before at least the mid-1970s. Inevitably there are bound to be delays—or lags—due to various causes, the first arising from the process of recognition of outside competition and the formulation of policy measures to counter it—a decision stage which is now almost over—and a second being the progress of technology or new training schemes, an aspect in which British clearing banks are well in advance. Further delays are bound to be introduced also by the difficulties of merging different bank structures. Again, substantial delays could be incurred through the tardiness of the authorities in providing an institutional environment which is simultaneously conducive to their task of monetary control and to the growth of the clearing bank system. In this context bank development will depend upon the re-appraisal, and possible reform, of present monetary methods and policies. Even so, despite many obvious hazards it is still possible—and tempting—to advance some generalisations about the sort of competition to be expected from the clearing banks in the future.

First, bank competition is likely to retain its emphasis on services although with less reliance perhaps upon the branch structure. Major improvements towards even quicker encashment and transfer services may be expected, with automatic cash dispensers in shops and other retail outlets, and a continuous development is likely towards a more rational cheque and credit card system, working to reduce the volume of transactions involving cheques or cash and based on the inter-bank computer service. It will then be more appropriate to talk of the clearing bank system, rather than a group of 'clearing' banks; the emphasis in the transfer mechanism would be a competition between the bank system and the Post Office giro, the Trustee Savings Bank, and others.

So far as bank asset policies are concerned, there is likely to be greater emphasis on the provision of credit or financial services where the rate of return is high in relation to the volume of credit extended—for example, credit cards or hire purchase. In another basic function—that of accepting and keeping in safe custody customers' funds—much greater sophistication may be expected, reflecting an appreciation of the need to intercept current savings rather than to act as residual takers of funds, along the lines already set by bank unit and investment trusts. Hence the banks may be expected to build up their deposit management functions, taking a commission for the management of customers' funds, through unit trusts and investment trust management—the retail and wholesale counterparts of deposit bank business. In the event of a substantial expansion of mortgage lending, one possible development could be that the banks' investment management subsidiaries would offer blocks of residential mortgages for purchase by institutional investors such as pension funds.

It seems certain that the banks will attempt to capture a much larger share of the consumer finance market. The provision of consumer 'working' capital could be supplied by an aggressive promotion of credit cards as a supplement to, and substitute for, more conventional but (to the banks) costly overdrafts, particularly where a large number of small loans is involved. In fact, of course, there would be no theoretical difference between these and overdrafts, other than technical details, except for the probability of reduced on-costs, although the borrower would not be paying the cost directly. Following from this, it would be natural for the banks to pay more attention to the whole area of instalment credit for personal expenditures, small businesses and agricultural borrowers. The extension of such credit to mortgage loans of conventional maturities will depend largely on decisions by the authorities—for example, on the introduction of (variable) reserve ratios for sight and time deposits.

Large medium or long-term loans and deposits, and the provision of specialist commercial finance, are more likely to continue to be the function of subsidiaries possessing special expertise—together, of course, with the ability to go into the market and bid for funds when necessary and to operate in both the capital and secondary 'money' markets.

7. The balance sheet structure

It follows from what has been said that the recent trend towards an increased reliance by the banks on their subsidiaries for expansion in many of the 'new' fields of activity is likely to be strengthened rather than weakened in the future. When medium- or long-term commercial facilities or other specialised commercial requirements are in demand it is probable that they will be increasingly provided by the subsidiaries and affiliates supporting the main services of each clearing bank.[20] Already a host of separate clearing bank institutions exist which have been established in order to provide fixed capital and other types of finance to small and medium-sized British companies, equity capital and other funds for established and developing businesses—perhaps prior to the flotation of a new issue—or the backing to finance a merger, funds for large-scale international development projects or medium-term export finance and other banking facilities, as well as associate and direct interests in factoring, leasing, hire-purchase, investment portfolio management, insurance broking, bullion broking, and general merchant and clearing bank activities and connections within Britain and abroad.

The implications for bank asset distribution may be best shown in imaginary and simplified balance sheets (Table 12). For the sake of illustration,

TABLE 12

A hypothetical balance-sheet, 1968 and 1980

BANK 'A' end 1968 (per cent of total) BANK 'A' end 1980

Liabilities		*Assets*		*Liabilities*		*Assets*	
Current, deposit and other accounts	100	Cash and Bankers' Balances	8	Current deposits	40	Cash and Bankers' Balances	6
		Balances with, and cheques in course of collection on, other banks	6	Savings and Time Deposits	60	Balances with, and cheques in course of collection on, other banks	2
					100		
		Money at call and short notice	13			Money at call and short notice	6
		British Government Treasury Bills	5			British Government Treasury Bills	5
		British Bills of Exchange	3			British Bills of Exchange	3
		Other Bills and Re-financeable Credits	3			Other Bills and Re-financeable Credits	3
		Risk Assets				*Risk Assets*	
		Gilt-edged investments	11			Gilt-edged investments	5

	Trade investments	1.6		Trade investments	12
	Investments in subsidiaries	1.4		Investments in subsidiaries	3
	Loans and Advances	46			
	Items in transit	2			
				Loans and Advances of which	
				Overdrafts (incl. amount outstanding on credit cards)	36
				Term Loans (incl. hire purchase agreements)	23
				Mortgages	5
				Items in transit	1
100		100	100		100

precise ratios for a variety of assets to deposits are shown although obviously no precise inferences can be drawn from what can be no more than hypothesis. The table assumes the existence of an institution engaged in operations most of which are currently being handled by bank subsidiaries and associates. In a speculative forecast for 1980, therefore, it is reasonable to expect, *ceteris paribus*, a higher volume of deposits and a higher ratio of advances. Cash and liquidity needs are already significantly in excess of what a large bank needs for its present operations—as the National Board for Prices and Incomes noted—and have been made more so by the mergers of the late 1960s amongst the clearing banks themselves. The size of a bank's deposits in relation to the total deposits of the banking system in which it operates will affect the extent to which that bank's payments are replaced without delay by new deposits.[21] The deposits of a large bank, therefore, will probably fluctuate proportionately much less from day to day than those of a small bank. On the occasion of bank mergers—and on the assumption that these result in a complete amalgamation—the requirement for bankers' balances with the Bank of England is clearly reduced for the banks concerned, since a proportion of what were previously inter-bank transfers involving the use of bankers' balances now become mere ledger or computer operations within one unit. Similarly any increase in size of any bank in relation to the total deposits of the banking system in which it operates reduces that bank's clearing risk.[22]

Looking ahead to 1980 it is reasonable to expect that the demand for cash in circulation will have been reduced by the development of an electronically-based credit card system. The two components of the bank's cash ratio, till money and bankers' balances, are thus both liable to downward revision, the first due to a reduced demand for cash and the second to a reduced clearance risk. In the case of the latter, however, it is possible that there could be an offset presented by the progress of a non-clearing-bank payments and remissions mechanism through the Post Office Giro and the Trustee Savings Banks, as well as increased domestic competition from other secondary banks. Even if deposits transferred from the clearing banks were more or less automatically restored, there would still remain a clearance risk for any individual bank (and for the clearing banks in aggregate) depending on the share of non-clearing banks in the total domestic deposits of the banking system; further, it is likely that part of the deposits so lost would be diverted into newly-issued government securities or, in the case of the Post Office and Trustee Savings Banks, placed directly into public deposits in the Bank of England Banking Department. As a result of the development of a fully mechanised clearing bank transfer system the volume of balances with, and cheques in course of collection from, other banks should decline, although, of course, for the banking system as a whole the item cancels out.

On the question of the liquidity ratios, if any, to be applied over the next decade or so, obviously nothing more than a guess can be attempted. To avoid excessive presumption a liquidity ratio of around 22 per cent is assumed, although this might be differentiated as between current accounts and savings and time deposits. If this were to be the case then the assumed composition of the bank's deposits—with a ratio of 2 : 3 between sight and time deposits—would probably permit a lower overall liquidity ratio than that shown in the table. It is further assumed that the traditional liquid assets, money at call and bills, will continue and retain their conventional composition, although even here minor changes could occur in, for example, the proportion of call money going outside the 'discount houses'. At the moment the clearing banks lend 60 to 70 per cent of their call money to the 12 discount houses, the remainder going to other banks, bill brokers outside the London Discount Market Association, jobbers, stock brokers and bullion brokers, as well as into specified currencies with banks in the UK and abroad. It is perfectly possible that the proportion extended to these markets by the clearing banks could fall still further if, for example, the definition of clearing bank liquid assets was extended by the authorities to include other markets beyond those already allowed or if the banks simply channelled an increased amount of their call money to their own subsidiaries, some of whom would be officially acceptable takers of funds. A marginal increase in clearing bank advances to the market might occur, on the other hand, with the growth of the sterling CD market if the clearing banks were to lend at last resort to the discount houses on the security of sterling CDs issued by the banks' subsidiaries. Bills, on the other hand, are as likely as not to retain their present pattern in the banks' portfolios, together with sundry extras such as ECGD re-financeable credits.

The more interesting, if even more speculative, developments are likely to arise in the banks' risk assets. Gilt-edged investments are still likely to form the residual item in the banks' risk assets, as well as serving as a secondary liquidity buffer, although possibly to a reduced extent, there being an increased emphasis on trade investments (in associates and affiliates) and investments in subsidiaries; even allowing for rapid book depreciation, the latter could still reach increased proportions. Trade investments and investments in subsidiaries together currently amount on average to about $2\frac{1}{2}$ to 3 per cent of the large clearing banks' deposits. Should all parts of the investment portfolio be written in at their full market value, however, it is likely that the proportion shown for trade and subsidiary investments would substantially exceed their book value—much more so than would be the case with their gilt-edged securities. In the banks' lending to business and the public various situations might occur, the ratios depicted in the table being but one possible combination. Overdrafts are likely to retain a large popularity for both business and personal customers and may find a prominent role in operation with credit cards. Term loans, together with hire purchase facilities, may or may not be handled by the main bank, depending on policy developments and on the nature of the deposit structure; if they are in fact retained, they would probably be concentrated on the small business and personal sector. Medium to long-term instalment credit to large companies, on the other hand, is more likely to remain the task of a merchant bank subsidiary. The provision of residential mortgages, however, could very well become a clearing bank function, capable of extensive development through the branch system, being carried either on the bank's books or sold in blocks to other institutional investors, including the banks' own subsidiaries. Long-term forecasts, however, suggest that in about ten years' time there will have occurred a substantial narrowing of the gap between supply and demand in the traditional building society mortgage market in any event. This being the case, the banks may be left with the riskier, interest-inelastic end of the market, a business which they may be justified in not pursuing. Individual banks might specialise to a certain extent in particular main areas of credit. Thus Bank 'B' could have 40 per cent of its deposits in overdrafts, including credit card loans, and 24 per cent in term loans, Bank 'C' 20 per cent in overdrafts, 36 per cent in term loans and 8 per cent in mortgages, Bank 'D' 29 per cent in overdrafts, 25 per cent in mortgages and 10 per cent in term loans. It is unlikely that there will be an equal concentration on term loans and mortgages to the virtual exclusion of other lending, not only because this goes too far against the banks' conception of what their main role should be—the provision of short-term finance—but also because heavy commitment in the long end of the market would influence the distribution of other risk assets; normal banking prudence will require an offsetting balance of liquidity in the banks' other lending. Tendencies towards specialisation already exist, with one bank—Barclays—already set fair to capture the lion's share of the credit card market. It may well be, however, that any such development will be no more than marginal; British banks on the whole are likely to prefer to adopt, through their branches, the role of financial general practitioners and to divert most extra-normal requirements to their specialist subsidiaries.

All this, of course, takes the discussion well into the realm of speculation. The history of the 1960s has been such that, while these possibilities are highly credible in the context of long-run development, in the immediate future the pressures upon the British economy in general, and on the clearing banks in particular, are likely to be such that progress towards them is bound to be severely limited by the constraints of official policy.

REFERENCES

1. See, for example, J. Sykes, *The amalgamation movement in English banking, 1825-1924,* London 1926, pp. 153-5.
2. 'Credit after the squeeze', *The Banker,* Vol. 109, No. 397, February 1959, p. 120.
3. National Board for Prices and Incomes, *Bank Charges,* Report No. 34, Cmd 3292, HMSO, London 1967, paras. 51-2.
4. *Ibid.*, para. 61.
5. Federal Reserve Bank of Chicago, May 1968.
6. E. P. Neufeld, 'The relative growth of commercial banks', *Essays in money and banking in honour of R. S. Sayers,* Oxford University Press, London 1968, p. 150.
7. See J. H. Coleman, 'Canada's new Bank Act: the challenge and the response', *The Statist World Banking Supplement,* London 1967, p. 97.
8. *Bank of England Quarterly Bulletin,* Vol. 8, No. 2, June 1968, p. 97.
9. See *Annual Abstract of Statistics,* No. 105, HMSO, London 1968, Tables 347 and 350 and *Financial Statistics,* No. 83, HMSO, London, March 1969, Table 31.
10. Monopolies Commission, *Barclays Bank Ltd., Lloyds Bank Ltd. and Martin's Bank Ltd.,* HMSO, London, July 1968, para. 178.
11. J. R. S. Revell, *Changes in British banking,* Hill, Samuel Occasional Paper No. 3, p. 23.

12. M. Ward, 'Are credit cards inflationary?', *The Banker,* Vol. CXVI, No. 485, July 1966, p. 450.

13. F. W. Gibson, 'The cashless revolution', *Westminster Bank Review,* February 1968, p. 24.

14. M. Ward, *loc. cit.*, p. 453.

15. J. Thomson, 'The case for the credit card', *The Banker,* Vol. CXVI, No. 485, July 1966, p. 46.

16. T. G. Hutson, 'Factoring', *The Bankers' Magazine,* Vol. CCVI, No. 1495, October 1968, p. 193.

17. Midland Bank Ltd., *Annual Report,* December 1968: revised memoranda of association, Clauses 2. 1. k and 3. 2

18. F. W. Gibson, *op. cit.*, p. 29.

19. *Ibid.*

20. W. F. Crick, 'Financial implications of economic growth', *Journal of the Institute of Bankers,* Vol. 85, Part I, February 1964, p. 20.

21. 'Bank Liquidity in the United Kingdom', *Bank of England Quarterly Bulletin,* Vol. II, No. 4, December 1962, p. 248.

22. E. W. Davis and E. T. Nevin, 'Monetary policy and the mergers', *The Bankers' Magazine,* Vol. CCV, No. 1489, April 1968, p. 271.

CHAPTER THIRTEEN

Control of the Credit Base

1. The return of monetary policy

One of the most striking features of the postwar history of the advanced economies of the world was the virtual unanimity with which they resorted to the use of 'orthodox' monetary techniques—meaning especially control through the price and/or volume of bank credit—in the course of little more than twelve months in 1950-51. After its almost total disuse for over a decade, and in many cases for nearly two decades, in the course of a year or so nearly every country in North America and Western Europe rediscovered credit control and dear money; for the United Kingdom the watershed is November 1951 and the return of the Conservative party to office.

That such a transformation should have occurred, virtually simultaneously, in so many countries is at first sight astonishing, even making due allowance for the emulation effect of the adoption of any given policy in a major economy on other economies dependent in greater or lesser degree upon it. The fact is that this almost universal restoration of credit control reflected the common economic and intellectual experience of the developed world and, equally, the changes occurring in their environment at the beginning of the 1950s.

On the one hand, the 'special' circumstances prevailing for some twenty years in Western Europe were giving way to 'normality' once again. In the 1930s there had been deep and protracted recession; then, the six years of world war; finally, the serious and apparently intractable external payments problems of the five or six postwar years. Each of these 'special' emergencies had been handled, in large degree, by extensive resort to government intervention in, or regulation of, domestic (and occasionally foreign) markets and control over the allocation of resources. Of necessity, the price and volume of credit had become secondary, if not irrelevant, considerations to the extent that ordinary market forces were superseded by official regulation. The progressive dismantling of this interventionist apparatus was a natural outcome of the reattainment of a full-employment normality in the economies of the industrialised world; the increased relevance of orthodox monetary policy was in turn a logical corollary of the diminished role of direct controls.

On the intellectual level, the late 1940s witnessed an increased awareness of certain limitations in the policy aspects of Keynes' *General Theory*—or, to be more precise, in the popularisations of it—which had so dominated economic thinking since its appearance in 1936. In the first place, the *General Theory* had presented a system of essentially medium- or long-term statics in which emphasis had been laid on the secular tendencies in the basic 'propensities' of the system—the propensities to consume and to invest. It had been written against a background in which both appeared to be steadily declining and prime importance was therefore attached to relatively long-term fiscal measures to offset this decline, especially in the field of income redistribution and public investment. The postwar world, however, proved to be one not of secular stagnation but of apparently continuous inflation marked by periodic short-run crises—for the solution of which, of course, the use of relatively slow-moving fiscal machinery was unsuited. Monetary policy, by contrast, seemed inherently more applicable to a situation marked by a series of short-run marginal crises rather than deep-rooted secular stagnation.

A second feature of popularised Keynesian theory had been the tendency to assume a low elasticity of the rate of interest with respect to changes in the quantity of money and, equally, a low elasticity of investment to changes in the rate of interest. Postwar experience indicated, however, that even if both assumptions were well-founded it by no means followed that reduction of the money supply would be without effect from a policy point of view. On the one hand, while the demand curve for money might be highly elastic within the relevant ranges of the rate of interest, the curve was also (as indeed Keynes himself had emphasised) a highly volatile one. Monetary techniques could therefore have their effect by causing the liquidity demand curve to shift about rather than by relying on movement along it.(1) On the other hand, while expenditure might be unresponsive to small changes in the rate of interest, it was increasingly appreciated that monetary policy worked through the availability of credit as well as—probably more than—its price. The real or alleged inelasticity of investment with regard to interest rates was therefore seen as something less than fatal to the cause of credit control.

The third element of the *General Theory* which had tended to push monetary policy into the background had been its concentration on the internal economy to the virtual exclusion of matters involving international trade and payments; as a theoretical system it had been closed as well as static. Again, the postwar world refused to fit this pattern and the international movement of short-term funds became an issue of increasing concern. Here was another sphere in which orthodox monetary policy had traditionally been regarded as particularly important and one in which, furthermore, other effective policy measures were singularly hard to discover.

For all these reasons, then, the beginning of the 1950s was a time peculiarly ripe for a return to the hallowed techniques of 'orthodox' credit control. They had been relatively little used in the industrialised world since the 1920s, but there was a sense in which the 1920s had been the last period of normality, a type of situation to which many hoped and believed the world was returning once the bulk of postwar reconstruction had been completed.

2. The banks and monetary control

A restoration of orthodox market control by the Bank of England over the operations of the commercial banking system was obviously a prerequisite for the return to conventional credit policy. At the end of 1951, however, the asset-structure of the British banks was scarcely conducive to this process. For reasons which have already been explained, the banking system was in possession of an enormous stock of Treasury bills and as a result enjoyed a liquidity ratio well in excess of the 'commercial' 30 per cent. As may be seen from Table 13 in October 1951 the clearing banks were operating with a liquidity ratio as high as 39 per cent. In the view of the authorities, so long as this position continued it was impossible for any effective control to be exercised by the Bank of England over the money supply. A reduction of cash through conventional open-market operations could easily be prevented, if the banks so chose, by simply allowing a corresponding volume of Treasury bills to run off at maturity and taking repayment in cash. The banks, in fact, were in a position to expand their advances very considerably at any time by switching out of liquid assets and without requiring any increase in their cash reserves.

The increase in Bank rate from 2 to 2½ per cent in November 1951—the first effective change in nearly twenty years—[(2)] was thus more psychological a gesture than normally, especially as the old 2 per cent rate was retained for Treasury bills. The more substantial measure was the issue of £1,000 million Serial Funding Bonds in exchange for Treasury bills; it was made clear to the commercial banks that they were expected to take up the greater part of this issue, which they duly did. As will be seen from Table 13, the result of this operation was that by the end of 1951 the clearing banks' holdings of bills had been reduced by some £360 million, bringing the liquidity ratio down to 33.2 per cent, while their investments had risen by £410 million. Allowing for the contraction of the Treasury bill supply normally experienced in the first quarter of the calendar year,[(3)] it could be said that the liquidity of the banking system had effectively been brought close to the conventional minimum.

The expected results followed. In December the banks announced that the rate of interest to be charged on advances would in general be increased by an amount equal to the rise in Bank rate.[(4)] They were also re-issued with a statement of the 'requests' which had been made to them earlier on the subject of credit priorities in association with the Chancellor's memoranda of guidance to the Capital Issues Committee; as a result they made it known that from this point on their attitude to loans and overdrafts would have to be a tougher one. Security prices fell and long-term interest rates rose; the classical medicine gave every appearance of working.

Looking back over the experience of 1952 this impression would at first sight be confirmed. In the first quarter of the year the measures of November 1951 had been augmented by a general tightening of the credit screws all round. Hire purchase regulations were made more stringent in February and again in April; Bank rate was pushed up to 4 per cent at the time of the Budget in March, although the special rate of ½ per cent below was retained for the discounting of Treasury Bills. The Budget itself imposed considerable penalties on consumption through reduced subsidies and higher expenditure taxes, although its other provisions in the realm of direct taxation probably neutralised the overall effects of this on aggregate demand.[(5)] Following upon all this, credit restriction seemed to be working; between March and December of 1952 advances by the clearing banks other than to nationalised industry fell by £190 million, while commercial bills discounted fell by £110 million.

Yet on closer inspection, it is possible to be distinctly sceptical concerning the degree to which the sharp fall in credit to the private sector was attributable to the orthodox medicine. On the one hand, during 1952 the authorities found themselves forced to put into reverse the technical measures of control over the banks adopted in November 1951. The requirements of Exchequer finance—including lending to the nationalised industries and the Post Office—involved a rise of some £1,000 million in official borrowing through the market, so that despite the funding operation of November 1951 the banks held £504 million more Treasury bills in December 1952 than in March 1952, and by the end of the year their liquidity ratio was back to 36 per cent. It is therefore difficult to argue that the fall in private borrowing from the banks was caused by pressure on bank liquidity.

On the other hand, events outside the credit system were such as to be capable in themselves of explaining the drop in private borrowing. Reference has already been made to the fiscal changes introduced by the 1952 Budget and the tightening of hire purchase regulations at the same time; it is also a fact that the stock-cycle characteristic of the postwar British economy was operating in the same direction, since the value of physical increases in stocks and work in progress dropped from £575 million in 1951 to a mere £50 million in 1952. Some might regard this as a consequence of the fall in the supply of private credit; others, with at least equal persuasiveness, could represent it as a major causative element in the diminished demand for credit.

The details of this first return to monetary orthodoxy are worth mention primarily because they typify the factors which obscured and complicated the operation of credit control in the years which followed. On the one hand, the complexities of the national debt situation, plus the needs of Exchequer financing, persistently prevented the authorities from achieving the control they believed necessary over the supply of Treasury Bills to the commercial banking system. As Table 13 shows, during the 1950s the average level of bank deposits followed an almost continuous upward trend, except during 1955-56; average Treasury bill holdings were some £130 million greater in 1959 than in 1952; the liquidity ratio never fell below an annual average of 32.5 per cent and was typically at a significantly higher level. The relative proportions of investments and advances remained virtually unchanged during 1952-58; the fact that the level of advances remained well below that regarded as 'normal' by the banks, despite their comfortable liquidity position, suggests that any restraint there may have been on bank lending arose from forces other than those of monetary policy.

On the other hand—and perhaps partly as a result of this apparent inability of the authorities to maintain a sufficiently close grip on bank liquidity—conventional monetary measures were almost invariably applied as part of a 'package deal' along with more direct controls—credit 'squeeze' directives to the banks by the Chancellor concerning the volume and direction of bank lending (usually in association with memoranda of guidance to the Capital Issues Committee), fiscal operations through the level of taxation and/or the rate of public investment expenditure and periodic manipulations of the regulations governing hire purchase credit.

As a result, throughout the 1950s it was exceedingly difficult to judge how far control over the economy was in fact being secured by monetary techniques of the orthodox kind and how far, on the other hand, such control as was achieved was attributable to other elements of the various policy packages. As it happened, the question was regarded as being a largely academic one; by 1957 a general conviction had gained ground that overall official control over the British economy, whether exercised through the banking system or otherwise, was in any event inefficient and inadequate. The economy, it seemed, was lurching from crisis to boom and

TABLE 13

London Clearing Banks, 1950-1959

	Oct. 1951	Dec. 1951	Annual averages									
			1950	1951	1952	1953	1954	1955	1956	1957	1958	1959
Total deposits, £mn.	6,204	6,333	6,014	6,162	6,083	6,256	6,495	6,454	6,288	6,432	6,636	6,935
Assets: £mn.												
Cash	514	521	497	511	505	509	528	529	516	526	543	565
Money at call	579	598	550	569	529	472	457	439	431	439	434	489
Treasury bills }	1,330	791	1,298	1,228	957	1,156	1,119	1,016	1,156	1,143	1,167	1,089
Other bills }		181			105	63	87	114	114	148	110	134
Total liquid assets	2,423	2,091	2,345	2,308	2,097	2,201	2,190	2,098	2,218	2,256	2,255	2,277
Treasury Deposit Receipts	177	102	430	247	7	—	—	—	—	—	—	—
Investments	1,555	1,965	1,505	1,624	1,983	2,163	2,321	2,149	1,978	2,008	2,149	1,836
Advances	1,897	1,931	1,603(a)	1,822(a)	1,776	1,666	1,731	1,941	1,820	1,868	1,923	2,522
% of total deposits:												
Cash	8.3	8.4	8.3	8.3	8.3	8.1	8.1	8.2	8.2	8.2	8.2	8.1
Liquid assets	39.0	33.2	39.0	37.5	34.5	35.2	33.7	32.5	35.3	35.1	34.0	32.8
Investments	25.1	31.0	25.0	26.4	32.6	34.6	35.7	33.3	31.5	31.2	32.4	26.5
Advances	30.6	30.5	26.7(a)	29.6(a)	29.2	26.6	26.6	30.1	28.9	29.0	29.0	36.4

(a) Until 1951 these totals include items in transit in respect of 8 banks. The 1952 total on this basis would have been £1,838 million or 30.2 per cent.

Sources: Monthly Digest of Statistics, No. 74, HMSO, London, February 1952, Table 142, pp. 114-5 and *Annual Abstract of Statistics,* No. 98, 1961, HMSO, London 1961, Table 328, p. 279. Small discrepancies in totals due to rounding.

back again to crisis with what appeared to be substantial indifference to the manipulation of various policy instruments by the authorities. Largely as a result of this feeling, in May 1957 a committee was appointed under the chairmanship of Lord Radcliffe to 'inquire into the working of the monetary and credit system, and to make recommendations'.

3. The Radcliffe Report

It cannot be said that the report of the Radcliffe Committee, published in 1959,(6) resolved in any definitive sense all the uncertainties which had accumulated during 1952-58 concerning the technique and effectiveness of monetary control. So far as the commercial banks were concerned, the report laid heavy emphasis on the role of liquid assets rather than cash reserves in determining the level of deposits. Given the almost theological conviction of the Bank of England that it was essential to maintain stability in the Treasury bill rate—and therefore its willingness to buy and sell bills freely in response to market demand—the banks, the report argued, could always adjust their cash to the desired level by (in effect) selling Treasury bills to, or buying them from, the Bank of England. Hence, the Committee concluded, 'The effective base of bank credit has become the liquid assets (based on the availability of Treasury bills) instead of the supply of cash.'(7)

Furthermore, the Committee believed that since the ratio of advances to total deposits was significantly lower than the banks would themselves have wished—and that of investments correspondingly higher—the level of advances was in fact determined by the demand for them rather than by the availability of cash reserves. Investments being predominantly short-term, they could be sold in most cases without great capital loss (and, indeed, a sizeable proportion would be approaching maturity at any given moment); any opportunity for profitable lending could thus be seized more or less at will by switching resources out of the 'investments' category and into the 'advances' category. And of course, so long as liquid assets were well above the 30 per cent minimum,(8) advances could be increased by simply allowing Treasury bills to mature.

The Committee concluded, therefore, that despite the nominal return to the use of orthodox techniques of monetary control in 1951, those techniques had not in fact proved effective. In its view, until the authorities were able drastically to reduce the floating debt and thus the liquidity of the banking system—and the pressures of Exchequer financing plus the constant need to replace maturing securities appeared to have made this generally impossible—the credit base had passed out of official control. Given, on the other hand, the continuance of large security holdings by the banks, both the ability and the incentive to expand loans and overdrafts were bound to be present. Only drastic increases in interest rates aimed at 'locking-in' the banks could meet this latter problem, but the authorities did not feel themselves to be in any position to adopt an aggressive attitude to the level of market prices and rates. They were apparently convinced that 'highly fluctuating rates in the money market would have served no useful purpose and might have been positively damaging'(9)—presumably on the same grounds as those underlying the Committee's conclusion that 'The intricate and highly developed network of financial institutions bases some of its strength on the existence of a large body of highly marketable Government bonds whose market values are assumed to have a considerable measure of stability.'[10] In so far as the authorities were able to regulate the volume of bank lending at all, therefore, they could do so only through the credit 'squeeze'—i.e. direct quantitative restrictions of loans—rather than through conventional channels.

There is considerable evidence that this had in fact been the case. During 1951-59 there were three periods of general restriction: 1951-52, 1955-56, and 1957-58. In the first of these, as has already been noted, the banks were instructed to adopt a 'tougher' attitude to the granting of credit facilities and made public their intention of doing so. Again, in July 1955 the Chancellor announced that, through the medium of a letter to the Bank of England, he had informed the banking system of the need to reduce bank advances and of his desire to see 'a positive and significant reduction' in such advances during the following months. In the 'squeeze' of the autumn of 1957 the required restraint on bank lending was expressed more precisely; in announcing various measures to meet the crisis in September the Chancellor had announced that 'the average level of bank advances during the next twelve months should be held at the average level for the last twelve months.' He had no doubt, he had added, that the clearing bankers would 'do their best to achieve this result'.

The admirers of orthodox monetary policy would clearly find it unsatisfactory that the ministerial directive should appear to be the only device through which bank lending could be controlled. In the first place, arbitrary, unpredictable and frequently imprecise interventions in the banking system could scarcely be conducive to a smoothly-operating system; further, as the banks themselves frequently pointed out, control of this kind was incompatible with any real competition amongst banks in attracting business. Leaving all this on one side, however, the Radcliffe Committee struck the cruellest blow of all at the traditional image of the operation of credit policy with its conclusion that, by whatever means the restriction of bank credit was secured, it would in any case be a matter of relatively little consequence so far as economic policy was concerned.

The reasoning behind this conclusion is well known; put briefly, the Committee's conviction was that spending decisions depend on liquidity—i.e. the ability to obtain purchasing power from whatever source—rather than on the immediate possession of, or access to, money alone. While bank credit was by no means regarded as totally unimportant, it was nevertheless only one component of this wider entity, liquidity over the economy as a whole.[11] It therefore followed that restriction of bank advances, by constricting merely one segment of overall liquidity, would merely divert pressure to other segments, rather in the manner of a man compressing part of an inflated inner tube. Projects in their early stages might perhaps be checked by such a procedure but in general the effect would merely be 'to drive frustrated borrowers to other sources of credit'—trade sources, finance houses, accepting and discount houses and insurance companies. The Committee concluded that 'The obstructions to particular channels of finance have had no effect on the pressure of total demand, but have made for much inefficiency in financial organisation.' Their criticisms, it was agreed, might be met by the extension to these non-bank financial intermediaries—both those in existence and others as yet unborn—of the sort of control exercised over the commercial banks but, given their general scepticism concerning the role of monetary measures in ordinary times, they did not consider 'such an elaborate extension of compulsory powers to be justified in the conditions immediately before us'.[12]

For the protagonists of orthodox monetary control through the banking system, then, the report of the Radcliffe Committee was a singularly depressing document. The authorities, it was argued, could certainly recover effective control over the banking system by making the 30 per cent liquidity ratio explicit rather than somewhat vaguely conventional; furthermore, they could acquire the power to vary this ratio from time to time as dictated by circumstances.[13] In the absence of similar controls over other financial institutions, however, the Committee thought it would be difficult to justify 'drastic action' of this kind. As an 'emergency' measure, the practice of imposing quantitative limitations on bank lending by directive—the 'credit squeeze' technique—could continue to be adopted, although the alternative procedure of restricting advances to a prescribed proportion of total deposits was, in the Committee's view, to be preferred. But this would be strictly a 'crisis' measure, and provided small comfort for the proponents of the regulation of bank credit as a continuing technique of normal, day-to-day control. For them, the overall, chastening message of the report was that 'Monetary measures can help, but that is all.' And even then, one feels the Committee were tempted to add, not much.

4. Interest rates and liquidity

In the early part of the twentieth century, following upon the formalisation of the quantity theory of money by Marshall, Pigou and Fisher, the main task of the monetary authorities had come to be regarded as the quantitative control of bank deposits through their cash base. Although the importance of interest rates was recognised, they were regarded as having less significance, their main function being conceived to be the filling of the subordinate role of making open-market operations effective. As was noted earlier, after the publication of the *General Theory* the main emphasis in the management of the economy tended to shift to fiscal policy and the direct control of investment and in good Keynesian tradition the Radcliffe Committee appeared to have relegated the supply of money to the second division. So far as that Committee was concerned, it was the 'whole liquidity position' which was relevant to spending decisions; official interest in the supply of money could be due only to its significance in that 'whole liquidity' picture.[14]

The interest rate mechanism—although in itself of disputed relevance as a direct regulator of spending decisions—was thus assigned to play the major role in the control of overall liquidity:

> Movements in interest rates have significant effects on the liquidity structure. If they could be uninhibited in their manipulation of interest rates, the authorities would have powerful influence on the entire liquidity position.[15]

The authorities were thus exhorted to have regard to the structure of interest rates rather than to treat the supply of money as the centrepiece of the monetary mechanism. The supply of money, although not unimportant, was held to be incidental to interest rate policy.

Within its 'slippery and ill-defined' concept of liquidity the Radcliffe Committee sought to embrace not only the liquidity of the banks but also that of other financial intermediaries and, indeed, the entire private sector. By so doing the report inevitably blurred the distinction between concepts of liquidity which were relevant to spending decisions and those which are appropriate to the analysis of financial intermediaries.(16) In so far as the intermediaries were concerned, the Radcliffe Committee concluded that it was important to control their rate of lending and that, in the absence of direct measures, this could be achieved by reducing their liquidity through their reserves.

The main instrument through which the Committee proposed that this end should be attained was variation of the level of interest rates. As part of a normal Roosa-type mechanism a rise in the level of interest rates was assumed to reduce the value of reserves; this would force the financial intermediaries to devote an increased proportion of their incoming deposits to the restoration of their reserve position, thereby, of course, reducing their rate of lending.(17) In so far as the clearing banks were concerned, the Committee readily recognised the limitations of this approach, given the substantial shortening of bank investment portfolios in the early 1950s. The banks, however, were subject to other, more direct measures of control which the Committee considered unsuitable for non-bank intermediaries. The latter, it was argued, as a consequence of a fall in the value of their reserves, would rebuild them by purchasing gilt-edged securities or bills from the authorities. It is doubtful, however, whether these institutions would in fact be perturbed by a 'paper' fall in reserve values, especially when the causative rise in interest rates could be expected to be no more than temporary; certainly an actual *reduction* of lending would be most unlikely. On the other hand, if and when they did make efforts to induce a switch of bank deposits and/or securities from the general public to themselves by offering higher rates, the major effect of this could well be that idle bank deposits would be activated and a fall in the velocity of circulation of money avoided. If the intermediaries chose to build up their reserve ratios by holding more cash, then the rise in interest rates would be effective from the policy point of view. On the other hand, if the incoming deposits were used to buy securities from would-be spenders in the private sector, then although reserves would be restored, cash would continue to be switched from savers to potential spenders.(18)

As has already been stressed, the Radcliffe Committee had concluded that the supply of money was incidental to interest-rate policy and that if the authorities could be uninhibited in their manipulation of interest rates, their influence could be a powerful one. In fact, an uninhibited use of the interest rate mechanism had not been a feature of postwar British monetary history owing to the official conviction that there existed a prior and well-entrenched constraint—somewhat grudgingly recognised by the Radcliffe Committee—in the shape of the management needs of the national debt. The main concern of the monetary authorities, according to their own evidence, had been the management of the debt with a view to the maximisation of the demand for gilt-edged securities, not only to provide for the finance of contemporary requirements but also for the refunding of a continuing flow of maturities.(19) From this stemmed a concern for the stability of interest rates, both short and long, at a level which minimised the burden on the Exchequer. By this commitment to a given structure of interest rates, of course, the authorities had *ipso facto* abdicated control of the money supply.

The authorities had thus been seeking to achieve stability in both the gilt-edged and the Treasury bill markets. In the case of the latter the stability was desired in order to influence international demand for sterling as well as in the interests of the management of internal markets in long-term securities—given the belief that irregularities in the bill market could spread to the gilt-edged market. Consequently the authorities had been prepared in general to deal freely between cash, Treasury bills and gilt-edged, so that neither the cash ratio nor the liquid assets ratio could provide a really firm fulcrum for an effective monetary policy.

One aspect of this basic principle of maximising the demand for long-term debt and the satisfaction of official financial requirements during the postwar decades was the continuing desire of the authorities to 'fund' the debt. Originally this arose from the wish to protect the Exchequer from maturities occurring at inconvenient or expensive moments, but increasing emphasis was subsequently placed on the need to reduce dependence upon short-term borrowing from the banks; by strengthening the demand for gilt-edged stock in the private sector the volume of tender Treasury bills outstanding could be reduced. When fiscal deficits necessitated increased borrowing, the authorities sought to have the choice of increasing sales of the funded debt, preferably to the non-bank public, rather than being forced to resort to residual—and allegedly 'inflationary' borrowing—from the banks.

The authorities were successful during most of the 1960s in managing drastically to reduce the volume of Treasury bills on offer to the private sector. The reduction was due partly to the fact that local government authorities were instructed to borrow directly from the private sector instead of—as before 1955—from the Public Works Loans Board. Another important factor was the considerable decline in the Treasury bill issue following the heavy fall in the gold reserves of the United Kingdom during 1964-65. Thirdly, high levels of interest rates prevailing throughout the mid-1960s on occasion enabled the authorities to sell unusually large amounts of medium and long-term gilt-edged securities; in 1966-67, for example, interest rates were expected to fall and this enabled the Exchequer to reduce its borrowing on Treasury bills.[20] A partial offset, on the other hand, was the decline—if not collapse—in the 'outside' demand for Treasury bills as companies switched to the new parallel markets as an outlet for surplus funds.

5. The debate on the credit base

As a result of the philosophy underlying the Radcliffe report, official attention was increasingly directed at the advances of the clearing banks and other lenders. Control was nominally exercised through the interest-rate mechanism—although its use, as has been noted, was severely inhibited by the prior concern for debt management—and also, in the case of the clearing banks, through the rather suspect technique of regulating the supply of tender Treasury bills. These were supplemented by the power of the Bank of England to make 'requests' as to, in particular, the level of bank liquidity ratios. Adequate testimony to the ineffectiveness of these policies, if only on a technical level, may be found in their more or less complete subordination in practice to direct controls in the form of Special Deposits and increasingly rigorous direct restraints upon the volume and structure of bank advances.

Responsibility for the shortcomings of the interest-rate mechanism can hardly be laid on the shoulders of the Radcliffe Committee, although it could be said to have underestimated the severity of the constraint imposed upon the authorities by the official conception of the requirements of debt policy. On the other hand, considerable criticism could be directed at the Radcliffe prescription for the control of the banks' credit base. The Committee, of course, had concluded that 'the effective base of bank credit has become the liquid assets (based on the availability of Treasury bills) instead of the supply of cash'.[21] The case for this liquid assets theory obviously rested on the assumption that control via the cash ratio was unworkable because of the excess liquidity of the banks—an excess based on the supply of Treasury bills and the readiness of the authorities to allow cash reserves to be preserved by the free exchange of Treasury bills. Various explanations were put forward in this context, two of which may be considered the most important. The first was that the Bank of England was unable to control the cash base of the clearing banks because of its commitment to the role of lender of last resort. Provided that the banks had a portfolio of Treasury bills, it was argued, they could always re-discount them at the Bank for cash.[22] Against this it could be argued that control could be retained through Bank rate, provided that the authorities were prepared to allow interest rates to rise sufficiently to discourage the exchange of Treasury bills for cash, and if such a policy were to be carried through to the exclusion of all other policy aims the banks would eventually be forced to reduce deposits.[23] Apart from the implications for these other policy aims, however, some difficulty and delay would be likely to be experienced in its operation.[24] The use of a 'penal' rate assumes that the market will cut its share of the Treasury bill issue by reducing its bid at the weekly tender while the increased rates would attract greater non-bank demand—with, of course, a deleterious effect on bank cash. During the 1950s, at any rate, the latter was a not unreasonable expectation but it became increasingly less realistic as the decade proceeded and through the 1960s because of the development of other private sector outlets for non-bank funds. In any case, even if a cash shortage occasioned by open-market operations was relieved via the 'front door' at penal rates, there was no reliable mechanism in operation which would force a multiple contraction of deposits on the banks if they possessed excess liquid assets which could be used—simply, if needed, by awaiting maturity—to oblige the authorities to re-create the lost cash.[25] More important, the successful implementation of a penal Bank Rate might require rates of such height and duration as to interfere intolerably with other policy objectives. (It may be pertinent to note here that Bank of England lending to the discount market via the front door has been very seldom used in recent years.)

An alternative version, propounded by Professor R. S. Sayers and similar to that contained in the Radcliffe Report, is that the authorities' lack of control over the cash base arises from their choice of a certain structure of interest rates to which bank cash must be fitted:

> The Bank of England remains... passive in deciding the amount of cash: the cash is simply fitted to the total of bank deposits coupled with the requirements of the public for circulation.[26]

The authorities can therefore choose either the level of interest rates or the size of the money supply but cannot regulate both independently of each other, a proposition, of course, which is scarcely novel. In the event—and in accord with the philosophy of the Radcliffe Committee—their decision throughout most of the 1960s was to plump for control of interest rates to the neglect of the quantity of money. Over most of the postwar era, therefore, the authorities have provided cash to meet the demands of the public and have made cash virtually interchangeable to the banks with Treasury bills via the 'back door'. The cash ratio as an instrument of regulation went by default.

There is certainly no theoretical reason why the authorities should not control the volume of bank deposits through a minimum ratio of liquid assets, provided that these are negotiable, are readily saleable outside the banking system, carry a rate of return lower than that on other funds [27] and, most important, have a source of supply which is within the effective control of the authorities. The official definition of what constitutes a liquid asset comprises private sector debt as well as public debt, the quantity of the latter not being closely determined by the former. Although at the time of its original conception the liquidity ratio was based largely upon the Treasury bill, therefore, there was nothing to prevent the banks from varying the volume of their liquid assets by securing a redistribution of the total supply of Treasury bills or by creating their own supply of officially acceptable 'private sector' substitutes. In the case of the former the banks, through the discount houses, could bid up prices so as to secure an increased allotment at the tender; they could also buy Treasury bills from outside holders, especially when the latter were likely to be discouraged by lower rates. What is more, the ability of the authorities to influence the demand of outside holders for Treasury bills, without resort to drastic swings in rates, has been progressively reduced by the development of the parallel markets.

More important, it was feasible for the banks, if they so chose, to 'manufacture' liquid assets by directly or indirectly encouraging prospective borrowers to offer bills for discount instead of seeking to borrow by way of overdraft, thereby increasing the supply of liquid assets and avoiding direct restrictions on advances. Similarly, they could indirectly increase the volume of liquid assets by being prepared to increase the extension of call loans to the discount houses on the security of commercial bills—or, for that matter, to allow them to purchase gilt-edged securities from the private sector. So far as the clearing banks were concerned, the role of the discount market increased in importance in this period compared with the 1930s, largely because it was able to substitute new sources of liquid assets, in the form of commercial bills and short-dated government securities, to compensate for the declining availability of Treasury bills. The clearing banks could also foster an additional supply of liquid assets by increasing their proportion of non-discount-market call money—for example, by short-term lending to stockbrokers or other banks—thereby further weakening the link between call money and holdings of public sector liabilities. As may be seen from Table 14, both developments in fact occurred during the early 1960s; between 1960 and 1963 a decline of some £165 million in holdings of Treasury bills was more than offset by a rise of more than £340 million in call money and 'other' bills. As a device for controlling bank liquidity, therefore, funding had been made largely ineffective by the ability of the banks to create new liquid assets within the private sector.[28] In other words, a fundamental error had been introduced into official thinking by the implicit identification of the

TABLE 14

London Clearing Banks, 1960-69

(Annual averages)

	1960	1961	1962	1963	1964	1965	1966	1967	1968	1969
Total deposits: £ mn.	7,236	7,395	7,611	7,971	8,550	8,989	9,376	9,772	10,431	10,610
Assets: £mn.										
Cash	588	607	623	647	696	739	767	798	851	879
Money at call	562	606	718	748	738	910	1,006	1,136	1,335	1,451
Treasury Bills	1,007	992	933	842	790	653	689	564	468	294
Other Bills	147	233	272	298	365	461	446	492	527	568
Total liquid assets	2,299	2,437	2,546	2,535	2,589	2,763	2,908	2,990	3,182	3,191
Special Deposits	74	174	159	—	—	56	137	194	208	213
Investments	1,407	1,122	1,194	1,244	1,220	1,087	1,137	1,341	1,375	1,201
Advances	3,123	3,357	3,408	3,880	4,328	4,653	4,732	4,725	5,075	5,328
% of total deposits										
Cash	8.1	8.2	8.2	8.1	8.1	8.2	8.2	8.2	8.2	8.3
Liquid assets	31.8	33.0	33.5	31.8	30.3	30.7	31.0	30.6	30.5	30.0
Investments	19.5	15.2	15.7	15.6	14.3	12.1	12.1	13.7	13.2	11.3
Advances	43.2	45.4	44.8	48.7	50.6	51.8	50.5	48.4	48.6	50.2

Source: *Annual Abstract of Statistics*, No. 105, 1968, HMSO, London 1968, Table 347, p. 309; *Financial Statistics*, no. 93, HMSO, London, January 1970, Table 38, pp. 48-9.

terms 'liquid asset' and 'Treasury bill' in the Radcliffe Report. The room for manoeuvre possessed by the clearing banks proved to be greater than the authorities had anticipated and was progressively increased by the development of secondary markets and the operation of the banks' own subsidiaries.

The basic incompatibility of the objectives of British economic policy, as enumerated by the Radcliffe Committee, have long been apparent; less evident, perhaps, has been the equally incompatible nature of the measures which the authorities conceived to be necessary in order to attain monetary and financial harmony. The basic inadequacy of the Radcliffe analysis, indeed, lay in its failure to recognise the extent of this latter dilemma. It could be claimed on behalf of the authorities that in electing to seek control over interest rates to the neglect of control over the quantity of money they were at least aiming at an attainable target in one category as against a commitment to the high cost and largely unpredictable effects associated with the old orthodox cash approach.(29) The various uncontrollable leakages and injections occurring in the expansion of bank credit in the evolving British financial system are such that the bank deposit multiplier is subject to considerable uncertainty. It was normally rather small, and was proving as unreliable for forecasting purposes as the simple Keynesian multiplier, even if the authorities were prepared to abandon control over interest rates.(30) It thus appeared more realistic to suppose that banks attempt to fit cash and liquid assets to their deposits rather than vice-versa. On the other hand, the failure to find a satisfactory solution to the problems of monetary control could be held to have contributed to the British economic malaise, amongst whose consequences are the highest recorded periods of Bank rate since the nineteenth century and the fall of gilt-edged prices to all-time lows, Consols falling from about par in 1946 to well below 30 by 1969.

It is here that the fundamental weakness of official thinking emerges in its full clarity. The official doctrine of what constituted effective debt management and of what was necessary for it proved to be wrong in execution and can be held to be wrong in concept. It was wrong in execution because it simply did not work. Despite the continuous intervention by the Bank in the name of maintaining stable markets to advance the cause of funding—a policy qualified only from 1969 onwards—throughout the 1960s the gilt-edged market slid steadily and almost continuously downwards. So far from inducing holders of gilt-edged to retain their stocks (and *a fortiori* to increase their holdings), the knowledge of official intervention had precisely the reverse effect; the penalty of moving a narrow market against himself being largely removed, the potential seller of gilt-edged was encouraged to become an actual one while, aware of all this, the potential buyer declined to enter a market where a congenital sagging tendency was being positively cultivated by the authorities. The official devotees of 'funding' should have pleaded for occasional sharp falls in the market, not embarked on an inherently losing battle against them.(31)

This leads on to the conceptual weakness in the official doctrine of debt management, as opposed to the ineptness of its execution. 'Funding' to the authorities was synonymous with increased sales of long-term stock in replacement of short-term issues. In its widest sense, however, funding the debt involves reducing its liquidity, which is a function of its price rather than its volume. What the authorities failed to perceive was that maintenance of stability in the market in order to facilitate funding in their sense of the term (even supposing they had achieved this end) was militating against funding in this wider, 'locking-in' sense. In this latter context, a steady decline over a protracted period of time—even a substantial decline—is no substitute for a succession of sharp falls interspersed between occasional sharp rises. At the beginning of 1968, private holdings of gilt-edged stocks of more than five years' maturity amounted to just over £10,000 million; the turnover of such holdings on the London Stock Exchange in the preceding year amounted to around £8,000 million.(32) The implication is clear—for most transactions a price decline more than one year old is past history; it is the short-term fall over a few weeks or months which has any locking-in effect. And it was precisely this type of instability which official policy was dedicated to remove. Until the abandonment of the official policy of automatic support for the gilt-edged market in 1969, then, official debt management policy could thus claim the remarkable achievement of failing to attain its own objectives (which were wrong) and simultaneously preventing the attainment of others which might have been right.

6. Direct controls

The failure to secure a satisfactory compromise between the needs of debt management and those of monetary policy during the 1960s—assuming such a compromise to have been possible—inevitably implied an increased resort to direct controls. During the war the clearing banks had become accustomed to working under official directives, while for a long time before this the Bank of England had been accustomed to making its views known behind the scenes. In 1946 this moral power was formalised in the Bank of England (Nationalisation) Act, Clause 4, sub-clause 3 of which provided that

> The Bank, if they think it necessary in the public interest, may request information from and make recommendations to bankers, and may, if so authorised by the Treasury, issue directions to any banker for the purpose of securing that effect is given to any such request or recommendation.

In the event, these statutory powers have never been implemented, although the knowledge that the authorities are able to enforce their 'requests' or 'directives' no doubt remains an effective sanction—as does the possibility that the Bank of England can refuse to continue to maintain an account for a particular bank.(33)

Apart from recommendations concerning the size of liquidity ratios, official requests or directives have been aimed at bank lending, both in its distribution and overall volume. Qualitative 'requests' have been used throughout most of the post-war period, their emphasis being varied according to need. Thus on different occasions the banks have been requested to give priority to lending for defence purposes, for financing exports or import-substituting industries such as agriculture, for regional development and for productive investment generally. Conversely the banks have been asked to curb lending for personal consumption and speculation, for the finance of hire-purchase, property development and for imports. Such selective restrictions have been accompanied on occasion by a quantitative restraint, the first such, in July 1955, requesting 'a positive and significant reduction' in advances over the following few months. In September 1957 the banks were asked to ensure that the average level of their advances during the following twelve months should not exceed that for the corresponding period in the previous year. In 1961 and 1964 the banks were asked to reduce the rate of growth of their lending.

In May 1965, however, this type of direction took on a more precise and drastic character, individual banks being asked to ensure that their advances to the private sector during the following year did not exceed 105 per cent of the figure at May 1965, a limitation which was also applied to the granting of acceptance facilities and the discounting of commercial bills. Subsequently even more rigorous restraints were imposed. In November 1968 the banks were asked to bring their sterling lending to the private and overseas sector by March 1969 within a ceiling of 98 per cent of the level of November 1967. The real impact of the reduction required—of the order of about £100 million in non-fixed-rate lending to the private sector—was of course all the greater in a period when prices were rising. The difficulties which the banks faced in achieving this target (according to their own account) were considerable, particularly because of the nature of their lending arrangements.

Advances, of course, are the most illiquid of all bank assets. For a bank to call back outstanding advances is in most cases difficult and often impossible, especially when funds have been spent; theoretically it could involve the liquidation or bankruptcy of the borrowers concerned, with a consequently higher risk of bad debts. The danger of the overdraft system lies in the fact that banks may have undertaken lending commitments far in advance of the anticipated date at which the facilities are liable to be needed. As a result, they have unused but still available credit facilities which may be greater than the total of advances outstanding at any one time; these can be drawn upon without prior warning or discussion. In periods of credit restraint, therefore, the banks may find themselves unable to resist a rise in advances without refusing virtually all new lending, if borrowers generally seek to draw upon credits originally placed at their disposal in easier conditions. Indeed, as was observed in chapter 12, it appears that the ratio of the total of advances outstanding to unused but committed credit facilities has tended to rise when credit is restricted.(34) A significant lag in the enforcement of lending restraints is therefore to be expected, as well as possible offsetting tendencies.

Associated with the use of directives, and commonly interpreted as a bludgeon to ensure their effect, has been the use of Special Deposits. Their original purpose, as described by the Chancellor of the Exchequer in 1960 on the first occasion of their use, was to provide an alternative to making a request to the banks which, it was hoped, would 'influence them in the direction of moderating their advances rather than selling gilt-edged stocks'.(35) In fact on that occasion the banks chose to continue the sale of investments in order to meet the demand for advances. As a result, directives were soon afterwards re-introduced.

Special Deposits are called from the banks in the form of a percentage of each bank's deposits to be placed with the Bank of England. Interest on these deposits was originally paid at a rate slightly under the prevailing bill rate, but in June 1969 the rate was halved in the course of a further attempt to bring pressure on the banks. Special Deposits are not acceptable as liquid assets, are not encashable and carry no specified term for repayment, and in essence the system operates as a liquidity ratio varied by mandate. Since the Budget of 1967 it became even more similar to a variable liquidity ratio, to 'be used in a new and more flexible manner... as a routine adjustment to conditions as they develop',[36] together with the use, when necessary, of official 'requests' or directives. Thus the official secondary liquidity ratio has been held at the constant figure of 28 per cent since 1963 while Special Deposits have provided the variable 'control' component.

It is apparent nevertheless that, like the traditional bases of central bank control—the cash ratio, open-market operations and the interest rate mechanism—these more recent techniques have been largely unsuccessful, primarily because of the familiar constraint of the official concept of debt management policy. Occasions when restrictions on bank advances were considered advisable often coincided with periods when it was difficult to sell large quantities of government debt to the private sector. The consequential resort to the banks for residual borrowing then generated the liquidity which frustrated official credit control. And it may be appropriate to note at this point that between 1969 and 1974 the British government will have to redeem or replace some £7,000 million maturing securities. The former course would necessarily entail an injection of cash into the private sector and an increase in the money supply, while the latter would require for its success policies incompatible with traditional measures of monetary control.

If the introduction of a mandatory liquidity ratio to compensate for the deficiencies in monetary control proved less than satisfactory, resort to more direct controls in the form of directives has involved inequitable burdens on certain classes of borrower as well as upon lenders; in any event, it is subject to lags in implementation and to offsetting action in other ways. This is not to deny the operational usefulness of directives: obviously they are effective in so far as the banks are concerned, even if in a blunt fashion. Sometimes overlooked, moreover, is the fact that they are made more necessary by resort to old orthodox prescriptions in an environment no longer suited to them. The incentive to private commercial borrowers to borrow from banks tends to be strong (and price-inelastic) at precisely those times at which the authorities are forcing up rates in the capital market—for example, by selling new issues of long-term stock; it is better to borrow short rather than long when interest rates are considered unusually high.

7. The revival of the Quantity Theory

Given the constraint which they believed to be imposed upon them by the need to manage the National Debt, over the postwar years the authorities opted for an attempt to maintain a given structure of interest rates to the neglect of the control of money supply. In the second half of the 1960s, this apparent lack of official interest in the money supply gave rise to concern not only abroad but, following the investigations of successive IMF missions, within Britain itself. The view gained ground that official attention has to be paid to the stock of money and, in particular, to changes in it. In the past, it was argued, the authorities far too often placed constraints on what were felt to be the key sectors in the banks' asset portfolios—their liquid assets or advances—while the total level of deposits (and hence bank holdings of gilt-edged stocks) was allowed to remain more or less free from official regulation. As a result, if the banks were unable to make loans to borrowers because of official restrictions on advances, they could still buy gilt-edged securities and thus indirectly put potential spenders in a position to spend. Given the extent of the government's own expenditure and the way in which this is financed, the key contributory factor in this process was conceived to be the readiness of the Bank of England to support the gilt-edged market. By 1969, as a result of all this, a significant shift in long-standing attitudes had become manifest with a changing emphasis on the part of the Bank of England in its management of the gilt-edged market.

It would appear that on both sides of the Atlantic academic argument emanating from Chicago and elsewhere had come to convince the authorities that control over the quantity of money is a more comprehensive and effective means of influencing total spending than simple operation on the level of bank advances. In many countries evidence has been produced which it is claimed reveals a strong correlation between the quantity of money and the price level during periods of inflation. In the United States, in particular, a substantial body of data has been assembled bearing on the association between the stock of money, or the rate of increase of the stock of money, and the level of economic activity.[37] In Britain, also, it is possible to point to an increase of approximately 400 per cent since 1939 in both the general price level and the volume of money.

Armed with data of this sort, academic writers have in effect resurrected the old quantity theory of money, developed it into a portfolio-balance version of Keynesian monetary theory and sought to restore primary emphasis on the stock of money, rather than on aggregate demand, as the basic determinant of expenditure.[38] Whereas the traditional Quantity Theory purported to explain the level of money income in terms of the stock of money, however, the new Quantity Theory stresses the importance of changes in the level of money income and, in particular, of expected changes in the general price level as causes of shifts in the demand for money—that is, it is a theory of the determinants of the income velocity of circulation.

Orthodox Keynesian economists have tended to dismiss the Quantity Theory of money because of what was regarded as its theoretical crudity. The velocity of circulation, it was held, could be extremely erratic in the short run and in the long run was liable to be subjected to the influence of factors which were considerably more sophisticated and complex than the rather *simpliste* quantity formulation allowed for. The Radcliffe Committee, for example, had concluded that the velocity of circulation was 'a statistical concept that tells us nothing directly of the motivation that influences the level of total demand'.[39] In contrast to this concept of a highly elastic and unstable velocity function, however, Friedman and his colleagues of the Chicago School argued that the velocity of circulation, while certainly not constant, possesses an in-built stability and is therefore predictable; there is, they maintain, an equilibrium ratio of money to income depending on various significant economic variables such as real income, the cost of money substitutes and expectations about future movements in the price level.[40] An increase in the quantity of money therefore results in a corresponding increase in its velocity of circulation so that money incomes rise by more than the rise in the quantity of money.

Empirical evidence for Britain shows that the income velocity of circulation of bank deposits varies and has risen noticeably since the second World War.[41] Although over the period 1877-1961 as a whole estimates of the reciprocal of 'V'—the ratio of the stock of money to the national income known as the Cambridge 'k'—seem to be fairly stable, they include large relative variations within the period. During the period of greatest recorded stability before the first World War, for example, there was still a 6 per cent coefficient of variation. For changes in income and changes in k between 1878-1961, however, a large negative association has been shown to exist, whereas there is a small positive trend effect between aggregate real income and k, a result similar to that obtained by the Chicago School investigators.

Evidence has subsequently been adduced to show that the money supply expressed in real terms has forecast consumption better than the standard Keynesian multiplier except during the depression years of the early 1930s, when the simple Keynesian multiplier provided a better fit.[42] In Britain a similar attempt to test the comparative performance of the two models has been made over five periods between 1878 to 1963.[43] Similar 'superior' results were obtained for the monetary multiplier for the years preceding 1914 although some scepticism may be entertained as to the statistical reliability of the estimated money series for the nineteenth century. Better results—i.e. a closer 'fit'—were obtained for the Keynesian multiplier for the inter-war period, although for the postwar period no sensible statistical pattern was obtained.

A fundamental criticism of all attempts to verify the quantity theory formulation, however, has always been that they reveal nothing on the vital matter of the direction of causation. The fact that both money income and money supply have risen together in no way establishes that the latter is the cause, in some sense, of the former. It could equally reflect the fact, it has been argued, that as money incomes have risen, under the pressure of aggregate demand, the authorities have allowed the money supply to rise more or less *pari passu* (or at a slightly slower rate) in order to pursue their own debt management aims. Had they not done so, it manifestly does not follow that the rise of money income would have been prevented. The upward pressure on interest rates which would have ensued might cause a significant rise in velocity as conventionally measured—a rise which the accommodating behaviour of the monetary authorities had previously rendered simply unnecessary. This criticism has undoubtedly lost much of its force as a result of the work by Friedman and Schwartz on the monetary history of the United States and by Cagan on the supply of money in the U.S.[44] This work can be said to have demonstrated that, in the United States at least, the supply of money has by no means been always passively determined in response to *de facto* changes in the economy and, conversely, has in turn exerted an independent influence on the economy.

More importantly, however, the historical evidence clearly reveals that sustained restriction upon one type of money supply generates in time the development of other types—a reaction observed in the invention of banknotes by goldsmiths, in the switch to deposit banking when note issues were forbidden to the country banks and, in more recent years, in the escalation of financial intermediaries providing credit which the joint-stock banks were prevented from supplying by official restrictions or their own inertia. What might appear as a rise in the velocity of money, as conventionally measured, might therefore reveal nothing more than that new types of money supply were coming into existence and that the initial definition of money supply had become obsolete. If in the short run (as seems consistent with the evidence) there is a more or less constant relationship between the money supply narrowly defined and this expanding wider range including substitutes, no great harm is done from a policy point of view. Over the long run, however, such a constant relationship is manifestly unlikely, so that policy may be seriously distorted by an implicit identification of the two concepts.

On the whole, therefore, the case for the new Quantity Theory remains only partially established. Its proponents have succeeded in demonstrating that in the short run the influence of changes in the volume of the money supply is almost certainly greater than it would have been fashionable to concede a decade earlier—although this is by no means to show that its significance is an overwhelming or definitive one. In the long run, the importance of the 'new monetarism' probably lies in its conceptual integration of wealth and income as influences on behaviour, the wealth in question including not only tangible real assets but human wealth also as contributors to the expected yield on wealth. The long-term role of the stock of money remains essentially permissive in the sense that the larger the stock of money the greater the freedom of manoeuvre within which a potential price rise has to operate—originated, as it may well be, by factors quite independent of the monetary situation.(45)

8. The problem of definition

From what has just been said, it is clear that not the least of the problems attaching to a scrutiny of the role of money arises from the difficulties of its definition. The controversy surrounding this may be regarded as the economists' hardy perennial, having made its first appearance in the nineteenth-century debates between the Bullionist, Currency and Banking Schools as to whether or not bank notes—and subsequently current account deposits—were to be counted as money or merely as a currency substitute tending to increase its velocity. Latterly attention has been focused upon the role of time (or deposit account) deposits and also on the deposits of non-clearing bank financial intermediaries. The role of money, as a means of payment and as a store of wealth, together with the existence of close substitutes for it, tends to make it difficult to treat money in total isolation, thereby raising serious conceptual problems of integrating income, wealth and interest. One illustration of this is given by the extension in the official definition of the money supply from currency and deposits of deposit banks (London Clearing Banks, Scottish Banks, Ulster Banks and a few others) to the inclusion of net deposits by UK residents with the whole of the banking sector—the latter comprising banks and the discount market and including both sterling and non-sterling current and deposit accounts. Thus the official definition now extends far beyond the simple means of payment, incorporating not only deposits in non-sterling currencies, but all deposits by UK residents with the whole of the banking sector.(46) The sophisticated quantity theorists within the International Monetary Fund have indeed added yet another dimension to the concept by introducing a version known as domestic credit expansion (DCE) which excludes the effects of changes in the balance of payments.(47)

It is clear that the inclusion of secondary bank deposits—arising from the activation of idle clearing bank balances—rather than an excessively expansionist debt management policy engineered through the clearing banks alone has provided the biggest proportionate contributor to the commonly discussed rapid increase in Britain's money supply in the late 1960s. According to the official definition, the total money supply rose by 40 per cent between 1963 and 1968; the liabilities of the deposit banks, however, increased by less than 30 per cent, whereas those of the secondary banks rose by no less than 227 per cent.(48) In other words, the money supply as traditionally measured showed a much more modest rate of growth—in fact, it had been a rate more or less in pace with the rise in national income.(49)

The crucial point, of course, is the significance of all this for the overall level of demand in the economy. The extent to which the growth of secondary bank deposits has contributed to the expansion of demand is, to say the least, debatable. Control of the quantity of money, defined to exclude such deposits, can scarcely be expected to be particularly effective if the supply of assets which can carry out the same functions of money is available at constant or relatively low cost. As a store of wealth, most secondary bank and other intermediary deposits are clearly acceptable—if not in fact superior—substitutes for those of the deposit banks proper. It is arguable, however, that the definition used for operational purposes should be primarily associated with money in the sense of immediate purchasing power, concentrating on its rating as a means of exchange. In this context deposits with secondary banks, building societies and finance houses, largely consisting of time deposits with relatively rigid withdrawal periods, might be argued to be less relevant than clearing bank deposits on either current or deposit account and more appropriately regarded as near money. Near money is not accepted in exchange for goods; such liquid assets must first be converted into clearing bank deposits (or into Trustee or Post Office Savings Bank deposits) before being usable for exchange.

This conversion will involve some cost in loss of interest but, except in the indirect ways already described, will not affect the total of clearing bank deposits. In this context, in other words, near money may be relevant to the level of aggregate demand in so far as holders consider that it adds to their overall liquidity and are accordingly influenced in their behaviour as consumers or investors. Whether or not near money can be regarded as cash thus depends essentially on the extent and nature of its substitutability. Its imperfections in this respect should not be overstated. Withdrawal requirements in some non-bank intermediaries—the larger building societies, for example—are not as rigid as is sometimes supposed, sums of over £500 being repayable on demand. Secondary banks, however, dealing in deposits of much larger sums matched against assets with corresponding time periods, are less likely to be so tolerant. However, limitations similar to those already described could be said to apply to clearing bank deposit accounts; these must technically be converted into current accounts and involve loss of interest if withdrawn before the required period. Furthermore, the development of current account services by non-clearing-bank intermediaries suggests that such conversion could increasingly occur as easily as from a clearing bank deposit account; institutions providing such facilities could be regarded without much doubt as banking institutions whose liabilities were acceptable as money.

Whereas traditional Keynesian theory would hold that an increase in the money supply would have the effect of lowering interest rates, the reverse applies in the case of the secondary banks and finance houses whose deposits have been increased precisely as a result of their competing through higher rates. In turn a significant factor responsible for this increase in the money supply, in its broader sense, has been the cartel operation of the clearing banks supported by the desire of the authorities for interest rate stability. The empirical evidence, for Britain at any rate, suggests that whether a narrow definition of bank deposits is adopted or a broader definition incorporating deposits of the Post Office, Building Societies, and so on, makes on the whole little difference.(50)

Whether the liabilities of secondary banks and non-bank financial intermediaries are regarded as money or not, however, it is impossible to ignore their asset creative powers. The traditional view that control of the clearing banks *ipso facto* constitutes control of the supply of credit is clearly no longer tenable, and the presence of a range of close substitutes for money has a number of implications for the velocity of bank deposits. It is generally agreed that the overall velocity of clearing bank deposits (and currency) depends in part on the existence and activities of non-bank intermediaries and secondary banks. Making due allowance for qualifications of, or inelasticities in, the personal sector's demand for clearing bank deposits, it is clear that the demand for money to hold will be related to the yield on close substitutes, together perhaps with the level of income possessed by the persons in question. It is possible in principle to distinguish between income and substitution effects in this context, both of them generally operating to promote the expansion of non-bank and secondary bank intermediaries. The income effect operates in so far as higher income levels generate a greater degree of sophistication in the personal demand for assets; just as increased income normally leads to increased reliance on bank deposits relative to the use of currency, so over a long period further income increases tend to cause people to adjust their asset portfolios so as to attain some desired or 'normal' ratio of cash plus bank deposits to *other* assets—including the liabilities of non-bank intermediaries. The substitution effect operates in so far as people are induced to switch out of cash or bank deposits in response to interest rate differentials. In reality the expansion of intermediary debt would appear to have resulted from both income and substitution effects. Generally it might be expected that the former would have greater relevance for the personal sector—stimulating switches to non-bank intermediary deposits and other assets—while the latter would predominate for the corporate or business sector, causing switches to deposits in secondary banks and finance houses.

Reference has already been made to the allegation by the National Board for Prices and Incomes of a decline of clearing bank deposits in relation to GNP. To the extent that, and during the periods in which, such a decline has in fact occurred, it may well have been due to the interest-rate differentials obtainable on any financial assets. On the other hand, it could equally be argued that any decline in clearing bank deposits relative to the growth of national income has represented no more than an adjustment towards an equilibrium situation. The facts indicate, indeed, that over the twentieth century as a whole such a decline has simply not occurred.(51) It would not have been unreasonable, after all, to expect a decline from the relatively very high levels of bank deposits and currency in the postwar years as asset portfolios were re-distributed towards the acquisition of increased holdings of less liquid assets. The rising velocity of bank deposits and currency in the postwar years, in other words, to a substantial degree may simply reflect a process of adjustment by asset owners rather than an inherent trend regulated in the long run by the activities of the non-bank financial intermediaries.

This hypothesis depends essentially on the assumed length of the adjustment period—that is, the assumed speed of reaction to disequilibrium—and, of course, on whether the short run or long run is the object of examination. It is pertinent to note that by the mid-1950s the ratio of clearing bank deposits and currency in circulation was already below the 1938 figure, which itself was substantially lower than the average for the 1930s as a whole. It continued its rapid decline until about 1957 by which time the legacy of the Dalton cheap money appears to have been worked out of the system. Subsequently the fall was much less marked, a phenomenon which has been associated in some quarters with the rise of the secondary markets and institutions whose activities—as argued in the preceding chapter—may have resulted in a partial restoration of clearing bank deposits previously finding their way into Treasury Bills.(52)

Certainly it is clear that empirical data do not provide conclusive proof—to put it mildly—that the rise in the income velocity of bank deposits and currency since the second World War had been due primarily to the activities of non-bank and secondary bank intermediaries; allowance has always to be made for the adjustment of excessively liquid portfolios towards an unknown equilibrium and the movement of long term interest-rates relative to short-term rates.(53) In connection with the latter, the major asset substitutions over the post-war period have not been confined to switches between money and various types of near money, but have rather been between, on the one hand, both near money and money itself and, on the other, the more risky, higher yielding assets such as equities and even real property which, in a persistently inflationary era, were considered to serve as better stores of value.

Short-run measures to stabilise the level of money incomes by control of the clearing banks have in the past encountered considerable resistance because of the short-term flexibility of monetary velocity in response to changes in interest rates. A high degree of this internal flexibility may arise from the activities of a large body of financial intermediaries, although as yet to an unknown degree. The policy problem arises from the extent of possible substitution between different liabilities—in other words, from the ease with which lenders and borrowers may switch from one institution or market to another. On the other hand, where financial assets and forms of credit are imperfect substitutes for each other, monetary policy will not be completely thwarted, although its effect may be less, and felt less rapidly, than it would have been in the absence of substitution. In so far as non-bank and secondary bank intermediaries can provide substitutes for clearing bank deposits in periods of restraint they will exert an expansionary influence, not only because of the increase generated in monetary velocity but because of their lower and variable cash ratios and consequently higher and more elastic credit multipliers.

Paradoxically, the invention of the concept of domestic credit expansion (DCE) and its importation into the policy 'rules' of the United Kingdom could have the effect of stultifying monetary policy to a much greater degree than the growth of financial intermediation—paradoxically, because it was apparently intended to have the reverse effect. The implications of the concept are that the money supply becomes a dependent variable of the state of the balance of payments in a manner highly reminiscent of the gold standard. Bound by the constraints of its rules over any given year, the authorities could well be driven to become less disposed, rather than more, to regard adjustments in the money supply as an independent instrument for offsetting tendencies towards disequilibrium before those tendencies had acquired cumulative momentum. The DCE concept, in other words, may import into monetary policy precisely those lags and rigidities characteristic of fiscal policy which, it was argued at the beginning of this chapter, helped to restore monetary policy to favour in the early 1950s. It is scarcely conceivable, however, that the DCE concept will long survive in any but a highly tenuated and modified form: the 1970s are highly unlikely to embrace a monetary system having all the disadvantages of the gold standard and none of its advantages. History will probably record it as little more than a psychological stimulus imposed by world creditors on a debtor showing a chronic (but no doubt curable) reluctance to shed the debtor's role.

9. Conclusion

It is perhaps appropriate that this final chapter of a study of the London clearing banks should have recorded disagreement and uncertainty concerning the role of the banks in the operation of monetary policy and, indeed, the role of monetary policy itself. The three centuries or so covered by the study are in fact distinguished by such uncertainty and debate precisely because of the constant evolution which has been a feature of the clearing banks over that period. Errors of policy and in its operation have occurred whenever this capacity for unceasing change has been overlooked. The drafters of the Bank Charter Act assumed that because bank notes and coin were currently the major element in the money supply, regulation of their issue was a sufficient safeguard, only to be proved wrong by the ensuing development by the banks of another form of money—the bank deposit—which ultimately became predominant. The clearing banks themselves, having achieved dominance in the credit mechanism, hardened into an oligopolistic, rather self-satisfied system, overlooking the possibility—which in the 1950s and 1960s became a reality—that by so doing they would not merely permit but stimulate the emergence of alternative institutions and assets which could threaten their predominance just as surely as the bank deposit challenged the supremacy of currency. The Radcliffe Committee implicitly assumed that the then existing dominance of the Treasury bill in bank liquidity would continue indefinitely and thereby pushed the technique of credit control on to a wrong track. The whole record shows that in the realm of British banking, more perhaps than in that of any other industry, to assume permanence of the status quo is the first step to disaster.

That having been said, the task of speculating on the future of the monetary policy is seen to be a hopeless one except in the very broadest of terms. It is clear that the belated realisation by the clearing banks that there are alternative forms of banking institution or methods and avenues of borrowing and lending has occurred far too late to prevent the permanent establishment of such institutions in Britain. The speed and flexibility with which the clearing banks respond to this fact is their only hope of preventing these 'secondary' banks from displacing them in the most rewarding avenues just as the country banks displaced the goldsmiths in an earlier epoch.

The implications of this fact for monetary policy are clear enough. The Radcliffe Committee were obviously correct in concluding that tight control of the clearing banks would be self-defeating in that it would merely stimulate the creation of new credit channels outside the reach of conventional central banking weapons. They were surely incorrect in concluding that the widening of official control to include such new channels would involve a hopeless continuous extension of official intervention in an ever-expanding network of institutions. The network of 'new' banks has flourished only because restrictions were imposed on 'old' banks alone. The lesson of banking history is that regulation should be defined in terms of function, not institution; future policy will be given a firm foundation only when official requirements are imposed on any institution—however described or organised—undertaking specified activities such as inviting from the general public deposits repayable at less than twelve months' notice or providing credit (however secured) on comparable terms. Once established, such regulations are unlikely to generate new agencies designed to circumvent them precisely because the incentive to create such institutions will have been removed. If credit control is to continue as a weapon of economic policy in Britain (and it is scarcely conceivable that it should not) it is in this direction that it is likely to move. In so far as official control has discriminated against the clearing banks in the past, this trend is likely to improve their competitive position. But neither this, nor a mere amalgamation into two or three institutions of dinosaur proportions, will in any way guarantee it.

The corollary of this from the official side is that the error of seeking to regulate banking institutions through the medium of assets whose supply is partly within the control of those institutions will need to be repaired. In the last resort, it is only through the supply of legal tender, deposits with the central bank or 'bankers'' government securities that certainty of control can be achieved. These are precisely identifiable and cannot be created by anyone other than the authorities themselves. The mix of requirements under these headings can be varied from time to time and, if thought necessary, from one type of institution to another. The 'Special Deposit' is merely one (not particularly elegant) variant on this theme. A variable cash ratio would appear to be infinitely simpler and equally effective.

Whether these changes in the scope and nature of future techniques of credit control are considered worthwhile depends largely on the enthusiasm the authorities are likely to display for monetary policy itself. The obstacles here are probably intellectual rather than institutional—inconsistency (if not incoherence) of attitude rather than physical inability to achieve specified aims. The contemporary retreat into the theoretical simplicity of a quantity-theory approach does not augur well; it would perpetuate the error of relating control to a defined entity (an official concept of the quantity of money) and thus embarking on a continuous pursuit of an entity whose capacity for rapid change is certainly greater than that of the constructors of official definitions and compilers of statistical series. But the London clearing banks have been grappling with similar tergiversations in official pursuits of monetary control for a century and a half and have prospered none the less; no doubt they will continue to do so.

Not that the matter is of concern only to the clearing banks themselves. The smooth and efficient operation of the British monetary machine, of which they still form an overwhelmingly important part, is of the utmost concern to the economy as a whole, and much of its halting, half-hearted behaviour in the postwar era is clearly attributable to official interventions not properly suited to it: the fiscal concern for a stable (and low-cost) market in the national debt, a reliance on quantitative credit squeezes rather than deposit control—for a similar motive—and the most recent retreat into the apparent automaticity of DCE. Official rigidity of this sort is no substitute for forceful and flexible manipulation of the levers of the machine, even at the cost of the occasional blunder. The arbitrariness and artificiality imparted by it into the system have already had important consequences for a wide circle of users of the machine, most especially for borrowers steered towards sources of credit distinguished by higher costs and less flexible terms. This must be of particular significance to the smaller, dynamic enterprises the economy can ill afford to hold back, the firms reliant on outside sources of finance by virtue of their size and meritorious of it by virtue of their capacity for growth. The small, high-cost, fringe money-lender is historically associated with an economy in which a sophisticated banking and credit system has not yet been established; it would indeed be ironic if the rigidities and incompatibilities of official policy were to succeed in re-creating the phenomenon in a country which could have claimed, not very long ago, to have possessed the most sophisticated and efficient system of banking in the world.

REFERENCES

1. As has already been observed, perhaps the most dramatic illustration of this phenomenon was the open intervention in the London gilt-edged market by the government broker in November 1949. Prices rose immediately and substantially, although it subsequently transpired that the actual magnitude of official buying was in fact very small.

2. As was mentioned earlier, Bank rate had been raised above 2 per cent for some two months at the outbreak of war in 1939—solely because tradition demanded it.

3. Tax receipts customarily reach their peak during this quarter (the final quarter of the fiscal year), so allowing the Exchequer to employ the surplus over expenditure in repaying short-term indebtedness accumulated during the earlier part of the fiscal year.

4. In June of 1951 the banks had announced an increase of $\frac{1}{4}$ to $\frac{1}{2}$ per cent in their lending rate in cases where it had previously been especially low, but this change had been dictated by what might be called administrative rather than policy reasons.

5. I. M. D. Little, 'Fiscal policy', *The British economy in the nineteen-fifties*, (Ed. Worswick and Ady), Oxford University Press, London 1962, Part III, Ch. 8, p. 259.

6. *Committee on the working of the monetary system*, Report, Cmd 827, HMSO, London 1959.

7. *Radcliffe Report*, Chap. V, para. 376, p. 128.

8. First officially recognised, apparently—in a characteristically vague fashion—by the Bank of England in 1957—*ibid.*, Chap. V, para. 352, p. 119.

9. *Ibid.*, Chap. VI, para. 430, p. 150.

10 *Ibid.*, Chap. VI, para. 491, p. 175.

11. *Ibid.*, Chap. VI, paras. 389-91, pp. 132-3.

12. *Ibid.*, Chap. VI, para. 511, p. 182.

13. Or, alternatively, adopt the Special Deposit system—formally created in 1958—by which resources could be transferred out of or into the liquid assets category, keeping the ratio constant. See *ibid.*, para. 508.

14. *Radcliffe Report*, para. 389.

15. *Ibid.*, para. 397.

16. W. T. Newlyn, *Theory of Money*, Oxford University Press, London 1962, pp. 132-4.

17. *Radcliffe Report*, para. 393.

18. R. J. Ball, *Inflation and the Theory of Money*, Allen and Unwin, London 1964, p. 200.

19. Radcliffe Committee, *Minutes of Evidence*, Qs. 1841-98; see also 'Official transactions in the gilt-edged market', *Bank of England Quarterly Bulletin*, Vol. VI, No. 2, June 1966.

20. See *Bank of England Quarterly Bulletin*, Vol. 8, No. 4, December 1968, Table 3.

21. *Radcliffe Report*, para. 376.

22. W. T. C. King, 'Should Liquidity Ratios be prescribed?', *The Banker*, Vol. 106, No. 363, April 1956; W. Manning Dacey, 'The floating debt problem', *Lloyds Bank Review*, No. 40, April 1956, and *Money Under Review*, Hutchinson, London 1960.

23. Newlyn, *op. cit.*, p. 27.

24. A. B. Cramp, 'Control of the money supply', *Economic Journal*, Vol. LXXVI, No. 302, June 1966, pp. 278-87.

25. A. B. Cramp, 'The control of bank deposits', *Lloyds Bank Review*, No. 86, October 1969, p. 23.

26. R. S. Sayers, 'The determination of the volume of bank deposits: England 1955-56', *Banca Nazionale Del Lavoro Quarterly Review*, Vol. VIII, No. 35, December 1955.

27. A. N. McLeod, 'Technical Controls over bank deposits in Britain', *Oxford Economic Papers*, July 1969, p. 180.

28. R. L. Crouch, 'The inadequacy of "new-orthodox" methods of monetary control', *Economic Journal*, Vol. LXXIV, No. 296, December 1964, pp. 924-30.

29. Cramp, 'Control of the money supply', *op. cit.*, p. 285.

30. *Ibid.*, p. 285.

31. See W. E. Norton, 'Debt management and monetary policy in the United Kingdom', *Economic Journal*, Vol. LXXIX, No. 315, September 1969.

32. *Bank of England Quarterly Bulletin,* Vol. 9, No. 2, June 1969, Table 13, p. 249.

33. 'Banking regulation in Britain—by "suasion not statute"', *Midland Bank Review,* November 1967, p. 16.

34. J. E. Wadsworth, 'Banking Ratios Past and Present', *Essays in money and banking in honour of R. S. Sayers,* Eds. C. R. Whittlesey and J. S. G. Wilson, Oxford University Press, London 1968, pp. 247-8.

35. *Hansard,* April 28th 1960, Col. 399.

36. *Ibid.,* April 11th 1967, Col. 100.

37. M. Friedman and A. J. Schwartz, *A monetary history of the United States, 1867-1960,* Princeton University Press, Princeton, N. J., 1963 and P. C. Cagan, *Determinants and effects of changes in the stock of money, 1867-1960,* Columbia University Press, New York 1965.

38. M. Friedman (Ed.), *Studies in the Quantity Theory of Money,* University of Chicago Press, Chicago 1956, esp. pp. 3-21. See also M. Friedman, *A Program for Monetary Stability,* New York 1960. Also Friedman (review) in *American Economic Review,* Vol. LI, No. 5, December 1961 pp. 1053-4.

39. *Radcliffe Report,* para. 391.

40. Friedman, *Studies in the Quantity Theory of Money.* See also L. C. Anderson and J. L. Jordan, 'Monetary and fiscal actions: a test of their relative importance in economic stabilisation', *Federal Reserve Bank of St. Louis Review,* Vol. 50, No. 11, November 1968.

41. A A. Walters, *Money in Boom and Slump,* Institute of Economic Affairs, Hobart Paper No. 44, pp. 29, 34. Note also the remarkable rise in the ratio of bank clearings to GNP during the 1960s revealed by Table 1, col. (9), of the Statistical Appendix.

42. M. Friedman and D. Meiselman, 'The Relative Stability in Monetary Velocity and the Investment Multiplier in the United States, 1897-1958', in *Stabilisation Policies,* Commission on Money and Credit, Prentice-Hall, Englewood Cliffs, New Jersey 1963.

43. C. R. Barrett and A. A. Walters, 'The stability of Keynesian and Monetary Multipliers in the United Kingdom', *Review of Economics and Statistics,* Vol. XLIII, No. 4 November 1966. See also N. J. Kavanagh in a Birmingham discussion paper (August 1965), quoted by Walters, *Money in Boom and Slump.*

44. See references cited in 37 above.

45. Ball, *op. cit.,* p. 224.

46. 'Money supply and the banks', *Midland Bank Review,* February 1969.

47. See 'Domestic credit expansion', Supplement to the *Bank of England Quarterly Bulletin,* Vol 9, No. 3, September 1969.

48. *Financial Statistics,* No. 86, HMSO, London, June 1969, Table 47, p. 54.

49. See Statistical Appendix, Table 1, col. 5.

50. Walters, *Money in Boom and Slump,* p. 24.

51. See Statistical Appendix, Table 1, Col. 6, and also Ball, *op. cit.*, pp. 213-5.

52. 'Money supply and the banks,' *Midland Bank Review*, February 1969, p. 4.

53. Ball, *op. cit.*, p. 216.

STATISTICAL APPENDIX

TABLE 1

GNP and Money Supply, 1900–68

Annual averages

Year	GNP at factor cost £ million	Currency in circulation £ million	LCB: Net Deposits £ million	Money supply (2 + 3)	(4) as % of (1)	LCB Deposits as % of GNP (3) as % of (1)	LCB Deposits as % of Money supply (3) as % of (4)	Bank clearings £000mn	Bank clearings Per £100,000 GNP
	(1)	(2)	(3)	(4)	(5)	(6)	(7)	(8)	(9)
1900	1,970	122	554	676	34.3	28.1	82.0	9.6	48.7
1901	1,989	122	554	676	34.0	27.9	82.0	10.2	51.3
1902	1,992	121	566	687	34.5	28.4	82.4	10.6	53.2
1903	1,962	119	554	673	34.3	28.2	82.3	10.7	54.5
1904	1,978	116	554	670	33.9	28.0	82.7	11.2	56.6
1905	2,043	117	572	689	33.7	28.0	83.0	13.0	63.6
1906	2,109	118	589	707	33.5	27.9	83.3	13.4	63.5
1907	2,172	120	596	716	33.0	27.4	83.2	13.5	62.2
1908	2,072	120	612	732	35.3	29.5	83.6	12.8	61.8
1909	2,144	123	626	749	34.9	29.2	83.6	14.2	66.2
1910	2,231	125	646	771	34.6	29.0	83.8	15.4	69.0

TABLE 1 (continued)

Annual averages

Year	GNP at factor cost £ million	Currency in circulation £ million	LCB: Net Deposits £ million	Money supply (2 + 3)	(4) as % of (1)	LCB Deposits as % of		Bank clearings	
						GNP (3) as % of (1)	Money supply (3) as % of (4)	£000mn	Per £100,000 GNP
	(1)	(2)	(3)	(4)	(5)	(6)	(7)	(8)	(9)
1911	2,328	131	669	800	34.4	28.7	83.6	15.4	66.2
1912	2,409	136	688	824	34.2	28.6	83.5	16.8	69.7
1913	2,527	143	728	871	34.5	28.8	83.6	17.3	68.5
1914	2,537	183	818	1,001	39.5	32.2	81.7	15.5	61.1
1915	2,978	216	857	1,073	36.0	28.8	79.9	14.4	48.4
1916	3,521	255	1,016	1,271	36.1	28.9	79.9	16.5	46.9
1917	4,173	296	1,173	1,469	35.2	28.1	79.9	20.6	49.4
1918	5,023	399	1,379	1,778	35.4	27.4	77.6	23.0	45.8
1919	6,274	435	1,630	2,065	32.9	26.0	78.9	30.7	48.9
1920	6,509	432	1,738	2,170	33.3	26.7	80.1	42.2	64.8
1921	5,128	392	1,764	2,156	42.0	34.4	81.8	36.7	71.6
1922	4,378	355	1,730	2,085	47.6	39.5	83.0	39.0	89.1
1923	4,178	343	1,629	1,972	47.2	39.0	82.6	38.4	91.9
1924	4,271	346	1,622	1,968	46.1	38.0	82.4	41.4	96.9
1925	4,549	340	1,610	1,950	42.9	35.4	82.6	42.3	93.0

TABLE 1 (continued)

Annual averages

Year	GNP at factor cost £ million	Currency in circulation £ million	LCB: Net Deposits £ million	Money supply (2 + 3)	(4) as % of (1)	LCB Deposits as % of: GNP (3) as % of (1)	LCB Deposits as % of: Money supply (3) as % of 4	Bank clearings: £000mn	Bank clearings: Per £100, 000 GNP
	(1)	(2)	(3)	(4)	(5)	(6)	(7)	(8)	(9)
1926	4, 301	336	1, 615	1, 951	45. 4	37. 6	82. 8	41. 5	96. 5
1927	4, 478	333	1, 661	1, 994	44. 5	37. 1	83. 3	43. 3	96. 7
1928	4, 532	331	1, 709	2, 040	45. 0	37. 7	83. 8	45. 9	101. 3
1929	4. 632	324	1, 743	2, 067	44. 6	37. 6	84. 3	46. 5	100. 4
1930	4, 576	321	1, 747	2, 068	45. 2	38. 2	84. 5	44. 9	98. 1
1931	4, 191	324	1, 711	2, 035	48. 6	40. 8	84. 1	37. 4	89. 2
1932	4, 024	331	1, 745	2, 076	51. 6	44. 5	84. 1	33. 4	83. 0
1933	4, 042	337	1, 906	2, 243	55. 5	48. 3	85. 0	33. 4	82. 6
1934	4, 295	344	1, 830	2, 174	50. 6	43. 8	84. 2	36. 8	85. 7
1935	4, 499	358	1, 947	2, 305	51. 6	44. 4	84. 5	38. 8	86. 2
1936	4, 664	390	2, 156	2, 546	54. 6	47. 5	84. 7	42. 0	90. 1
1937	5, 010	437	2, 220	2, 657	53. 0	45. 6	83. 6	44. 2	88. 2
1938	5, 310	442	2, 213	2, 655	50. 0	42. 9	83. 4	40. 9	77. 0
1939	5, 659	454	2, 175	2, 629	46. 5	39. 7	82. 7	37. 8	66. 8
1940	6, 718	519	2, 408	2, 927	43. 6	37. 3	82. 3	41. 4	60. 7

TABLE 1 (continued)

Annual averages

Year	GNP at factor cost £ million	Currency in circulation £ million	LCB: Net Deposits £ million	Money supply (2 + 3)	(4) as % of (1)	LCB Deposits as % of: GNP (3) as % of (1)	LCB Deposits as % of: Money supply (3) as % of (4)	Bank clearings: £000mn	Bank clearings: Per £100, 000 GNP
	(1)	(2)	(3)	(4)	(5)	(6)	(7)	(8)	(9)
1941	7, 800	603	2, 849	3, 452	44. 3	38. 1	82. 5	44. 5	57. 1
1942	8, 610	763	3, 145	3, 908	45. 4	38. 0	80. 5	50. 1	58. 2
1943	9, 180	928	3, 544	4, 472	48. 7	40. 1	79. 2	58. 3	63. 5
1944	9, 398	1, 098	4, 012	5, 110	54. 4	44. 2	78. 5	63. 6	67. 7
1945	9, 371	1, 255	4, 541	5, 796	61. 8	50. 1	78. 4	68. 0	72. 6
1946	8, 851	1, 332	4, 922	6, 254	70. 7	57. 6	78. 7	70. 3	79. 4
1947	9, 455	1, 351	5, 454	6, 805	72. 0	59. 8	80. 2	74. 7	79. 0
1948	10, 520	1, 229	5, 703	6, 932	65. 9	56. 2	82. 3	81. 9	77. 8
1949	11, 136	1, 238	5, 761	6, 999	62. 8	53. 6	82. 3	87. 9	78. 9
1950	11, 740	1, 244	5, 800	7, 044	60. 0	51. 2	82. 3	96. 3	82. 0
1951	12, 961	1, 291	5, 918	7, 209	55. 6	47. 5	82. 1	111. 1	85. 7
1952	14, 012	1, 370	5, 782	7, 152	51. 0	43. 4	80. 8	112. 6	80. 4
1953	15, 065	1, 462	5, 946	7, 408	49. 2	41. 5	80. 3	125. 5	83. 3
1954	15, 923	1, 551	6, 152	7, 703	48. 4	40. 8	79. 9	146. 6	92. 1
1955	16, 975	1, 657	6, 093	7, 750	45. 7	38. 0	78. 6	155. 1	91. 4

TABLE 1 (continued)

Annual averages

Year	GNP at factor cost £ million	Currency in circulation £ million	LCB: Net Deposits £ million	Money supply (2 + 3)	(4) as % of (1)	LCB Deposits as % of GNP (3) as % of (1)	LCB Deposits as % of Money supply (3) as % of (4)	Bank clearings £000mn	Bank clearings Per £100,000 GNP
	(1)	(2)	(3)	(4)	(5)	(6)	(7)	(8)	(9)
1956	18, 420	1, 765	5, 921	7, 686	41. 7	34. 1	77. 0	163. 3	88. 6
1957	19, 522	1, 842	6, 038	7, 880	40. 4	33. 0	76. 6	175. 2	89. 7
1958	20, 385	1, 905	6, 230	8, 135	39. 9	32. 6	76. 6	183. 4	90. 0
1959	21, 389	1, 969	6, 499	8, 468	39. 6	32. 4	76. 8	201. 8	94. 4
1960	22, 767	2, 062	6, 743	8, 805	38. 7	31. 8	76. 6	228. 2	100. 2
1961	24, 367	2, 151	6, 909	9, 060	37. 2	30. 4	76. 3	245. 2	100. 6
1962	25, 458	2, 161	7, 084	9, 245	36. 3	29. 9	76. 6	275. 6	108. 3
1963	27, 190	2, 210	7, 409	9, 619	35. 4	27. 2	77. 0	305. 2	112. 2
1964	29, 351	2, 332	7, 891	10, 223	34. 8	26. 9	77. 2	358. 7	122. 2
1965	31, 304	2, 483	8, 316	10, 799	34. 5	26. 6	77. 0	411. 6	131. 5
1966	32, 889	2, 637	8, 675	11, 312	34. 4	26. 4	76. 7	455. 5	138. 5
1967	34, 494	2, 700	9, 024	11, 724	34. 0	26. 2	77. 0	561. 9	162. 9
1968	36, 358	2, 827	9, 645	12, 472	34. 3	26. 5	77. 3	600. 3	165. 1

TABLE 2

Liabilities of the London Clearing Banks, 1921-68

(Annual averages)

Year	Current Accounts (£ million)	Deposit Accounts (£ million)	Other Accounts (£ million)	Total Liabilities (£ million)	Index 1958 = 100	(1) as % of (4)
	(1)	(2)	(3)	(4)	(5)	(6)
1921	1,025	729	58	1,812	27.3	58.4
1922	998	709	67	1,774	26.7	58.5
1923	966	648	60	1,674	24.8	59.8
1924	950	666	55	1,671	25.2	58.8
1925	923	680	59	1,662	25.0	57.6
1926	921	688	56	1,665	25.1	57.3
1927	932	727	54	1,713	25.8	56.2
1928	954	755	57	1,766	26.6	55.8
1929	940	789	62	1,800	27.1	54.1
1930	921	820	60	1,801	27.1	52.9
1931	897	802	61	1,760	26.5	52.7
1932	867	883	41	1,791	27.0	48.4
1933	978	930	45	1,953	29.4	50.1
1934	953	886	41	1,880	28.3	50.7
1935	1,054	904	41	1,999	30.1	52.7
1936	1,197	982	37	2,216	33.4	54.0

TABLE 2 (continued) (Annual averages)

Year	Current Accounts (£ million)	Deposit Accounts (£ million)	Other Accounts (£ million)	Total Liabilities (£ million)	Index 1958 = 100	(1) as % of (4)
	(1)	(2)	(3)	(4)	(5)	(6)
1937	1,233	1,011	43	2,287	34.5	53.9
1938	1,244	1,033		2,277	34.3	54.6
1939	1,252	996		2,248	33.9	55.7
1940	1,487	1,018		2,506	37.8	59.3
1941	1,885	1,085		2,970	44.8	63.5
1942	2,148	1,128		3,275	49.4	65.6
1943	2,455	1,222		3,677	55.4	66.8
1944	2,765	1,388		4,153	62.6	66.6
1945	3,127	1,566		4,692	70.7	66.6
1946	3,377	1,720		5,097	76.8	66.2
1947	3,690	1,959		5.650	85.1	65.3
1948	3,850	2,062		5,913	89.1	65.1
1949	3,940	2,034		5,974	90.0	66.0
1950	3,979	2,036		6.014	90.6	66.2
1951	4,095	2,067		6,162	92.9	66.5
1952	3,907	1,938	238	6,083	91.7	64.2
1953	3,938	2,051	367	6,256	94.3	63.0

TABLE 2 (continued)

(Annual averages)

Year	Current Accounts (£ million)	Deposit Accounts (£ million)	Other Accounts (£ million	Total Liabilities (£ million)	Index 1958 = 100	(1) as % of (4)
	(1)	(2)	(3)	(4)	(5)	(6)
1954	4, 078	2, 094	323	6, 495	97. 9	62. 8
1955	4, 054	2, 070	330	6, 454	97. 3	62. 8
1956	3, 932	2, 008	348	6, 288	94. 8	62. 5
1957	3, 905	2, 139	388	6, 432	96. 9	60. 7
1958	3, 769	2, 442	425	6, 636	100. 0	56. 8
1959	4, 064	2, 431	440	6, 935	104. 5	58. 6
1960	4, 207	2, 515	514	7, 236	109. 0	58. 1
1961	4, 157	2, 638	600	7, 395	111. 4	56. 2
1962	4, 186	2, 747	678	7, 611	114. 7	55. 0
1963	4, 486	2, 781	704	7, 971	120. 1	56. 3
1964	4, 836	2, 922	792	8, 550	128. 8	56. 6
1965	4, 869	3, 292	828	8, 989	135. 5	54. 2
1966	4, 955	3, 536	885	9, 376	141. 3	52. 9
1967	5, 084	3, 769	919	9, 772	147. 3	52. 0
1968	5, 334	4, 177	920	10, 431	157. 2	51. 1

TABLE 3A

Assets of the London Clearing Banks, 1921-68

(Annual averages, £ million)

Year	Cash inc. balances at the Bank of England	Money at call and short notice	Treasury Bills	Other bills	Treasury Deposit Receipts	Total Liquid Assets	Special Deposits	Invest-ments	Advances	Advances as % of GNP
	(1)	(2)	(3)	(4)	(5)	(6)	(7)	(8)	(9)	(10)
1921	211	105	363		—	679	—	331	833	16.2
1922	206	113	340		—	659	—	391	750	17.1
1923	197	110	275		—	582	—	356	761	18.2
1924	195	105	244		—	544	—	341	808	18.9
1925	196	117	226		—	539	—	286	856	18.8
1926	195	120	216		—	532	—	265	892	20.7
1927	198	137	218		—	553	—	254	928	20.7
1928	196	150	237		—	584	—	254	948	20.9
1929	194	145	229		—	568	—	257	991	21.4
1930	192	140	264		—	596	—	258	963	21.0
1931	182	121	256		—	560	—	301	919	21.9
1932	187	116	308		—	611	—	348	844	21.0
1933	212	102	354		—	663	—	537	758	18.8
1934	212	134	230		—	576	—	560	753	17.5

TABLE 3A (continued) (Annual averages, £ million)

Year	Cash inc. balances at the Bank of England	Money at call and short notice	Treasury Bills	Other bills	Treasury Deposit Receipts	Total Liquid Assets	Special Deposits	Invest-ments	Advances	Advances as % of GNP
	(1)	(2)	(3)	(4)	(5)	(6)	(7)	(8)	(9)	(10)
1935	215	142	266		—	623	—	615	769	17.1
1936	221	158	313		—	692	—	614	839	18.0
	228	165	320		—	713	—	643	865	18.6
1937	235	167	281		—	683	—	652	954	19.0
1938	241	151	280		—	672	—	637	976	18.4
1939	244	149	255		—	648	—	608	991	17.5
1940	268	148	369		73	859	—	666	995	14.2
1941	311	134	231		495	1,171	—	894	858	11.0
1942	345	133	234		642	1,355	—	1,069	798	9.3
1943	386	152	185		1,002	1,725	—	1,147	747	8.1
1944	437	180	171		1,387	2,175	—	1,165	750	8.0
1945	492	206	188		1,811	2,697	—	1,156	768	8.2
1946	523	300	457		1,492	2,772	—	1,345	888	10.0
1947	473	450	723		1,308	2,954	—	1,474	1,107	11.7
1948	486	473	744		1,284	2,987	—	1,479	1,319	12.5
1949	496	510	914		983	2,903	—	1,505	1,440	12.9

TABLE 3A (continued)

(Annual averages, £ million)

Year	Cash inc. balances at the Bank of England	Money at call and short notice	Treasury Bills	Other bills	Treasury Deposit Receipts	Total Liquid Assets	Special Deposits	Invest-ments	Advances	Advances as % of GNP
	(1)	(2)	(3)	(4)	(5)	(6)	(7)	(8)	(9)	(10)
1950	497	550	1,298		430	2,775	—	1,505	1,603	13.7
1951	511	569	1,228		247	2,555	—	1,624	1,822	14.1
1952	505	529	957	105	7	2,104	—	1,983	1,838	13.1
1953	509	472	1,156	63	—	2,201	—	2,163	1,666	11.1
1954	528	457	1,119	87	—	2,190	—	2,321	1,731	10.9
1955	529	439	1,016	114	—	2,098	—	2,149	1,941	11.4
1956	516	431	1,156	114	—	2,218	—	1,978	1,820	9.9
1957	526	439	1,143	148	—	2,256	—	2,008	1,868	9.6
1958	543	434	1,167	110	—	2,255	—	2,149	1,923	9.4
1959	565	489	1,089	134	—	2,277	—	1,836	2,522	11.8
1960	588	562	1,007	142	—	2,299	74	1,407	3,123	13.7
1961	607	606	992	233	—	2,437	174	1,122	3,357	13.8
1962	623	718	933	272	—	2,546	159	1,194	3,408	13.4
1963	647	748	842	298	—	2,535	—	1,244	3,880	14.3
1964	696	738	790	365	—	2,589	—	1,220	4,328	14.8
1965	739	910	653	461	—	2,763	56	1,087	4,653	14.9

TABLE 3A (continued)

(Annual averages, £ million)

Year	Cash inc. balances at the Bank of England	Money at call and short notice	Treasury Bills	Other bills	Treasury Deposit Receipts	Total Liquid Assets	Special Deposits	Invest-ments	Advances	Advances as % of GNP
	(1)	(2)	(3)	(4)	(5)	(6)	(7)	(8)	(9)	(10)
1966	767	1,006	689	446	—	2,908	137	1,137	4,732	14.4
1967	798	1,136	564	492	—	2,990	194	1,341	4,725	13.7
1968	851	1,335	468	527	—	3,182	208	1,375	5,075	14.0

TABLE 3B

Assets of the London Clearing Banks, 1921-68

(% of gross deposits)

Year	Total Liquid Assets	Special Deposits	Investments	Advances
	(1)	(2)	(3)	(4)
1921	37.5	—	18.3	46.0
1922	37.1	—	22.0	42.3
1923	34.8	—	21.6	46.3
1924	32.6	—	20.4	48.4
1925	32.4	—	17.2	51.5
1926	32.0	—	15.9	53.6
1927	32.3	—	14.8	54.2
1928	33.1	—	14.4	53.7
1929	31.6	—	14.3	55.1
1930	33.1	—	14.3	53.5
1931	31.8	—	17.1	52.2
1932	34.1	—	19.4	47.1
1933	34.2	—	27.5	38.8
1934	30.6	—	29.8	40.1
1935	31.2	—	30.8	38.5
1936	32.3	—	28.7	39.2
	32.2	—	29.0	39.0

TABLE 3B (continued) (% of gross deposits)

Year	Total Liquid Assets	Special Deposits	Investments	Advances
	(1)	(2)	(3)	(4)
1937	29.9	—	28.5	41.7
1938	29.5	—	28.0	42.9
1939	28.8	—	27.1	44.1
1940	34.3	—	26.6	38.1
1941	39.4	—	30.1	28.9
1942	41.4	—	32.6	24.3
1943	46.9	—	31.2	20.3
1944	52.4	—	28.0	18.1
1945	57.5	—	24.6	16.4
1946	54.4	—	26.4	17.4
1947	52.3	—	26.1	19.6
1948	50.5	—	25.0	22.3
1949	48.6	—	25.2	24.1
1950	46.1	—	25.0	26.7
1951	41.5	—	26.4	29.6
1952	34.6	—	32.6	30.2
1953	35.2	—	34.6	26.6
1954	33.7	—	35.7	26.6

TABLE 3B (continued) (% of gross deposits)

Year	Total Liquid Assets	Special Deposits	Investments	Advances
	(1)	(2)	(3)	(4)
1955	32.5	—	33.3	30.1
1956	35.3	—	31.5	28.9
1957	35.1	—	31.2	29.0
1958	34.0	—	32.4	29.0
1959	32.8	—	26.5	36.4
1960	31.8	1.0	19.5	43.2
1961	33.0	2.4	15.2	45.4
1962	33.5	2.1	15.7	44.8
1963	31.8	—	15.6	48.7
1964	30.3	—	14.3	50.6
1965	30.7	0.6	12.1	51.8
1966	31.0	1.5	12.1	50.5
1967	30.6	2.0	13.7	48.4
1968	30.5	2.0	13.2	48.6

TABLE 4

Major UK Liquid Assets, 1900-68

(Annual averages: £ million)

Year	Currency in circulation	Post Office Savings Bank Deposits	Trustee Savings Bank Deposits	National Savings Certificates	Defence Bonds	Premium Savings Bonds	Building Society Shares & Deposits	Gross Clearing Bank Deposits	Total	9 as % of GNP	8 as % of 9
	(1)	(2)	(3)	(4)	(5)	(6)	(7)	(8)	(9)	(10)	(11)
1900	122	133	56	—	—	—	52	446	809	41.1	55.1
1901	122	138	57	—	—	—	53	446	816	41.0	54.7
1902	121	143	57	—	—	—	54	457	832	41.8	54.9
1903	119	146	57	—	—	—	56	446	824	42.0	54.1
1904	116	147	57	—	—	—	58	446	824	41.7	54.1
1905	117	150	58	—	—	—	60	457	842	41.2	54.3
1906	118	154	59	—	—	—	62	475	868	41.2	54.7
1907	120	157	59	—	—	—	63	477	876	40.3	54.4
1908	120	160	60	—	—	—	64	512	916	44.2	55.9
1909	123	163	61	—	—	—	66	542	955	44.5	56.8
1910	125	167	63	—	—	—	69	570	994	44.6	57.3
1911	131	173	64	—	—	—	65	595	1,028	44.2	57.9
1912	136	180	66	—	—	—	60	615	1,057	43.9	58.2
1913	143	185	68	—	—	—	61	649	1,106	43.8	58.7
1914	183	189	70	—	—	—	62	778	1,282	50.5	60.7
1915	216	189	69	—	—	—	62	851	1,387	46.6	61.4
1916	255	192	68	38	—	—	62	1,011	1,626	46.2	62.2

TABLE 4 (continued)

(Annual averages: £ million)

Year	Currency in circulation	Post Office Savings Bank Deposits	Trustee Savings Bank Deposits	National Savings Certificates	Defence Bonds	Premium Savings Bonds	Building Society Shares & Deposits	Gross Clearing Bank Deposits	Total	9 as % of GNP	8 as % of 9
	(1)	(2)	(3)	(4)	(5)	(6)	(7)	(8)	(9)	(10)	(11)
1917	296	200	68	106	—	—	61	1,198	1,929	46.2	62.1
1918	399	219	71	188	—	—	62	1,415	2,354	46.9	60.1
1919	435	251	81	268	—	—	68	1,677	2,780	44.3	60.3
1920	432	267	89	309	—	—	76	1,798	2,971	45.6	60.5
1921	392	266	92	354	—	—	84	1,812	3,000	58.5	60.4
1922	355	266	95	403	—	—	94	1,774	2,987	68.2	59.4
1923	343	271	101	432	—	—	108	1,644	2,899	69.4	56.7
1924	346	277	105	452	—	—	125	1,671	2,976	69.7	56.2
1925	340	283	109	467	—	—	145	1,662	3,006	66.1	55.3
1926	336	285	111	484	—	—	169	1,665	3,050	70.9	54.6
1927	333	285	113	488	—	—	195	1,713	3,127	69.8	54.8
1928	331	287	118	483	—	—	230	1,766	3,215	70.9	54.9
1929	324	287	123	481	—	—	270	1,800	3,285	70.9	54.8
1930	321	288	129	488	—	—	319	1,801	3,346	73.1	53.8
1931	324	290	138	487	—	—	370	1,760	3,369	80.4	52.2
1932	331	298	149	476	—	—	418	1,791	3,463	86.1	51.7
1933	337	317	163	481	—	—	457	1,953	3,708	91.7	52.7
1934	344	341	177	494	—	—	496	1,880	3,732	86.9	50.4
1935	358	373	190	504	—	—	542	1,999	3,966	88.2	50.4
1936	390	411	205	511	—	—	586	2,216	4,319	92.6	51.3

TABLE 4 (continued)

(Annual averages: £ million)

Year	Currency in circulation	Post Office Savings Bank Deposits	Trustee Savings Bank Deposits	National Savings Certificates	Defence Bonds	Premium Savings Bonds	Building Society Shares & Deposits	Gross Clearing Bank Deposits	Total	9 as % of GNP	8 as % of 9
	(1)	(2)	(3)	(4)	(5)	(6)	(7)	(8)	(9)	(10)	(11)
1937	437	452	219	515	—	—	635	2,287	4,545	90.7	50.3
1938	442	490	232	518	—	—	683	2,277	4,642	87.4	49.1
1939	454	530	244	564	30	—	708	2,248	4,760	84.1	47.2
1940	519	602	263	666	155	—	703	2,506	5,414	80.6	46.3
1941	603	738	302	880	342	—	691	2,970	6,526	83.7	45.5
1942	763	914	355	1,115	488	—	690	3,275	7,600	88.3	43.1
1943	928	1,123	418	1,371	597	—	696	3,677	8,810	96.0	41.7
1944	1,098	1,366	493	1,643	707	—	718	4,153	1,078	108.3	40.8
1945	1,255	1,634	569	1,835	861	—	747	4,692	11,593	123.7	40.5
1946	1,332	1,879	640	1,951	1,035	—	785	5,097	12,719	143.7	40.1
1947	1,351	1,959	706	2,052	1,072	—	846	5,650	13,636	144.2	41.4
1948	1,229	1,943	768	2,120	1,005	—	921	5,913	13,899	132.1	42.5
1949	1,238	1,949	826	2,141	966	—	1,009	5,974	14,103	126.6	42.4
1950	1,244	1,943	878	2,158	945	—	1,113	6,014	14,295	121.8	42.1
1951	1,291	1,906	913	2,192	906	—	1,316	6,162	14,586	112.5	42.2
1952	1,370	1,844	931	2,235	849	—	1,325	6,083	14,637	104.5	41.6
1953	1,462	1,781	946	2,277	802	—	1,463	6,256	14,987	99.5	41.7
1954	1,551	1,738	979	2,332	794	—	1,655	6,495	15,544	97.6	41.8
1955	1,657	1,713	1,018	2,382	791	—	1,864	6,454	15,879	93.5	40.6
1956	1,765	1,643	1,055	2,420	760	33	2,035	6,288	15,999	86.9	39.3

TABLE 4 (continued)

(Annual averages: £ million)

Year	Currency in circulation	Post Office Savings Bank Deposits	Trustee Savings Bank Deposits	National Savings Certificates	Defence Bonds	Premium Savings Bonds	Building Society Shares & Deposits	Gross Clearing Bank Deposits	Total	9 as % of GNP	8 as % of 9
	(1)	(2)	(3)	(4)	(5)	(6)	(7)	(8)	(9)	(10)	(11)
1957	1,842	1,683	1,102	2,422	722	106	2,197	6,432	16,506	84.6	39.0
1958	1,905	1,662	1,143	2,457	765	181	2,381	6,636	17,130	84.0	38.7
1959	1,969	1,663	1,199	2,549	883	235	2,614	6,935	18,047	84.4	38.4
1960	2,062	1,695	1,277	2,621	1,007	282	2,850	7,236	19,030	83.6	38.0
1961	2,151	1,724	1,359	2,655	1,067	331	3,044	7,395	19,726	81.0	37.5
1962	2,161	1,749	1,466	2,676	1,099	374	3,324	7,611	20,460	80.4	37.2
1963	2,210	1,776	1,616	2,706	1,132	416	3,758	7,971	21,585	79.4	36.9
1964	2,332	1,803	1,798	2,713	1,099	466	4,257	8,550	23,018	78.4	37.2
1965	2,483	1,818	1,962	2,637	1,188	521	4,834	8,989	24,432	78.1	36.8
1966	2,637	1,808	2,091	2,558	1,092	567	5,521	9,376	25,650	78.0	36.6
1967	2,700	1,789	2,212	2,590	1,001	610	6,437	9,772	27,111	78.6	36.0
1968	2,838	1,798	2,422	2,602	917	690	7,377	10,431	29,075	80.0	35.9

NOTES ON STATISTICAL APPENDIX

The following abbreviations are used throughout:

LCES: *The British Economy: Key Statistics, 1900-1966,* published for the London and Cambridge Economic Service by Times Newspapers Ltd., London 1967.

ABHS: B.R. Mitchell and P. Deane, *Abstract of British historical statistics,* Cambridge University Press, London 1962.

AA: *Annual Abstract of Statistics,* HMSO, London.

MDS: *Monthly Digest of Statistics,* HMSO, London.

FS: *Financial Statistics,* No. 84, April 1969, HMSO, London 1969.

BESS: Bank of England *Statistical Summary.*

TABLE 1

Col. (1) *1900-62:* (except for 1915-19 and 1939-45) LCES, Table A, col. 8. The wartime estimates were derived by using as an index Prest's series for net national income at current prices (ABHS, Chap. XIII, Table 2B, p. 368). In each case the immediate pre-war LCES figure was indexed forwards and the immediate postwar LCES figure was indexed backwards; the wartime estimates were then derived as the arithmetic average of the two estimates so obtained for each year. *1963-68:* estimates were taken from *Preliminary estimates of national income and balance of payments, 1963-1968,* Cmd. 3983, HMSO, London 1969, Table 1, p. 4. There is thus a slight discontinuity between 1962 and 1963 onwards, but the 1963 figures in the two sources differ by only some 0. 5 per cent.

Col. (2) *1921-66:* LCES, Table M, col. 8. 1900-20: series indexed back by total notes held by the public, ABHS, Chap. XV, Table 6, for 1900-1904 and by BESS, November 1932 for 1905-20. 1967-68: FS, Table 49.

Col. (3) *1921-66:* LCES, Table M, col. 15. 1905-20: BESS, November 1932. Note that in all the London Clearing Bank series data relating to the District Bank are included from 1937 onwards. 1900-1904: The figure for 1905 was indexed back by *The Economist* series (an arithmetic mean being taken in each case), ABHS, Chap. XV, Table 3, Part A *less* total Bank of England deposits shown in *ibid.,* Table 2B. *1967-68:* FS, Table 35.

Col. (8) *1900-1938:* ABHS, Chap. XV, Table 5; *1939-1967* AA, various; *1968* FS, Table 50.

TABLE 2

Cols. (1)-(4) *1921-44:* BESS; *1945-67,* AA; *1968,* FS, Table 35.

TABLES 3A, 3B

Col. (1)-(9) As for Table 2.

TABLE 4

Col. (1) As for Table 1, col. (2).

Cols. (2) and (3) *1900-39,* ABHS, Ch. XV, Table 7 (averages of year-end figures); *1940-67:* totals outstanding as at March 31st, Pember and Boyle, *British Government Securities in the twentieth century;* 1968, FS, Table 23.

Col. (4) *1916* onwards: as for cols. (2) and (3) totals include accrued interest.

Col. (5) *1939* onwards: as for cols. (2) and (3) totals include British Savings Bonds and National Development Bonds from the dates of their introduction.

Col. (6) *1956* onwards: as for cols. (2) and (3).

Col. (7) *1900-1965,* LCES, Table M, col. 17. Totals shown are averages of two year-end figures except for 1900 which refers to end—1900 only; *1965-68.* FS, Table 55.

Col. (8) As for Table 1, col. (3) except that the LCES column used as a base is Table M, col. 9.

Index